FOREVER SENNA

To my dear friend, Arnaud Chambert-Protat, with whom I have shared so many moments of camaraderie on the Formula 1 circuits and beyond. Arnaud, you left us too soon; you will be greatly missed. My warmest thoughts go to your wife, Anne-Laure, children, and grandchildren. This book, "Éternel Senna", highlighting the immense champion we have admired so much, is for you.

Dominique Leroy

The Author, Dominique Leroy, is a photographer from Nîmes, author, and director. A true photography enthusiast, he has made the Formula 1 paddocks his playground for over 25 years. A privileged witness to Ayrton Senna's rise in the world of Formula 1, he photographed the Brazilian driver throughout his career.

Daniel Ortelli covered Formula 1 and the entire motorsport scene for AFP for more than ten years all around the world. He has already published several books on the history of Formula 1, its world champions since 1950, and the biographies of the two most recent, Lewis Hamilton and Max Verstappen (with Thomas Woloch).

Thomas Woloch is a young author specializing in motorsports. Born in Nantes, he graduated from the School of Journalism in Cannes and holds a Certification in Journalism from Laval University (Canada). A sports enthusiast, Thomas Woloch is also the author of the biographies of Max Verstappen (with Daniel Ortelli) and Sebastian Vettel (with Loïc Chenevas-Paule).

Publisher: Helmin & Sorgenfri under license from Glénat

Helmin & Sorgenfri
Nivå Strandpark 21
DK-2990 Nivå
Denmark

1. edition, 1. circulation

The photos in this book are now part of the Grand Prix Photo Agency's archives.

Layout: Julie Lotte
Prepress and manufacturing: Glénat production

The paper used for this book comes from sustainably managed forests.

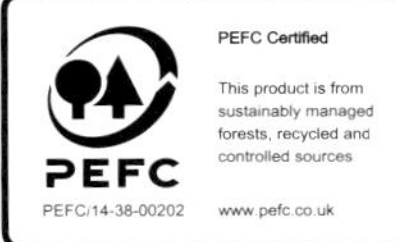

Printing was completed in April 2024 in Spain by Indice S.L.
ISBN: 978-87-94190-48-0

FOREVER SENNA

PHOTOS Dominique Leroy
TEXT Daniel Ortelli et Thomas Woloch

FRIENDS' FOREWORD Jean Alesi
Gerhard Berger
Thierry Boutsen

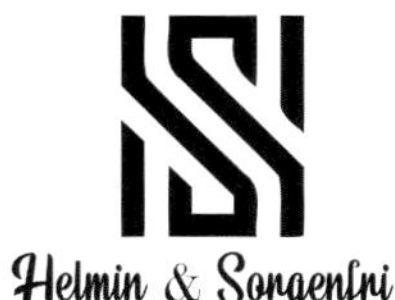

FRIENDS' FOREWORD

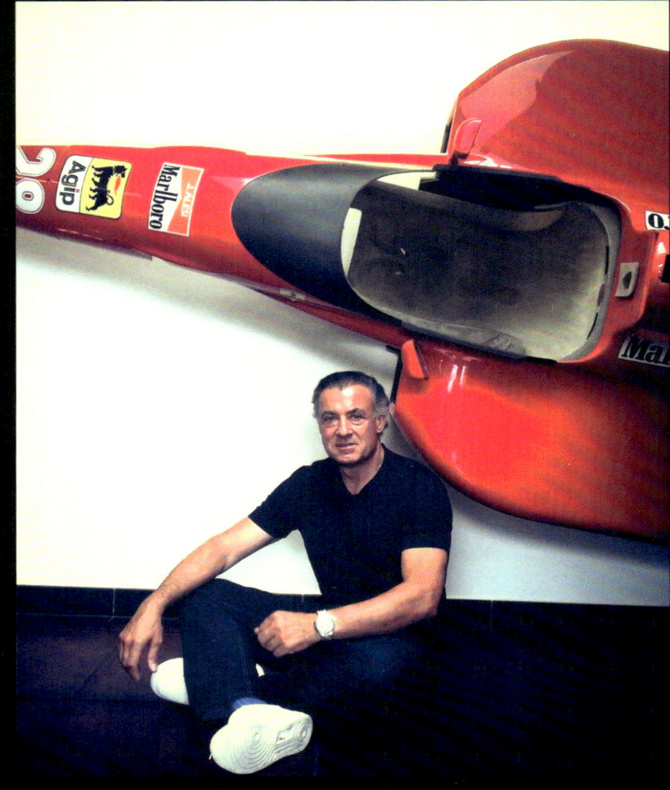

JEAN ALESI

"My friendship with Ayrton stems from my friendship with Gerhard. Long before we were teammates at Benetton, Gerhard and I had a lot in common through our shared interests and sense of humor! So it was because of him that I became one of Ayrton's close friends following two personal events with Ayrton.

Phoenix in 1990, just after a semi-season in 1989, I was fighting with Ayrton during more than half a race, and I retook the lead just after he overtook me for the first time. In the end, he finally overtakes me, but the first podium of my life had a special meaning, especially thanks to the congratulations he publicly gave to me. I had the feeling of entering a new world... his.

And Barcelona in 1991, one grand prix, two duels between us. From lap 14 to 29, then in lap 42 to 50, when I climbed on a curb, risking taking both of us out, but... I got through! In both these situations, we really had some fun. And as we sometimes say, 'It's a bonding experience.' Other circumstances and similarities have strengthened our relationship, which is undoubtedly one of the most rewarding I've ever had."

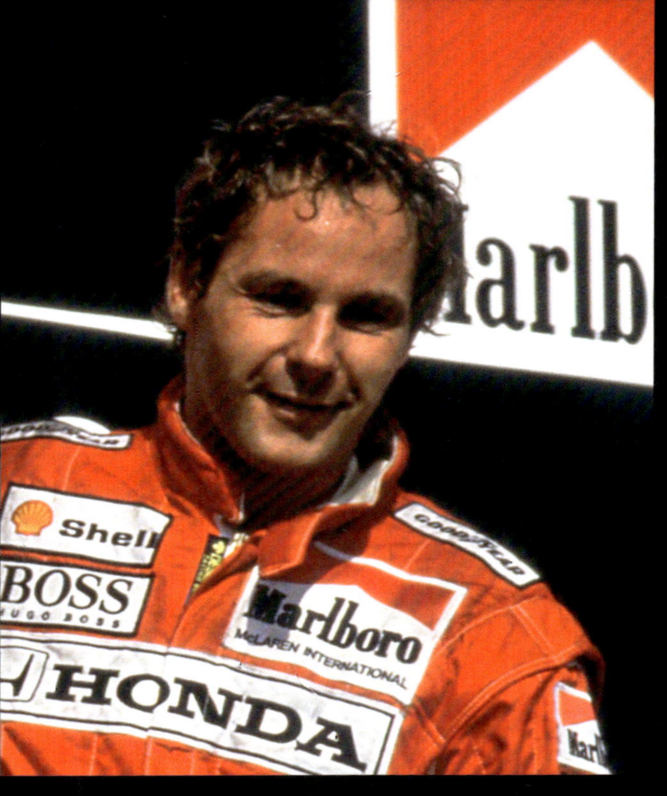

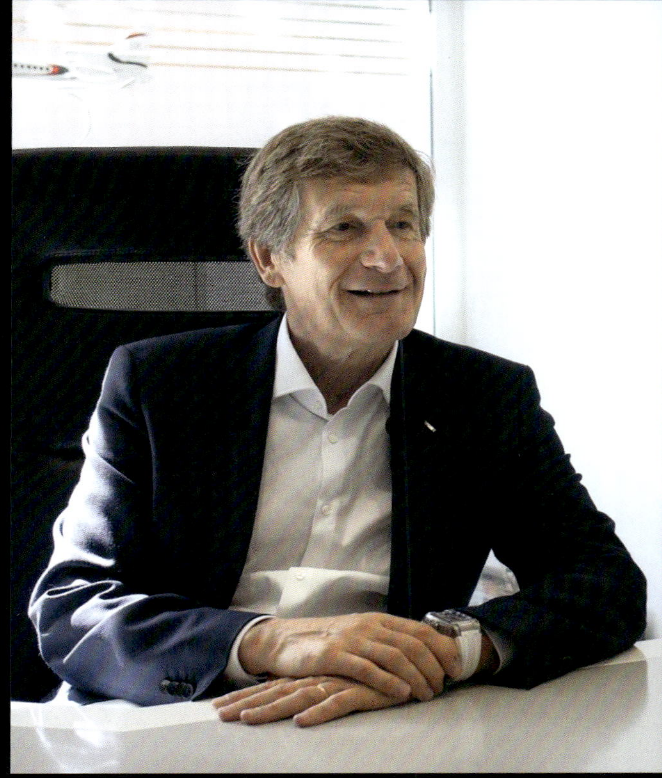

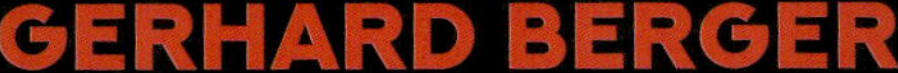

GERHARD BERGER

“The first time I met ‘that guy’ (back then, in F3, everyone was, for the most part, just a new rival with no previous reputation), it was weird, strange! He won, but he wasn’t happy I got the best lap ‘instead of him,’ as he told me on the podium. I didn’t really care about it. I wanted to laugh about it and told him to file a claim. I would have even wanted him to win that thing, as I didn’t care about getting my name on a simple line. Nonetheless, the message was pretty clear: he hated losing and was ready to win at all costs.

Seven years later, we had become friends and teammates in F1 and, in a certain way, the biggest rivals as we had the same materials to work with. And to my surprise, when I was doing better than him, Ayrton was the first to congratulate me! And four years later, I lived something that can easily resume our friendship.

At the start of a race in Italy, as the announcer introduced the drivers on the grid one by one, the audience applauded loudly when my name was announced. Ayrton winked at me from his cockpit, pleased by the ovation. It was our last exchange of glances. It’s engraved forever in my eyes, in my head, in my heart, everywhere inside me, still vibrating on my skin. That was at Imola.”

THIERRY BOUTSEN

“Sadly, I never had the opportunity to be teammate with Ayrton. And as he didn’t really have any bonds with other drivers, I have fond memories of our friendship. I don’t really remember how it happened. Maybe it was just like discovering a new guy, like a newcomer at the office. Feelings of sympathy and human sincerity quickly prevailed over all others.

On vacation at his place or elsewhere, we shared great moments of exchange and trust and were often in confidence on many subjects, including God, that he was thanking every time he won a race. Some media even claimed that he was doing that for his image. I guarantee you that it wasn’t for that. His sincere faith pushed him, and even if he was naturally a really good driver, it helped him by reinforcing his confidence, putting him on a level no one ever got since then. When my wife Patricia and I asked him to be the godfather of our son, it wasn’t because of our friendship. Knowing he had a really strong faith, we knew he would have been the ideal person for that. He accepted. Unfortunately, Cédric was born three weeks ‘after.’ Ayrton thus never became his godfather, but I am sure that anywhere he is, he is still keeping an eye on him.”

This book contains 16 exclusive interviews with those who crossed paths with Ayrton Senna in Formula 1:

JEAN ALESI
GIOVANNA AMATI
GERHARD BERGER
THIERRY BOUTSEN
JOHNNY CECOTTO
CLIVE CHAPMAN
NUNO COBRA
ERIK COMAS
BOB DANCE
JEAN-MARC GOUNON
STEVE HALLAM
STEFAN JOHANSSON
JEAN-LOUIS SCHLESSER
PATRICK TAMBAY
LEO TURRINI
MIKE WILSON

CONTENTS

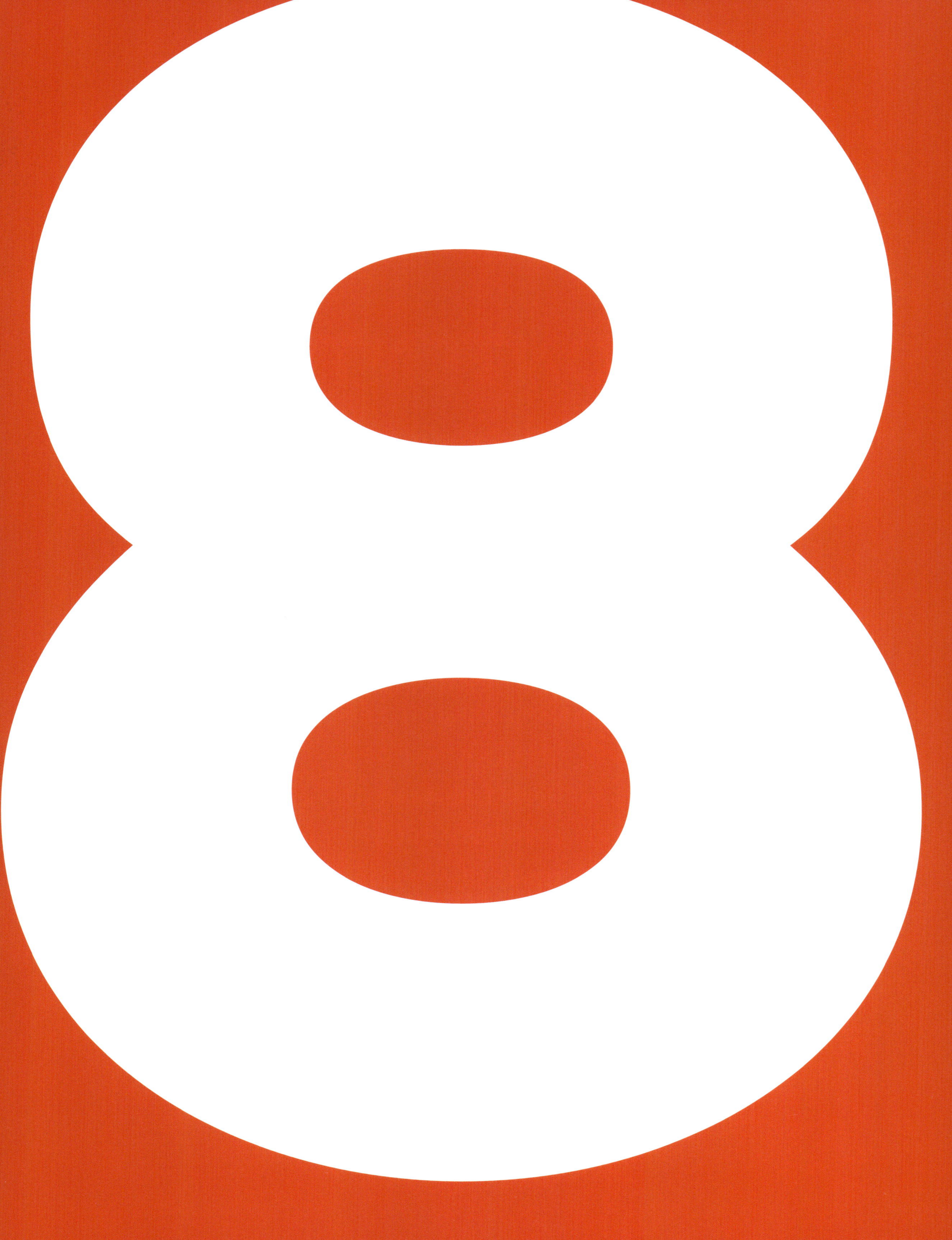

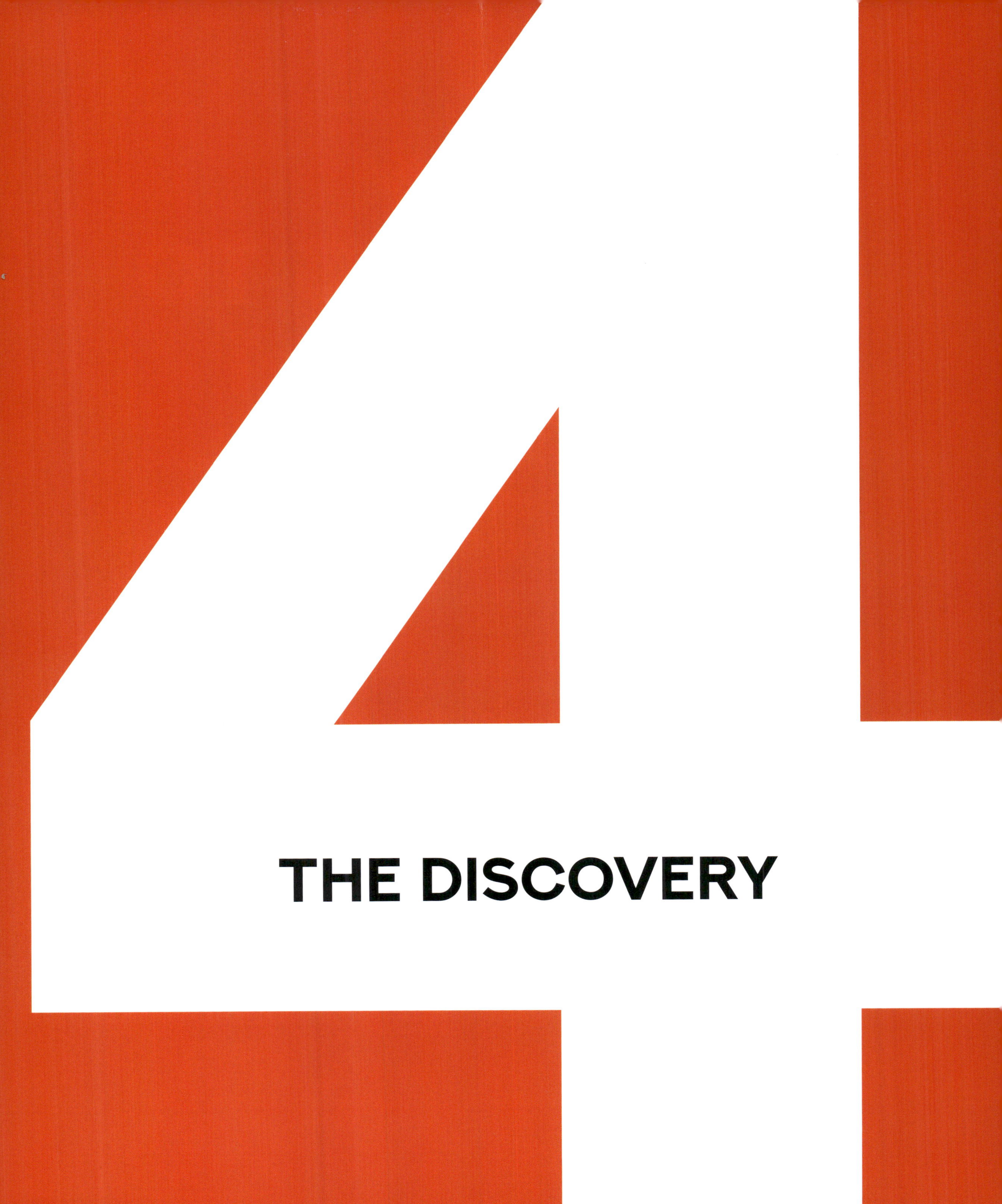

THE DISCOVERY

FROM FORMULA 3 TO FORMULA 1

AYRTON SENNA'S NUMEROUS VICTORIES IN ENGLAND, FIRST IN FORMULA FORD, THEN IN FORMULA 3 (10 VICTORIES IN 1983), GAVE HIM THE OPPORTUNITY TO SHOWCASE HIS TALENT.

Senna's trial session with Williams, who didn't want to sign a contract with Senna because they already had contracts with drivers Rosberg and Laffite, may have convinced Ron Dennis of McLaren to learn a tad more about him. However, Dennis had already decided to recruit Alain Prost to form a duo with Niki Lauda, who was aiming for a third world champion title. And while Peter Warr of Lotus would have loved pairing Senna with driver Elio de Angelis, the British sponsors of Nigel Mansell put some pressure in favor of the hot-headed Briton, who ultimately kept his place on Lotus's racing team that was founded by the late Colin Chapman, who passed away in 1982.

PIQUET'S VETO

With Williams, McLaren, and Lotus unwilling to contract with Senna, only two teams remained open to him: Brabham and Toleman. Since July of 1984, Bernie Ecclestone was aware that Senna was free for the 1984 racing season. There were only two problems: Parmalat, the main sponsor of the team Ecclestone bought in the beginning of the 1970s, would have preferred having an American driver with Nelson Piquet. The double world champion (1981, 1983) was aware of the potential and the danger coming from his young fellow countryman. He vetoed that decision. In the following years, he would deny it several times, but Herbie Blash, Brabham's general director at the time, and Christ Witty, the boss of Toleman, were aware, and Ecclestone knew that this wouldn't work: "Nelson was really irritated when he discovered we wanted to recruit Senna and talked to Parmalat. I told Parmalat that it was stupid to have two Brazilians, that they would never get along. I also explained to Parmalat that Senna was faster than Piquet, therefore he didn't want him on the team."

A DEPARTURE CLAUSE AT TOLEMAN'S

Senna thus signed with Toleman, but with a departure clause in his contract. He knew he was going to struggle with his F1 debut. If the car provided by Toleman was not good enough to meet the expectations of the driver, Senna had no problem going forward, so long as he could leave for another team at the end of 1984. The final negotiations happened in

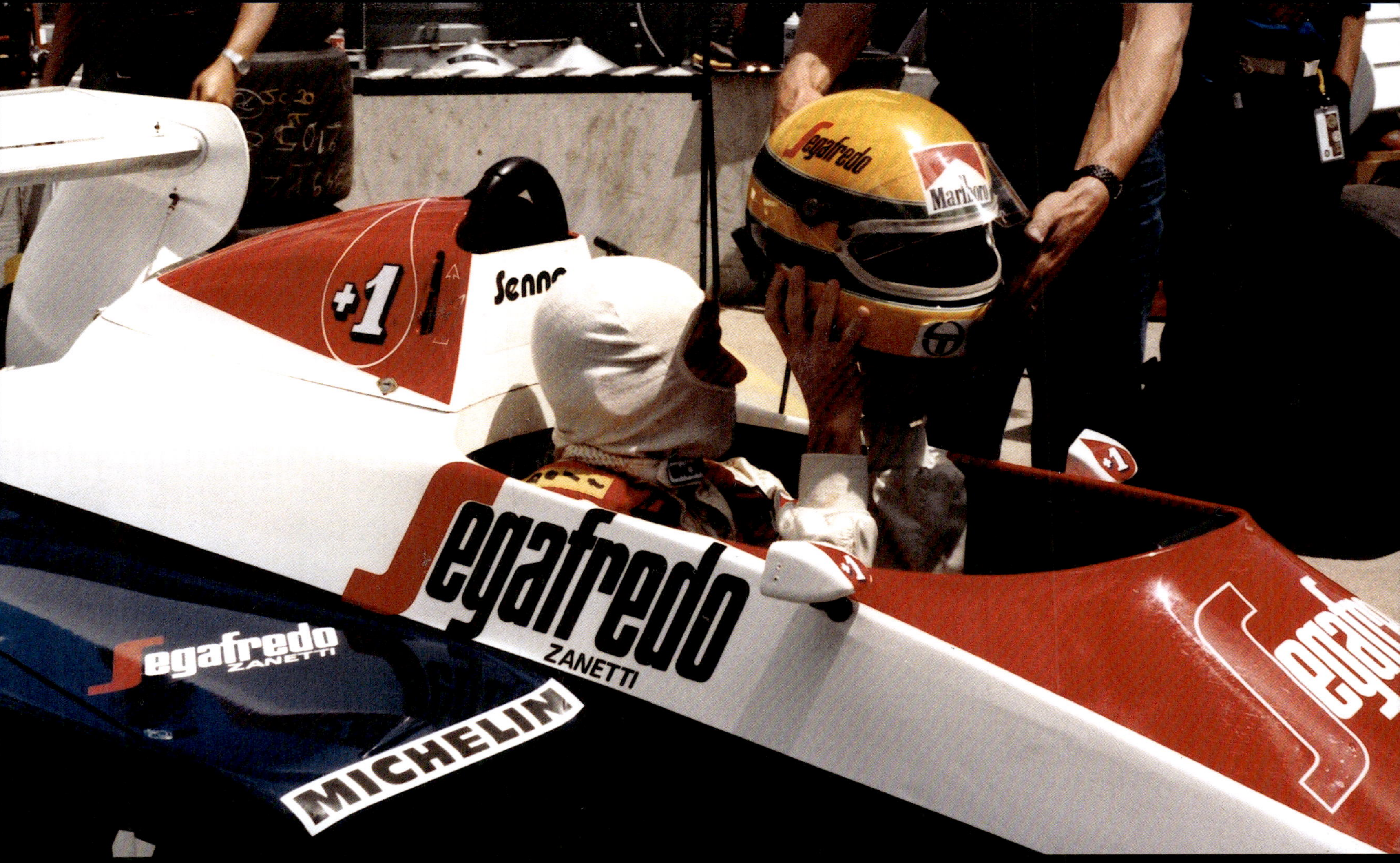

On March 25, 1984, at the age of 24, young Ayrton Senna officially debuted in F1 with the British Toleman team at the Jacarepaguá circuit in Brazil.

England, with every line, every clause, and every sentence being translated, checked, and validated over the phone by Senna's lawyers in Sao Paulo.

NO HELMET BIG ENOUGH AT ARAI

In the meantime, Senna, with the assistance of Keith Sutton, founder of the photography agency Sutton Images, was negotiating a sponsorship contract with Arai, a Japanese manufacturer of motorcycle and F1 helmets. The amount Senna asked from this potential new business partner far exceeded the original $60,000. Arai was shocked and simply sent this response to the daring Senna: "Sorry, but we don't have any helmets that could fit your head."

LATE PREPARATION WITH NUNO COBRA

Toward the end of 1983, as Senna was preparing for his F1 debut the following year, he thought he was having trouble with his heart. He booked an appointment with Nuno Cobra at the University of Sao Paulo. Their first meeting was not so great. Cobra had never worked with an F1 driver before and thought Senna was "a bit puny," but ultimately accepted the challenge of "making that young guy stronger" by helping him mentally and physically prepare for F1 racing. The preparations started in the beginning of January 1984, just a few weeks before his grand debut at the Brazil Grand Prix at the Jacarepaguá track.

RACE AFTER RACE

1984

BRAZIL GRAND PRIX: AN UNLUCKY NEWBIE

The 1984 Formula One World Championship held its first race on the track of Jacarepaguá. That Sunday, March 25, 1984, Ayrton Senna woke up at 5:00 a.m. in preparation for his first Grand Prix. And luckily for him, the first race took place in his country, in the region of Rio de Janeiro. He felt everything but euphoria, which wasn't typical of him.

On the Friday morning before the race, instead of going to the track he went to the dentist, where he underwent anesthesia to have an infection cleaned out. After that, he arrived at the track around noon and, as he had had anesthesia, he couldn't easily communicate with his team. On the Saturday before the race, a new problem emerged. Senna and his Toleman TG183B couldn't get out of the pit for part of the afternoon. The problem? The Pirelli set of tires were blistered in a manufacturer's defect and the turbo was acting up. Though the team changed the tires, the situation didn't improve. As Senna angrily stated, "I finished one lap, and on the second one, when I tried to push, the car became impossible to drive. In my mirrors, I could see parts of my tires flying all over the place!" Nonetheless, he still managed to qualify for the race in 17th position. One of the best newbies. Despite being in front of a crowd that was rooting for local hero Nelson Piquet, Senna managed to enjoy a certain amount of attention. On the morning of the race in unbearable heat, Senna signed autographs before meeting with his team to discuss their strategy. The plan was as follows: the team would change the tires on the 30th lap. Unfortunately, Senna would only complete eight. Just like the day before, the turbo barely worked and betrayed him. Senna was used to being in the front in the lower categories, but on that day, he was the first to withdraw. Watched by his mom, Neyde, and his father, Milton, Senna calmly testified before the media, "I drove slow, very slow, so I wouldn't destroy the tires. Having mechanical problems happens. What we must do now is find out what is wrong with the engine and prepare the car for the next race. Of course, I'm bummed, but who wouldn't be?"

Crossing the finish line for the first time in a Grand Prix would have to wait.

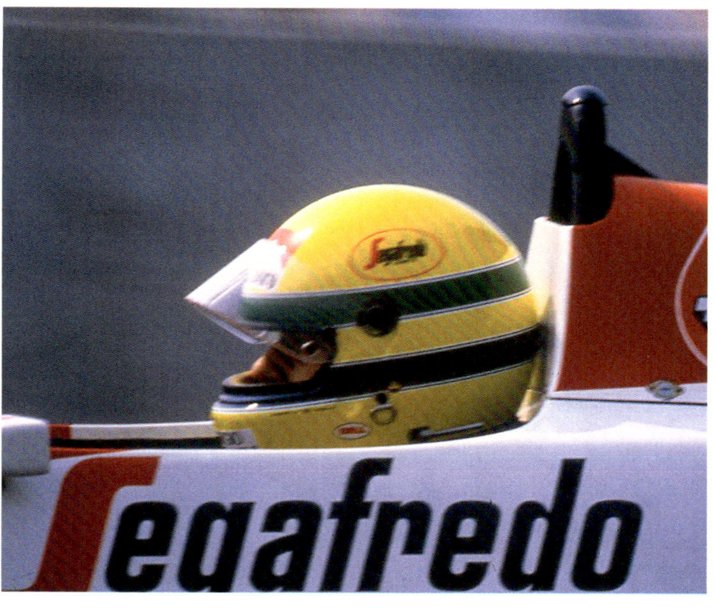

Ayrton Senna's yellow and green helmet, which was designed by Sid Mosca and became legendary, featured the dominant colors of the Brazilian flag.

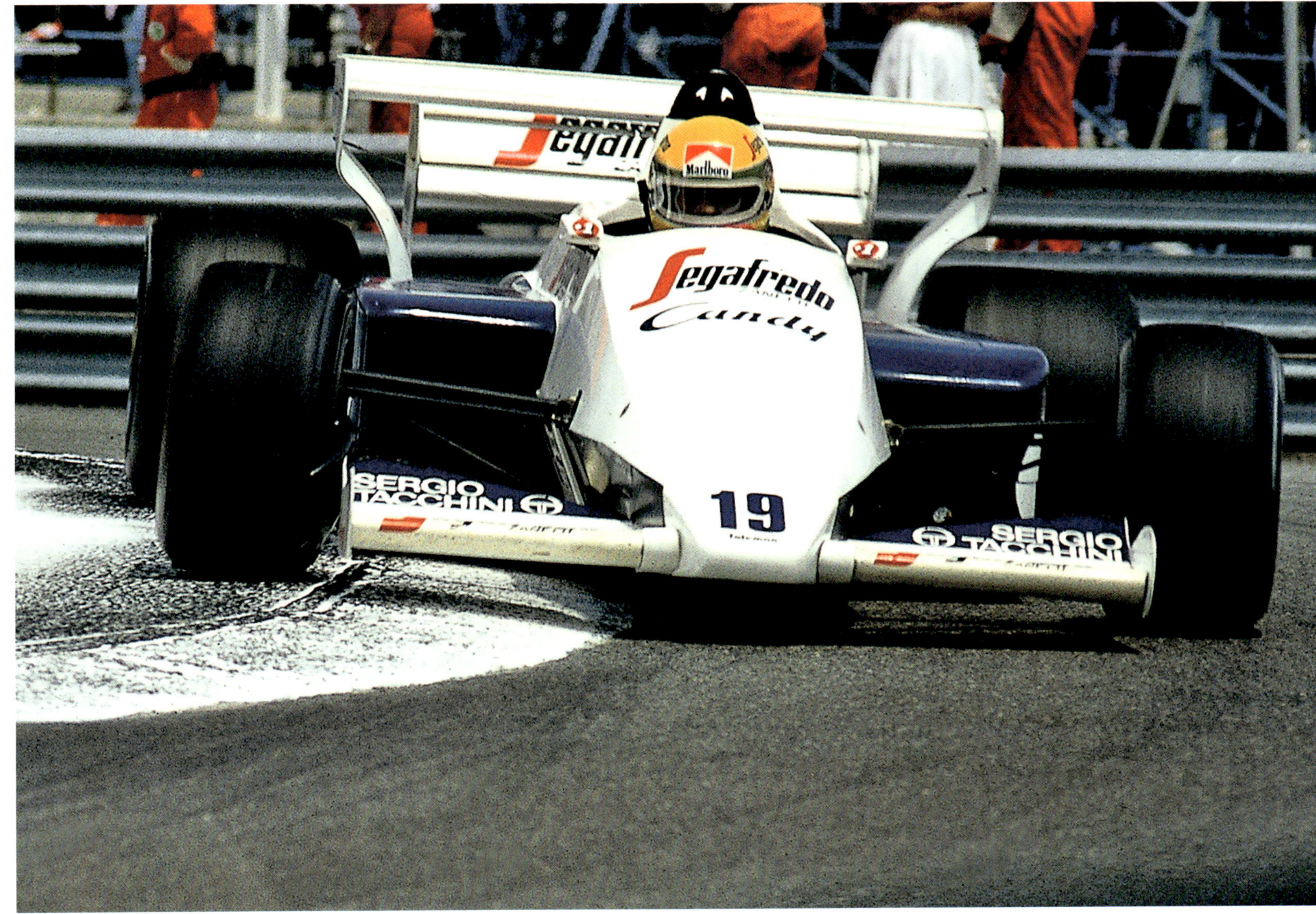

At the Monaco Grand Prix in May 1984, Ayrton Senna revealed himself to the world by finishing second, just behind Alain Prost. Due to rain, the race was stopped with a red flag.

MONACO GRAND PRIX: THE ICKX FACTOR

When Senna arrived in Monaco on May 30, 1984, to drive in the most anticipated Grand Prix of the year, he was in an unpleasant surprise: his passport had disappeared when his bag was stolen from an assistant of the Toleman team. That small inconvenience didn't stop him from concentrating on the first free practice sessions in the streets of Monaco. Thanks to some new Michelin tires, he placed 13th on the grid, just like in Dijon-Prenois. And that number 13 seems to have been lucky because, despite the torrential rain, he was able to properly showcase his talent for the first time, and with a major advantage: he was using the same Michelin tires as McLaren's Lauda and Prost, which perform better in the rain. Why? Toleman, which is a team with a limited budget, negotiated a "cheap" contract with Michelin that said they must use, in theory, tires from the prior season. But, Michelin didn't have 1983 rain tires, and therefore had to give brand new tires to Senna and Cecotto. The result lived up to this unforeseen gift. Senna got an excellent start and by the end of the first lap he was already in ninth, and he continued passing all the grid stars, including Rosberg and Lauda as well as Ferrari's drivers, Alboreto and Arnoux. On the 19th lap, Senna was in second and catching up with Prost, gaining one second each lap. On the 30th lap, the torrential rain became even worse. The visibility was very limited, and Prost was having trouble with his brakes. He was literally idling on the track, but not Senna. When Jacky Ickx decided to wave the red flag on the finishing lane, Senna was barely three seconds behind Prost. The race had to come to an end for safety reasons, but Senna thought he'd won. The situation was thoroughly confusing. It was Senna's first podium in Formula 1, but he was frustrated by the circumstances of the race. He skipped the evening gala, choosing instead to dine with close friends and family, including Alex Hawkridge and two Brazilian journalists, Galvao Bueno and Reginaldo Leme.

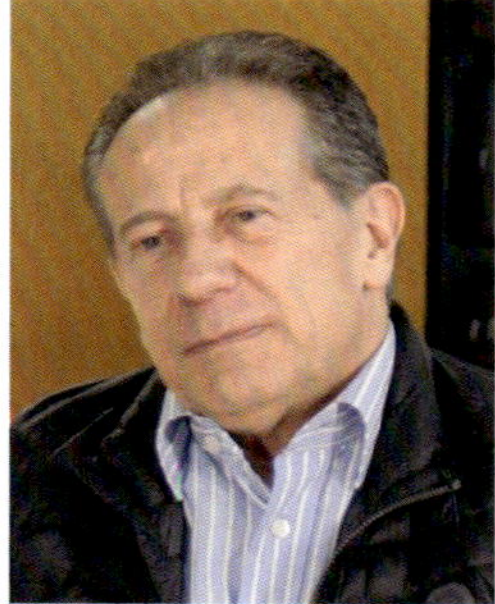

JOHNNY CECOTTO

Johnny Cecotto, Ayrton Senna's 1984 teammate at Toleman, talked about their relationship

"In the beginning, it was really good. We had a good relationship. Of course, he was the number one driver because he arrived before me and had signed the number one contract. The team couldn't make two of the same cars. For example, the engines were different. Ayrton had the new version—the one from 1984—with an electronic injection system. The difference is in speed, power, and many other things. Normally, Ayrton did all the tests and preparation, and

I could only drive the car during the race weekends. One day, I was called to run some trials together at Donington (Park). It was only for one day and we only had a single car. We were alternating. At the end of the day, I was slightly faster than him, and for him, this was unacceptable. He didn't like it. He couldn't accept it. And so, our relationship started degrading. Many years later, Ayrton talked about it in Autosprint when someone asked him the following question: 'Who was the teammate who impressed you the most?' He said that it was me."

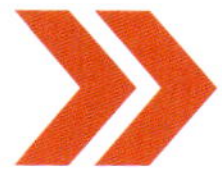

In 1984, Ayrton Senna competed in 14 Grand Prix races with the Toleman, experiencing the intricacies of F1 in the TG184 with a Hart engine.

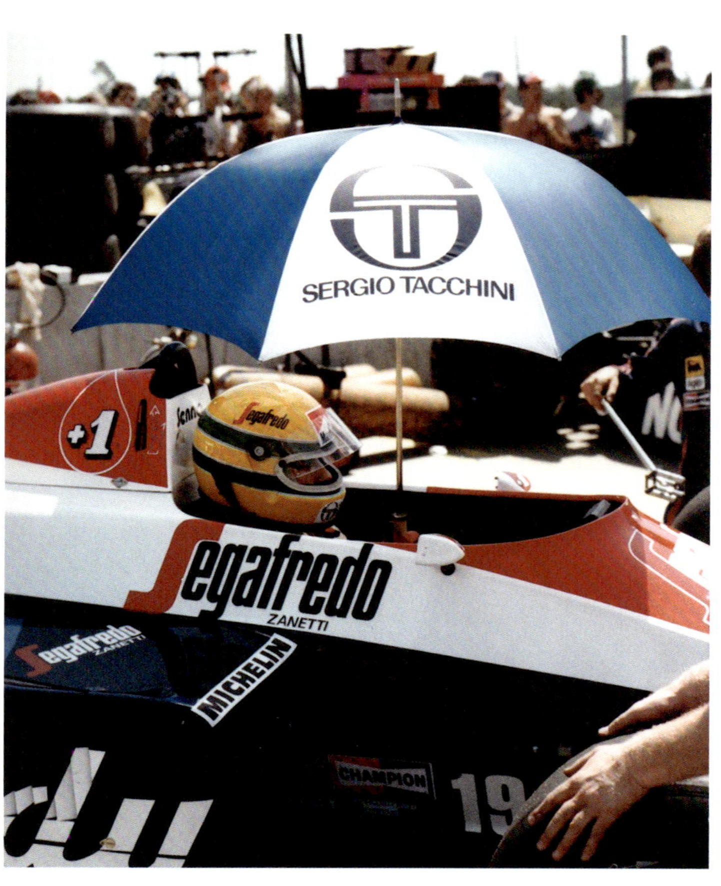

DALLAS GRAND PRIX: ANGER AS BLACK AS THE TRACK

In Dallas, on the third street circuit of the 1984 season, after Monaco and Detroit, it was so hot that the track melted, cracked, and crumbled. Some teams filled trashcans with water and ice to soak the drivers' helmets to help them withstand the heat during the free practices. The heat wasn't a problem for Senna, whose physical preparation with Cobra six months prior had enhanced his heat resistance. He ended up on the third line of the grid in fifth place. Pleased with Senna's placing, the team's manager, Peter Gethin, asked Senna not to come back to the track to try for a better starting position. Senna was literally boiling with anger at the request but managed to keep his cool, though he did take a close-up look at all the sections of the circuit that had been repaired by the organizers where the asphalt had melted. His objective? To get back on the track. But Gethin got his way and Senna returned to the hotel, furious and pointedly ignoring his bosses. The next day, after spending most of the race at the rear of the pack, he had to withdraw on the 47th lap due to a broken transmission.

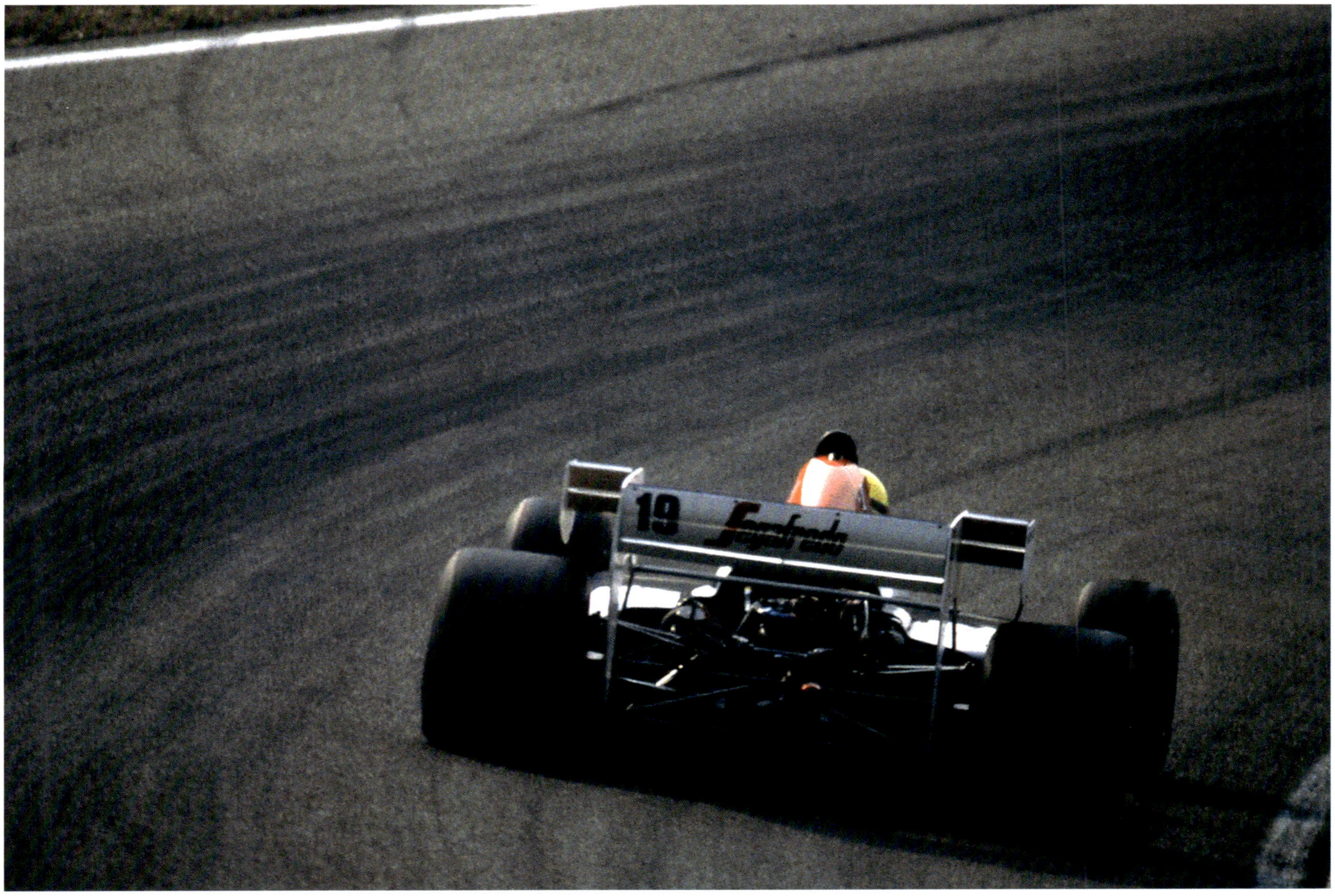

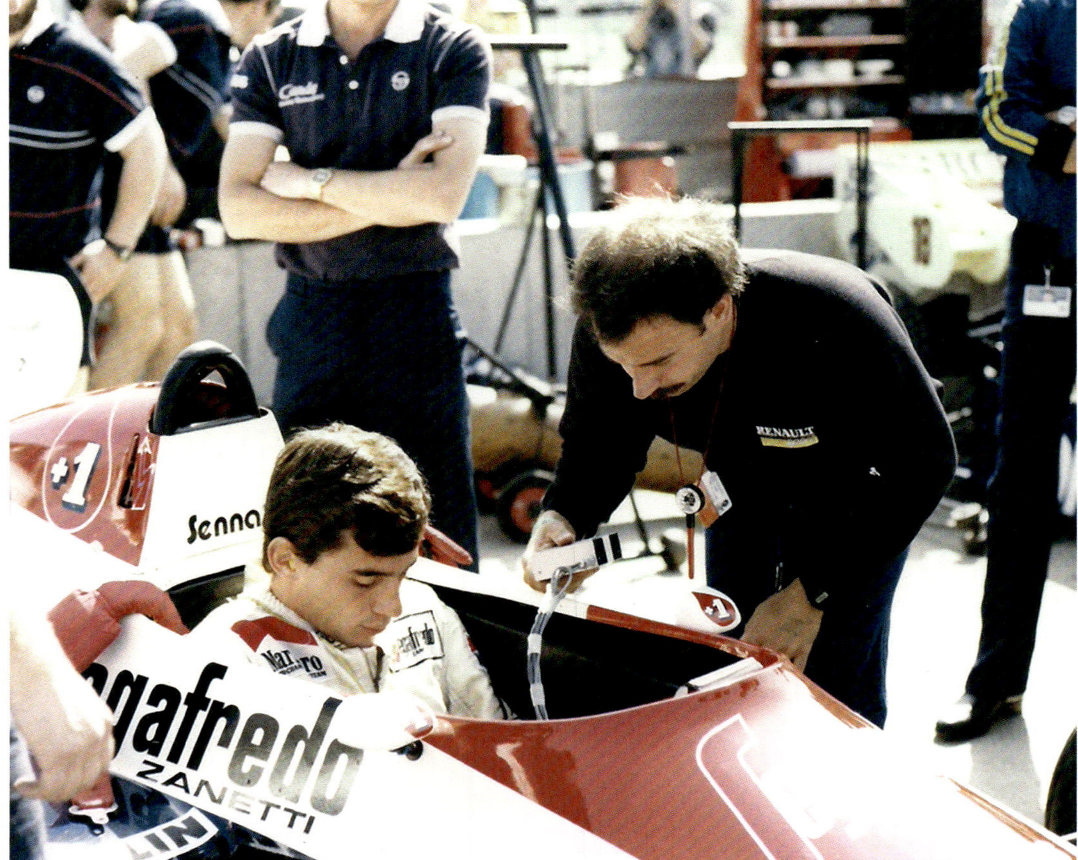

Top: In 1984, the Toleman TG184 was not the most performance-oriented car on the grid; however, it allowed the young Brazilian to complete the first 549 laps of his F1 career.

Bottom: Meticulous by nature, Ayrton Senna never started a Grand Prix without wrapping his hands in bandages to avoid blisters.

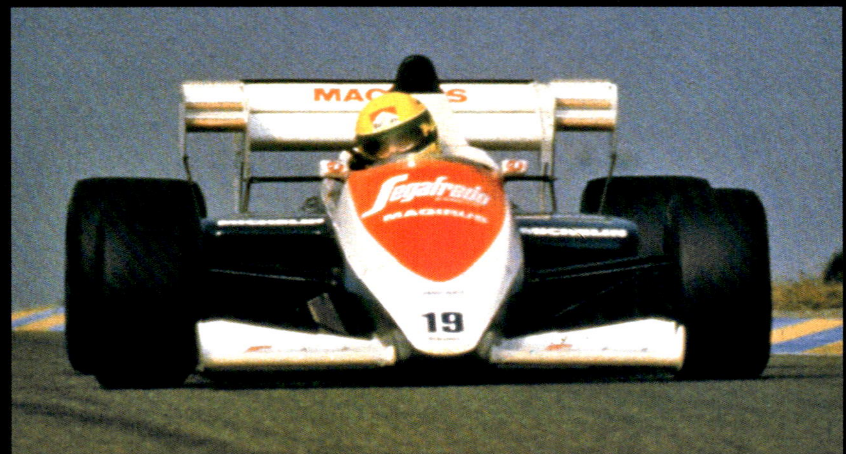

THE CARS: TOLEMAN TG183B / TOLEMAN TG184

The Toleman TG183B was the first Formula 1 car officially driven by Ayrton Senna in the world championship. It was a difficult car to handle for any debut driver. Designed by Rory Byrne, the TG183B was angular, heavy, and had no power steering. The physical effort to make the most of it was colossal. Which would limit the British F3 champion, faced with purely physical limits to its piloting. Even Pat Symonds, Senna's track engineer, acknowledged that the TG183B "is a complicated car to drive and configure, but when you finally get the right setup, it can be pretty fast." The TG183B featured a radiator mounted directly on the spoiler that was powered by a homemade 600-horsepower Hart turbo engine whose reliability was not its strong point. Between that and the Pirelli tires, the TG183B struggled to compete with its rivals who were equipped by Goodyear and Michelin.

After three races and one missed race, which Senna had failed to qualify for, Toleman officially retired the TG183B and replaced it with a newer version: the TG184. Speaking about this car, Byrne said, "The suspension and the monocoque were essentially the same as those of the 183, but we removed the Venturi system from the front wing, as it made the car too sensitive to pitching, and moved the oil and water radiators to the right-hand pontoon. The result was an increase in downforce of around twenty-five percent." Thus, the car was far easier to configure and drive. Furthermore, the TG184 was designed to use and was equipped with Michelin tires, same as their rivals Ligier, Renault, Brabham, and McLaren. The Toleman budget was far inferior to those of McLaren or Ferrari, but the team found some solutions. Starting with the Monaco Grand Prix, Senna would enjoy a new electronic injection system, unlike his teammate Johnny Cecotto, who still had to drive with a mechanical system. Driving the TG184, Senna hit the podium three times, and these were the only podiums Toleman would ever have.

STEFAN JOHANSSON

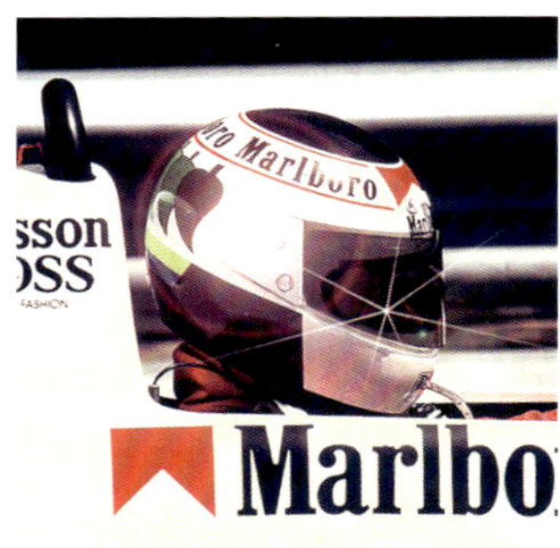

Stefan Johansson, Ayrton Senna's other teammate at Toleman in 1984, talked about Senna's talent, his exceptionally high standards, and compared their relationship with the friendlier one he had with Alain Prost.

"With the engine department, with the folks from Michelin, everything had to perfect, everyone had to give Senna an answer concerning the handling of the car. He was very impressive, and he absolutely wanted to score big, by any means. He expected everybody to do their best because he was performing his best on the track. He was young, but very hard and demanding, saying, 'I want this, and that, and this.'

It wasn't like that with Alain (Prost). With him, it was more of a personal relationship, with a certain level of friendship. First, we would talk about the car, but when we were done, we would talk about everything else. Ayrton was different. There were no social links, but that wasn't too bad since he didn't care about it. He was so ambitious, so resolved to get some results. Alain too, but he had a different way of living."

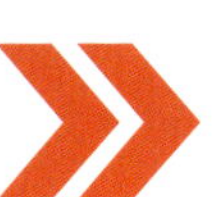

He was young, but very hard and demanding

STEFAN JOHANSSON

GERMANY GRAND PRIX: DISCOVERING FRUSTRATION

On the fourth lap and in fifth place at the Hockenheim track, Senna was going approximately 155 mph (250 kph) when the Toleman TG184's rear spoiler detached. He lost control of the car, hit the safety rail, and plunged into the Hockenheim Forest. Thankfully, Senna was not injured. The car, however, was badly damaged, as was his ego. Full of anger, he threw his steering wheel on the ground, then walked from the crash to the pit, which gave him time to think about what had happened. "I had everything," Senna said. "The car was perfect. I had no doubts about my rhythm. I'm sure I could've finished between Prost [winner] and Lauda [second]." This was the fourth time that season that Senna had been victim to a mechanical failure during a race.

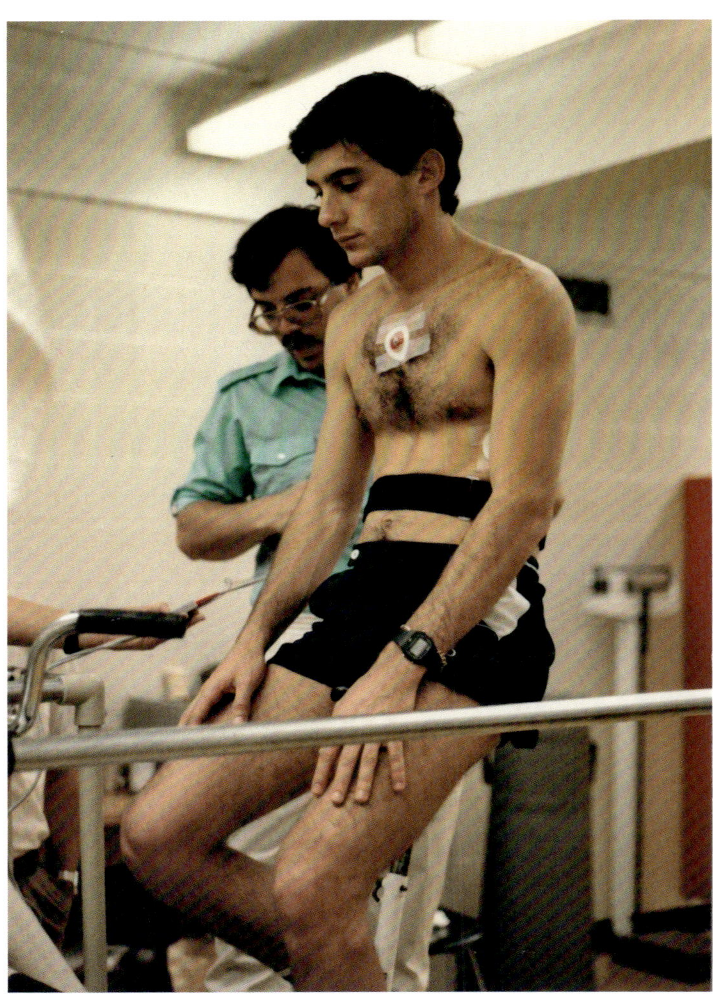

Upon entering F1, Ayrton Senna had a rather slender stature and appeared very fragile to the eyes of the man who would become his physical trainer and confidant: Nuno Cobra. Here, the driver's physical abilities were assessed at McGill University a few days before the 1984 Canadian Grand Prix.

GÉRARD DUCAROUGE, ONE OF SENNA'S EARLY FANS

There's no shortage of anecdotes about Senna's maiden season in F1. He was extremely assertive and self-confident for a debutant in the premier class. His temperament was not always easy to handle, particularly for his boss, Alex Hawkridge. But for Rory Byrne, the designer of the Toleman cars, it was far more satisfying.

Senna was already a hard worker, and he explained that, since June 1984, he felt the need to be respected. "I would like to be respected for my work, my willpower and the sacrifices I've made," Senna reported the French magazine, AutoHebdo. As soon as Senna joined F1, he overcame his shyness to say hello to Lotus's star engineer, Gérard Ducarouge, when they were seated at nearby tables in a restaurant with his inseparable journalist friends Reginaldo Leme and Galvao Bueno from TV Globo.

As Ducarouge later recalled to his friend, journalist Lionel Froissart, who had also authored a few books about Senna, "[Senna] talked to me in Italian. I speak this language since I have to use it at Alfa Romeo. Ayrton, who I didn't know at all, congratulated me on all my achievements. He knew everything about my career: my debut at Matra in their endurance races, my lengthy collaboration with Ligier, then Alfa Romeo, and then my arrival in England, with Lotus, the year prior. He made it clear that he absolutely wanted to work with me and that one day it would happen. This was all the more astonishing given that he had just arrived in F1 and had just begun working with Toleman."

A few months later, Senna would sign with Lotus, and would work with Ducarouge as his technical manager.

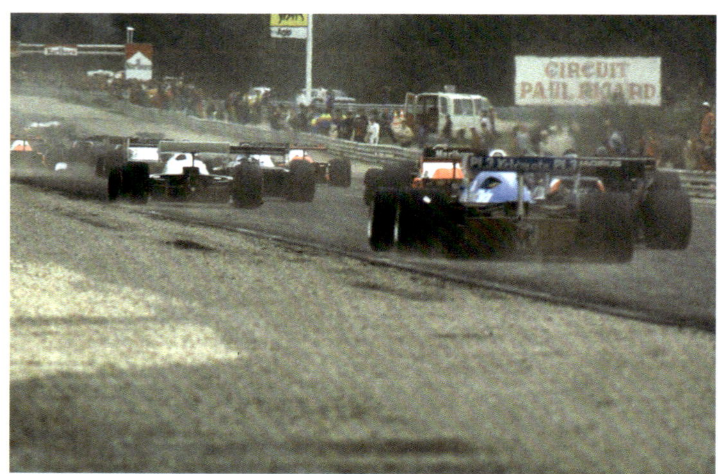

PORTUGAL GRAND PRIX: BYE, BYE, TOLEMAN!

The Portugal Grand Prix was the final race of the 1984 season. It was also a chance for Senna to perfectly finish his first season in F1 by getting a third podium for Toleman, after Monaco and Brands Hatch at the British Grand Prix. Starting third on the grid, Senna ended up in the same position at the end of the race behind the McLaren drivers, Prost and Lauda, the latter being a three-time world champion.

The next day, just for fun, Senna returned to the Estoril track because Alex Hawkridge made him an offer he couldn't refuse: try to score the best time, in a private session, against lesser-rated rivals than Prost, Lauda or Piquet. On the track in a Toleman mule outfitted with soft tires, Senna competed against Roberto Moreno, Manfred Winkelhock, Jan Lammers, and Ivan Capelli. Senna completed a dozen laps, the best being 1 minute 21.7 seconds, which was three thousandths of a second faster than Piquet's pole position two days earlier in a Brabham equipped with qualifying tires. In the downhill that preceded the stand lines, a man observed Senna's last laps driving a Toleman equipped with the turbo engine he himself fully designed. That man was Brian Hart.

Top left: In 1984, no less than 26 cars took part in several races, ensuring a spectacle at the beginning of some events.

Top right: With his Toleman, Ayrton Senna started in F1 in the shadow of Niki Lauda (McLaren) and the Brabham team, still led by Bernie Ecclestone.

Bottom right: The Toleman was not always very effective; however, it allowed Ayrton Senna to stand out on some circuits.

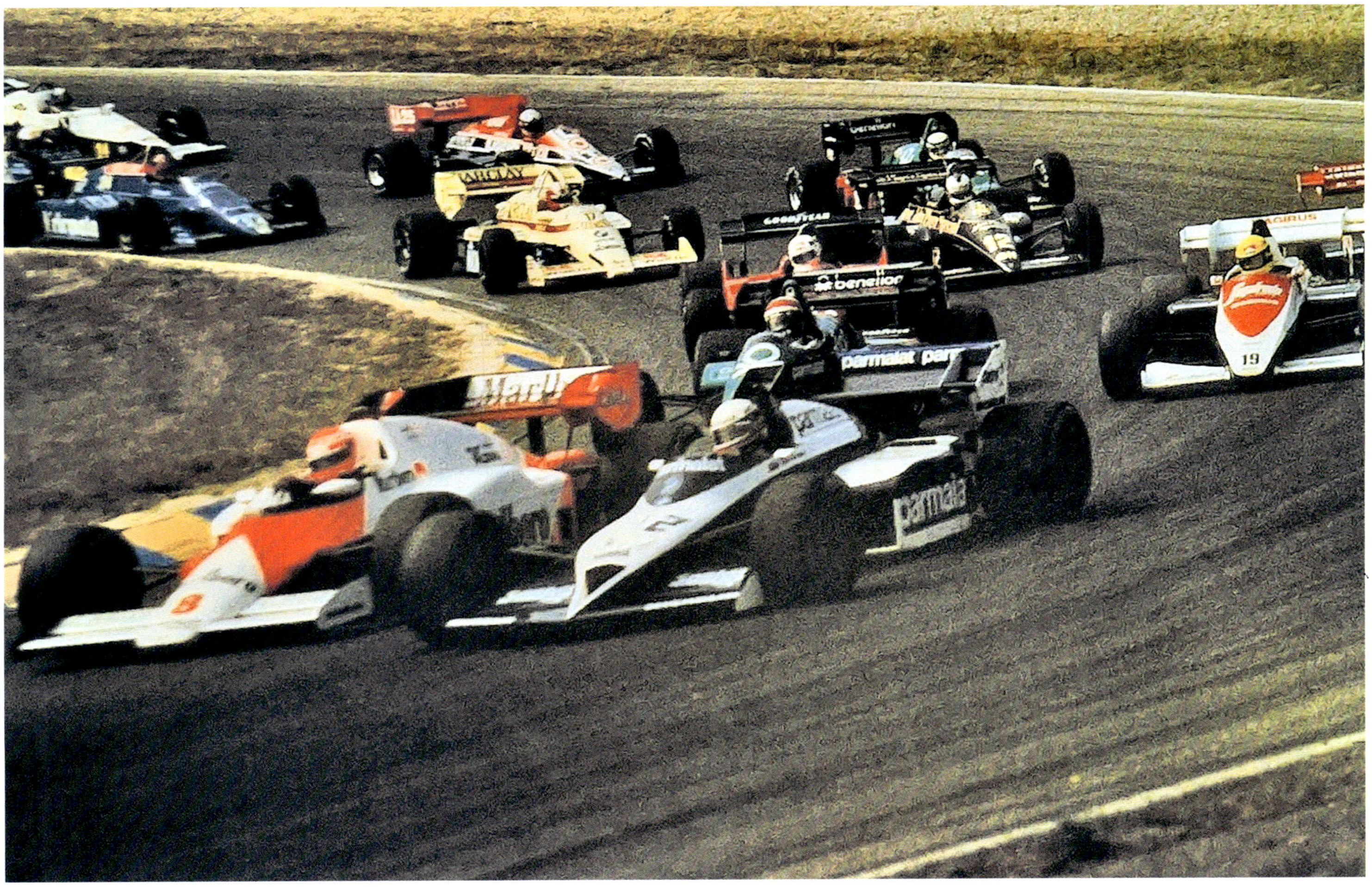

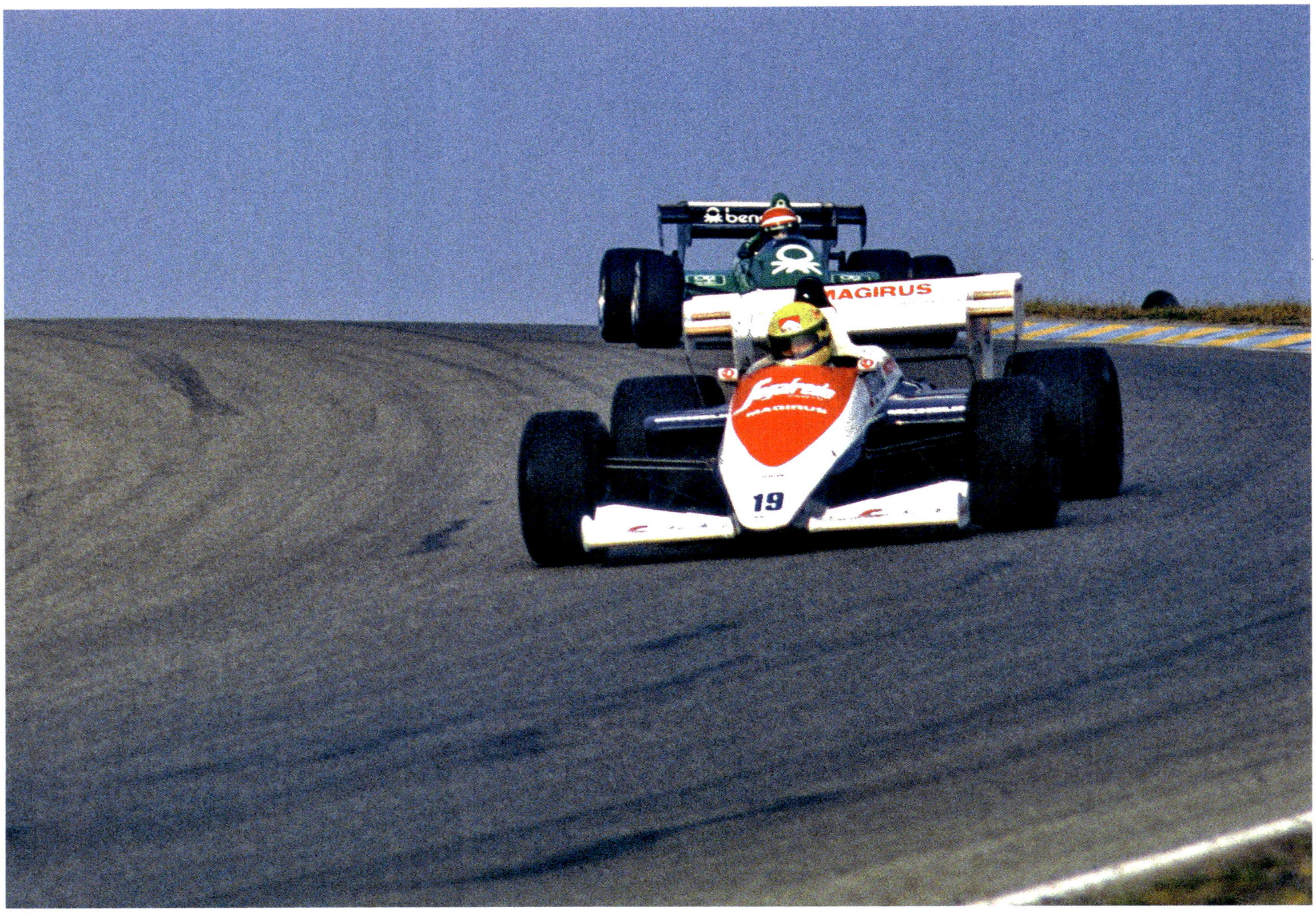

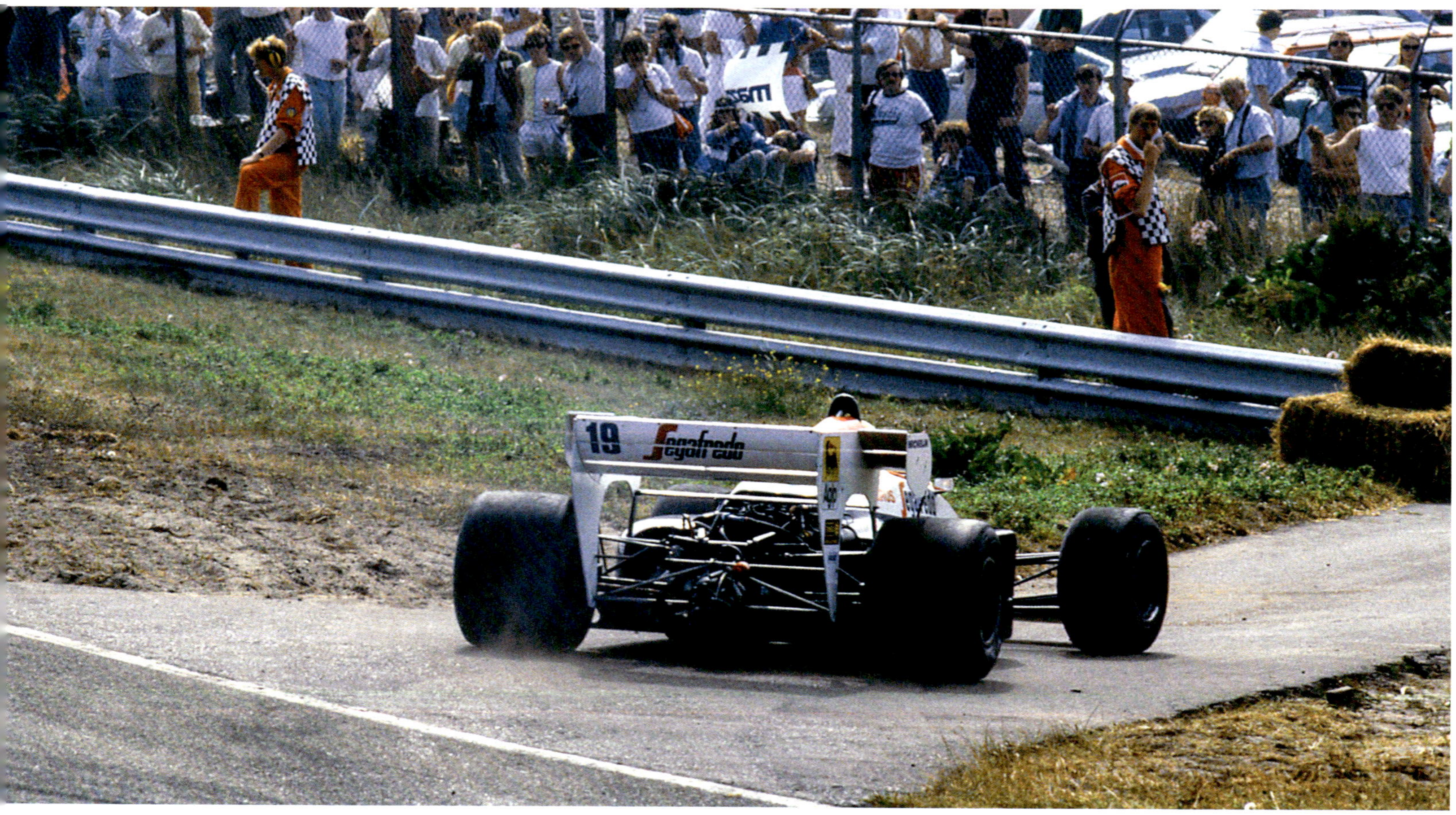

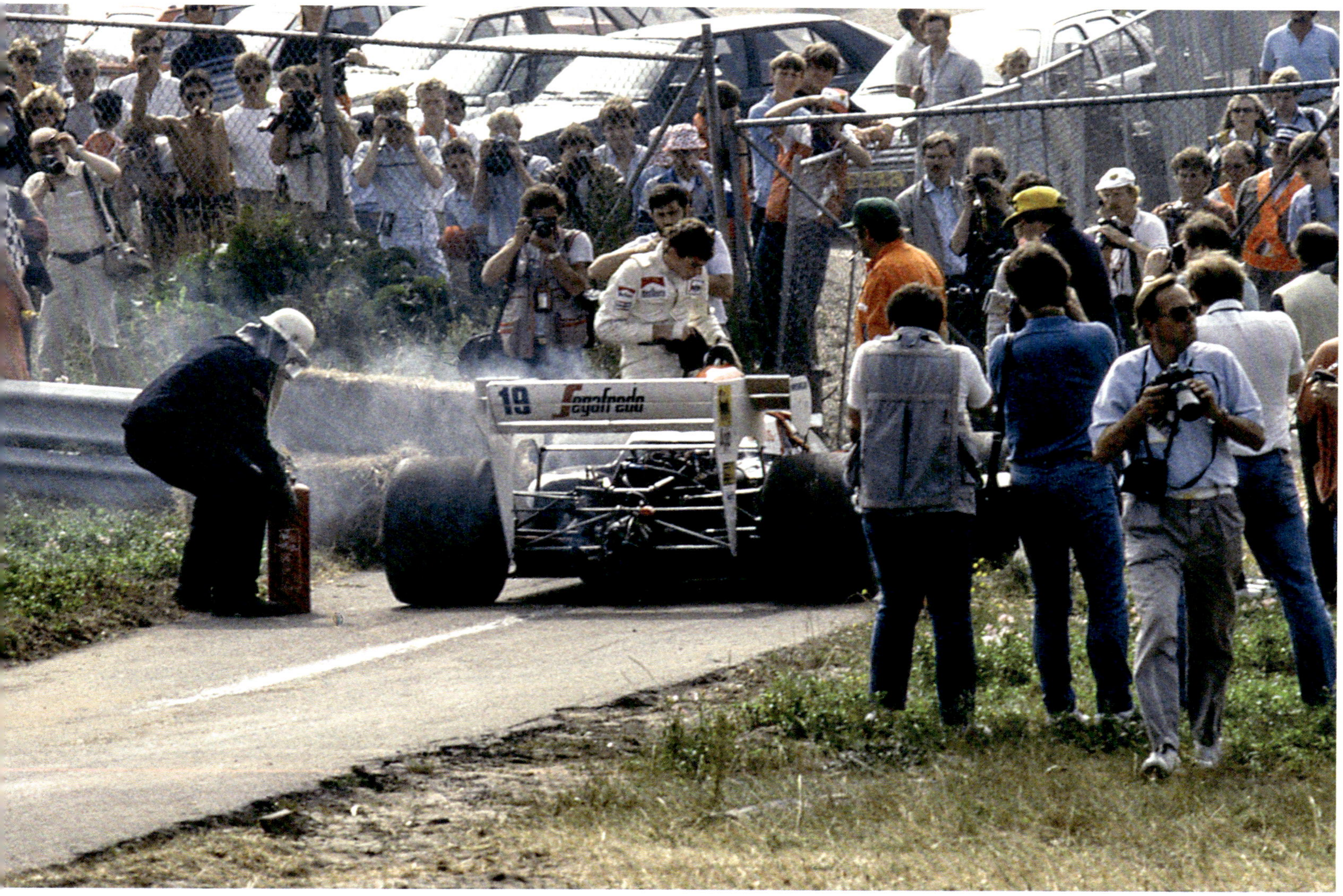

Top: Turbo or engine problems with Ayrton Senna's Toleman often prevented him from showing his full potential.

Bottom: In total, Ayrton Senna retired eight times in his first 14 Grand Prix races in F1.

Right: Ayrton Senna led Nigel Mansell, who was then with Lotus. The two drivers would meet again a few years later, competing at the forefront in much more competitive cars: a McLaren for the Brazilian and a Williams for the mustached Briton.

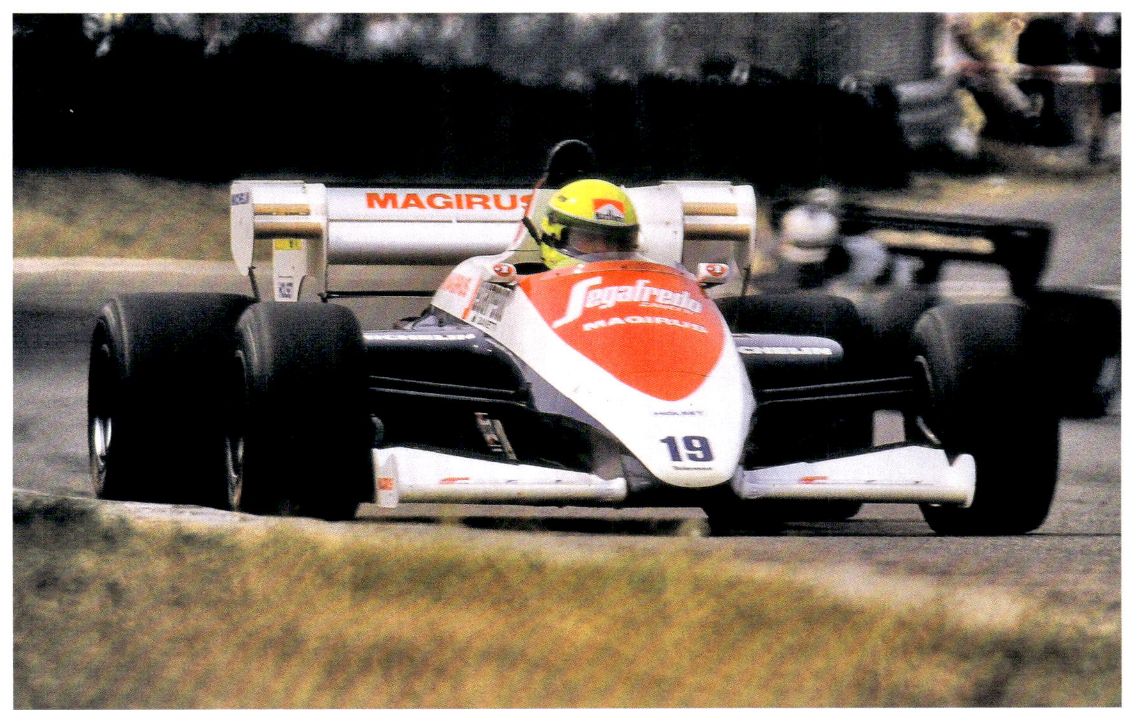

THE 1984 SEASON IN FIGURES

GRAND PRIX	QUALIFIERS	RACE
BRAZIL	16TH	DNF (TURBO)
SOUTH AFRICA	13TH	6TH
BELGIUM	19TH	6TH
FRANCE	13TH	DNF (TURBO)
MONACO	13TH	2ND
CANADA	9TH	7TH
DETROIT	7TH	DNF (CRASH)
DALLAS	6TH	DNF (TRANSMISSION)
GREAT BRITAIN	7TH	3RD
GERMANY	9TH	DNF (CRASH)
AUSTRIA	10TH	DNF (OIL PRESSURE)
NETHERLANDS	13TH	DNF (ENGINE)
EUROPE	12TH	DNF (CRASH)
PORTUGAL	3RD	3RD

RANKING: NINTH PLACE IN THE FORMULA ONE WORLD CHAMPIONSHIP

(13 POINTS, 3 PODIUMS, 1 BEST LAP)

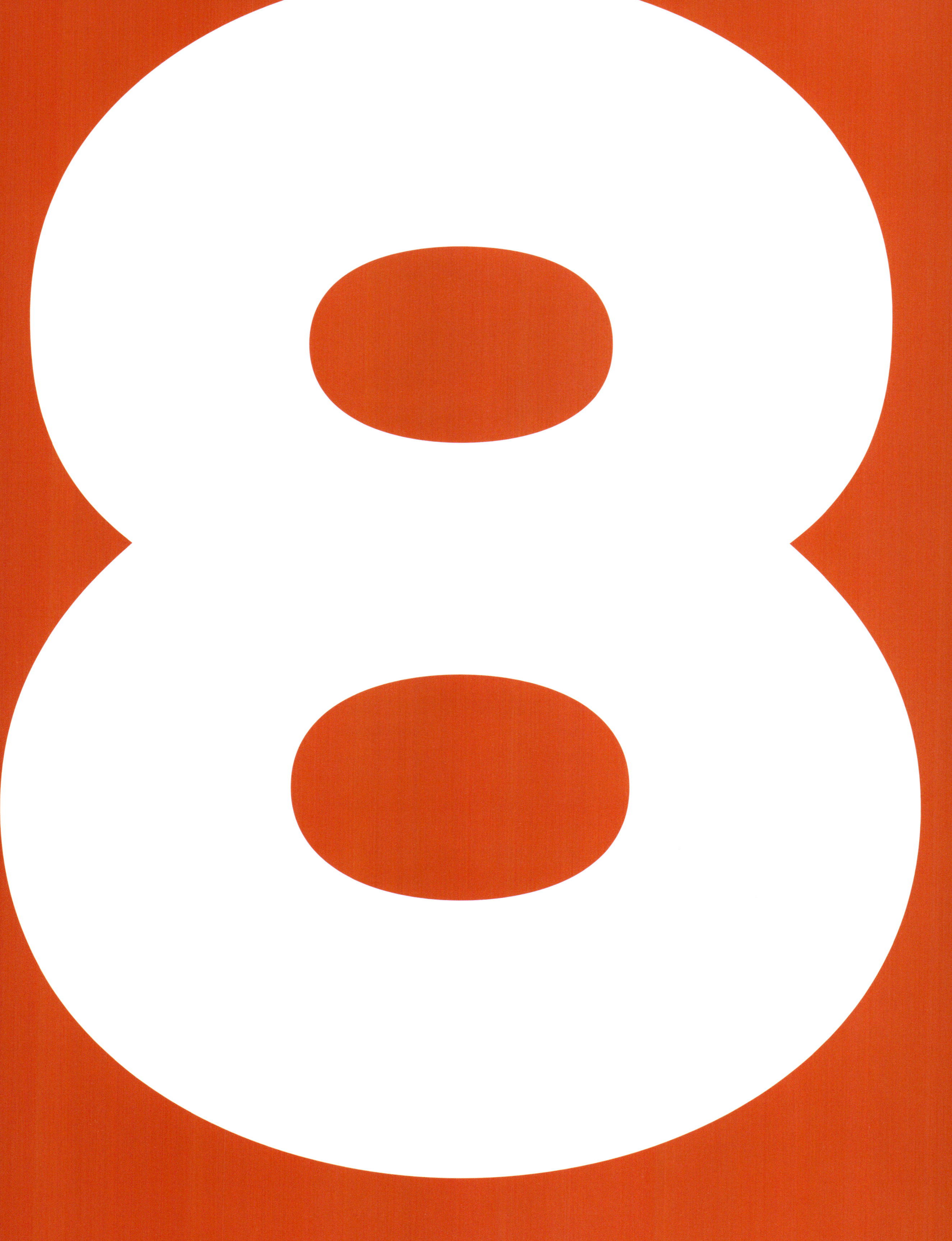

5

A SEAT AT LOTUS

THE CONFIRMATION

FROM TOLEMAN TO LOTUS.

AFTER SPENDING A YEAR WITH TOLEMAN AND LEARNING WHAT FORMULA 1 REALLY WAS, SENNA'S MOVE TO LOTUS IS THE BEGINNING OF A DREAM.

The young Brazilian has already showcased all of his talent, and the British racing team, orphaned since 1982 after the death of Colin Chapman, its founder, is still one of the strongest teams of the '80s thanks to some very powerful Renault engines. And to make things even better, the black and gold design of the cigarette manufacturer, John Player Special, is back, just like in the fruitful years of the '70s, when another Brazilian, Emerson Fittipaldi, and many other talented pilots, like Ronnie Peterson and Mario Andretti, won many, many races.

The first time Ayrton enters the Lotus 97T with his Renault engine is in early February 1985 on the Rio de Janeiro track, where the Brazilian Grand Prix is supposed to take place. Bob Dance, the head mechanic at Lotus, still perfectly remembers those first laps: "We had instruments glued on the dashboard. They were indicating the temperature and the pressure in the tires during the laps. Senna told us, 'There's dozens of instruments, and I won't remember what they say during a single lap. I'm going to watch six of them. You'll be able to take notes. Then I'll do another lap, and I'll check the information I've missed.'" He was also communicating smoothly with the engine manufacturer; would it be with Renault or Honda (in 1987)? He had a natural talent, but he was also giving 100% because he knew that the more he gave to the team, the more they would give him.

The year prior, the whole Lotus team saw what Senna was made of during his "one man show" in the streets of Monaco (second place behind Prost, race stopped because of torrential rain). Bob Dance also remembers: "It was raining, and everyone thought, 'Wow! What a way of driving!' So, Peter Warr, our

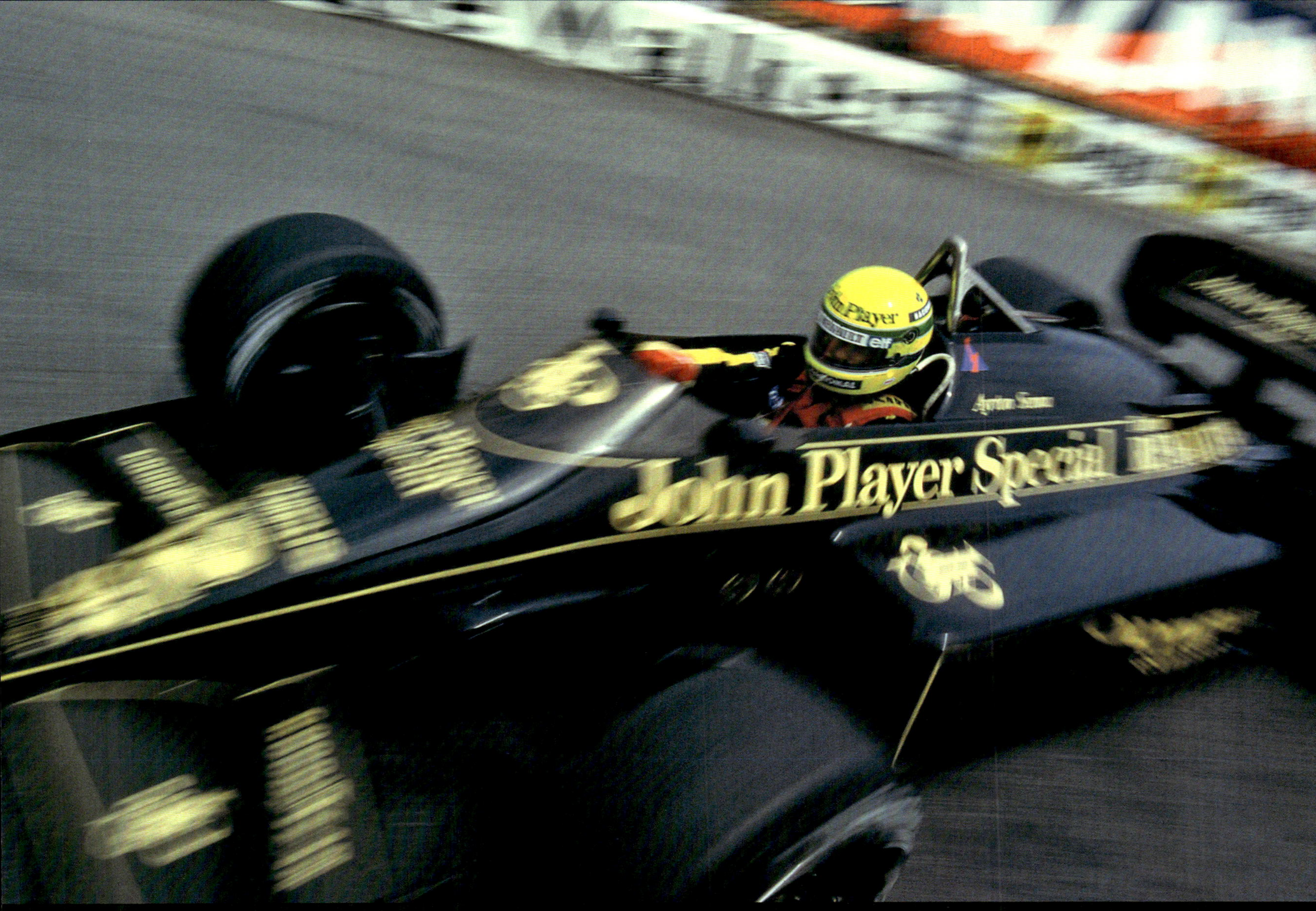

The Lotus 97T has left a beautiful mark in the history of F1, adorned in the colors of a famous tobacco sponsor. Behind the wheel, Senna's talent did not go unnoticed.

team manager, was immediately interested in the possibility of bringing him into our team, and negotiations began. He was very enthusiastic about the idea of joining Lotus, especially as we could count on Renault engines, which were very good." And starting with the Brazilian Grand Prix, at home, after the qualifying, he finally discovered his brand-new Formula 1. He had to drop out by lap 48 (due to an electrical problem) as he was nearly securing a new podium, the first with Lotus, behind Prost and Alboreto, after having been in second place for a short period of time. He was furious about getting back to the stand, but everyone in the team was feeling great. The second chapter of his incredible career was already starting…

RACE AFTER RACE

1985

PORTUGUESE GRAND PRIX: THE BRAZILIAN EQUILIBRIST

Two weeks later, Senna is ready for round two and aiming for a good result in Portugal. He has just turned 25 (on the 21st of March) and is supported by his parents. In qualifying, he is the best in the free practices on a track that fits him just perfectly. He even destroys the track record of seven-tenths of a second, with a lap time of 1:21.007. What makes it even better is that this record was the property of his fellow countryman, Nelson Piquet, the year before. "We had a lot of power, and everything seemed to be ticking. This track suits us well as everything comes down to the straights," he says to the journalists. Calm and relaxed, the Brazilian will start in front of the grid for the first time in his life in Formula 1.

At Estoril, the weather will be horrendous; rain, cold, and wind will be the main factors on the 21st of April. The weather conditions are so bad that the last warm-up session before the race has to be postponed by 30 minutes as the medical helicopter can't get up in the air. The race starts in terrible conditions. In the Lotus stand, the Sport Auto journalist, Gérard Crombac, a close friend of the Chapman family, can even hear the engineers shaking. But the man in the yellow helmet doesn't care at all about the weather—maximum concentration, no margin for error. His crazy speed is worrying everybody. And the "slow" signs shown by his engineer, Gérard Ducarouge, at every lap don't seem to have any effect on the fearless Ayrton. A fine strategist, the kid from São Paulo makes life difficult for his peers and doesn't turn on his red light in the back of his car. The last thing he wants is to help Lauda, Prost, and the other pilots have better adherence by driving in his path. And on the 67th lap, the race directors have had enough. The race must finish, two laps short of the end. Thus, Senna wins his first race with a one-minute gap, and Alboreto takes second place in his Ferrari, all the other opponents having been lapped.

The Lotus team, led by Gérard Ducarouge, invades the track and celebrates, a celebration that displeases the FISA and its French president, Jean-Marie Balestre, who will very soon forbid this practice and will also impose a $1,000 fine on the British team. But the first victory of Lotus in three years is worth every cent of this fine, even if Colin Chapman is no longer there to congratulate the winner. On the podium, as the first chords of the Brazilian anthem start echoing out, Senna is on the verge of crying. In addition to a telegram, he also gets a call from the President of Brazil, José Sarney, who says, "We Brazilians are proud of your performance. You succeeded in bringing joy to the country today." In just two hours of racing, Formula 1 has found itself a new king, and Brazil its new idol.

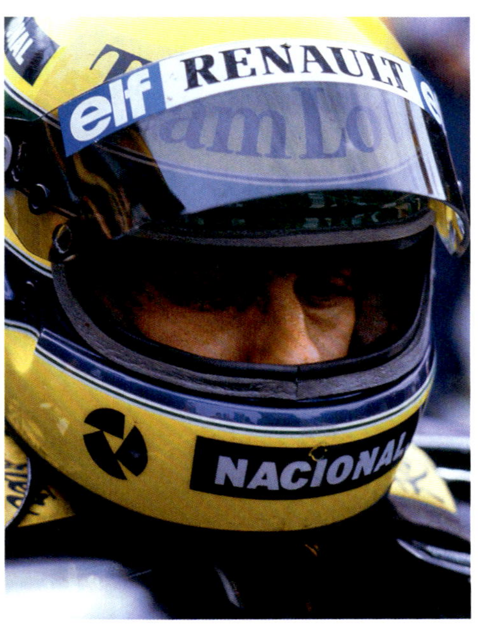

Upon joining Lotus, Senna was aware that he was taking another step toward the pinnacle of the premier category of motorsports.

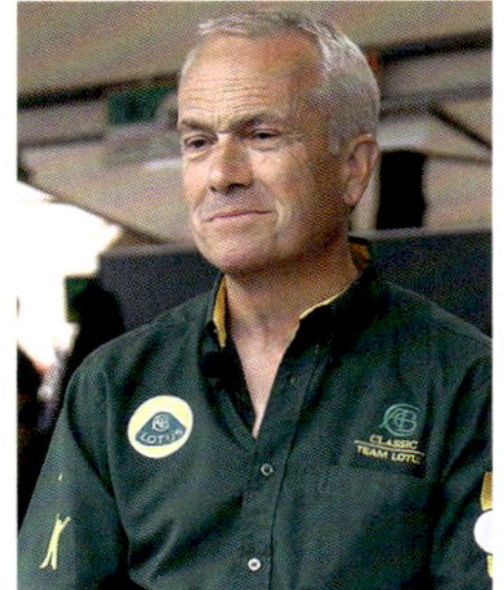

THE OPINION OF CLIVE CHAPMAN (SON OF LOTUS FOUNDER, COLIN) ON AYRTON SENNA

"Ayrton was a very skilled driver. He was a winner. He could spot any opportunity to gain the slightest advantage over his opponents. That's exactly what my father did. Ayrton was mentally very strong. There might have been some friction between them, but they shared a common ambition: Ayrton wanted to win the drivers' championship, and my father wanted to win the constructors' championship. Together, I think they would have been very successful."

Ayrton was a very skilled driver. He was a winner.

CLIVE CHAPMAN

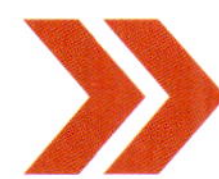

In early 1985, a sudden facial paralysis worried Ayrton Senna and his close ones. Fortunately, it turned out to be more fear than harm for this ambitious driver, who was already mindful of his image.

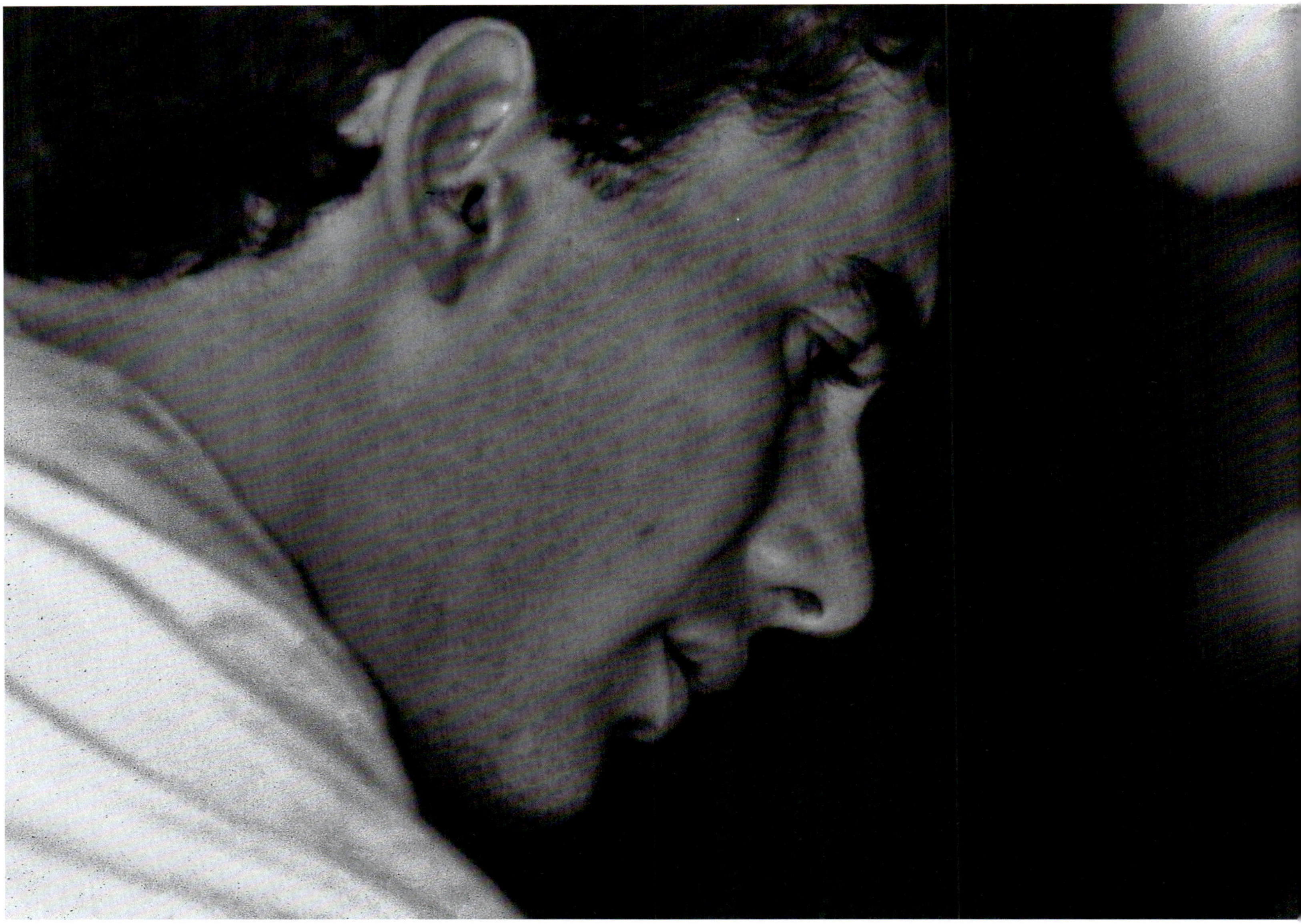

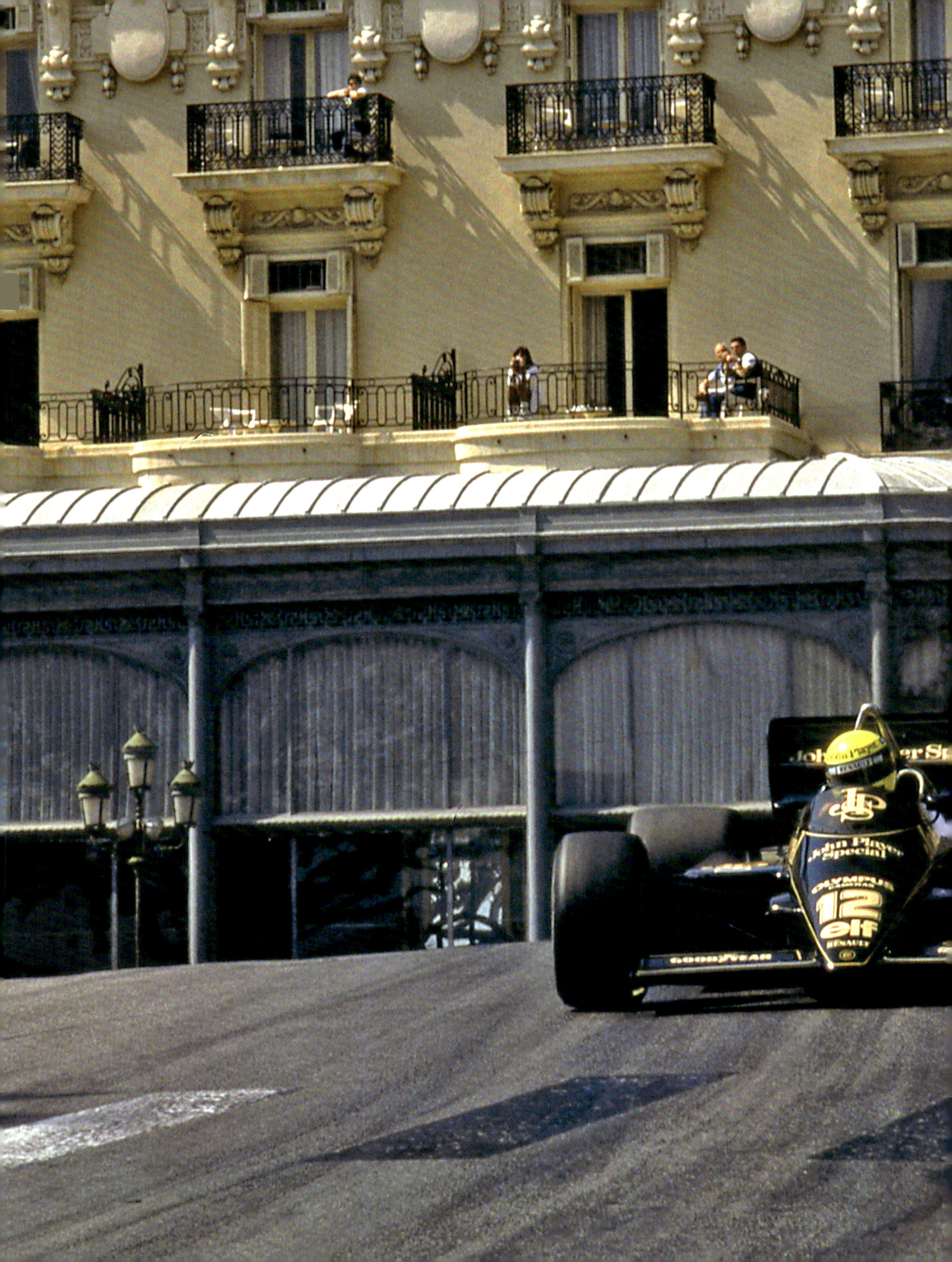
John Player Special
OLYMPUS
12
elf
GOODYEAR
RENAULT

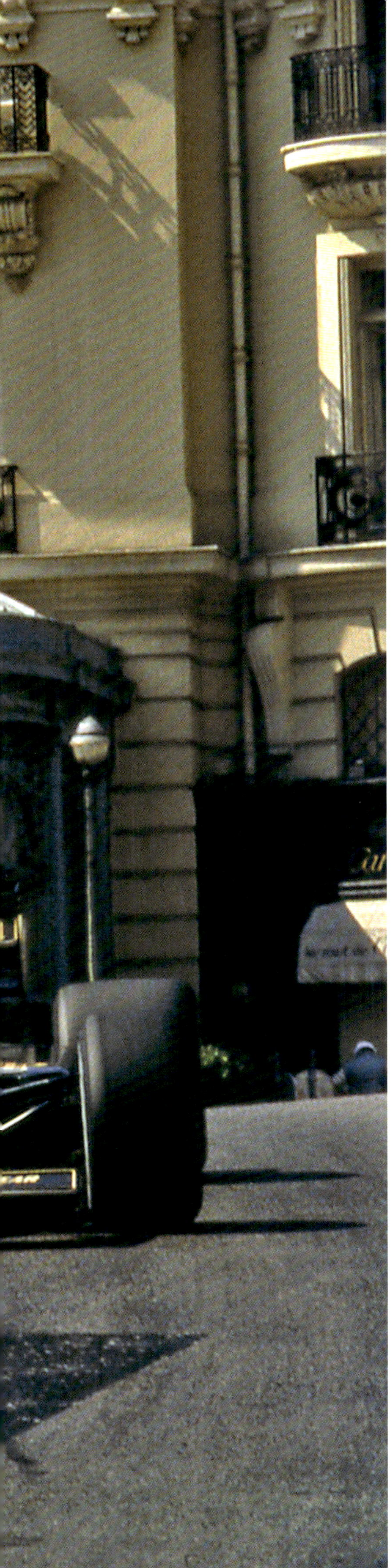

MONACO GRAND PRIX: NOT SO NICE

As he arrives in Monaco, after a new pole position and a withdrawal for running out of fuel, three laps from the end of the race at the San Marino Grand Prix in Imola, Senna is ready for the fight like never before. He goes in pole, again, for the third consecutive time, but his rivals are upset. Alboreto, the Ferrari driver, and Lauda, the running world champion, blame the Brazilian for getting in the way, braking and slowing them down on their fastest lap. "It's easy to achieve pole in these conditions," the McLaren driver says angrily, and in revenge, Alboreto also gets in the way of Senna in the Rascasse turn, nearly pushing him into the railings. "A pilot can be faster than the other, but he has to show sportsmanship," adds the Italian. But as Prince Albert and Princess Stéphanie are invited into the Ferrari stands, he gives up shouting at the Brazilian after the qualifying. On the Sunday, the Brazilian starts off with cold tires due to a short-circuit on his heating blankets, but he still takes the lead until lap 13, when his Renault engine fails. In front of Alboreto and De Angelis, Prost wins in the other Lotus. Eighteen years later, during an interview, the team manager of Lotus at that time, Peter Warr, takes full responsibility for Senna's behavior during this Monaco qualifying. He says that it was his idea and explains that the Brazilian regretted his attitude right after exiting his cockpit after the qualifying. "Peter, I never want to do that again. If someone is faster than me, then that's alright," the pilot said to him.

In 1985, Ayrton Senna claimed the third pole position of his career in Monaco. An engine problem prevented him from finishing the race, but in the following years, he would find solace by making the principality his own.

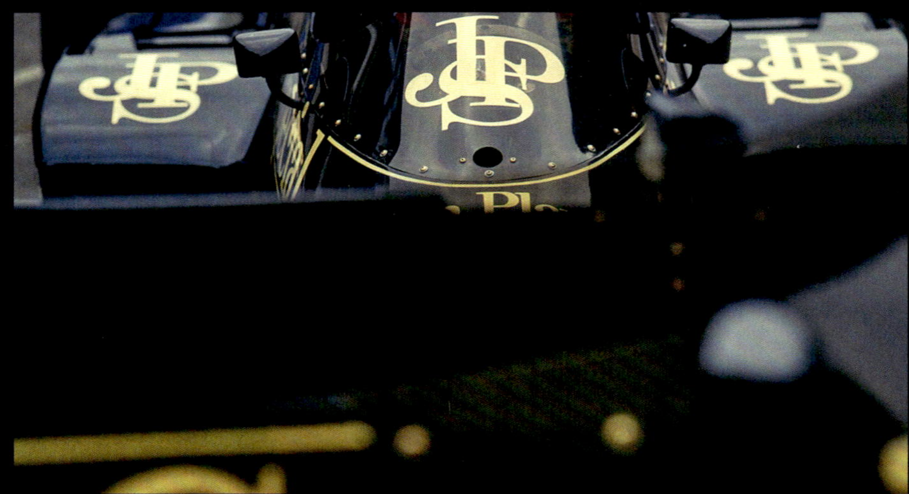

THE CAR: LOTUS 97T

A MYTHICAL LIVERY FOR A PILOT SOON TO BE CALLED "MAGIC."

On Friday the 8th of February 1985 at 5:15 p.m., Ayrton Senna exits the Jacarepaguá stands, driving his Lotus 97T. After a few laps across the track, everyone is seeing that he finally has a car that can really showcase all of his potential, not because it's timelessly elegant, but simply because it's fast. Gérard Ducarouge and his assistant, Martin Ogilvie, were responsible for its design. The late Colin Chapman's teams worked on this car at the same time as on the Lotus 96T, which was originally intended for the American CART Championship. It would never run in the US, but the Norfolk team would use this aborted project to install a few more aerodynamical elements. On the front, the beginnings of what is today known as side deflectors can be seen. These bargeboards, as the engineers call them, direct the airflow around the car. As a result, aerodynamic performance is better and the Lotus benefits from more downforce—perfect for Ayrton Senna's balance skills.

This 97T is powered by a V6 turbo engine of 1.5L, manufactured by Renault, which develops around 760 hp. In the cockpit, there are a dozen liquid-crystal displays showing the oil temperature, the turbo power and also how much fuel the car is carrying. This is something that Senna absolutely loves as he is always striving for more data, as do the Renault engineers, who are always on the lookout for new data. Fast and agile, this black and gold car, a dear sponsor of Lotus, is unfortunately not very reliable. During the 1985 season, Senna would withdraw seven times for mechanical failures. But it also helped the kid from Santana Street to earn his first two victories.

THE MAIN CHARACTERS

ELIO DE ANGELIS, THE GENTLEMEN TEAMMATE

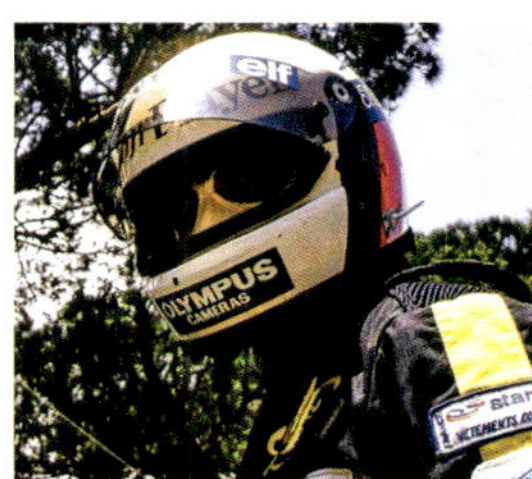

When Ayrton Senna arrives at Lotus, Elio de Angelis is already firmly installed, knowing he is a very talented pilot and not really expecting what is going to happen next. He has been in Formula 1 since 1979, and he has just taken third place in the 1984 World Championship, grabbing four podiums behind the unbeatable McLarens, driven by Lauda and Prost. He is also a close collaborator of Gérard Ducarouge, the head engineer in the British racing team. He has spent five seasons with Lotus, with his main highlight being his victory in the 1982 Austrian Grand Prix, five hundredths of a second faster than the Williams driven by Keke Rosberg, father of Nico and future world champion.

In 1985, the world of De Angelis is taken by storm, mainly because of Senna's talent. The Roman native doesn't understand it yet but continues getting some points. He even wins his second Formula 1 race on the track of Imola due to a combination of circumstances: Piquet, Senna, and Johansson run out of fuel three laps from the end, and Prost is disqualified after the race as the weight of his McLaren wasn't in conformity. At the end of the season, Elio finishes fifth in the World Championship, five points shy of Senna, but understands that the situation is not looking good for him at Lotus. He would then join his fellow countryman, Riccardo Patrese, in the Brabham team but would unfortunately be the victim of a tragic accident. On the 15th of May 1986, during a private free practice session on the Paul Ricard track, his wing would detach as he was entering the Verrerie S, and his Brabham would be launched into the air at more than 180 km/h. Elio would never get out of his car. He was 28 years old.

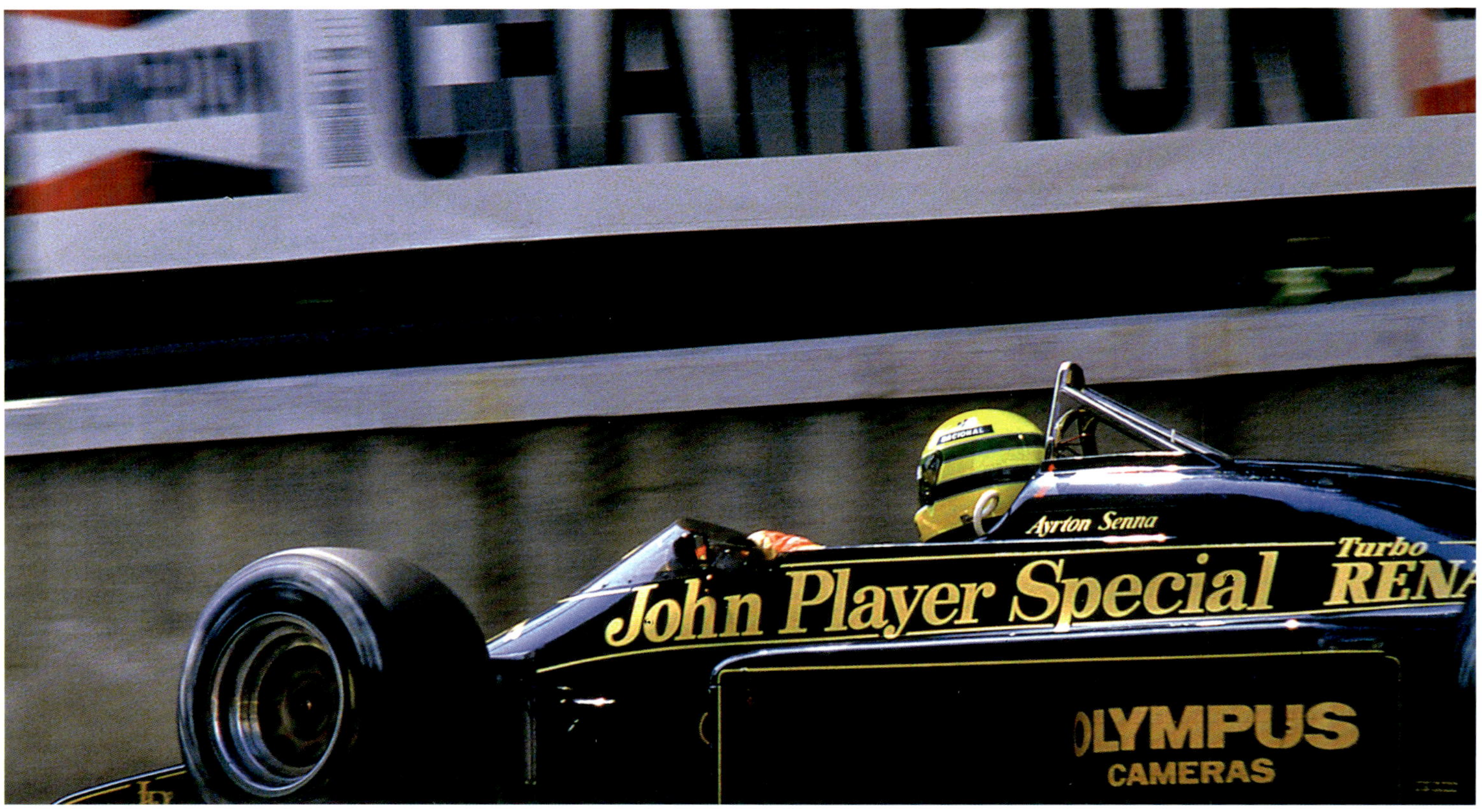

Ayrton Senna exploited the full potential of his Lotus 97T through his fast and aggressive driving.

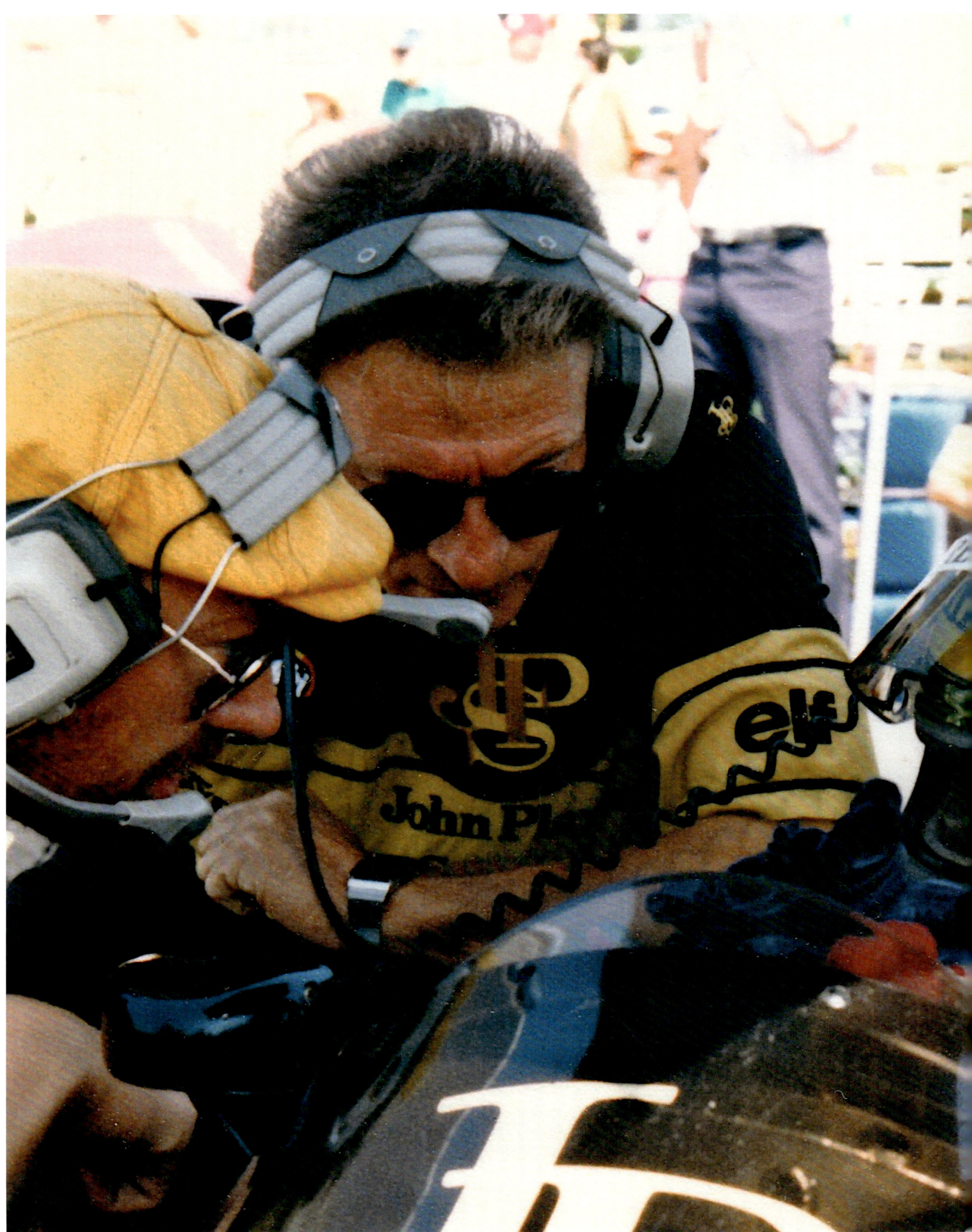
John
elf

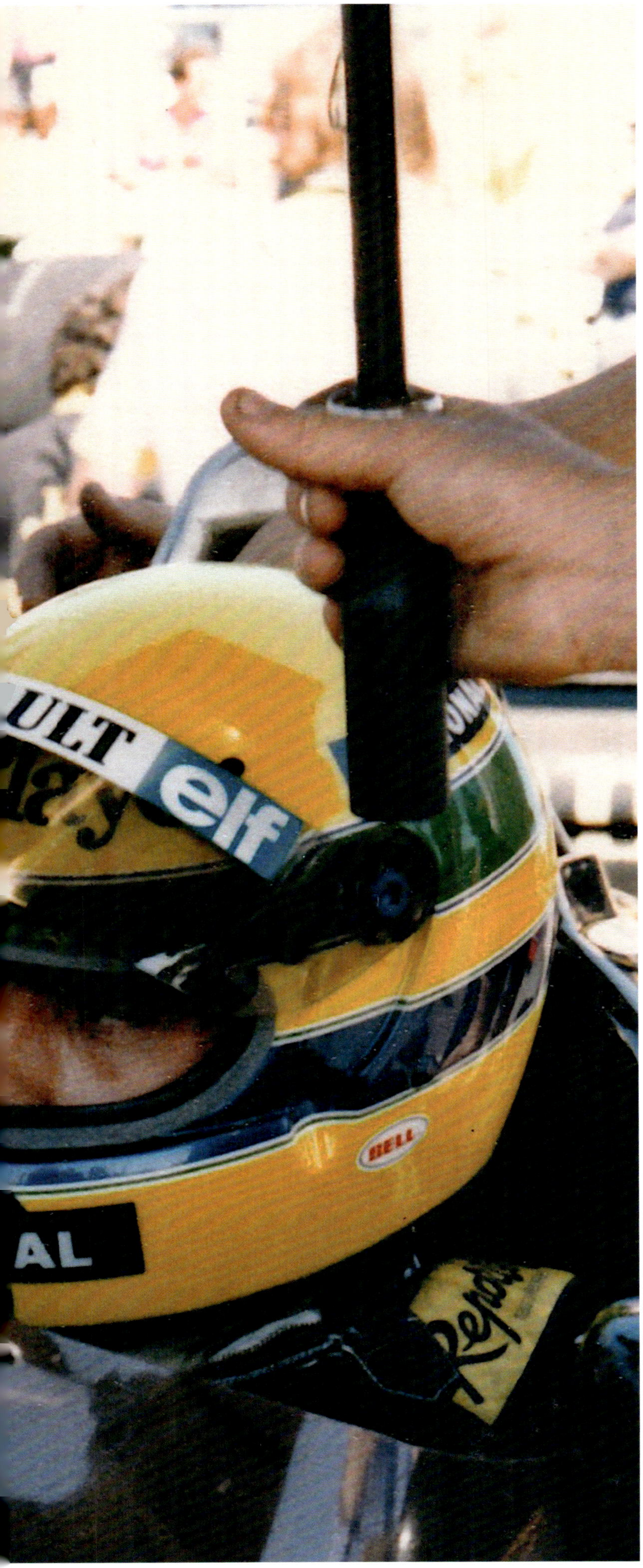

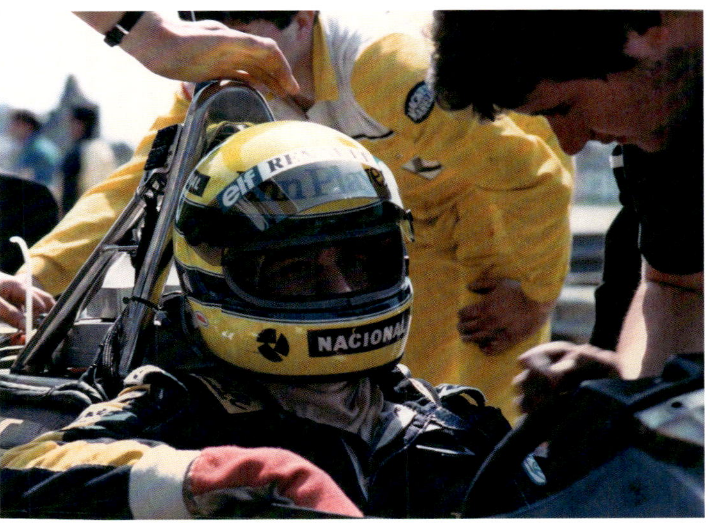

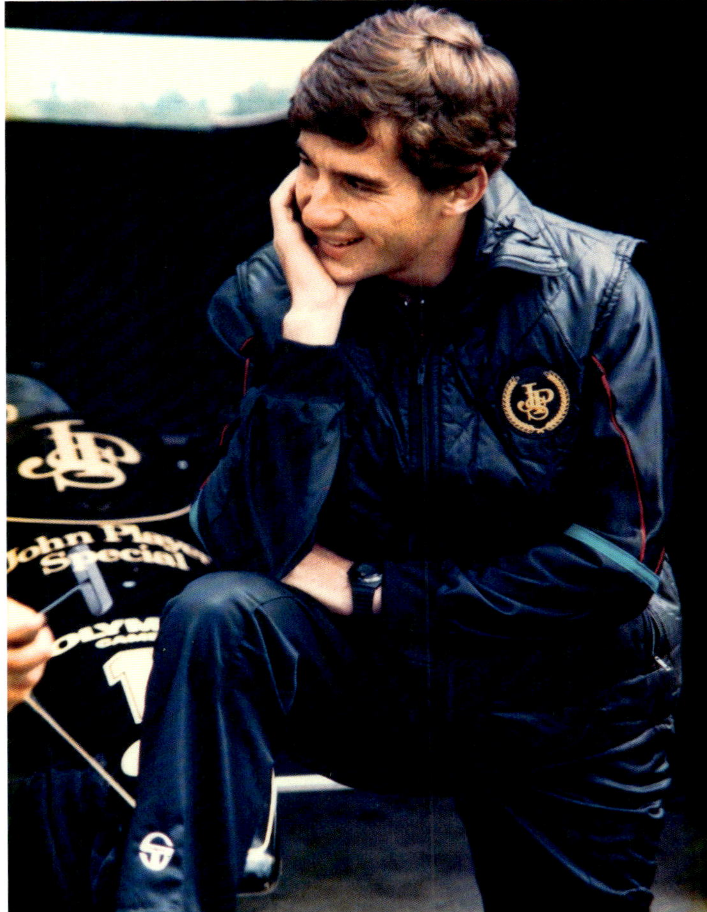

Left: Eager for any information, Ayrton Senna spent a lot of time with his team to improve the settings of his Lotus under the expert eye of the French engineer, Gérard Ducarouge.

Top: After a learning season with the Toleman, Ayrton Senna advanced in the team founded by the brilliant Colin Chapman.

Bottom: A demanding guy, Ayrton Senna also knew how to be cheerful and playful with his mechanics when the pressure subsided a bit.

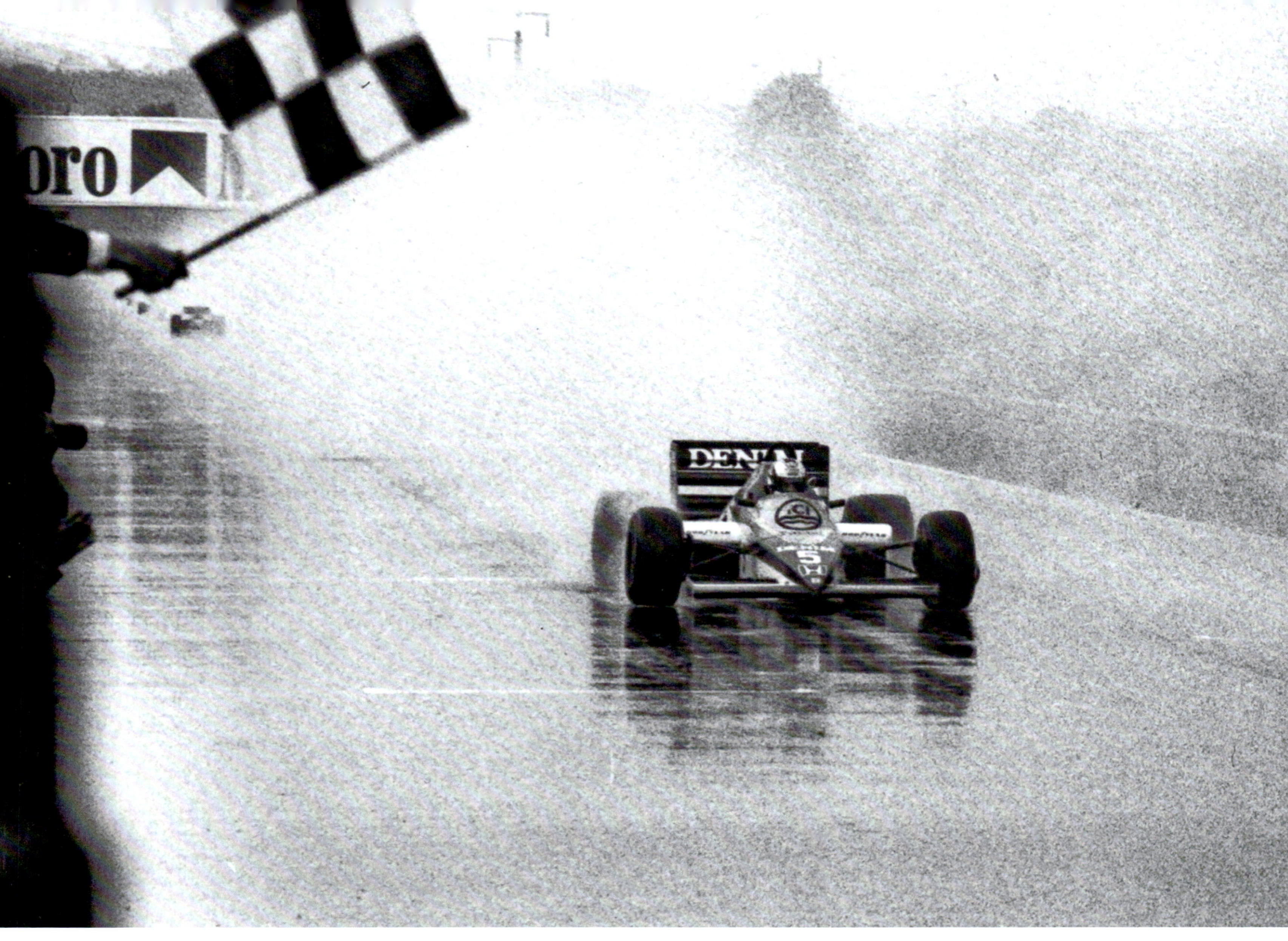

BELGIAN GRAND PRIX: "MAGIC'S" CONFIRMATION

Originally scheduled for June, the Belgian Grand Prix is postponed until the 15th of September. With four races remaining, Ayrton Senna is in fourth place, just behind teammate Elio De Angelis. And the weekend starts in a less than ideal way. On the morning of Friday the 13th, his gearbox is stuck in second gear—kind of a bother on a seven-kilometer-long track. The gearbox of Lotus 12 is changed, and the car starts again. But trouble arises. Again. Smoke escapes from his engine—the turbo just gives up. And as if that wasn't enough, his mule catches fire in the afternoon. Twice. "A better Friday the 13th couldn't have happened," says the pilot of the black and gold car. Fortunately for him, all this bad news is behind him. In qualifying, Senna is doing great, and so is his Lotus. The car looks balanced, reliable, and easier to drive. Bernard Dudot from Renault remembers the briefing: "During 45 minutes, he described a single lap, how he felt, all the technical data, the engine speed, the oil pressure, etc. We also compared the telemetric data. They were all the same. That was crazy!" With struggling tires, he is just 97 thousandths of a second behind Alain Prost, who takes the pole.

It is raining during the race, and the pilot with the yellow helmet makes a better start than the French. And then, his racing senses help Senna choose the ideal moment to put on slick tires, and he is soon tearing every other pilot apart. That was anything but a coincidence; during the morning warm-up session, Ayrton walked a kilometer by foot on the track in order to feel how the adherence was at different places. His small engine problems in the straights of the magnificent Belgian track wouldn't stop him from finishing first, in front of Nigel Mansell and Prost. That was his fourth consecutive podium, and also his second Formula 1 victory, which was very well deserved.

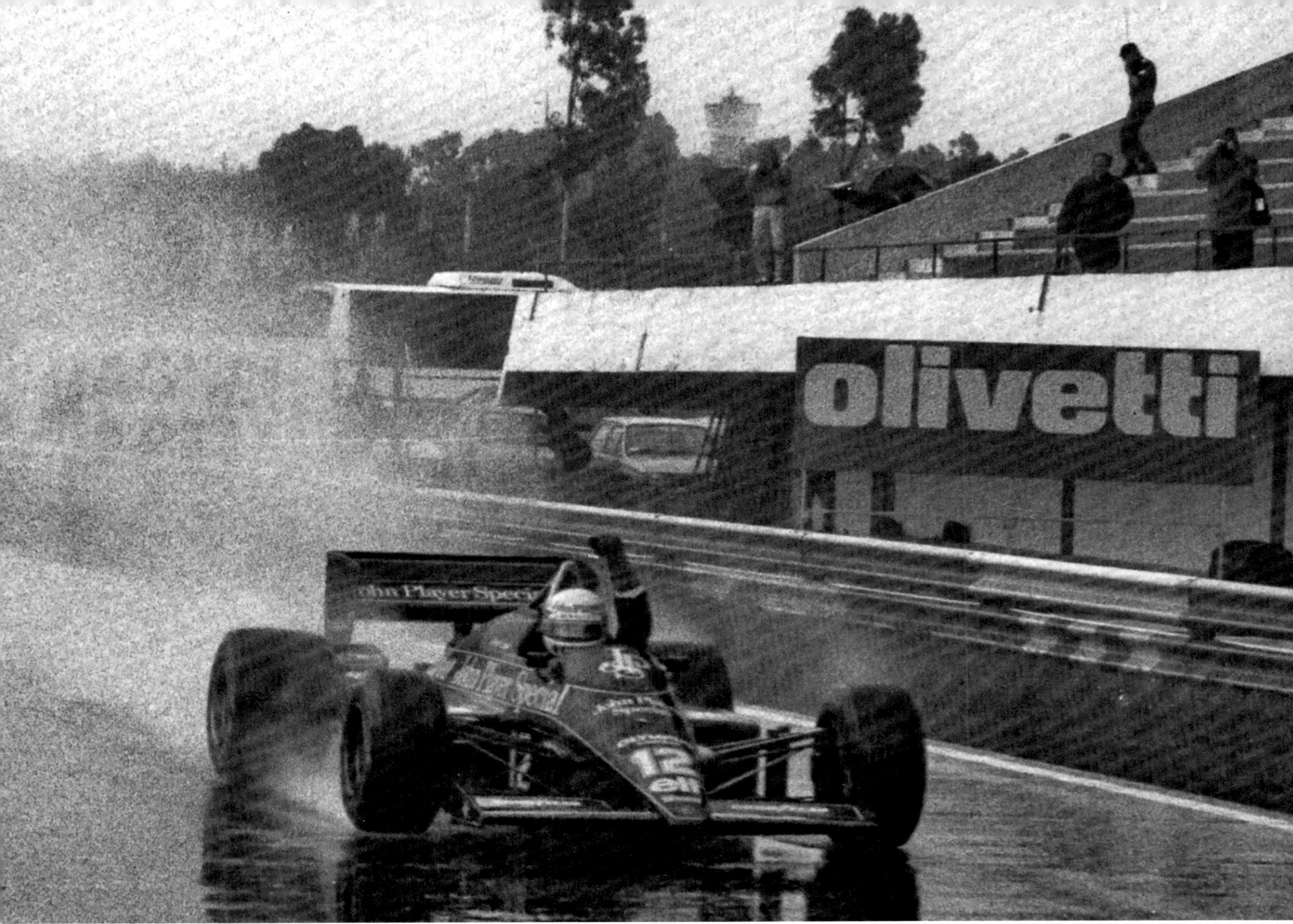

The day Ayrton Senna became "Magic": his very first victory in F1, achieved in style at the Portuguese Grand Prix in the rain, at the Estoril circuit.

AUSTRALIAN GRAND PRIX: SENNA'S SAMBA

The 1985 season comes to an end in Adelaide, Australia. On this urban track, which is made up of several twists and turns, Senna will again astonish the world with his talent in qualifying. In the free practices, he already shines on this new track, ending with the second-best lap, just behind Keke Rosberg in his Williams. The gap between the two drivers was just one thousandth of a second. Then came qualifying, and the young Brazilian made his mark by elevating Formula 1 driving to an art form. His time of 1:19.843 makes him the poleman and also the only pilot to break the 1:20 barrier. His closest rival, Nigel Mansell, is six hundredths of a second behind him, and Rosberg is two whole seconds away!

During his best lap, the native of São Paulo rides through the circuit like a genius. His black and gold Lotus seems like it is dancing the samba. Even with heavy oversteering, the Lotus 97T stays on track, and the 800 hp it is producing are perfectly driven by the pilot. We knew Ayrton Senna was something special, but with this outstanding lap, giving him the pole, the Brazilian showcased something a bit different. A bit better. So much so that at the press conference, the 200 journalists present applauded the daredevil in the yellow helmet. They can rest assured: he still has a lot left in the tank.

"Beco" will again be putting everyone on the edge of their seat. Even if it is Niki Lauda's last Grand Prix, the public only has eyes for the incredible driving of the Portuguese Grand Prix. Audacious passings, including one on the first lap on Mansell, wide trajectories, and driving at the limit make him a crowd favorite. Sixty-two laps of maximum risk-taking was a bit too much for his Renault engine, which took the easy way out. The season of Senna ends as it started, by a withdrawal. But all the Formula 1 spectators are saying one thing: the 25-year-old Brazilian will be a great champion.

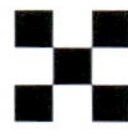

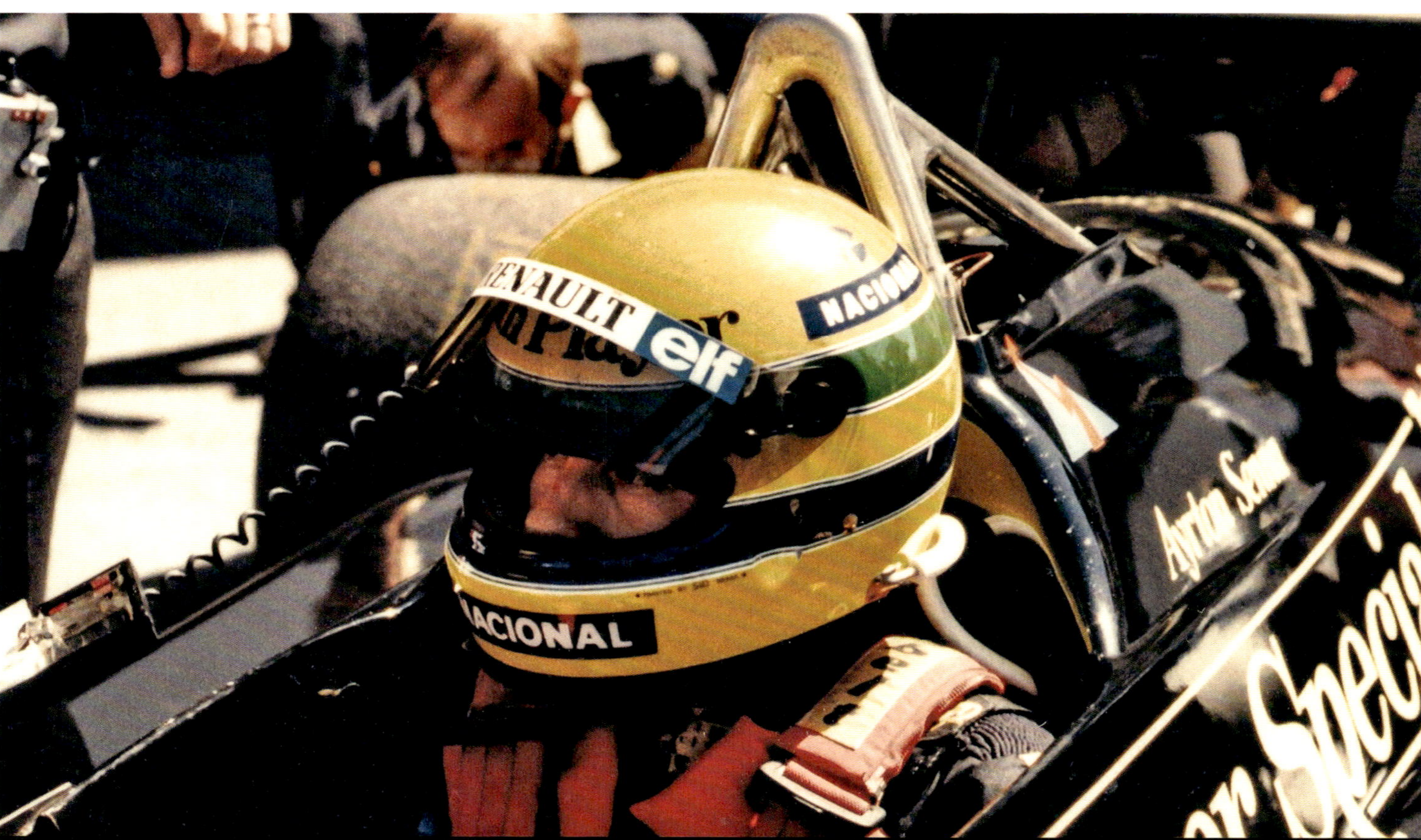

THE PRIDE OF BANCO NACIONAL

1985 is a big year for Senna and his sponsor. It's in that year that in his suit and helmet, he will appear with a very special sponsor: Banco Nacional. In late 1984, the Brazilian bank is looking for ways to rejuvenate its image and make itself more popular. Thus, it associates itself with TV Globo, Jornal Nacional, and with the football clubs Fluminense and Vasco de Gama. But the board of directors wants something bigger. They then receive a proposal from Ayrton Senna's entourage. At first glance, Nacional's management is perplexed by the driver's approach. Then the bank tries something unusual—being his exclusive sponsor. Senna's entourage is skeptical. Nacional's money is no match for the cash that could be provided by various sponsors.

To put pressure on the bank—and to get more money—Armando Botelho, one of Senna's closest advisors, coyly says that a rival bank, Bradesco, is also trying to sponsor the Brazilian. Nacional is worrying that they are going to lose that juicy deal. To earn more than what was proposed, the councilors of the pilot propose an idea to the bank: if he finishes fourth or better, he gets a bonus. The contract with Nacional is for a year. The timing is ideal, and the success is immediate. In commercials and on posters, Banco Nacional benefits from the image of the sportsman and gradually enters the minds of Brazilians. This contract would hold until the tragic death of the pilot. And interestingly enough, the bank wouldn't survive his death. In dire economic health and pinpointed for questionable internal management, Banco Nacional would run out of business in 1995, one year after Senna's death. The remaining assets were transferred to the Itaú Unibanco bank, and Banco Nacional disappeared. Nevertheless, the image of Nacional remains forever associated with that of Brazil's most legendary sportsman.

Before starting his engine, Ayrton Senna's mechanics await a hand signal from their driver.

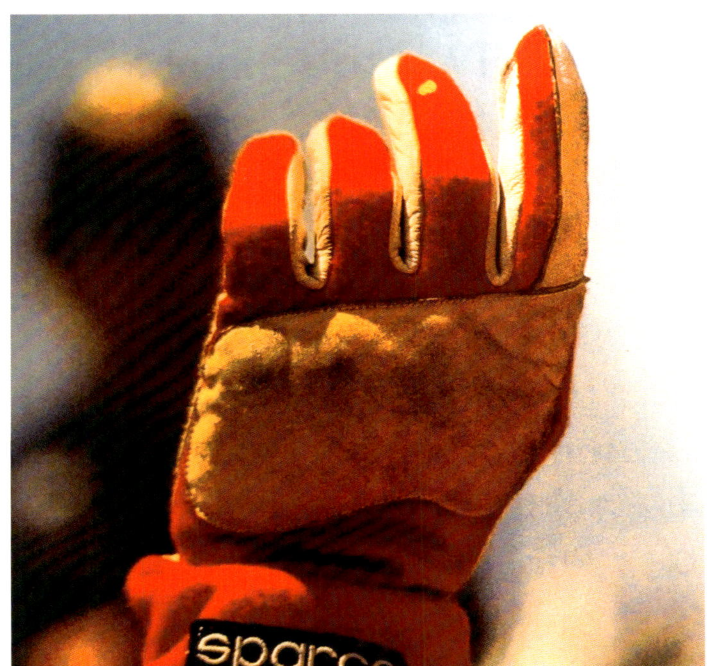

THE 1985 SEASON IN FIGURES

GRAND PRIX	QUALIFIERS	RACE
BRAZIL	4TH	DNF (ELECTRICAL PROBLEM)
PORTUGAL	POLE POSITION 1	VICTORY 1
SAN MARINO	POLE POSITION 2	7TH (NO FUEL LEFT)
MONACO	POLE POSITION 3	DNF (ENGINE)
CANADA	2ND	16TH
DETROIT	POLE POSITION 4	DNF (CRASH)
FRANCE	2ND	DNF (ENGINE)
GREAT BRITAIN	4TH	10TH (FUEL SUPPLY)
GERMANY	5TH	DNF (GASKET)
AUSTRIA	14TH	2ND
NETHERLANDS	4TH	3RD
ITALY	POLE POSITION 5	3RD
BELGIUM	2ND	VICTORY 2
EUROPE	POLE POSITION 6	2ND
SOUTH AFRICA	4TH	DNF (ENGINE)
AUSTRALIA	POLE POSITION 7	DNF (ENGINE)

RANKING: 4TH IN THE FORMULA 1 WORLD CHAMPIONSHIP

(38 POINTS, 2 VICTORIES, 6 PODIUMS, 7 POLE POSITION, 3 BEST LAPS)

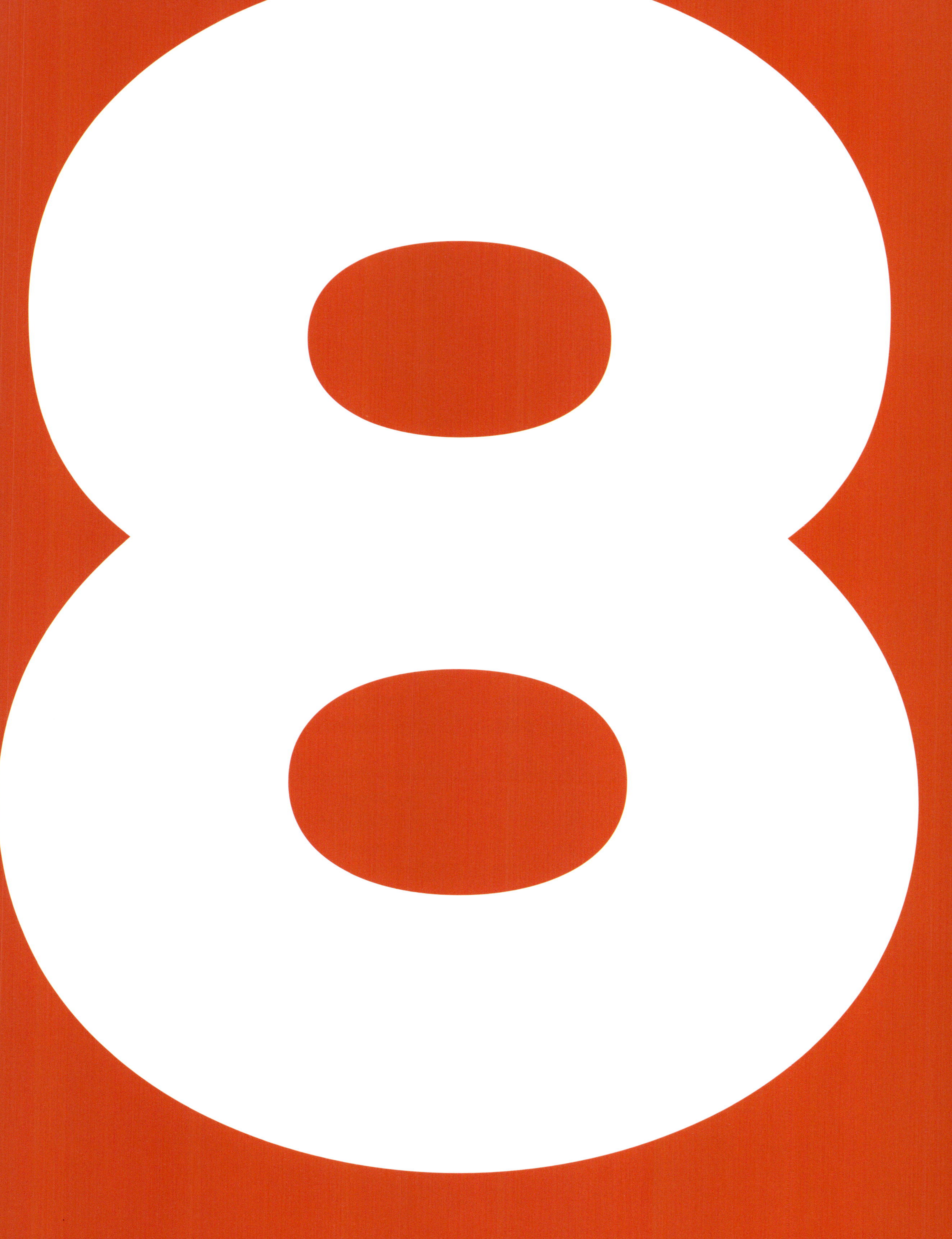
8

6
THE TURBO MASTER

ONE LAST RIDE WITH RENAULT

THE 1986 SEASON WAS AYRTON SENNA'S THIRD IN FORMULA 1. IT WAS ALSO THE LAST IN WHICH HE WAS POWERED BY A RENAULT TURBO ENGINE IN HIS LOTUS. AND SO, WITH THE FANTASTIC POWER OF HIS FRENCH ENGINE, HE ENDED UP IN THE FORMULA 1 HALL OF FAME.

The ideal package to string pole positions like pearls: 8 in 16 Grand Prix. This confirmed something that everyone pretty much already knew: Senna was the fastest pilot in the world.

During the races, the situation became more difficult, with too many withdraws (6) and lots of frustration, but there were still some nice consolation prizes, similar to those in the previous season: two victories (in Spain and Detroit) and a fourth place in the Drivers' Championship, for the second consecutive year. While Senna's car was far from being the best on the grid, his talent shone all over F1 during the qualifying sessions and during each Grand Prix: at the end of every race, he was on the podium!

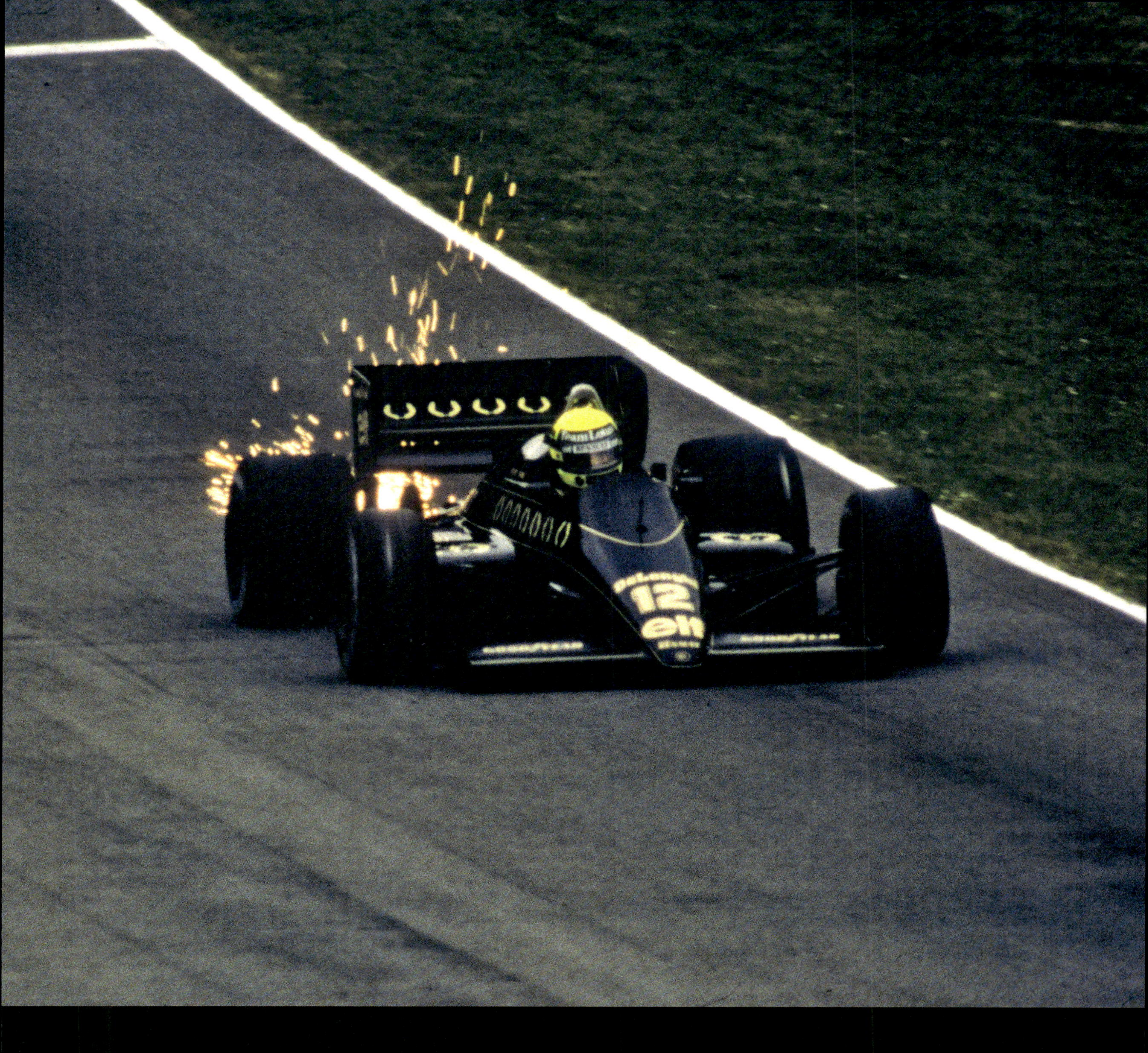

In the three seasons with Lotus, from 1985 to 1987, Ayrton Senna won 6 Grand Prix races and secured 16 pole positions.

RACE AFTER RACE

1986

SPAIN GRAND PRIX, JEREZ DE LA FRONTERA: FOR FOURTEEN THOUSANDTHS OF A SECOND

In 1986, the Spanish Grand Prix was back on the schedule, five years after it had totally disappeared, following a number of disagreements between the Formula One Constructors Association (FOCA) and the Royal Automobile Club of Spain, the owner of the Jarama track just outside Madrid. But by 1986, everyone was getting along once again, and Bernie Ecclestone decided to reintroduce F1 in Spain, since it had a massive car market and a very strong media. To make things even better when starting again from scratch, it was decided that the race would take place in the Jerez de la Frontera track, on a brand-new circuit near Sevilla in Andalusia, a region with fuel running through its veins. At a total cost of $10 million, the circuit was built in nine months, with a seven-year contract signed between FOCA and Andalusia.

It was only the second race of the season, following a Brazilian duet in which the older Piquet (Williams–Honda) led the youngster, Senna (Lotus–Renault). The qualifying sessions on this new Andalusian track were incredibly fast, with an average speed of 175 km/h compared to the 135 km/h average that the engineers had expected. Just like in Brazil, Senna found himself in pole (in front of both Williams of Piquet and Mansell), Team Lotus's hundredth pole in F1. While there were only 15,000 spectators in the stands to enjoy that first race in Jerez, they watched a fantastic race, animated by Senna, as well as the Williams, McLarens, and also the Ligiers of Arnoux and Laffite.

The race ended up being a fuel consumption fight, something that Senna was not so good at, given his racing technic. Mid-race, in lap 36, Senna was ahead of Mansell (by less than a second), Piquet, Prost, Rosberg and Laffite. The British pilot with his mustache passed Senna on lap 40, just as Piquet had to withdraw after his Honda engine broke down, leaving Prost in third. Taking air in front, Mansell was leading by four seconds at most, but he ended up damaging his back left tire, driving on a debris, which gave Senna the chance to catch up. The Williams driver hesitated, debating whether he should change tires, as they were ready in the stands, but on lap 63, he finally stopped, 20 seconds behind Senna, whose tires had been ruined. Nine laps remained.

Both Senna's and Prost's tires were done, and Mansell was wearing new tires. He passed the French driver, three laps before the end of the race and was closing the gap with the leader. On the 72nd and last lap, both drivers finished the last corner with Mansell being just a few centimeters behind Senna. He ended up leaving the corner on the left of the Brazilian's tail, got closer, closer, and accelerated. But then Senna crossed the line, fourteen thousandths of a second in front! This was the closest finish of a Grand Prix since the Italian Grand Prix in 1971. Mansell was convinced he had won as he got back to the stands, soaked, tired, and disappointed. "Hopefully, Frank had some fun watching the television…" he whispered, because his boss was in the hospital. He had changed his tires far too late: had he changed them earlier, he would have won. As for Senna and Prost, their fuel consumption figures were radically different. The Lotus had a liter and a half left in its tank, while the McLaren had 18 liters left in it; the McLaren's on-board computer was far too cautious in its recommendations. Senna led the championship and Mansell calculated the cap at the end of the race: only 93 centimeters. "It was like sprinting in the 100 m race in the Olympics. If the finishing line had been five meters after, I would have won!" Once across the finish line, the two men insulted each other all the way to the podium.

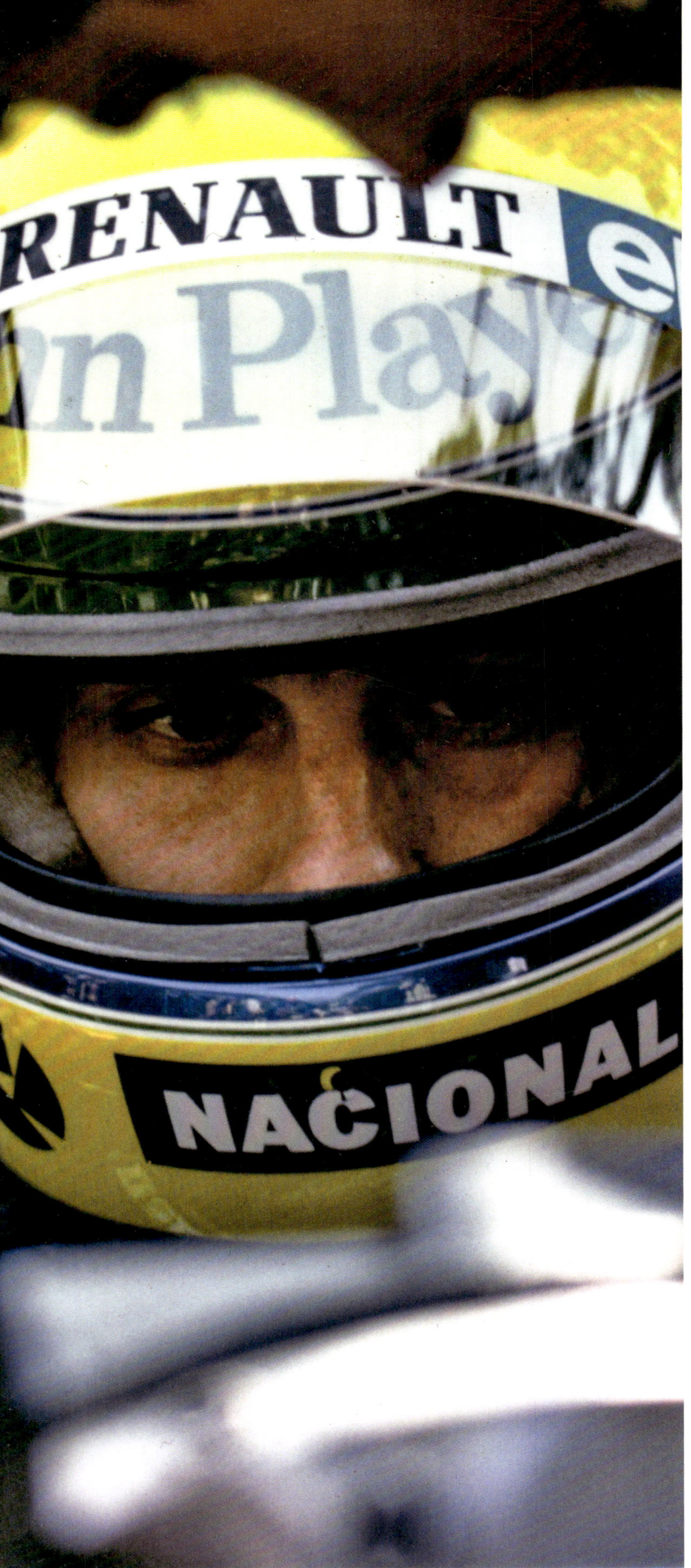

Every time Ayrton Senna put on his yellow helmet, he entered a bubble of concentration that allowed him to push the limits of his performance.

THE MAIN CHARACTERS

PETER WARR, THE "PARTNER IN CRIME"

The British often describe two people who get on well together and who, thanks to their complementary intelligence, pull off big moves as "partners in crime". This is one of the images that could be associated with the sometimes turbulent complicity of Peter Warr and Ayrton Senna during his Lotus years in which the Brazilian prodigy gained his first six F1 victories.

The son of a British soldier stationed in Iran, Warr was a talented pilot, but he was not good enough, or rich enough, to gain a seat in a Formula 1 car. His hiring by Colin Chapman, initially to manage the sales of the British brand, was followed by a promotion in 1966, at the age of 28, to director of Lotus Components. In 1970, he became the team manager of the racing team, winning the championship in 1970, despite Jochen Rindt's fatal crash at Monza, and in 1972, with Emerson Fittipaldi driving. This caught the eye of Canadian billionaire Walter Wolf, and Warr became the team manager of Walter Wolf Racing, the surprise winner during its very first Formula 1 Grand Prix in Argentina in early 1977, thanks to Jody Scheckter.

In 1979, the Wolf F1 team had to stop, and Warr joined Emerson and his brother Wilson, at Fittipaldi Automotive, which then became Copersucar. But the team struggled to gain good results and Warr decided to come back to Lotus, just before the death of its fantastic founder, Colin Chapman, in 1982. In 1983, the team concluded a contract with Renault to get some strong turbo engines, and in 1985, the first victory of the Warr–Senna duo was achieved, at the Estoril track in Portugal. Five fantastic victories would follow, including the Monaco Grand Prix of 1987, with a Honda engine, before the Brazilian wonder left, having been spotted and coveted by Ron Dennis, to join McLaren. Lotus never recovered from this departure, despite Warr's genius.

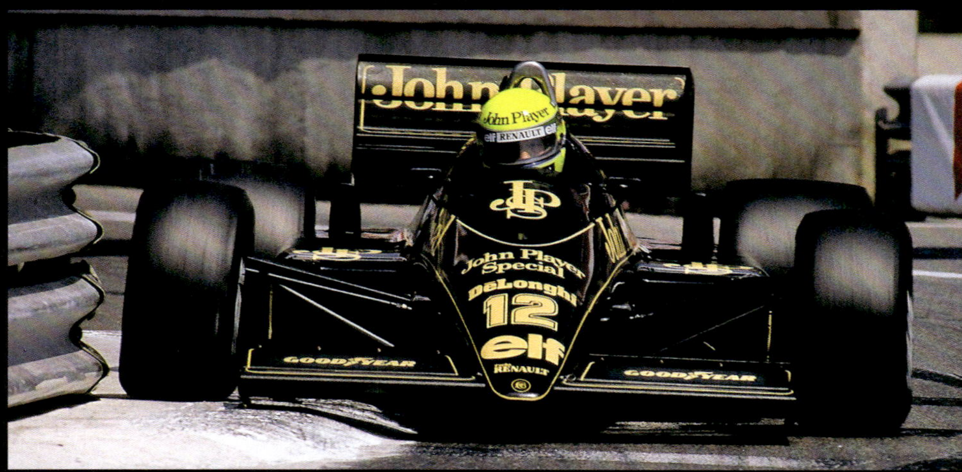

THE CAR: LOTUS 98T

THE END OF "NO-LIMITS" TURBO ENGINES

The Lotus 98T allowed Senna to fully live his passion: qualifying. With this car, the Brazilian found himself at the top of the grid eight times and earned as many podiums in 16 races in 1986. That Lotus would be the last to sport the black and gold colors of the John Player Special, powered by a Renault engine with two turbos and producing as much as 1,300 hp in qualifying. Designed again by Gérard Ducarouge and Martin Ogilvie, that car is still a racing demon. While its simply perfect features were ideal for a driver like Senna, the French–British car's "flat out" configuration was unable to hold for more than a few laps.

Lower and lighter than the 1985 version of the car, the Lotus 98T was also slightly more reliable, but that reliability came at the expense of the car's top speed. Although Ayrton would only reach the top step of the podium twice (in Spain and the USA) with this version, he suffered half as many withdraws and was able to aim for the world crown right up to the final races. However, this more reliable Renault engine had a massive problem: it drank a lot of fuel, and drank even more when facing the Brazilian's particular type of driving. The new micro-computer in the car that indicated the real-time fuel consumption was unable to help the situation.

Against the very strong Honda engine equipping the Williams and the TAG–Porsche engine used by McLaren, the Lotus 98T and its 900 hp was incapable of fighting in the same category. Nonetheless, that car is now considered a legend. The very few cars that were produced were carefully looked after by their owners, including McLaren CEO Zak Brown, and for good reason: in 1987, the FISA decided to limit the pressure of the turbos to restrain their efficiency, and two years later, the FISA totally banned the use of turbos in the engines, which brought the saga of the Lotus 98T to an end.

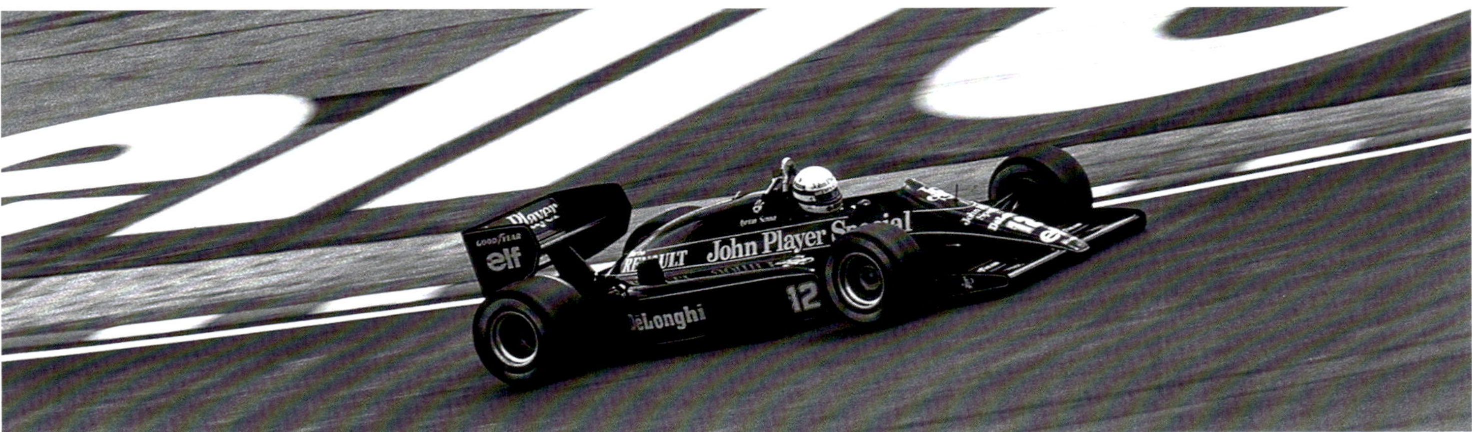

In 1986, the Lotus 98T marked the end of an era of cars equipped with powerful turbo engines.

PATRICK TAMBAY

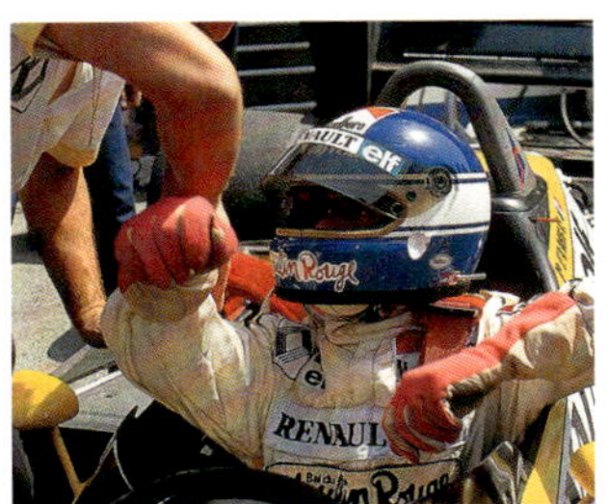

Patrick Tambay was still competing in F1 during Senna's first three seasons, from 1984 to 1986. After one Austrian Grand Prix, Tambay went water-skiing with the Brazilian, provoking his irritation because of his skiing skills. The Frenchman, a former member of the French junior winter sports team, was indeed very gifted at this sport.

"Ayrton had an enormous ego, that's for sure. It allowed him to feel he was better than anyone else. To be on top, you have to be like that. We went to the Austrian Grand Prix, that was on Thursday evening. We had nothing left to do on the track, so Ayrton told us to come with him: 'We'll do some water skiing, I'll show you'. We then went to the lake and Ayrton got in the water: he does a bit of slalom, getting through some left and right buoys and then falls into the water. There were some people on the boat. I started upright from the pontoon, got into the slalom and made some turns. He didn't like that at all. He turned around, went ahead and never looked back. He didn't say a word to me. Maybe he'd found someone with more ego than he had. Even if water-skiing wasn't Formula 1 (smile)."

BELGIAN GRAND PRIX

At the Belgium Grand Prix, the atmosphere in the paddock was dire. The recent death of Elio De Angelis during private trials at the Paul-Ricard track was still on the minds of everyone, including Senna, who had been De Angelis's teammate the previous season. "During a moment like this, the small disagreements we had at Lotus are all forgotten," he said to the Brazilian media. Sitting in his car, the youngster was not satisfied with how his car had been doing during the free practices. The insufficient torque of the Renault engine was to blame, as was the chassis, which Ayrton had not been able to successfully tune, while poor front suspension put further strain on the driver of Lotus No. 12. However, for some experts among the Brazilian media, such explanations were nothing more than excuses. Celso Iteberê, in O Globo, dared to write: "The Brazilian driver's eternal complaints about his car and his team are nothing more than a tactic to justify possible failures and enhance positive results."

Senna achieved fourth place in qualifying, far from his expectations, and as if that wasn't enough, Nelson Piquet, his Rio rival, had qualified to start first. However, things often change between the qualifying sessions on Saturday and the race on Sunday. Once the race began, Senna overtook Berger and Prost on the left at the source hairpin and set off in pursuit behind Piquet, only to be caught by the second Williams, driven by Mansell. The British driver passed him in lap three but spun two laps later, giving Senna the opportunity to retake his place. On lap 17, Piquet was forced to withdraw (engine), putting Senna one place ahead. However, some trouble arose in his stand, which gave Mansell the chance to overtake him once again. Realizing that he was consuming too much fuel and that his Renault engine was not as powerful as that of Mansell, Ayrton was forced to come to the serious conclusion that the Brit's Williams was, on that day, too fast for him. So he began to slow down. Was that a sign that he had finally grown up? Was he beginning to understand that aiming for a win in every race is not always the ideal thing? Maybe. Nevertheless, there was still one good thing to remember from this Grand Prix: during the race, Senna took back the top spot in the World Championship rankings.

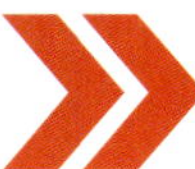

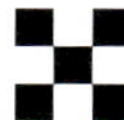

SENNA AND HIS DRIVING: A MASTER OF THE TURBO

Here's a question many observers, like his teammates, rivals, engineers and mechanics, asked themselves: what made Ayrton Senna the pilot he was? First of all, it is important to understand how he drove. Many people compared his way of driving to someone dancing Samba because, yes, Senna was a part of an era where sliding was a part of driving, a very aggressive, virulent way of driving that allowed him to get the very small detail that would get him pole position. To understand this, it was important to listen to his car.

Generally speaking, in Formula 1, the attack on a corner is broken down into three acts. First, the driver brakes. Then, he turns the steering wheel to start the curve. Finally, on exit, he gradually re-accelerates. This method is simply called brake–steer–throttle. But the mid-1980s saw the advent of turbocharged engines, and "playing" with the turbo could be very beneficial. Senna was quick to understand this. When braking in a corner and gradually accelerating again, the Lotus driver noticed a slight slowdown in his engine, which is normal. During the time when Senna was not pressing the accelerator pedal, the turbo stopped working. As a result, he had less grip, less power and therefore less speed. In such moments, adapting one's driving style becomes a necessity.

Senna, however, had an idea. During the corners, the Brazilian didn't simply push the throttle. He turned and then tapped his accelerator pedal aggressively and repeatedly, right in the middle of a corner. In this way, the turbo continued to be supplied and was always running at maximum rpm, which also gave his car more grip. For the ears and the stopwatch, it was a treat. But for his fuel consumption, it could be troublesome. His car used far more fuel than his rivals who were driving in a more classical way. This explains, partially, why the Brazilian so often ran out of fuel.

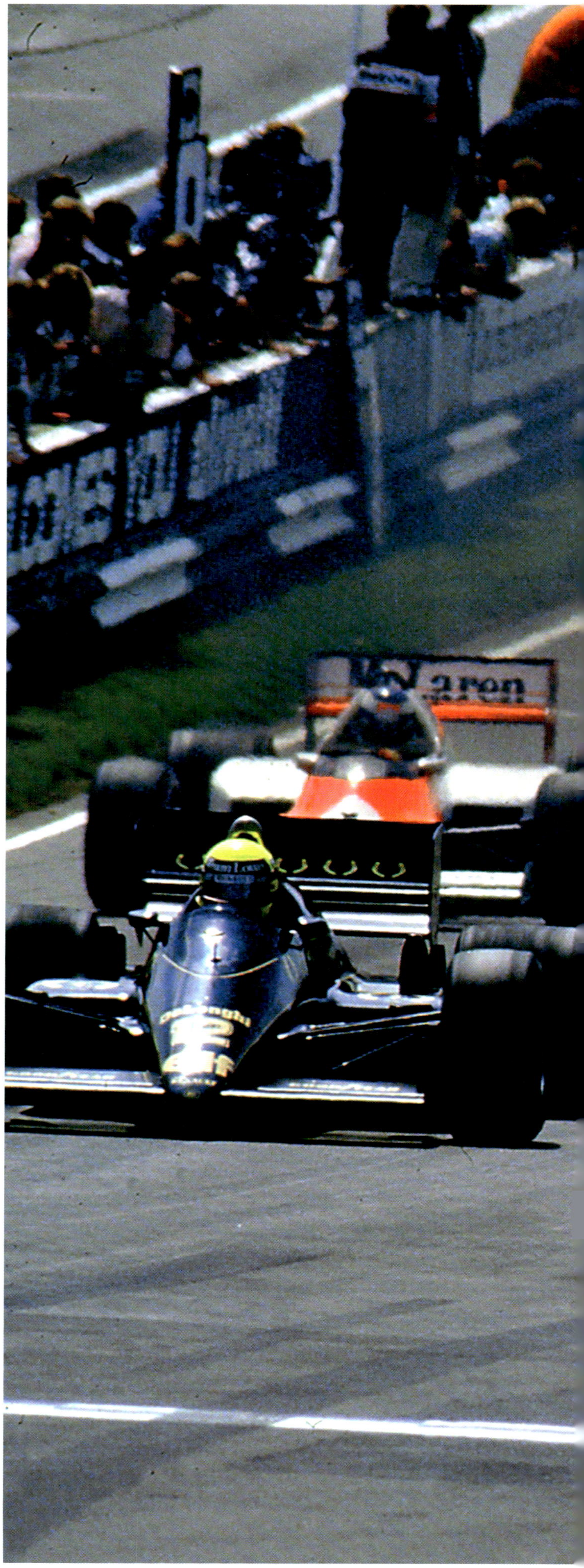

Third on the grid at the 1986 British Grand Prix, Senna was betrayed by his gearbox on the 27th lap. The race was won by Nigel Mansell (in the foreground).

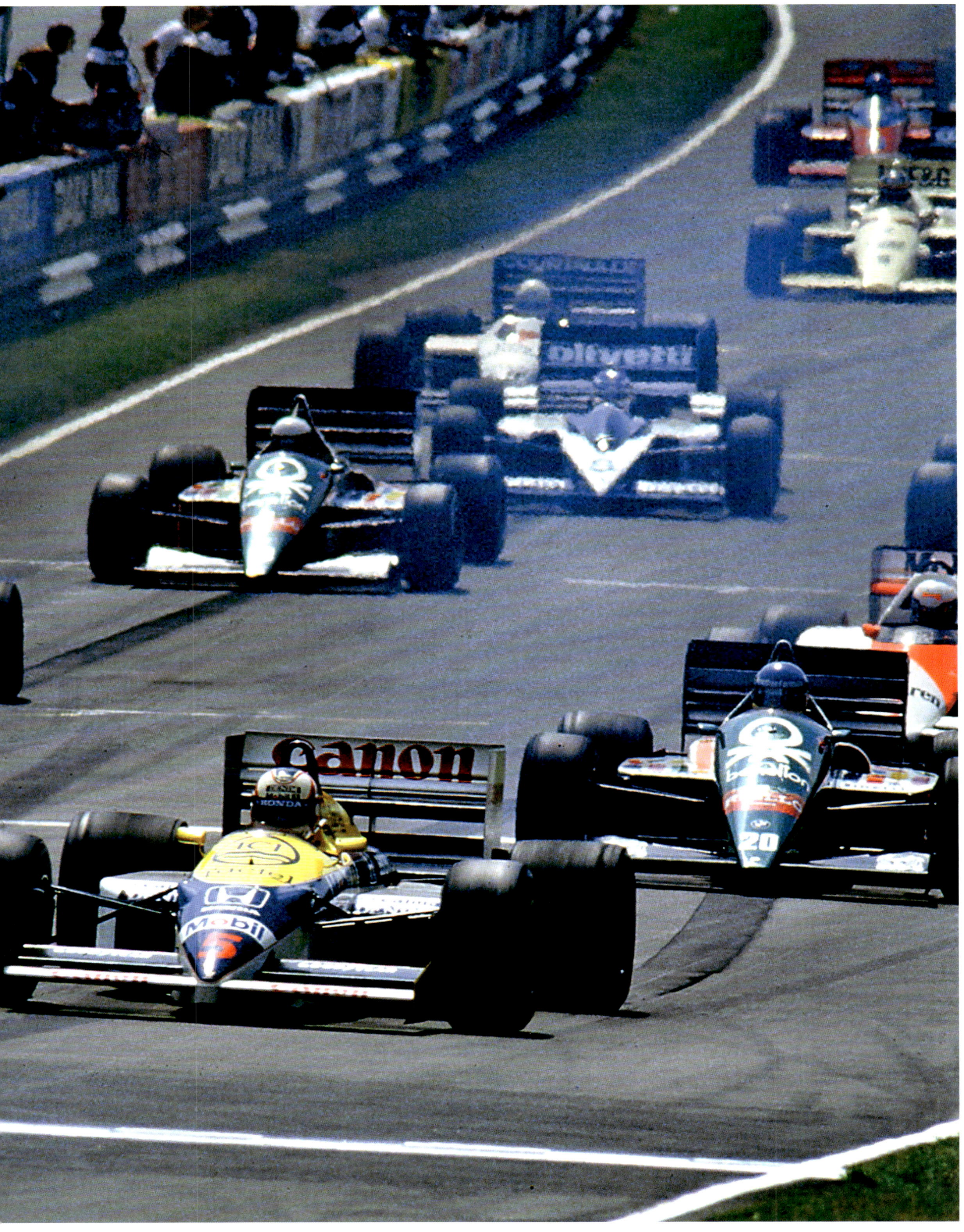
Canon
Mobil
20

BERNARD DUDOT, THE FANTASTIC ENGINEER

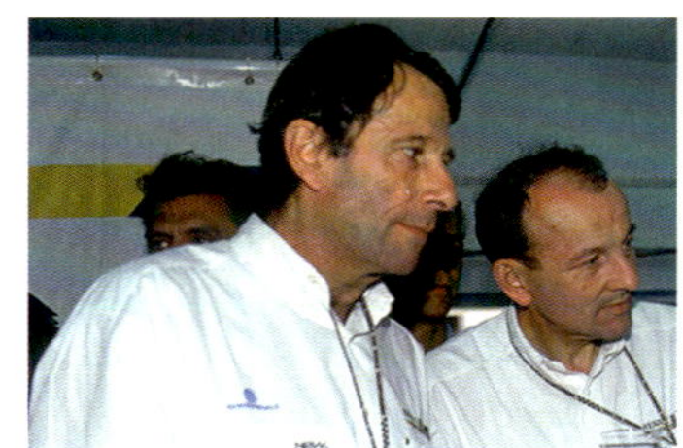

During Senna's small but essential stint at Lotus, another important character appeared: the French engineer Bernard Dudot, father of all the Renault engines powering Formula 1 since their very first stint in Formula 1 in 1977. As the technical director of Renault Sport, Dudot created, during two full seasons (1985 and 1986), incredible engines and gave sound advice to the British team and the young Brazilian star, who usually had a great performance in qualifying, thanks to the incredible power of the engines; these performances were, however, also thanks to the relentless demands of the driver in the yellow helmet. In 1986, at the Portugal Grand Prix, the engineer and his colleagues had a slightly bad experience of these demands. "We were just done with the development of a new turbo that pushed even stronger. It arrived in the suitcase of one of our engineers, Philippe Coblence, on Friday. We then installed it in Ayrton's car on Saturday, for the qualifying." Nobody told Senna about it, and being the king of pole positions, he got the best time. But he was incredibly angry when he exited the car. During his run, he "felt" the new turbo. Dudot could only witness the anger of the Sao Paulo native. "I can still hear him: 'But if you had told me, you made that change, I would have driven differently and went even faster!' That was Ayrton. He set very high standards for himself, and he expected us to set the same for him."

UNITED STATES GRAND PRIX, DETROIT: FOR THE SELEÇAO

Upon arriving in the United States, at a track they did not like at all, the drivers were furious to learn that they would have to pay 30% of their winnings to the American tax authorities, with an additional penalty dating back to 1982. To avoid a cancellation, Bernie Ecclestone took charge of negotiations with the American authorities and then paid $600,000 in full settlement. The circuit was in a terrible state, but the event brought in a lot of revenue, so the Grand Prix had to happen. At this time, the teams were discussing the future technical regulations that would come in to force in 1989. Would the turbos be banned or bridled? Would it happen or not?

Following on from Jacarepagua, Jerez, and Imola, Detroit was Senna's fourth pole, having beaten Mansell's Williams (by half a second) and Piquet, and finishing in front of Arnoux (4th) and Laffite (6th) in their Ligiers. But the Brazilian did not come to the press conference, and instead sent an attaché with a tape recorder on which he had recorded how he felt. He had already gone back to his hotel room to watch the Football World Cup quarterfinals between France and Brazil in Mexico; Prost, Laffite and Arnoux were also watching TV at the same time, rooting for Les Bleus of Michel Platini. After a French win during a penalty shoot-out, the Seleçao were eliminated, and Senna decided to stay in his hotel.

The next day, everyone except the Lotus drivers and Keke Rosberg opted for soft tires. On the second lap, Mansell took the lead after Senna missed a gear change, something that did not happen to him very often, but Senna overtook Mansell on lap 8, when the Brit was having some troubles with his back brakes. On lap 14, with a slow puncture in his back tires, the Brazilian was forced to come back to his stand and fell into eighth place. This left the two Ligiers "Made in France" in the lead, in front of Piquet and Senna, who were not far behind. It was as if the France–Brazil nightmare had begun once again. However, no-one anticipated that the Ligiers's tires would start to destroy themselves, and then a botched tire change for Piquet gave Senna first place. Then Piquet, on the attack, hit a vibrator on lap 42 and smashed his Williams into the wall, in a very dangerous position. Five laps later, the yellow flags were no longer waving, but the Williams was still in the same place, and Arnoux, who was chasing Senna, narrowly avoided him, only to be hit by Boutsen as he tried to get around the obstacle. Senna was untroubled and cruised to victory, his fourth F1 victory and second of the year; there would be no other for him in 1986.

During his victory lap, Ayrton grabbed a Brazilian flag waved by a fan, with the help of a steward who did not understand his request, and paid tribute to the Seleçao, who had been beaten by Les Bleus the previous day. He also revealed that he too had almost collided with Piquet's Williams, which had been abandoned in the middle of the trajectory: "What happened was scandalous, criminal. You never leave an abandoned F1 car on the track. It was a colossal danger." He regained the World Championship lead, three points ahead of Prost. It was purely symbolic, but the Seleçao had been avenged!

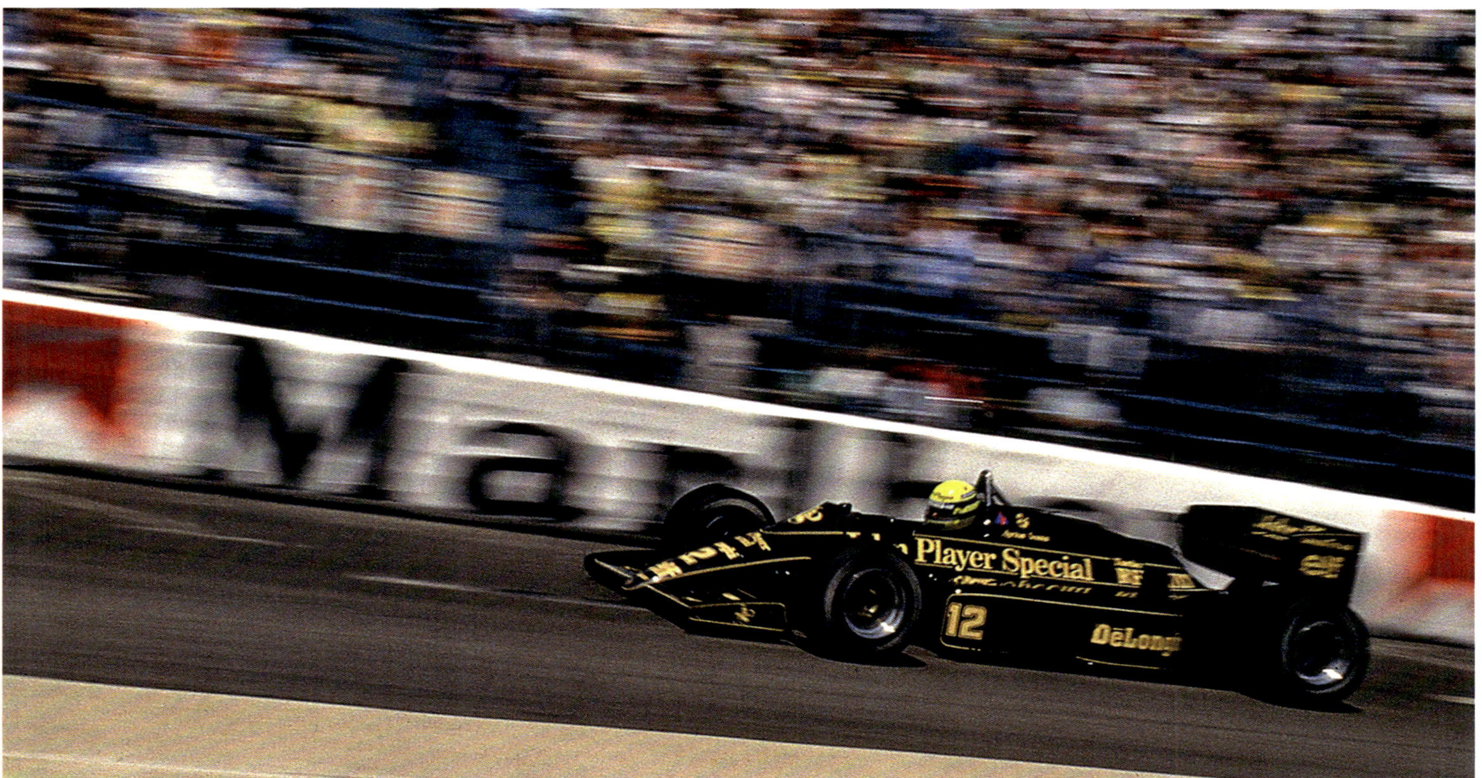

In 1986, Ayrton Senna secured 8 new pole positions, confirming his undisputed mastery in the highly specialized exercise of qualifying.

THE 1986 SEASON IN FIGURES

GRAND PRIX	QUALIFIERS	RACE
BRAZIL	POLE POSITION 8	2ND
SPAIN	POLE POSITION 9	VICTORY 3
SAN MARINO	POLE POSITION 10	DNF (WHEEL BEARING)
MONACO	3RD	3RD
BELGIUM	4TH	2ND
CANADA	2ND	5TH
DETROIT	POLE POSITION 11	VICTORY 4
FRANCE	POLE POSITION 12	DNF (CRASH)
GREAT BRITAIN	3RD	DNF (GEARBOX)
GERMANY	3RD	2ND
HUNGARY	POLE POSITION 13	2ND
AUSTRIA	8TH	DNF (ENGINE)
ITALY	5TH	DNF (TRANSMISSION)
PORTUGAL	POLE POSITION 14	4TH
MEXICO	POLE POSITION 15	3RD
AUSTRALIA	3RD	DNF (ENGINE)

RANKING: 4TH IN THE FORMULA 1 WORLD CHAMPIONSHIP

(55 POINTS, 2 VICTORIES, 8 PODIUMS, 8 POLE POSITIONS)

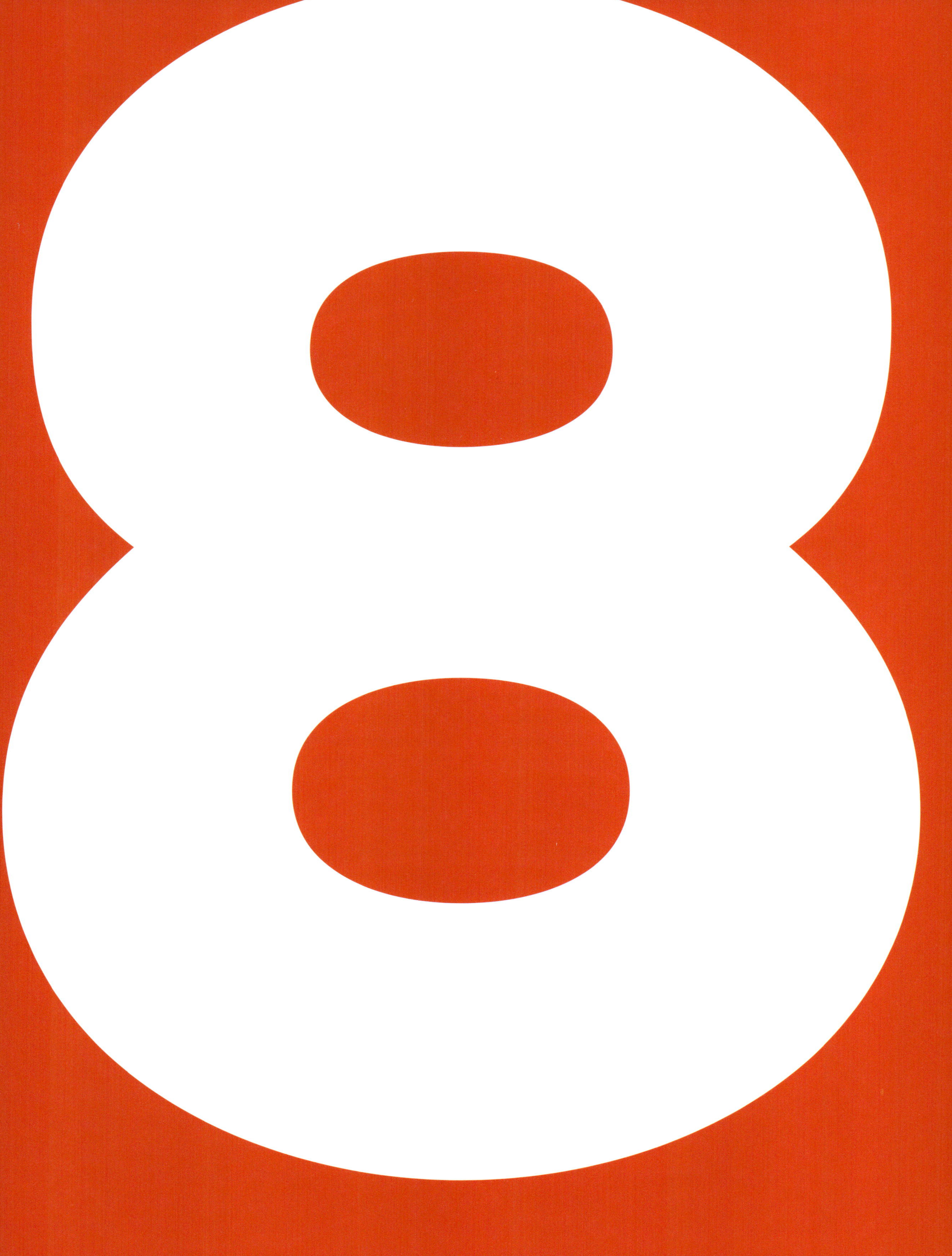

IN PRAISE OF CONSTANCY

LAST RIDE WITH LOTUS, FIRST WITH HONDA

SENNA'S LOTUS IS POWERED BY A HONDA ENGINE, WHICH IS LESS POWERFUL THAN THE RENAULT ENGINES HE HAD KNOWN THE PREVIOUS TWO SEASONS.

He must do his best, but must not complain too much because he knows that the following year, he is going to be working with Honda again, as he is leaning toward joining the Honda-powered McLaren team. Nothing is yet signed, but everybody knows it is a done deal, at least in Japan, in the upper circles of the Japanese manufacturer. Ayrton achieved just one pole position, at Imola at the start of the season, but the main thing was that he stepped onto the podium eight times in 16 races and was rewarded with a place on the final World Championship podium, finishing third, behind the two Williams–Honda drivers, Nelson Piquet and Nigel Mansell. He was four points shy of the British driver, who won twice as often as his teammate—six victories to three—but finally had to concede. And as always with Lotus, Senna won twice, winning in Monaco for his 50th Grand Prix victory and following up in Detroit, just like the previous year. He won at the two city circuits, each very different from the other, where his street-brawler driving attitude combined with the first active suspension in F1 history.

In 1987, for internal sponsorship reasons, Lotus traded its iconic black and gold John Player Special livery for the entirely yellow one of another tobacco sponsor, Camel. Here, on the last Lotus driven by Ayrton Senna in F1.

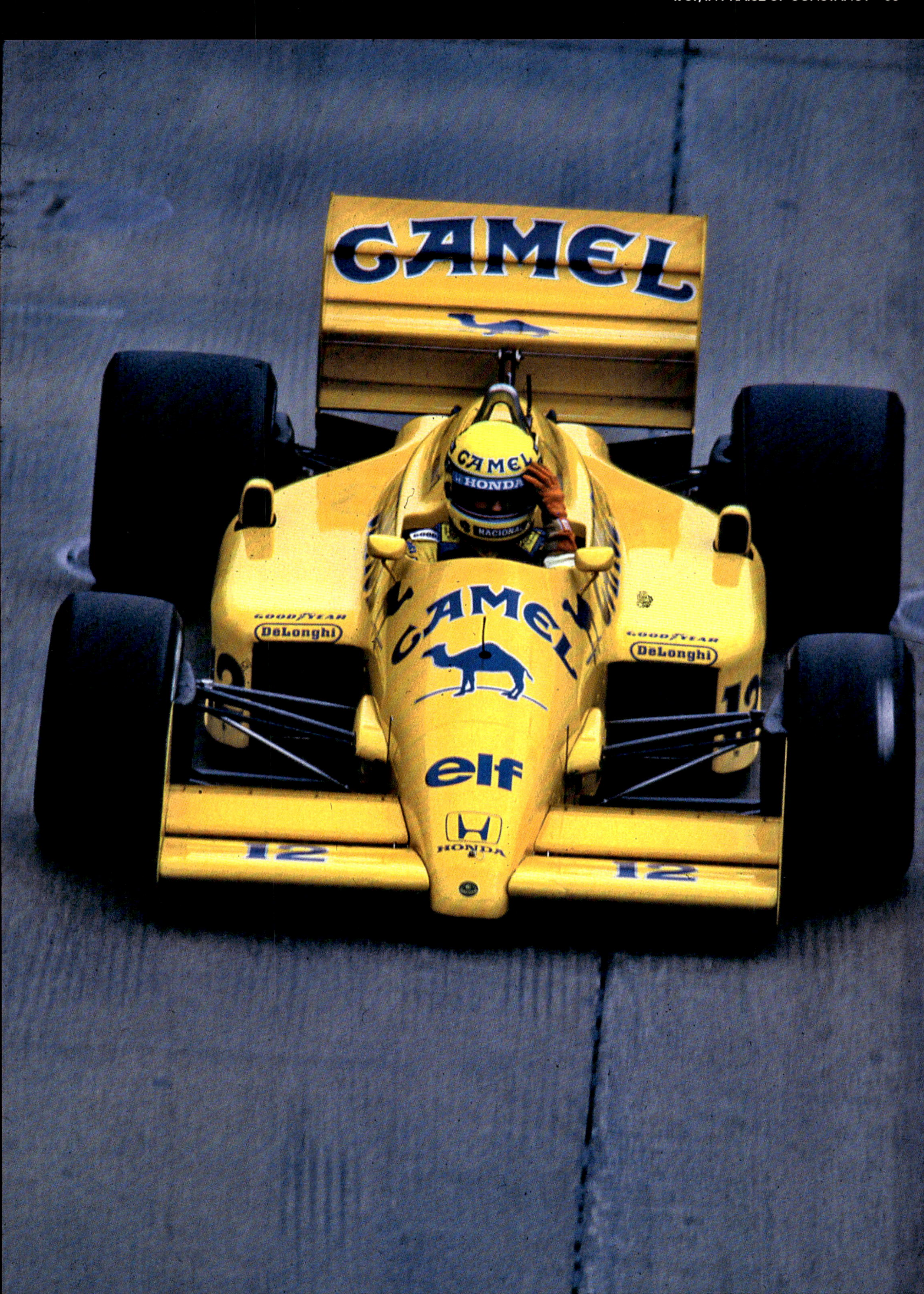
CAMEL
CAMEL
HONDA
NACIONAL
CAMEL
GOODYEAR
DeLonghi
GOODYEAR
DeLonghi
elf
HONDA
12
12

RACE AFTER RACE

1987

MONACO GRAND PRIX: THE WINNING 50TH!

Upon arriving in Monaco, the duel between the two Brazilians is something everyone is talking about. Piquet, the older of the two, is still in pain after his crash in Imola and has trouble sleeping. On top of that, he dislikes city circuits. Senna, the younger of the two, has just settled in Monaco, where he has never yet won, having finished second in 1984 and third in 1986. The feeling is pretty good among the Japanese engineers, who love to handle the technical data that the Lotus driver loves to produce and discuss. His acute sensitivity and astounding memory make him just as effective in some respects as the telemetry of the era.

This quality comes in very handy when it comes to fine-tuning the Lotus 99T's active suspension, the settings of which have to be redefined for every race. It is an enormous workload for the Team Lotus engineers and their manager, Gérard Ducarouge. The British team is one big step ahead in that field compared to Williams and McLaren. However, the rest of the car's development is slowed down by the active suspension design, which offers Senna more comfort but gives him less of a feel for the car. This does not stop him from getting second place on the grid between the two Williams cars. Mansell relegates the Brazilian to second, seven-hundredths of a second behind him, with twice as much back to his teammate, Piquet, who is one and a half seconds behind in third—a virtual abyss. Just before the start, the FISA president, Jean-Marie Balestre, summons Senna and Mansell to talk about the incident in Spa-Francorchamps, and Senna agrees to shake hands. As expected, Mansell starts like a rocket and gets away quickly, opening up a lead of 10 seconds on Senna before, on lap 30, his turbo decides not to function anymore, forcing him to withdraw. The Brazilian takes the lead. Nobody would ever see his back wing again. He just gets a little hot under the collar on lap 65, when he misses a gear in the S de la Piscine and comes very close to hitting the barriers. He recovers control of his Lotus easily and finishes 40 seconds ahead of a resigned Piquet. Third place on the podium is claimed by Michele Alboreto, who had a massive crash during Friday's free practice. Prost's engine blows up two laps short of the finishing line while he was in third place, one minute behind Senna.

On the podium, a delighted Ayrton is joined by Peter Warr and a few mechanics. He does not know the special Monaco protocol, so he sprays everyone when he opens his bottle of Moët & Chandon, including His Serene Highness Prince Rainier III and the rest of the princely family. Then he recounts his race:

Great car, great engine, great suspension! At the start of the race, I maintained an almost relaxed pace, letting Mansell go to preserve my tires and brakes. When I took the lead, I did three or four laps at full speed to see if everything was working perfectly and keep my concentration intact. Then I eased off again because nothing could worry me anymore.

Lotus had not won in the principality since Ronnie Peterson in 1974. It is the first victory for a Formula 1 car with active suspension. After the royal gala, where he greets the singer Jeane Manson, Ayrton joins his team at the Tip Top, a trendy bar, but he only stays for an hour. On Monday, he debriefs with "Ducared." Then, the following weekend, he is off to Brazil for a rest and to launch his clothing brand in a Rio de Janeiro nightclub. The Senna brand will start to shine.

BOB DANCE

In 1987, we changed our Renault engine for a Honda. Ayrton got on well with everyone on the team and was a great source of motivation. We were staying in an old house in the countryside and had a sort of stable to work in. That year, our advantage was based on our advanced knowledge of active suspension. Ayrton believed that this technical advance would enable him to beat his rivals. He did everything necessary during the tests and worked a lot with the people involved in this innovation. I think that without this, in his third season with us, he wouldn't have stayed. He would have joined McLaren, who were trying to snatch him from us. On city circuits like Monte Carlo and Detroit, it was an advantage. But we had to do a lot of testing and we suffered from a certain lack of reliability. Besides, we couldn't hold such a talented guy any longer.

The active suspension helped us retain Ayrton at Lotus...

BOB DANCE

At the 1987 Monaco Grand Prix, Ayrton Senna achieved his first success on the streets of the principality. Later, he would win the most glamorous Grand Prix on the F1 calendar 5 more times.

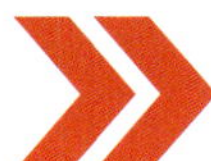

Following double page: The bright yellow livery of the Lotus 99T inspired Ayrton Senna to change the color of his helmet to be completely coordinated, showing his attention to detail.

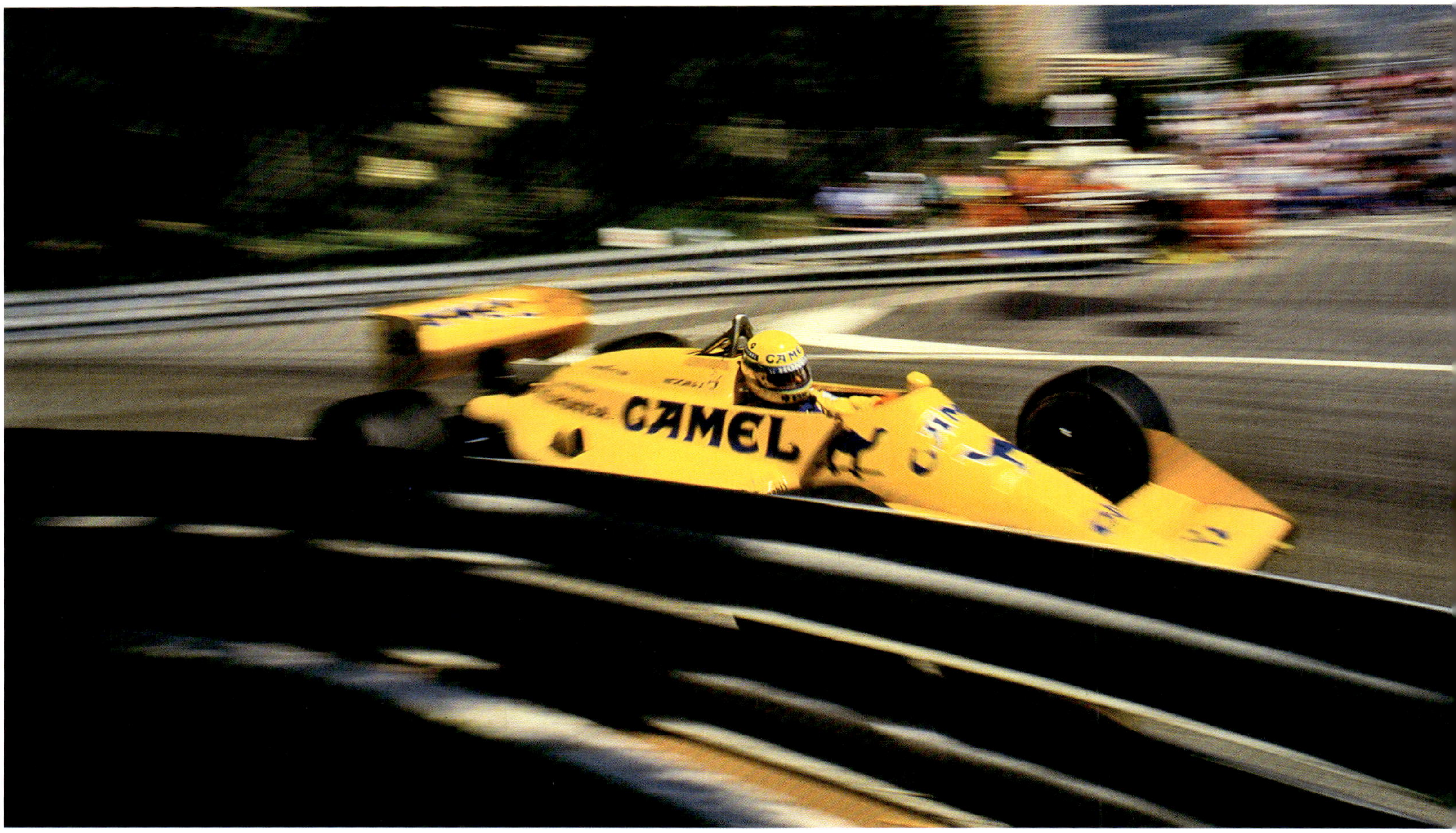

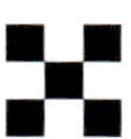

HONDA AND SENNA: THE LONG-AWAITED MARRIAGE

In 1987, Ayrton Senna finally got to use the Honda engines, which was a relief for the boy who had always wanted the best toys to play with. It is further proof of his commitment to his task as a driver inside and outside of the cockpit. He can now count on eight Japanese engineers to check every kilometer of their engine's performance and produce reports packed with detail. Sometimes, crewmembers from Honda would fly from Tokyo to London, and then, when they landed, they would go straight to a meeting for a few hours without even taking the time to shower or eat—a true sign of their dedication that Senna could only love. His driving also gets better. His feeling for the car, already near perfect, becomes even better. As proof of this, during a meeting with Honda, he asks for a light to flash on his steering wheel every 50 rotations per minute of his engine, instead of the 200 rotations initially planned. The Japanese are taken aback by the Brazilian's possible perception of this parameter. His response was brief and to the point: "I can feel it."

There is a notable example of that talent. During a free practice session, Senna returns to the pits seemingly for no reason, having only done a few laps. Helmet still on, he explains, "The engine was going to break. I had to stop so you could check what was wrong with it." Yoshitoshi Sakuaru, the team manager of Honda F1, cannot believe what he has just heard. The engineers check the engine but find nothing: No smoke, no problems on the surface of the engine. Was Senna, the "computer," mistaken? To make sure nothing had been missed, the engine has to be disassembled at the British center of the Japanese manufacturer. Every part of it is checked, and they find that the crankshaft is showing a bit of wear. It is a small detail that could have had massive consequences. The engine could have blown up a few laps later. But "Magic" had felt it all.

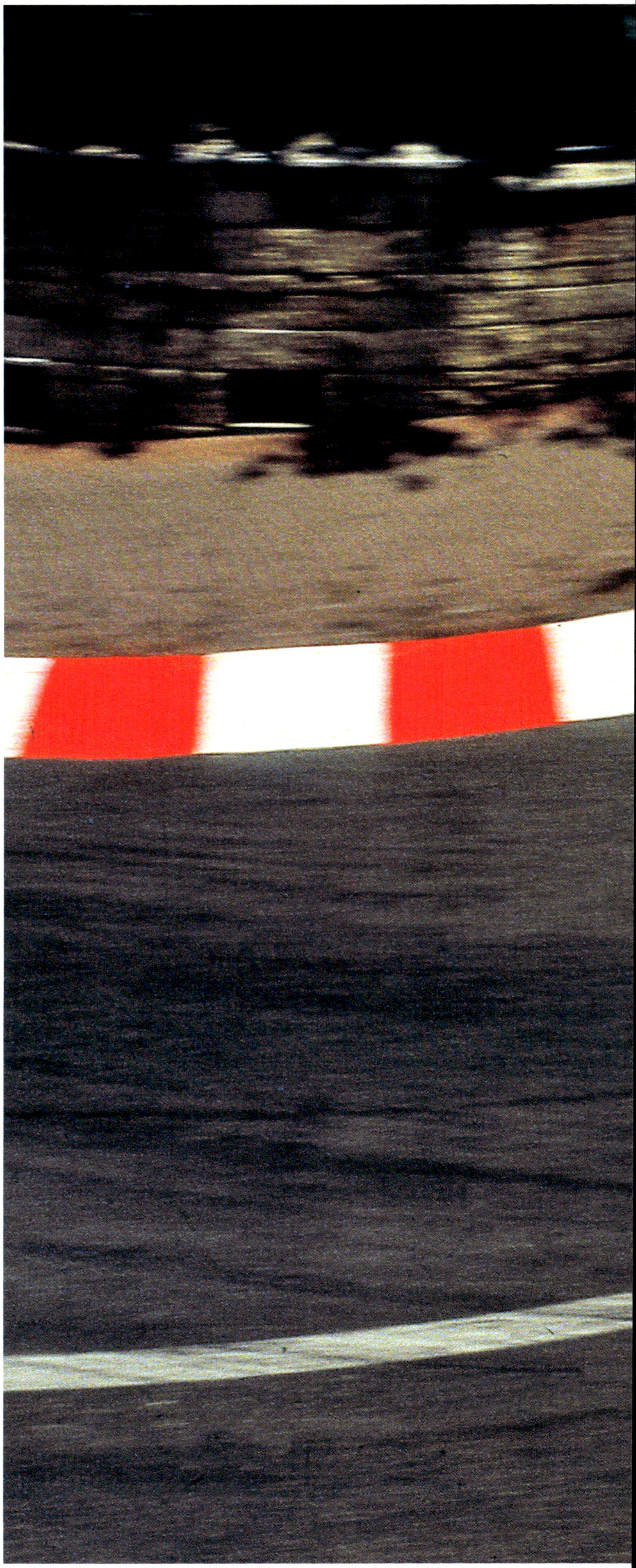

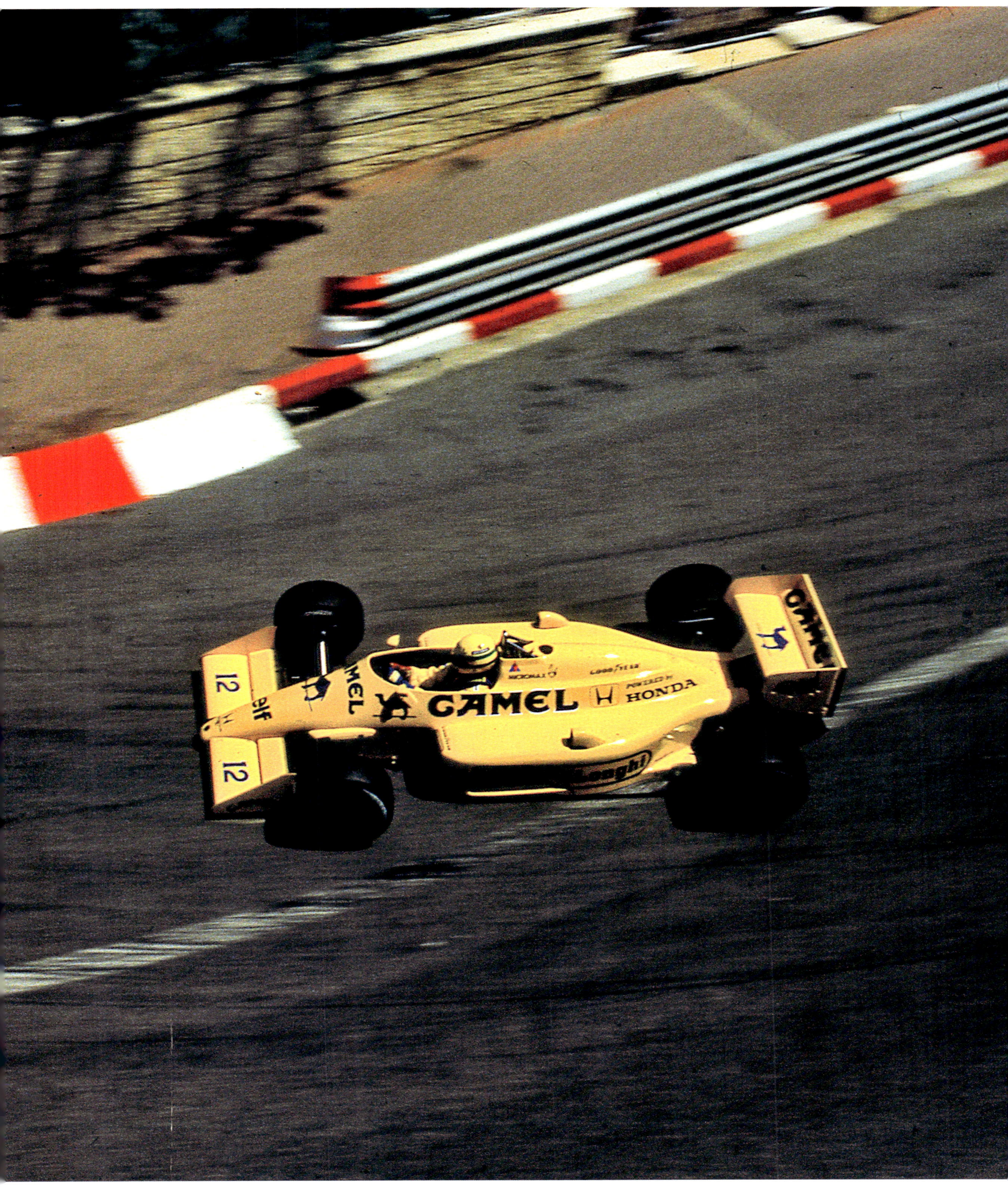
12
CAMEL
HONDA
12

SENNA VS. PIQUET THE FIGURES

From 1984 to 1991, when Piquet and Senna raced together in F1, both experienced highs and lows. But Ayrton, arriving in F1 later than Piquet—who had already won two world championship titles in 1981 and 1983—had more highs than his older rival, who became less and less motivated. The figures are decisively in favor of Senna.

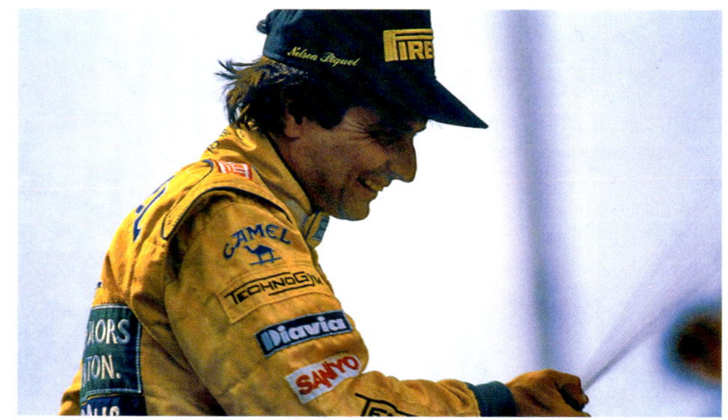

1984-1991	VICTORIES	PODIUMS	POLE POSITIONS	BEST LAPS	TITLES
SENNA	33	66	60	17	3 (1988, 1990, 1991)
PIQUET	13	37	16	14	1 (1987)

NELSON PIQUET, THE JEALOUS RIVAL

In the last 50 years of Formula 1 history, there has seldom been a rivalry greater than the coming together of these two Brazilian stars. The man from Rio de Janeiro, Nelson Piquet—the older of the two—is approaching the end of his career as the younger Ayrton Senna, a native of Sao Paulo, is rising through the racing firmament. Ultimately, their track record is fairly identical: three world championships each, but in very different conditions. And their respective legacies are quite different.

Born in 1952, the son of a politician, Nelson Piquet had to wait until 1978 before driving in Formula 1 and until 1980 to win his first Grand Prix, in Long Beach. He also benefits from the ideas of two geniuses: Bernie Ecclestone for his business nous and Gordon Murray for his design flair. Piquet would drive for Brabham for a long time. What was unusual about his three world championship titles is that each time he became champion, he won just three times during the season. He thus won by very small margins in 1981 and 1983, finishing one point ahead of Carlos Reutemann in the Williams and then, two points ahead of the young Alain Prost in his Renault. A consistent performer, he took third place in 1987 at the expense of his Williams teammate Nigel Mansell, despite the British driver's six victories.

The handover occurred in 1987, when Ayrton Senna left Lotus to join McLaren and was replaced in Colin Chapman's team by Nelson Piquet, who never managed to win in a Lotus in two seasons before ending up on a freewheel at Benetton, with three wins in total in 1990 and 1991. During the time that the two Brazilians were side by side in the paddock, Piquet first played on his young compatriot's inappropriate sense of humor, and then seemed downright bitter, confronted every weekend with the absolute adoration Senna aroused among Brazilian F1 fans. Piquet was respected and cheered by Brazilians when he won races, of course, but he was never worshipped like Senna.

The rivalry between Piquet and Senna was intense, especially in Brazil. Some even say they hated each other and exchanged insults. Even today in Brazil, Piquet's fans are convinced that he was better than Senna, but Senna was more popular because he was also the "Globo Boy." The Brazilian TV channel in charge of the official F1 broadcast in the country followed him very closely throughout his career. Forty years or so before the advent of Netflix, Globo always did its utmost to keep Senna in the news. But in addition to the media side of things, Senna was also known for his demonstrations of love for his country. Proud of the auriverde (gold-and-green) banner, he often took it with him onto the podium and made millions of Brazilians fall in love with him. This was something that Piquet would have to deal with on several occasions.

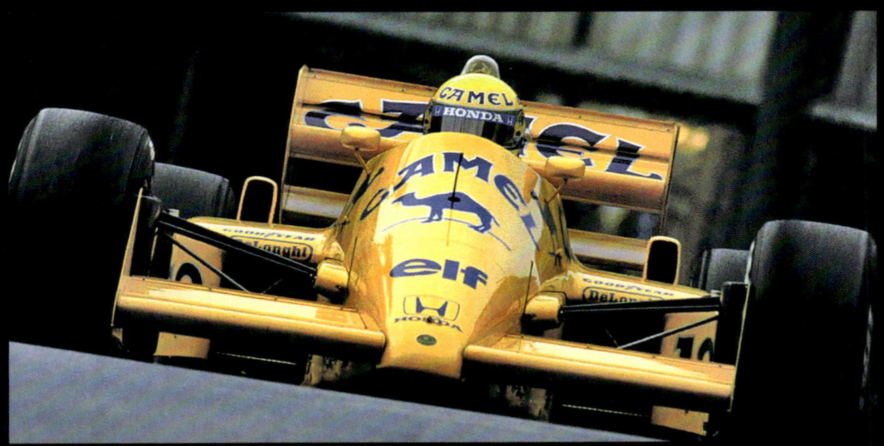

THE CAR: LOTUS 99T

SAYONARA RENAULT AND KONNICHIWA HONDA!

The Lotus 99T would end up being the last car from the Norfolk team to be driven by Ayrton Senna. It is also the first to be powered by a Honda engine, an engine he has wanted for a long time. The V6 Honda RA166E engine that powers the Lotus 99T is far bigger than the Renault engines from Viry-Châtillon. As a result, the Japanese and British work together to bring it all together. Despite this, the chassis is not the most effective and suffers from insufficient aerodynamics, not to mention the fact that the mythical sponsor, JPS, has given way to Camel and its garish yellow livery. A shame for purists.

Under the radar, hard work is underway to provide the Senna–Nakajima driving duo with an innovation it is hoped will be a revolution: active suspension, the first of its kind and a way of retaining Senna for another year. Ayrton thought, “If we had active suspension, we could probably beat our rivals.» Bob Dance admits in retrospect that without the active suspension, Senna would not have completed his third season with Lotus and would have joined the McLaren team. Colin Chapman had laid the foundations for this technology earlier in the 1980s but did not have the time—or the technical means—to develop it further.

In fact, the active suspension is simpler. A computer in the car analyzes the track variations. The computer then sends the information to the four suspensions, which then adapt accordingly. Thus, driving is far more comfortable, and the car is balanced like never before. But in 1987, not everything was yet computerized in Formula 1, and the technology developed by Lotus was miles away from that soon to be developed by Williams–Renault in 1992. Furthermore, errors often occur. The active suspension is highly sensitive and unreliable and becomes more of a burden than an advantage. Nonetheless, it helps Senna get two victories, in Monaco and Detroit, but it does not stop him from leaving Lotus at the end of 1987 to join McLaren.

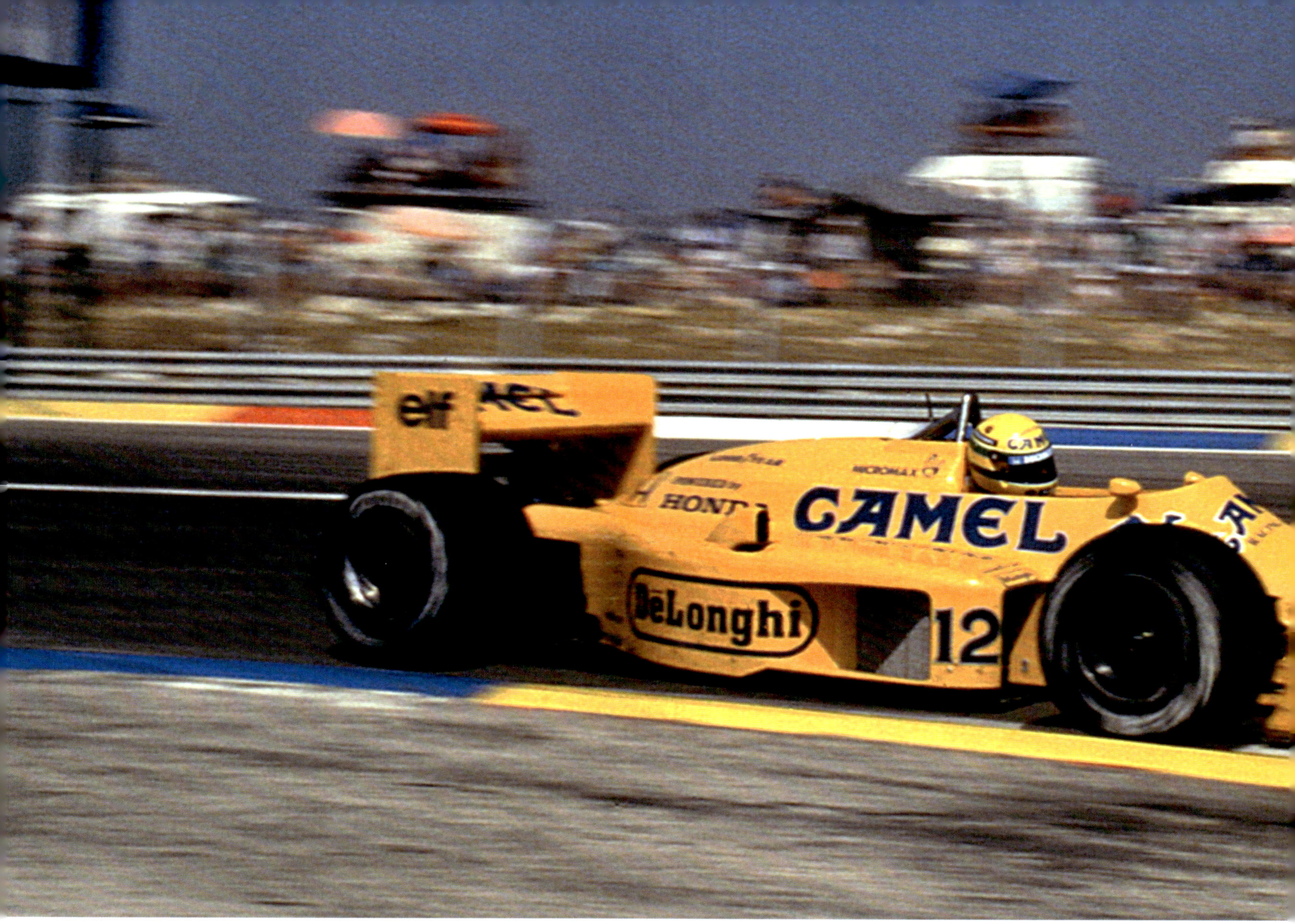

SATORU NAKAJIMA, THE IDEAL TEAMMATE

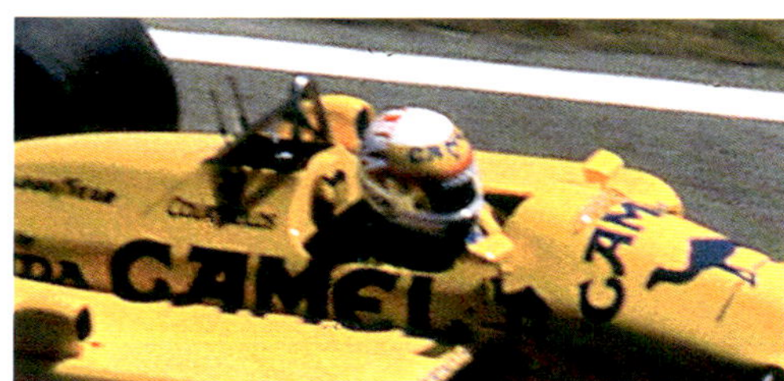

Senna's teammate at Lotus during the 1987 season was, at Honda's request, Satoru Nakajima, who would become the first regular Japanese driver in Formula 1. Having won many titles in Japan in F2 and F3000, he was ready to race in F1. Recruited as the second driver at Lotus, he would score seven points in his first season, including a fourth-place finish in the British Grand Prix. After driving in a Tyrrell, where he took the Honda engine with him, Satoru would completely change trajectories, working in advertising before becoming the team manager of the Formula Nippon racing team, which went on to win four titles between 1999 and 2009.

One story perfectly sums up the relationship between Ayrton and Satoru that year. When the Japanese driver arrived at the Monaco GP for the first time, the Brazilian made him a bandage for his hands, warning him that driving in the streets of the principality would be very tiring. He acted like his older brother, giving out plenty of advice to his teammate, who was seven years older than him! At the end of the qualifying session, when Satoru compared his time to Senna's (1'28.89 against 1'23.711, a difference of over five seconds), he simply said, "That's something I'll never be able to do myself."

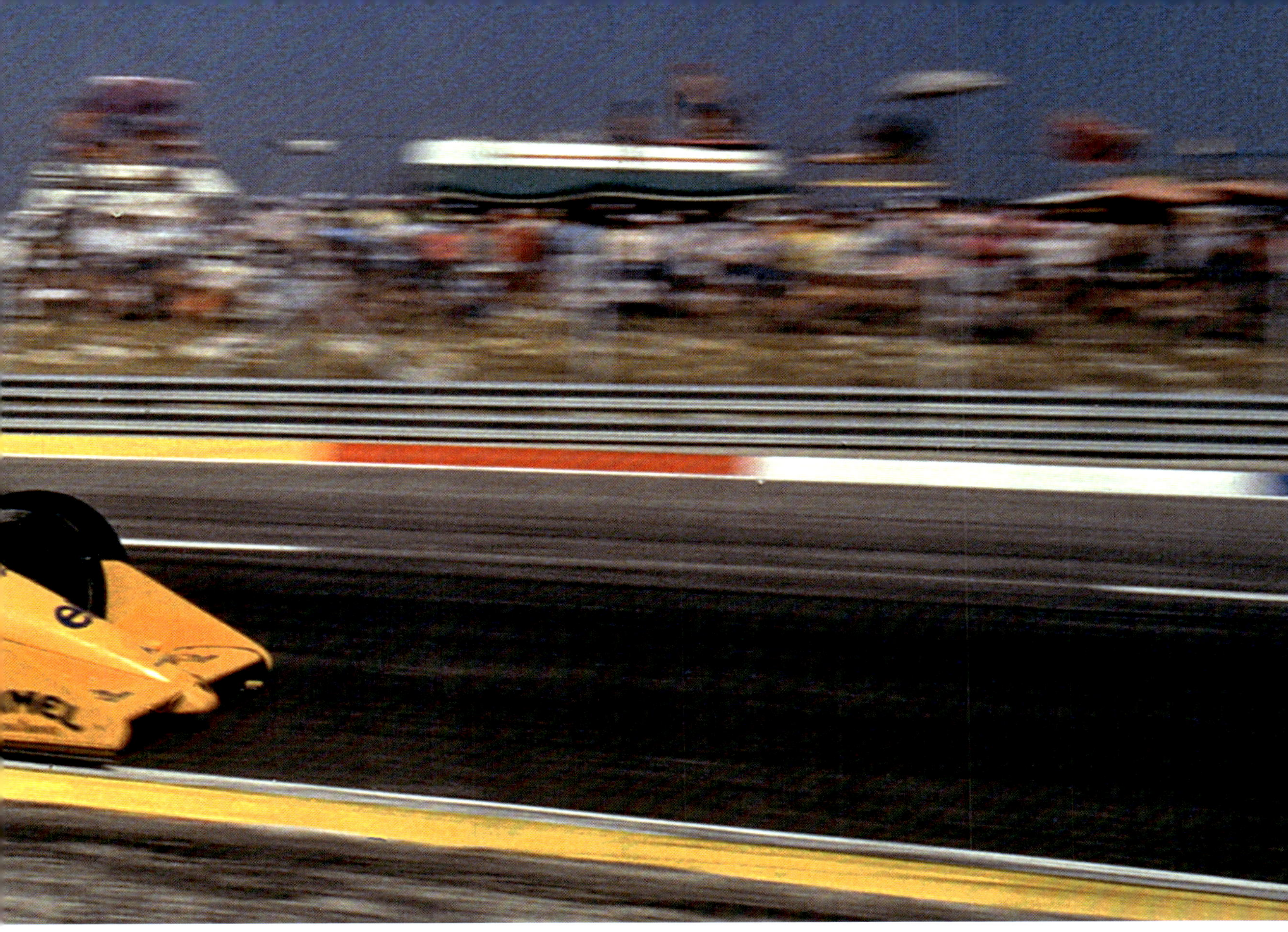

The Lotus 99T, powered by Honda, inaugurated for Ayrton Senna the driving of a single-seater propelled by the Japanese manufacturer. A first time but surely not the last...

GERMAN GRAND PRIX: SENNA BRAKES, PIQUET WINS

Having been voted the nation's favorite sportsman in his native Brazil, Senna arrives in Germany full of confidence. Nonetheless, a few days before the race, he gives himself a scare on the German track. A sudden puncture, which fortunately results in no major problems, causes him to lose control of his car for a distance of 400 meters. But he is already focused on his next task: to make his Lotus progress and win again, like in Monaco and Detroit. During the free practices, the situation with Piquet heats up. He overtakes his fellow countryman and shows what he is made of. Piquet is furious and the media goes crazy. The qualifying duel between them is won by Senna, who takes second on the grid again, behind Mansell but in front of Piquet. Ready to race, the Sao Paulo native tells the media about his consuming ambition: "I think that sooner or later my work will be crowned by a title. F1 demands sacrifice, and only those who dedicate themselves religiously to it will succeed." A prophetic statement, with a little dig at Piquet, the flamboyant character from Rio, only fourth on the grid despite having the best car in the field.

Senna starts with a mule, as his suspension breaks down, his wing collapses, his brakes do not respond correctly, and to top it all off, he has an oil leak. On lap 38, Peter Warr asks Senna to withdraw, but he refuses, stopping three times in the pits and finishing third behind Piquet and Stefan Johansson in the Ferrari. Climbing out of his car, he asks the mechanics to take a look at something: "You guys better check the brake pedal, as it got further and further away during the last laps." The mechanics get their flashlights; the pedal is deep, and because of Senna's pressure, a small hole has appeared. Ayrton's feet were thus just a few millimeters away from the asphalt. Enraged, Ayrton asks Gérard Ducarouge to hold an urgent meeting to discuss his Lotus's reliability. Meanwhile, Ron Dennis is ready to strike and starts planning the 1988 season.

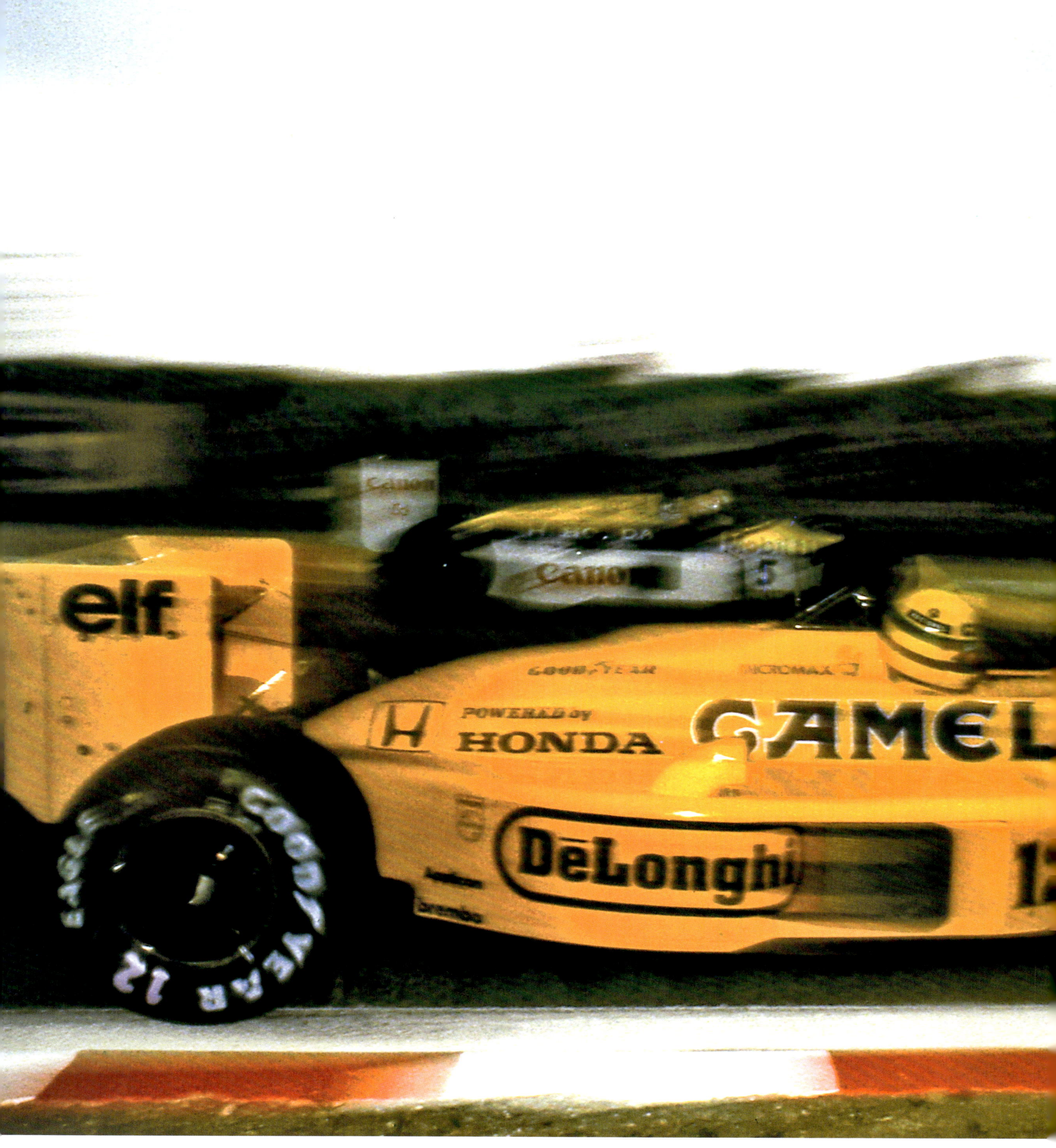
elf
HONDA
GOODYEAR 12

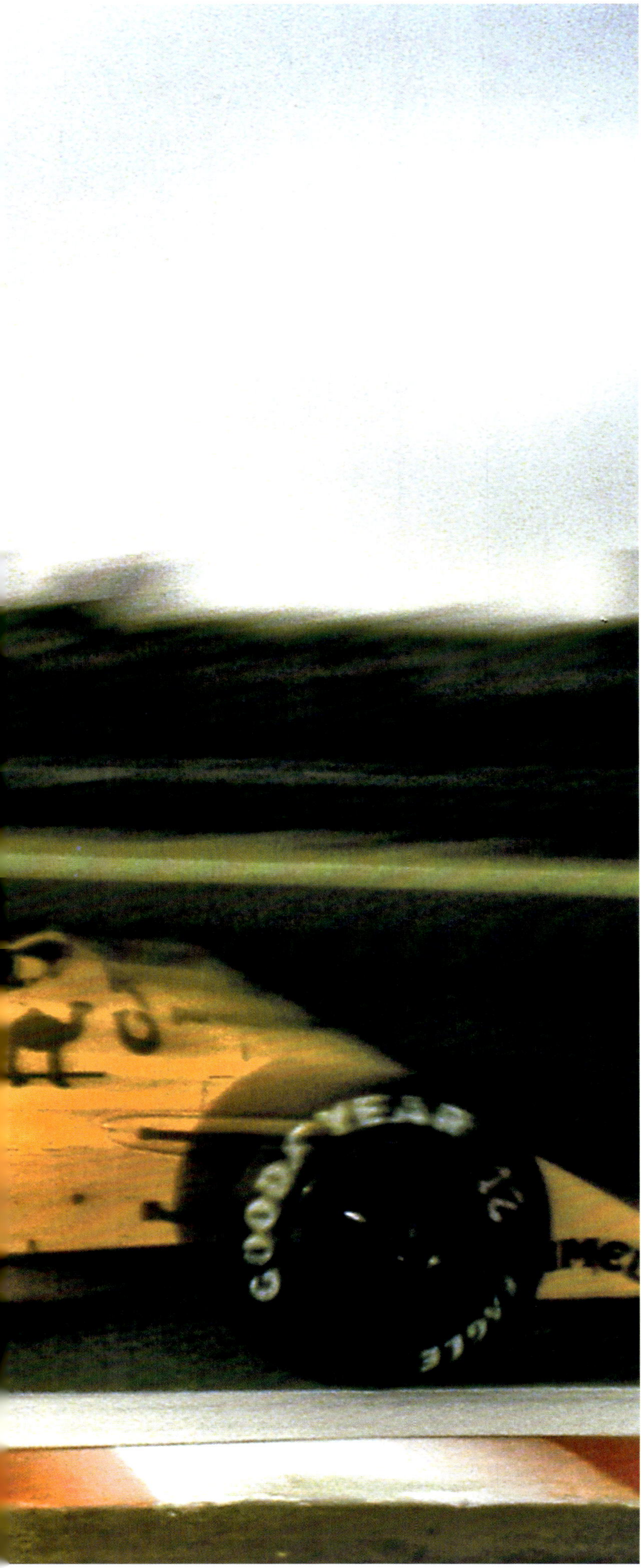

BEHIND THE SCENES IN THE PADDOCK

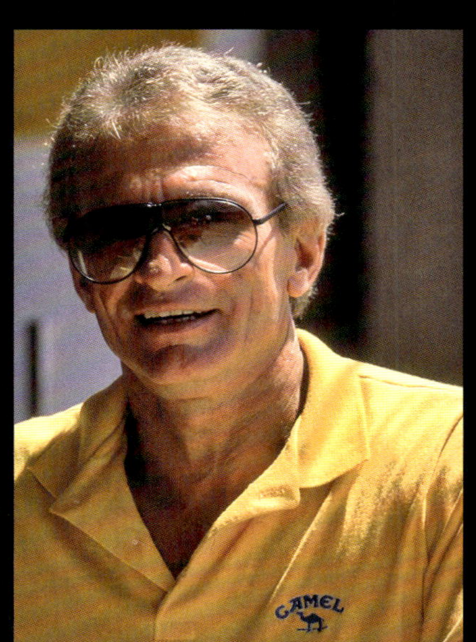

DUCAROUGE'S LETTER

Before the Japan Grand Prix, Senna's penultimate race with Lotus, his main engineer, Gérard Ducarouge, wrote him a lengthy farewell letter. What Ducarouge had not expected was that Senna was going to read it before coming to the track for the first free practice session. Upon his arrival in the pits, Ducarouge sees Senna and realizes that he has already read the letter. Senna is nearly crying and Gérard is also overwhelmed. He immediately regrets having given his driver an emotional shock, particularly when he is about to get in the car and drive at 300 km/h on one of the most grueling circuits on the calendar.

In his letter, Ducarouge, one of the most famous F1 engineers of that era, explains that he has decided not to formally say farewell to his favorite pilot since he does not feel like looking him directly in the eyes. He also says sorry for not giving him a car that was on a par with his talent during these three years and says that this frustration would follow him all his life.

During the 1987 season, Ayrton Senna (Lotus) and Nigel Mansell (Williams) often fought at the front.

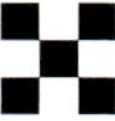

A PASSION FOR AVIATION

Just before the 1987 Brazil Grand Prix, Ayrton Senna co-piloted an F5E fighter of the Brazilian Air Force over Rio de Janeiro with Silvio Potengi, the usual pilot. Flying at almost the fighter's top speed of around 1,000 km/h, in several loops, they follow the long straight line of the Jacarepaguá circuit from above. Although he is ecstatic, he passes out a few times in the cockpit. Recounting this experience later to his friend Tchê, he stresses that it was one of the most electrifying moments of his life. After a steep dive followed by a low pass just a few meters above the sea in the Ubatuba region, Potengi makes a sudden 180-degree maneuver. Upside down, with the water close to the cockpit resembling another sky, Ayrton feels something he is completely unaccustomed to—panic. He finishes the 40-minute journey pale and dazed, but happy and filled with a curious sense of patriotism and thinks, "If all Brazilians could experience what I felt, maybe they'd have more love for their country."

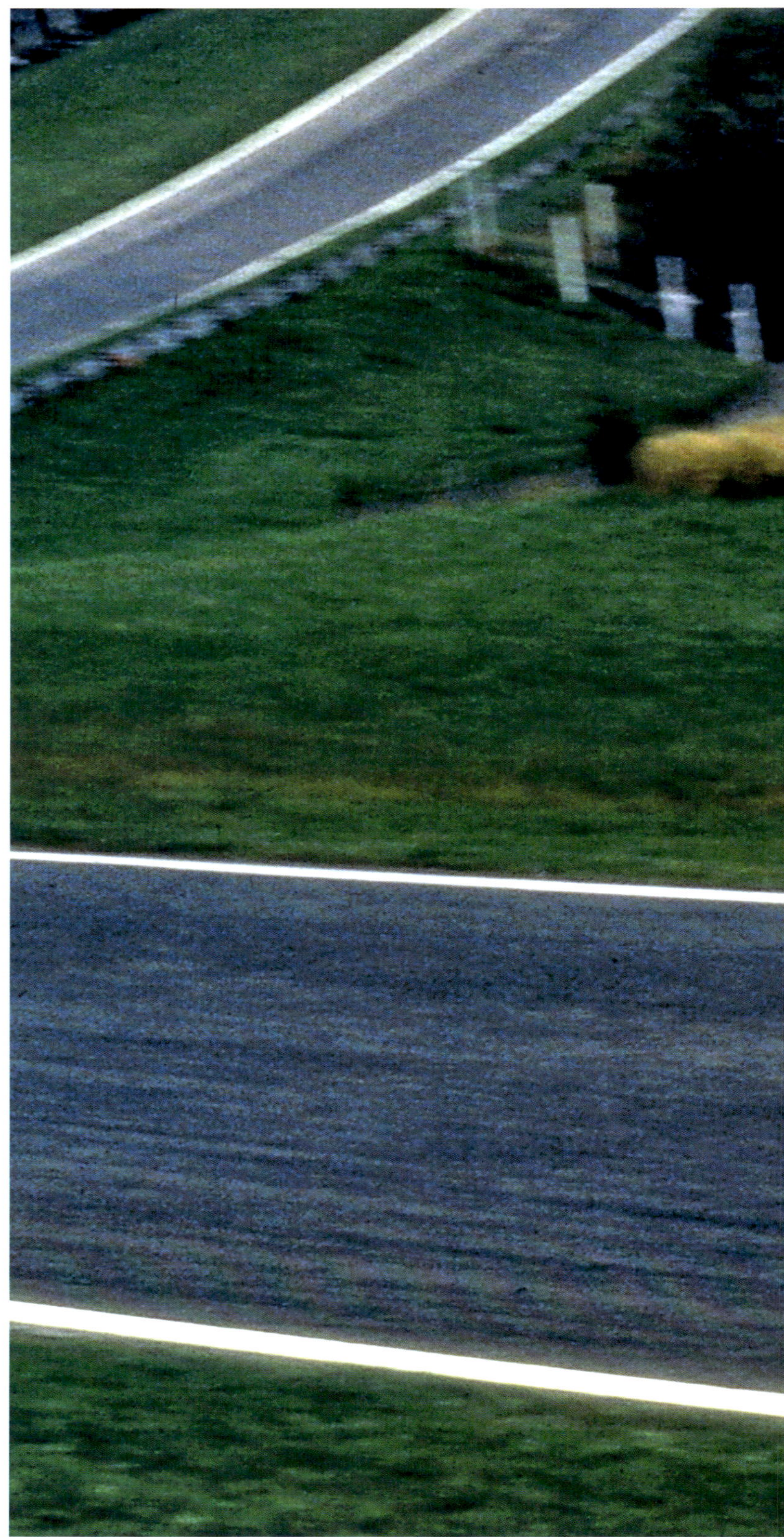

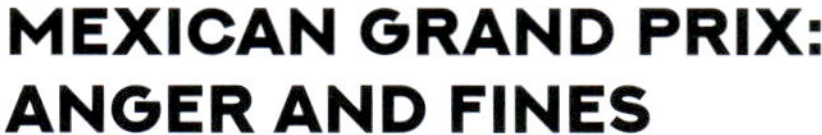

MEXICAN GRAND PRIX: ANGER AND FINES

On arriving in Mexico, Senna can technically still be World Champion. He needs to win the last three races of the season for that miracle to happen. But he does not believe in that dream anymore. The title will be contested between Mansell and Piquet. That way, he will not be disappointed. He knows all about the Lotus 99T and its reliability problems. During the Saturday session, Senna has a terrific crash on the Rodriguez Brothers track. On one section of the track, his Lotus takes a bump just as he shifts into fifth gear. It becomes airborne, and he loses control as it makes contact with the ground again. Stunned, he is taken to the medical center for examination. This triggers an angry outburst from the Brazilian: "Only my car needs to be taken care of, not me. You know what hurts the most? Not being able to compete for the victory, to hear my anthem."

Ayrton's troubles are not over yet. After starting from seventh in a chaotic Grand Prix that features two starts, the Paulista spins on lap 55 (out of 63) while in third place. The fault, according to him, is a recalcitrant clutch. But the worst is yet to come. He wants the race stewards to push his car so he can start driving again. One of the stewards approaches the car and pushes the Lotus a little, allowing him to start again all by himself. Consequently, Senna is in the middle of the track, idling for

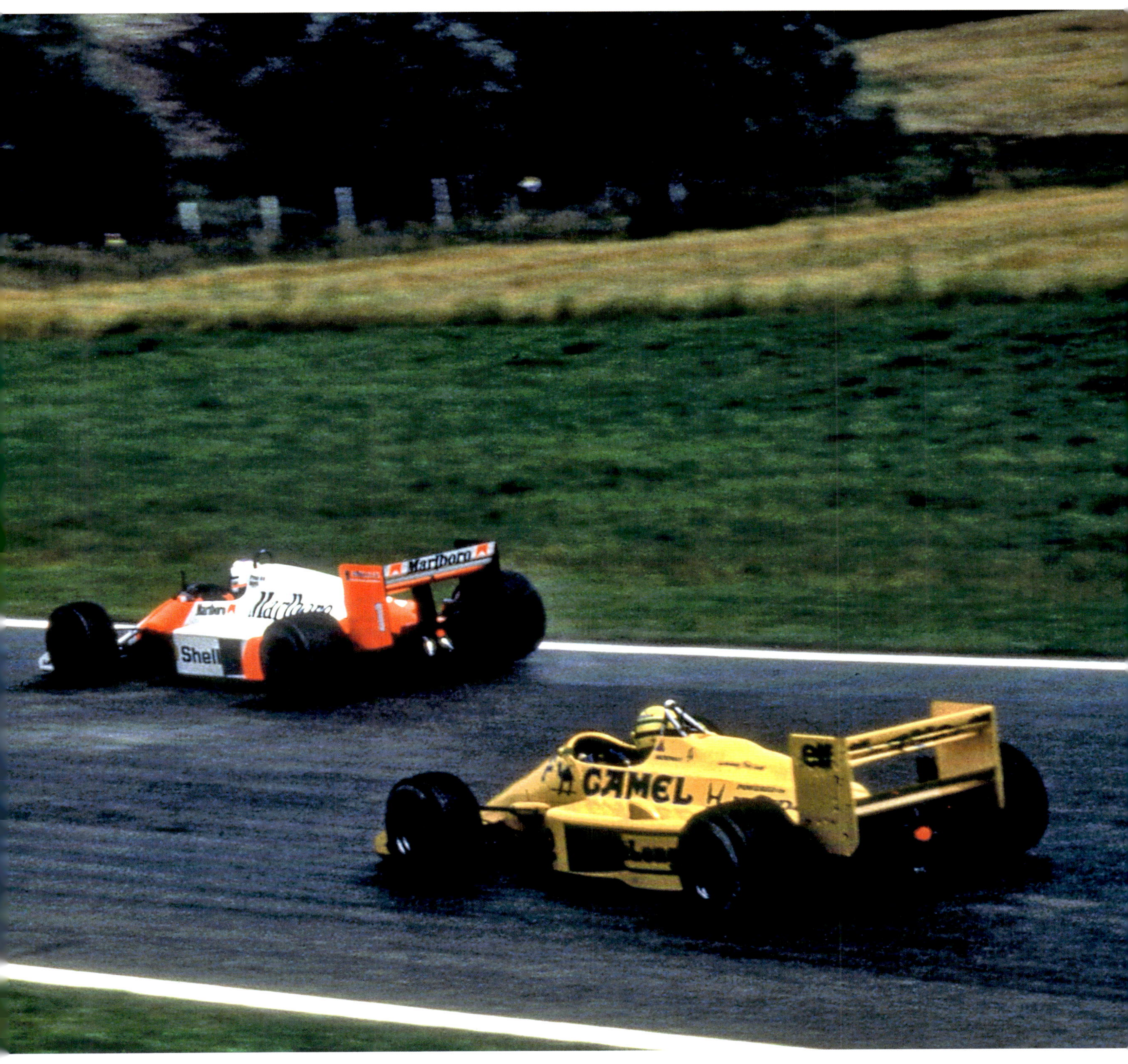

Alain Prost (McLaren) ahead of Ayrton Senna (Lotus). In the following season, they would compete on equal terms.

20 seconds—an eternity in Formula 1. His third place goes up in smoke. Then, some other stewards come to his rescue, but instead of restarting the Lotus, they cause it to slow down and stall. The Brazilian is absolutely furious. As he gets out of his car, he punches one of the stewards in the face and aims a kick at another. The scene is captured by television cameras and enrages the FISA, which fines him $15,000.

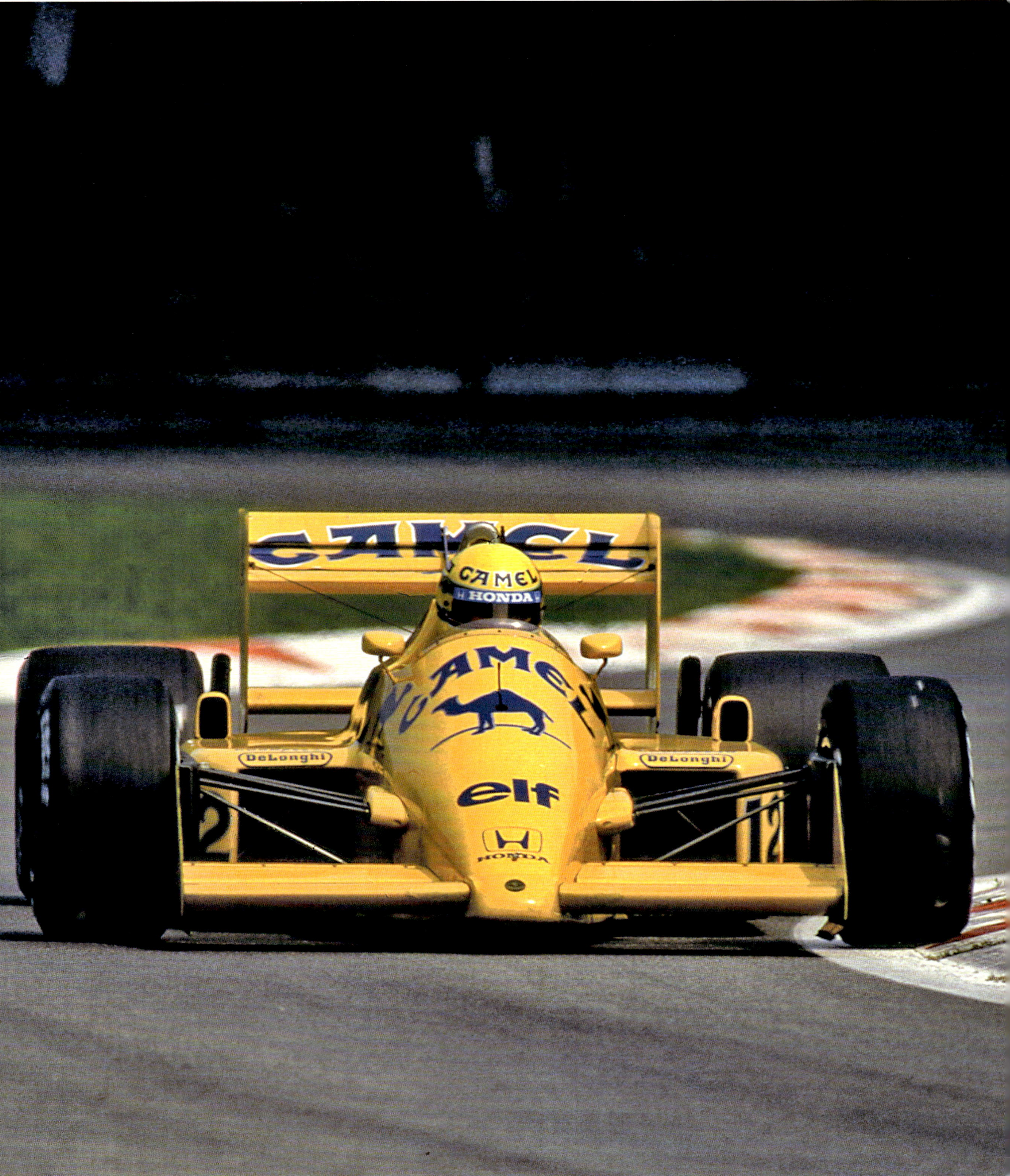
CAMEL
CAMEL
HONDA
DeLonghi
DeLonghi
elf
HONDA

Left: In 1987, Ayrton Senna and the Honda engine supplier worked tirelessly. The initial stages of this sacred alliance allowed the Brazilian to finish fourth in the F1 World Championship.

Right: Attentive to every detail, Ayrton Senna listened and observed every element that could enhance his performance.

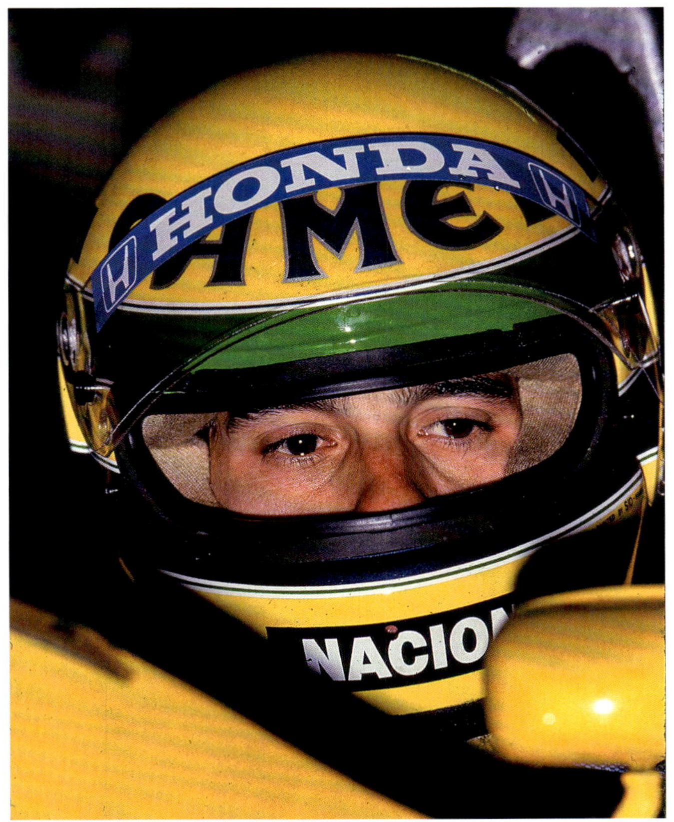

THE 1987 SEASON IN FIGURES

GRAND PRIX	QUALIFIERS	RACE
BRAZIL	3RD	DNF (OIL PRESSURE)
SAN MARINO	POLE POSITION 16	2ND
BELGIUM	3RD	DNF (CRASH)
MONACO	2ND	VICTORY 5
DETROIT	2ND	VICTORY 6
FRANCE	3RD	4TH
GREAT BRITAIN	3RD	3RD
GERMANY	2ND	3RD
HUNGARY	6TH	2ND
AUSTRIA	7TH	5TH
ITALY	4TH	2ND
PORTUGAL	5TH	7TH
SPAIN	5TH	5TH
MEXICO	7TH	DNF (SPUN)
JAPAN	7TH	2ND
AUSTRALIA	4TH	DSQ (NON-COMPLIANT BRAKES)

3RD IN THE FORMULA 1 WORLD CHAMPIONSHIP
(57 POINTS, 2 VICTORIES, 8 PODIUMS, 1 POLE POSITION)

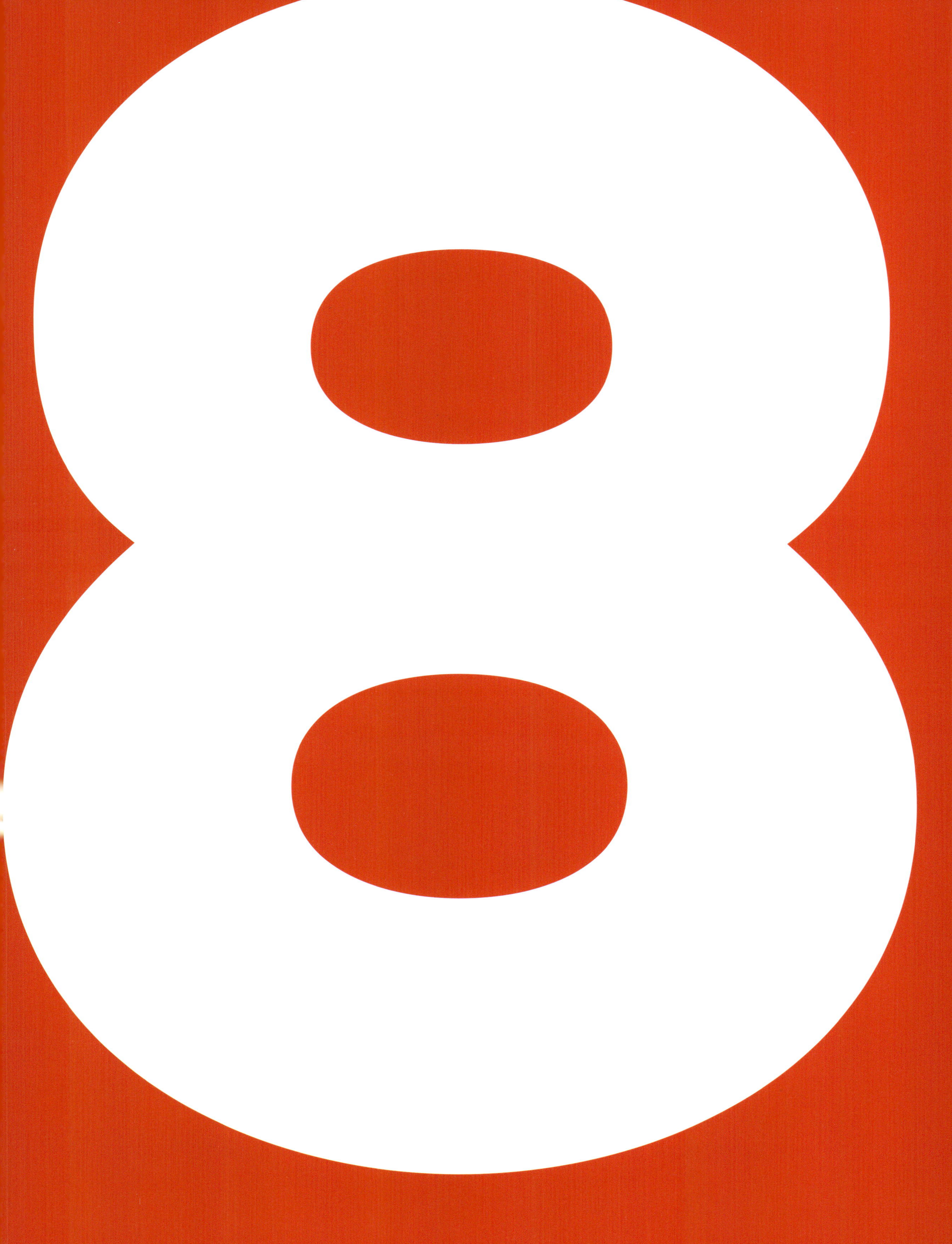

8

CONSECRATION

WORLD CHAMPION FOR THE FIRST TIME, AGAINST PROST

IN HIS FIRST SEASON DRIVING A MCLAREN-HONDA, AFTER BEING BRUTALLY DISQUALIFIED IN HIS FIRST RACE OF THE SEASON, SENNA ACHIEVED A FANTASTIC SEASON IN HIS HOME COUNTRY, BRAZIL, AND BAFFLED EVERY FORMULA 1 SPECTATOR, INCLUDING THOSE WHO WERE LOOKING FORWARD TO SEEING HIM IN A TOP TEAM AFTER HIS SUCCESSFUL STINT WITH LOTUS.

And if we take a look at his performance that season, the results are pretty satisfactory (eight victories, 11 podiums and 13 pole positions), as he was driving the same car as Alain Prost, who already won two titles as part of Ron Dennis' team. The master of Woking won his risky bet—associate two very strong pilots—and achieved an incredible season. Prost could look back on a year in which he scored more points than the Brazilian (105 to 94) even if the rules, which aimed to reward performance (11 best results out of 16 races), deprived him of a third title. Far behind the McLaren boys, only one pilot could win a race that season—Gerhard Berger at Monza, in his Ferrari. The Austrian ended the season with 41 points, or half of his untouchable rivals: eight victories for Senna and seven for Prost, which meant 15 wins out of 16 races for Master Ron's team.

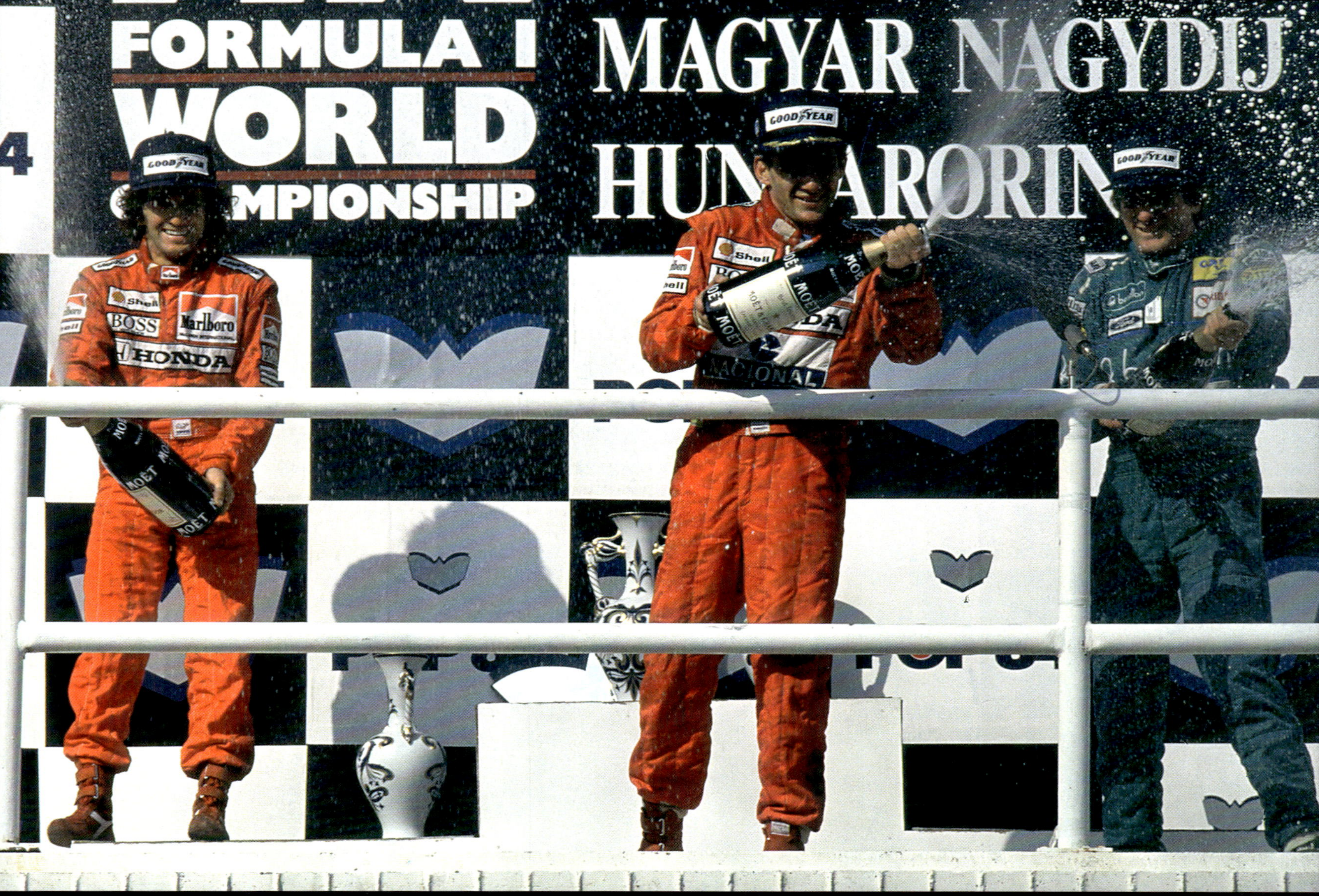

Ayrton Senna, the winner of the day, surrounded by Alain Prost and Thierry Boutsen on the podium of the 1988 Hungarian Grand Prix. A few weeks later, Senna became World Champion for the first time.

RACE AFTER RACE

1988

BRAZIL GRAND PRIX: MASSIVE DISAPPOINTMENT!

It was the first official race of the "Dream Team" assembled by Ron Dennis, and the free practices were already dominated by the McLaren-Honda, enough to freeze the rival teams even though the temperature was relatively hot. Senna got his first pole of the year, ahead of Mansell (2nd) and six-tenths ahead of Prost (3rd). It was very hot on the Jacarepaguá track in Rio de Janeiro, and the engineers were quite worried. Two problems arose: the cooling of the cars and the durability of the Goodyear tires. As Senna was on the grid, in pole position, his gearbox handle broke, and he started flapping his arms. But that's not all: smoke was rising out of his car, a sign of overheating. The race director, Roland Bruynseraede, stopped the start procedure.

Senna ran to his stand and sat in his mule, intending to start from the stands. But what Senna didn't know was that changing his car during the start procedure was forbidden. Senna risked being disqualified, but nobody had the heart to say it to the Brazilian champion, not even Ron Dennis, who knew the rules by heart.

Senna thus started from the stands, and Mansell was the first on the grid. He took a better start than Prost, but the Frenchman caught up and overtook him, establishing a comfortable lead. Senna was 18th and started climbing up. He was 13th on lap 5, then 8th on lap 10. Nothing could stop him, and, in front of his fans, he continued his overtaking spree. When Mansell withdrew on lap 19, Senna was 3rd. On lap 27, he went into the stands for a tire change, chatted with Ron Dennis, and asked his mechanics to clean up his radiators, which were blocked by some trash. On lap 31, a race stewards got the black flag out, with No. 12, Senna's number—he was disqualified for his car change. And Prost won the Brazil Grand Prix for the fifth time, by a very thin margin, his fuel tank nearly empty.

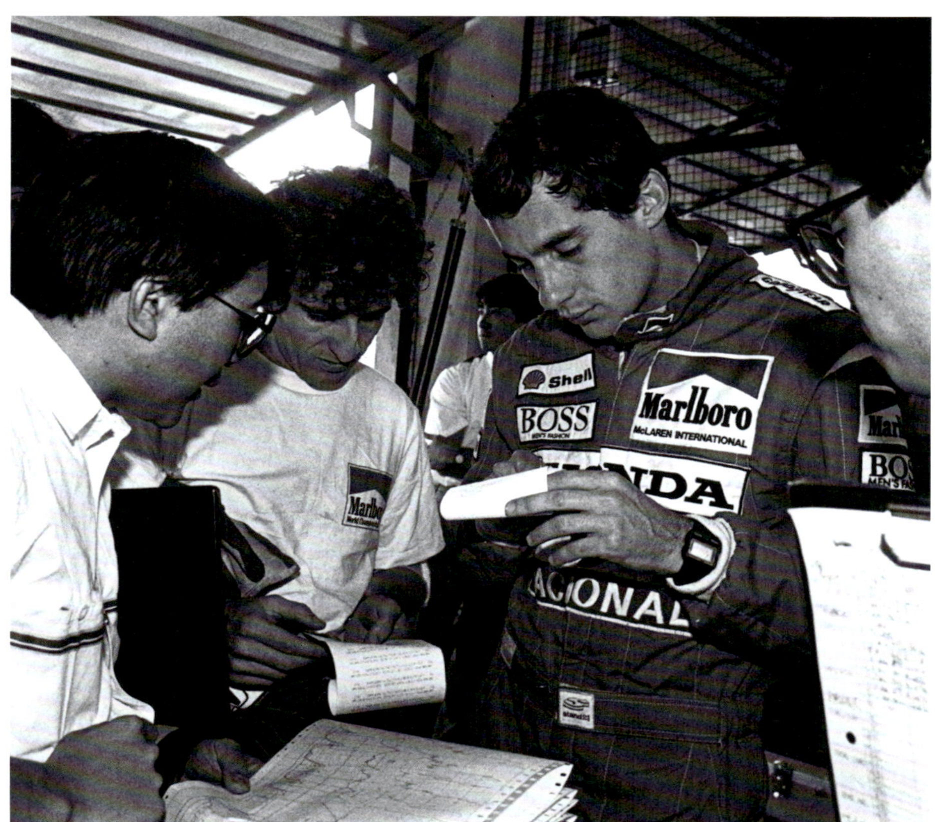

Left: Telemetry data was meticulously studied by Senna and Prost, with the assistance of McLaren and Honda engineers.

Right: Joe Ramírez, Ayrton Senna, and Alain Prost: a well-known trio for followers of the McLaren-Honda team in 1988.

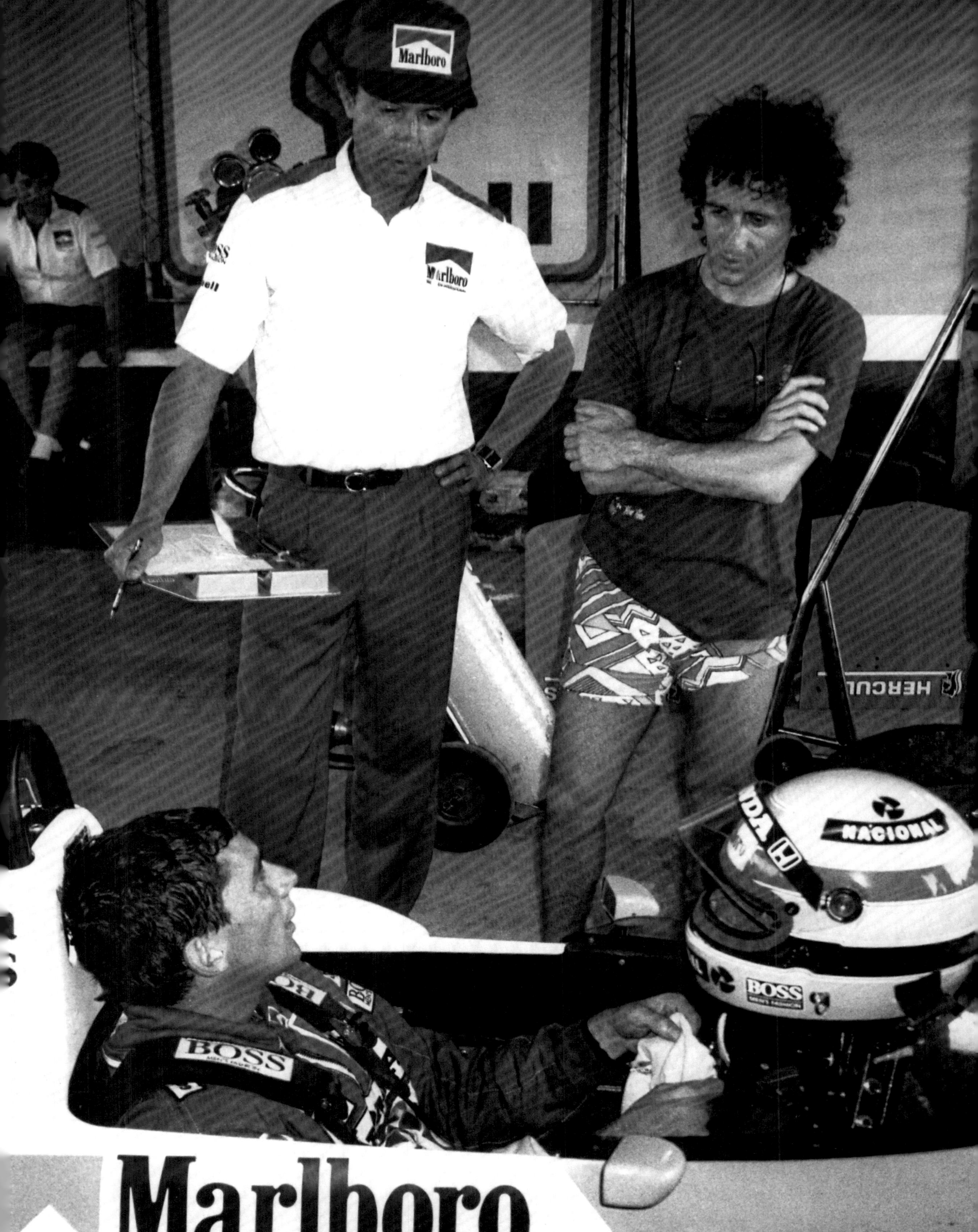
Marlboro
Marlboro
BOSS
NACIONAL
BOSS
BOSS
HERCUL
Marlboro

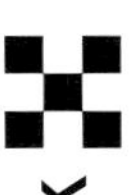

AYRTON SENNA, THE METICULOUS

It's no secret that Ayrton Senna was extremely demanding of both himself and his machine. His attention to detail gave his engineers plenty of headaches. But it was Senna's total commitment to the sport that put him at the pinnacle of motorsport. Before each race, Honda and McLaren would run computer simulations of Senna's potential pace the following weekend. "Normally, a driver's actual time is slightly slower than the best theoretical time from the simulation. But Ayrton was always slightly faster, because we couldn't copy what he did with the engine-tire combination," said engine engineer Takeo Kiuchi; proof that, at his best, man could be stronger than machine. Like an opera master, Senna spent a lot of time with his engine specialists. One day, he even tried to make the Japanese engineers hear a change in the sound of the Honda engine between 8,500 and 8,700 rpm. "It sounded like a musician looking for the perfect note," recalled suspension engineer Hiro Teramoto.

If Senna's technical skills impressed the engineers, his attention to detail went even further. Senna demanded that his hoods be made in a special way. Unlike many other drivers, Senna's hoods did not cover his mouth, forehead, or nose. He also insisted that the seams should not touch the top of his head, for fear that he might scratch himself with sweat and risk losing concentration for even a moment. Amazed at first, his equipment manufacturers finally agreed to his requests and sewed his hoods on the outside.

Alain Prost and Ayrton Senna review the data transferred by their team before driving on the Monaco Grand Prix circuit.

Next double page: at the end of the Beau Rivage climb, in the Massenet turn leading to the famous Monte-Carlo casino, spectators lean over to admire the Brazilian...

MONACO GRAND PRIX: MAGIC LAP AND LIFE LESSON

Before he arrived in Monaco, Senna had just won in Imola and managed to take two consecutive pole positions with his McLaren MP4/4. During the qualifying race, he was leading again, with at least a one second gap ahead of the peloton. So, he exited the track and went to the stands. That was for the best, as Ron Dennis didn't want to take the risk of damaging the car. But Senna tried to change his director's mind: "Please, just one more lap." The director agreed. Senna needed just under 84 seconds to complete one of the fastest and most impressive laps in F1 history. With a record of 1:23.998, he knocked a second and a half off the record set by his great rival, Alain Prost. The performance was outstanding; Senna came within nine-tenths of Mansell's pole the previous year, even though the Englishman's Williams-Honda had 300 more hp! Many enthusiasts and experts said that this was the greatest lap ever. Unfortunately, no images were recorded during Senna's lap, as cameras and the media weren't as ubiquitous as they are today. But luckily, the memories were unforgettable for those who were there that day. As the English team's coordinator Jo Ramírez reminisced, "After the session, Alain said to me, 'He's bloody fast.' I turned to Ayrton, who had a big smile on his face and winked at me." Senna waited two years to recount his experience. When he did, he described it as akin to entering "the zone," when control was total and concentration at its peak. "I was driving instinctively. I was in another dimension, as if I were in a tunnel. That day, I said to myself: 'This is my maximum. I can't do any better.' I've never felt that sensation again."

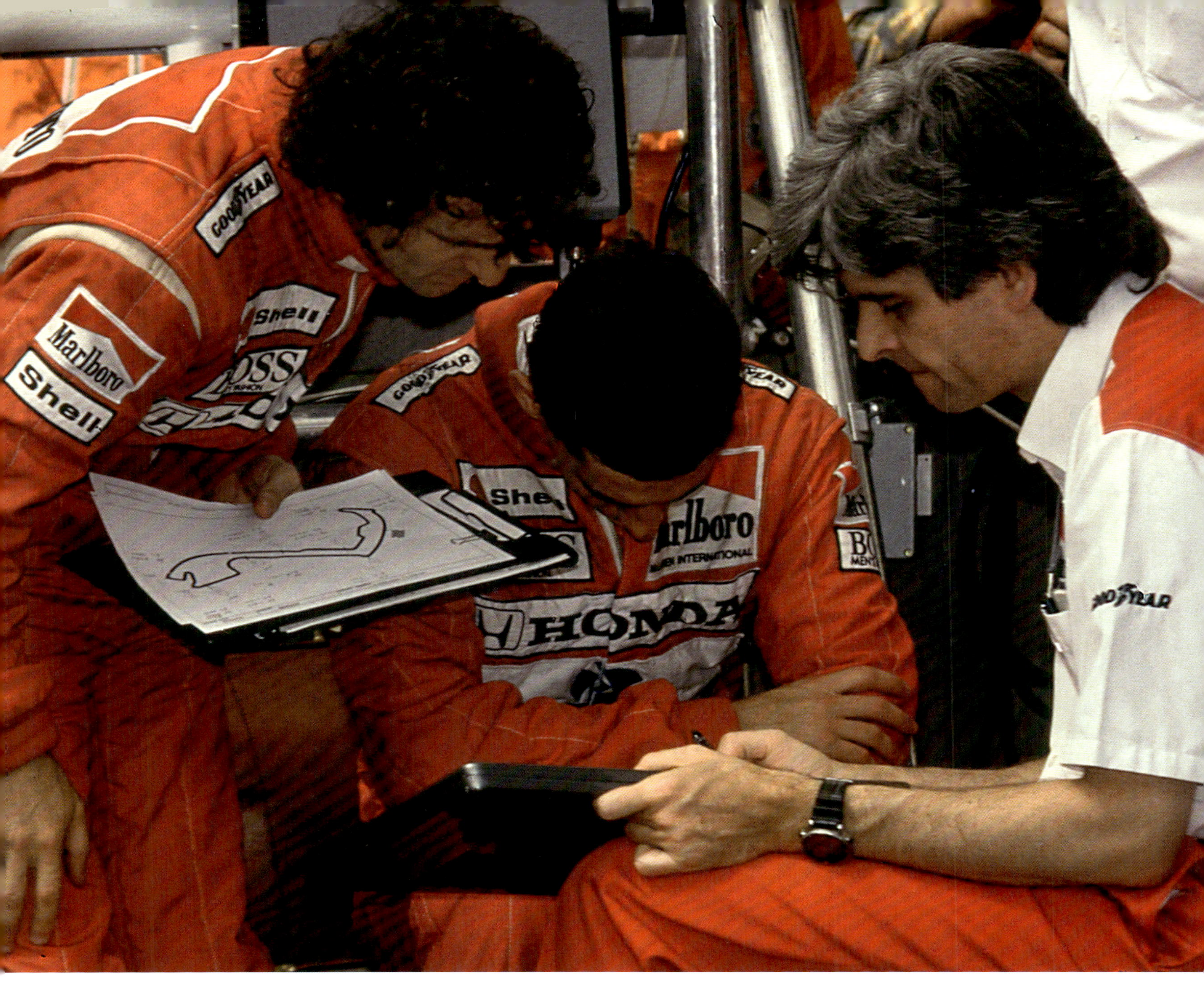

During the race, just like the day before, Senna wanted to destroy his rivals. Keeping his eye on Prost's performance, he was blocked behind Gerhard Berger, who was 2nd. On lap 55, the Frenchman overtook the Austrian, but he was still 48 seconds behind Senna. Senna was unhinged, driving faster and faster. Then, on lap 64 of 78, Ron Dennis spoke to him through the radio, saying, "Slow down, he is not going to overtake you!" One lap after that, the gap was 54 seconds. But the situation couldn't continue safely. On lap 67, the driver in the yellow helmet crashed his McLaren in the Portier corner and gave up his victory to Prost. Fuming in anger, Senna exited his car and didn't even go to the McLaren stands. Instead, he went to his own apartment in nearby Houston Palace to isolate himself. Jo Ramírez managed to get him on the phone. "I'm the stupidest man in the world," said Senna. At McLaren, a team member who preferred to remain anonymous summed up, "Senna made three mistakes: increasing his pace when it wasn't necessary, taking too long to respond to a radio instruction and making a calculation error [concerning the distance of the rails]." That situation would never happen again.

In the following day's edition, the French newspaper Nice-Matin wrote in praise of the McLaren driver, "Few were the world champions who did not combine talent and intelligence. The future will reveal the progress made by the Brazilian, to become number 1 in Formula 1." At the end of the season, once he had pocketed his first title, Senna said that the accident and the blunder had served him well. "I lost my concentration and made a stupid mistake. It made me think about myself a bit. My mistake in Monaco woke me up psychologically."

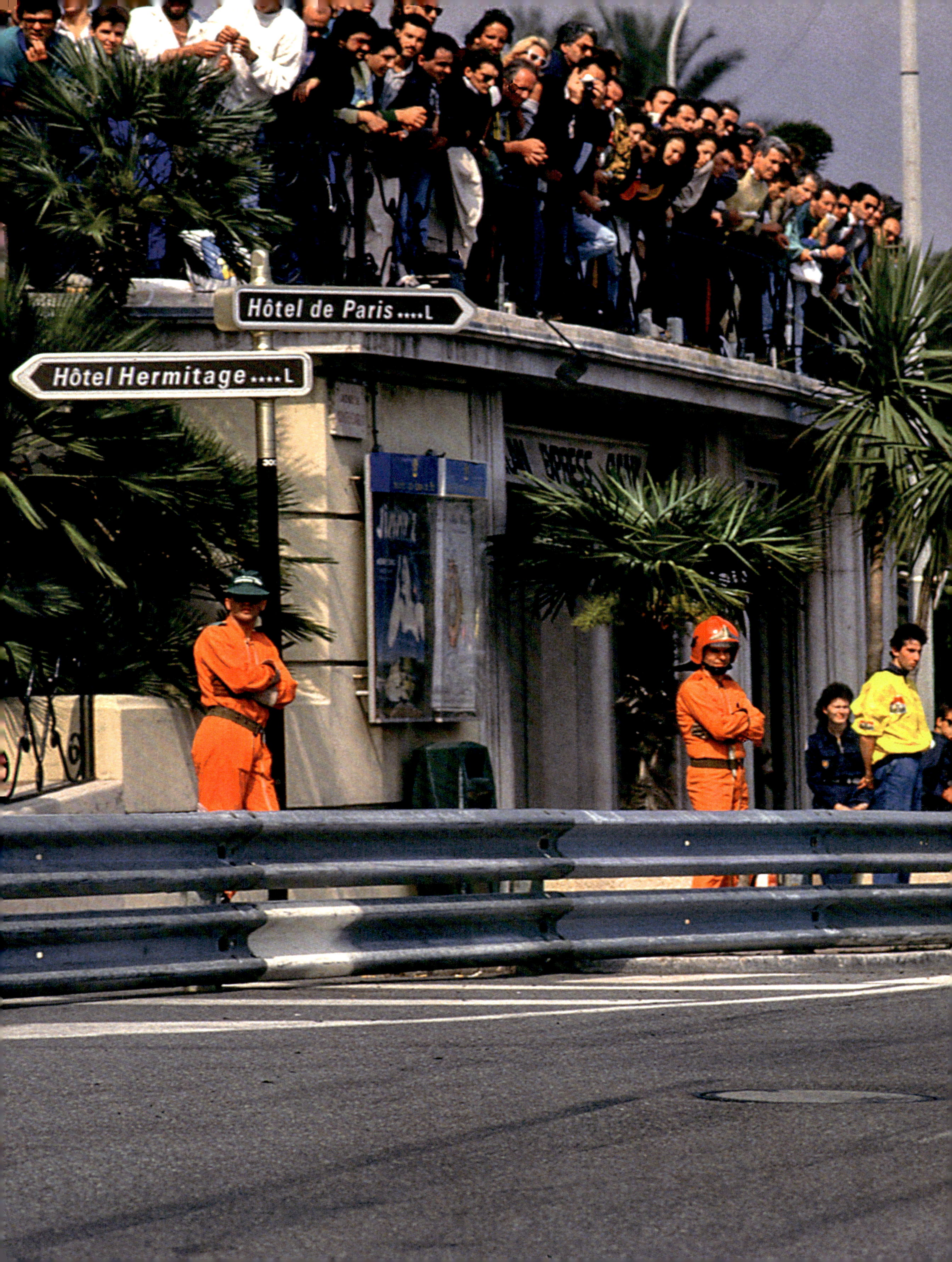
Hôtel de Paris L
Hôtel Hermitage L

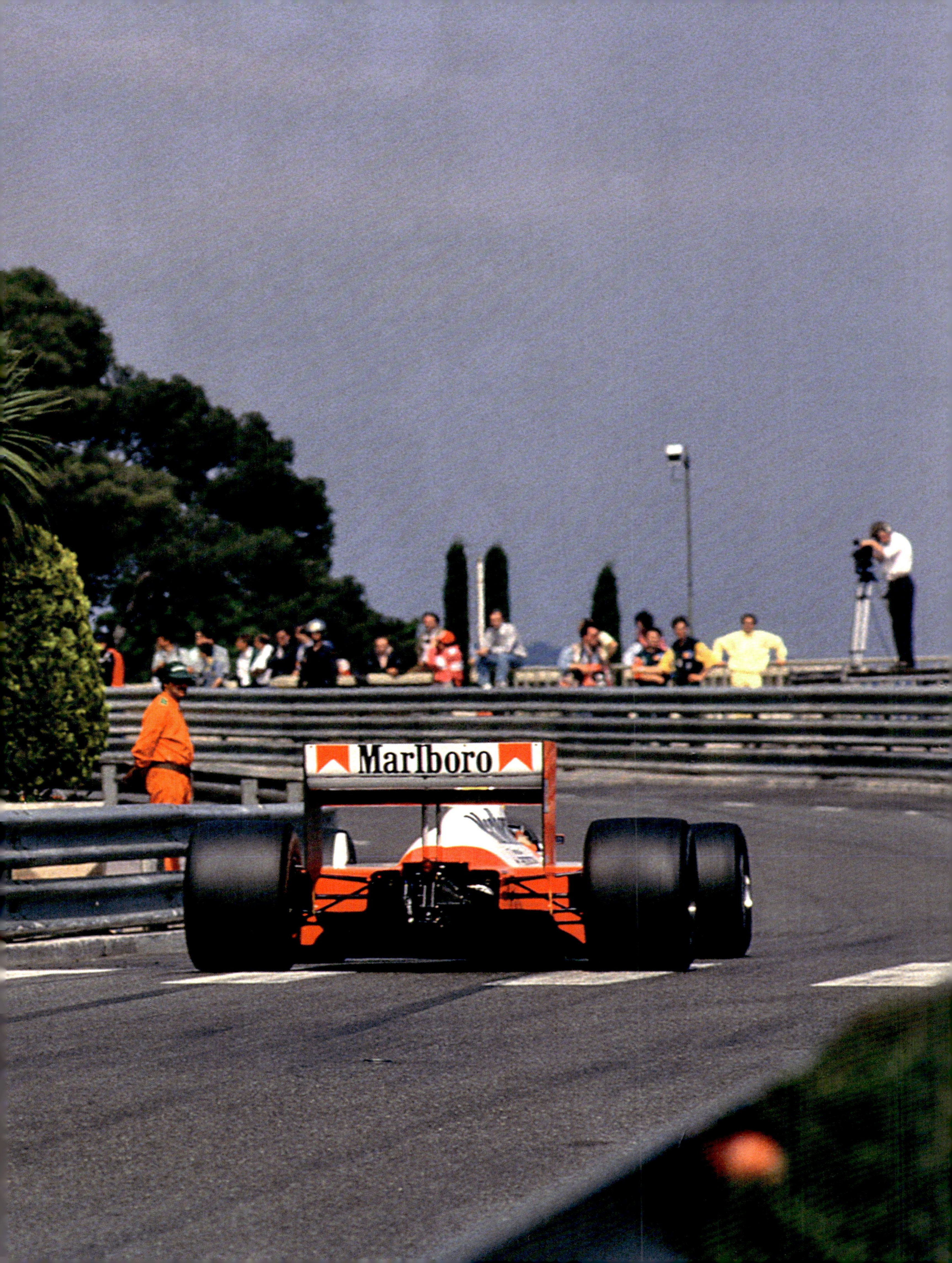
Marlboro

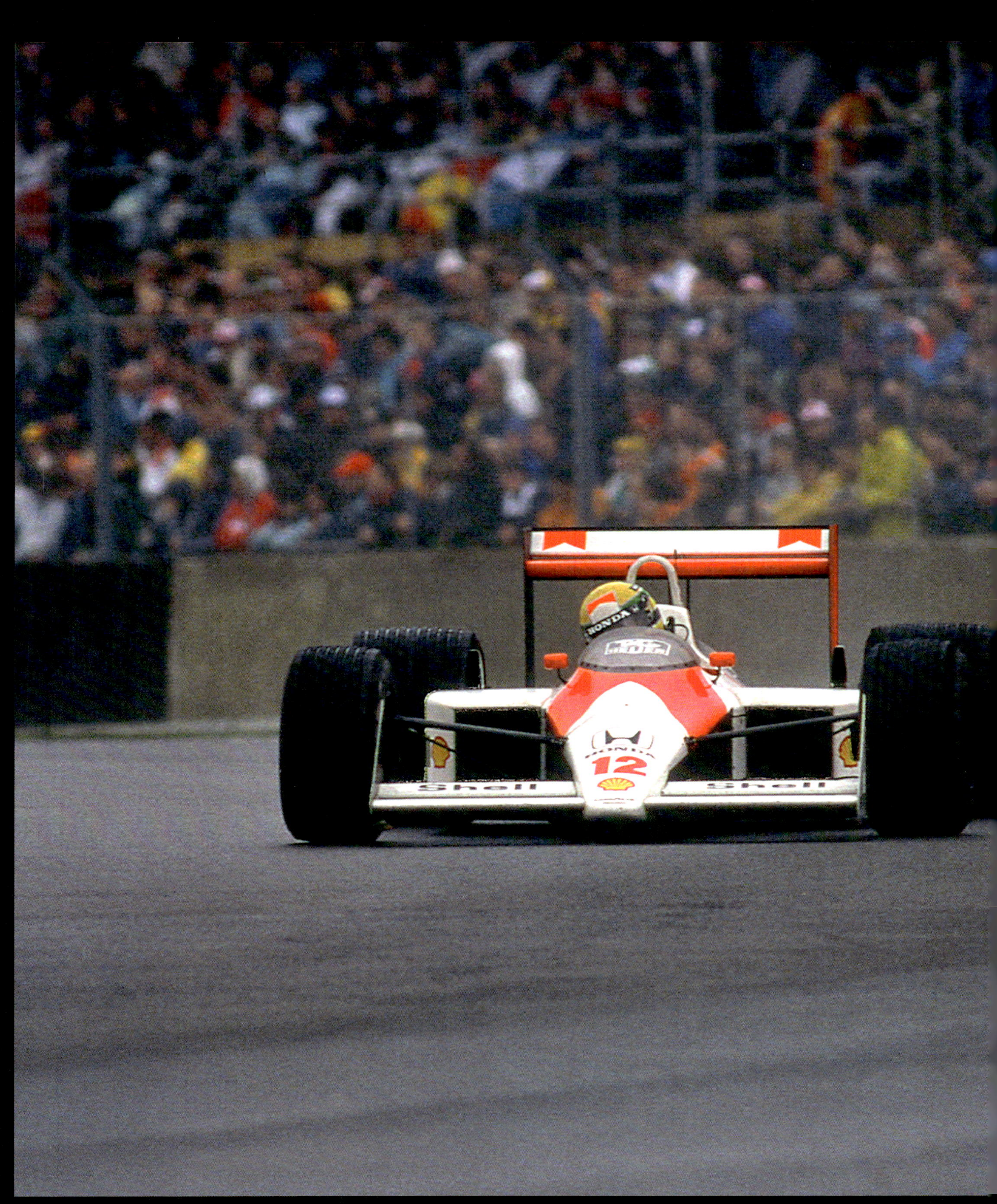
HONDA
12
Shell
Shell

THE CAR: MCLAREN MP4/4

The McLaren MP4/4 is probably one of the best cars ever to be part of Formula 1. It was the one that made all the enthusiasts dream and made all its rivals seethe. That particular car won 15 races out of 16, made it 15 times in pole, and led during 1,003 laps out of 1,031 in 1988—nearly total domination. The McLaren MP4/4 was very fast and became a legend. So much so, in fact, that Steve Nichols, its chief designer, and John Barnard, its technical director, are still battling over the project's paternity.

The McLaren story got off to a late start—August of 1987, to be precise. We learned that Honda would power the cars instead of TAG-Porsche. The arrival of Senna happened a few days after that announcement. The pressure was rising on the shoulders of the Woking men. "I was checking and re-checking [every detail of the car] and I left nothing to hazard. I think, in a strange way, a lot of the success of this car is down to my lack of confidence," said Steve Nichols with a smile. His colleague, Gordon Murray, tried to get some inspiration from the Brabham BT55 that he designed in 1986. Hired by McLaren, he got all the plans he designed at Brabham with him.

The Japanese team from Honda rolled up their sleeves and supplied an all-new Honda RA168E V6 twin-turbo engine, at the request of Gordon Murray, who wanted to lower the engine into the chassis. McLaren designed a gearbox with three shafts instead of two, a bold move. Recent regulations required a reduction in fuel tank capacity from 195 to 150 liters for turbo engines, for which this would be the last season. At the same time, the International Federation limited boost pressure to 2.8 bar, down from 4.0—a drastic reduction in engine power. The British team was also lowering the driver's seat and offering a 30-degree driving position, rather than the usual 45. This gave the car a lower center of gravity, giving Prost and Senna greater control, as well as improving the MP4/4's aerodynamic performance.

Presented during the last free practices in Imola, on Wednesday the 23rd of March, the McLaren MP4/4 was very competitive. Two days earlier, Senna finished a lap in 1:21.14 driving the 1987 model. With the new one, he was going two seconds faster! To keep from scaring off the rest of the field, Prost whispered in Ron Dennis's ear that Senna shouldn't show off too much of the new McLaren's capabilities. The Brazilian complied but couldn't contain his joy; "This car is really good," he said in the English motorhome. It was with this car that he would win his first world title.

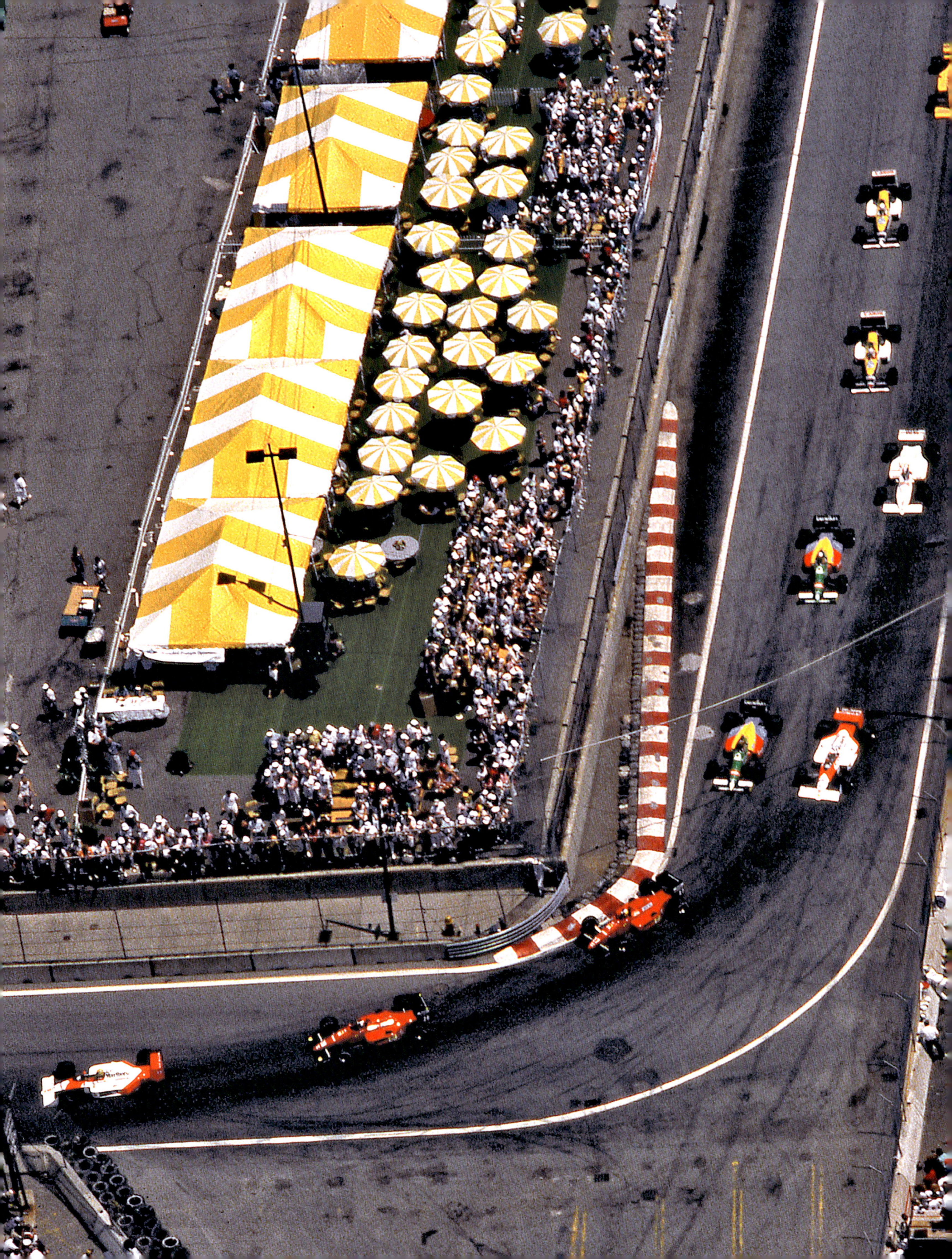

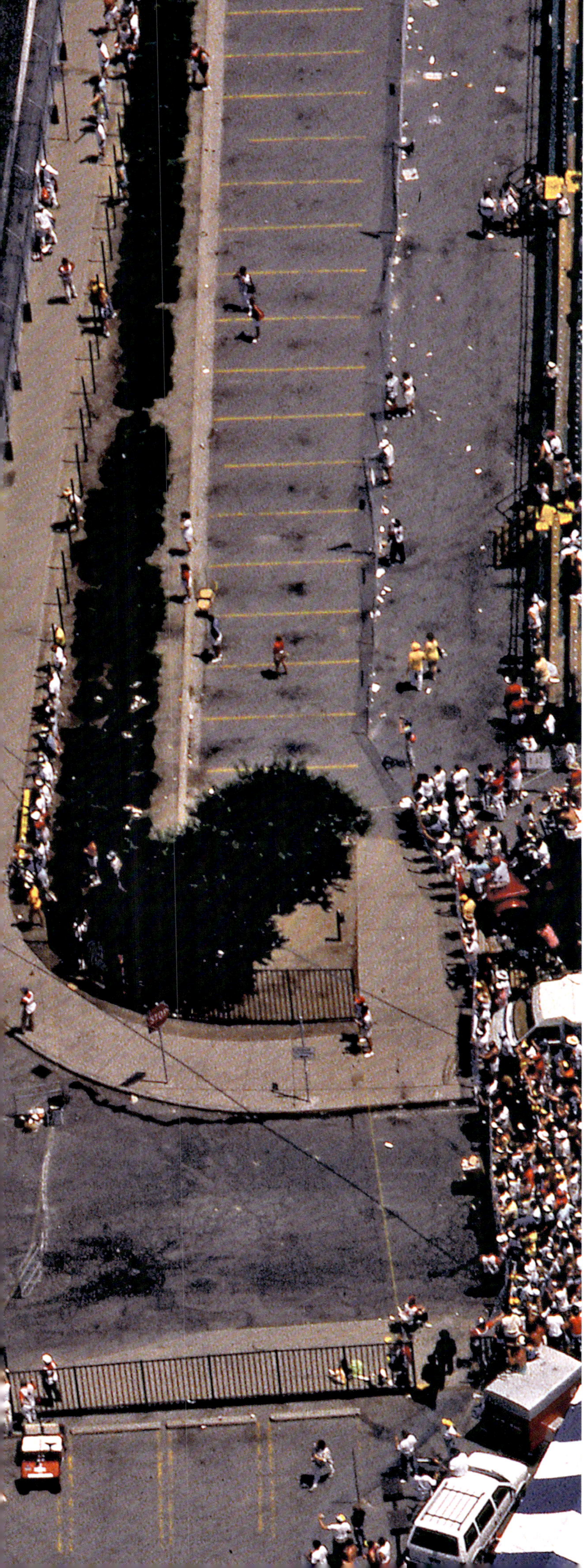

CANADA GRAND PRIX: DRIVE FOR FUEL

On Montréal Island, the McLaren-Honda dominated the free practices, and Senna got his fifth consecutive pole, one hundred eighty-two thousandths of a second ahead of Prost. The Ferraris (Berger 3rd, Alboreto 4th) were on the second line of the grid but already one second behind, in front of the Benettons (Nannini 5th, Boutsen 7th), and the Lotus-Honda of Piquet was in 6th place. This race went smoothly, as the fastest driver of the weekend won the race. Senna stopped just a few meters after the finishing line, as he barely had fuel left in his car to make an honor lap. Prost secured 2nd place and McLaren-Honda's third one-two finish of the season, ahead of Boutsen (3rd), who scored a podium with a naturally aspirated engine in an incredible performance. Piquet was far behind, placing 4th. The spectators, including many South Americans, were ecstatic about the victory of their idol, who pushed at the right time without wasting too much fuel.

"As it was a race for fuel, I had to be patient," Senna said. "The engineers of Honda told me my computer would be more precise, that it was important for me to follow its instruction. I had to wait for the right occasion. When I saw Prost having trouble overtaking the lapped guys [Arnoux and the Arrows], I didn't hesitate." Prost answered, "I could have closed the door but that's not the person I am… Having troubles with my consumption, and my water temperature being a bit high, I had rather let him overtake. Especially as we were at the start of a long race. I thought it was all going to come down to the last drop of fuel." In the end, Prost had to reduce his boost pressure to not run out of fuel, taking second place and its six points. In the World Championship rankings, Prost was 15 points ahead of Senna (39 to 24) and two-thirds of the Championship were still to be raced (11 laps out of 16).

Ayrton Senna leading the pack on a city circuit: not a surprising image.

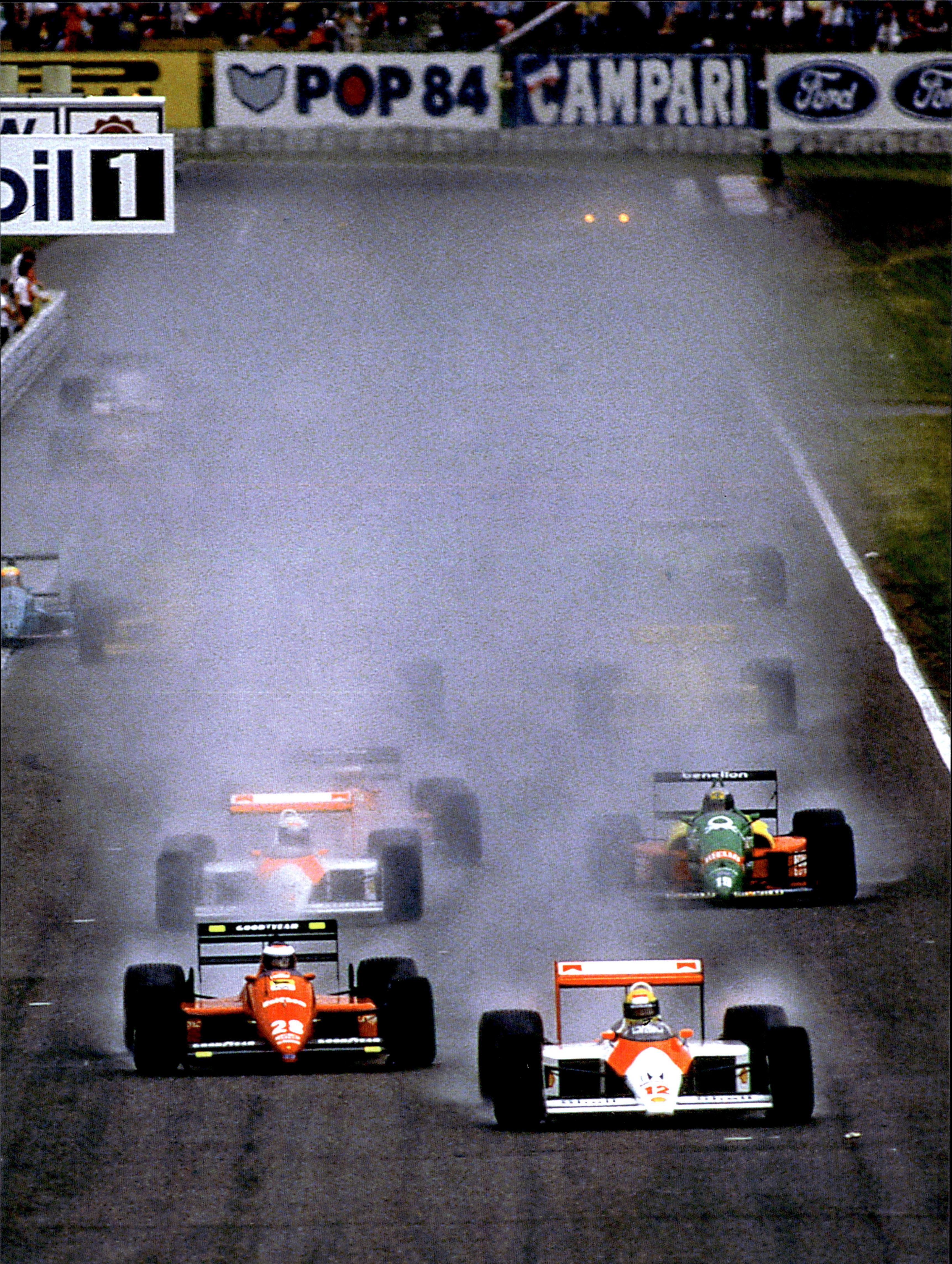
POP 84
CAMPARI
Ford
oil 1
benetton
GOODYEAR

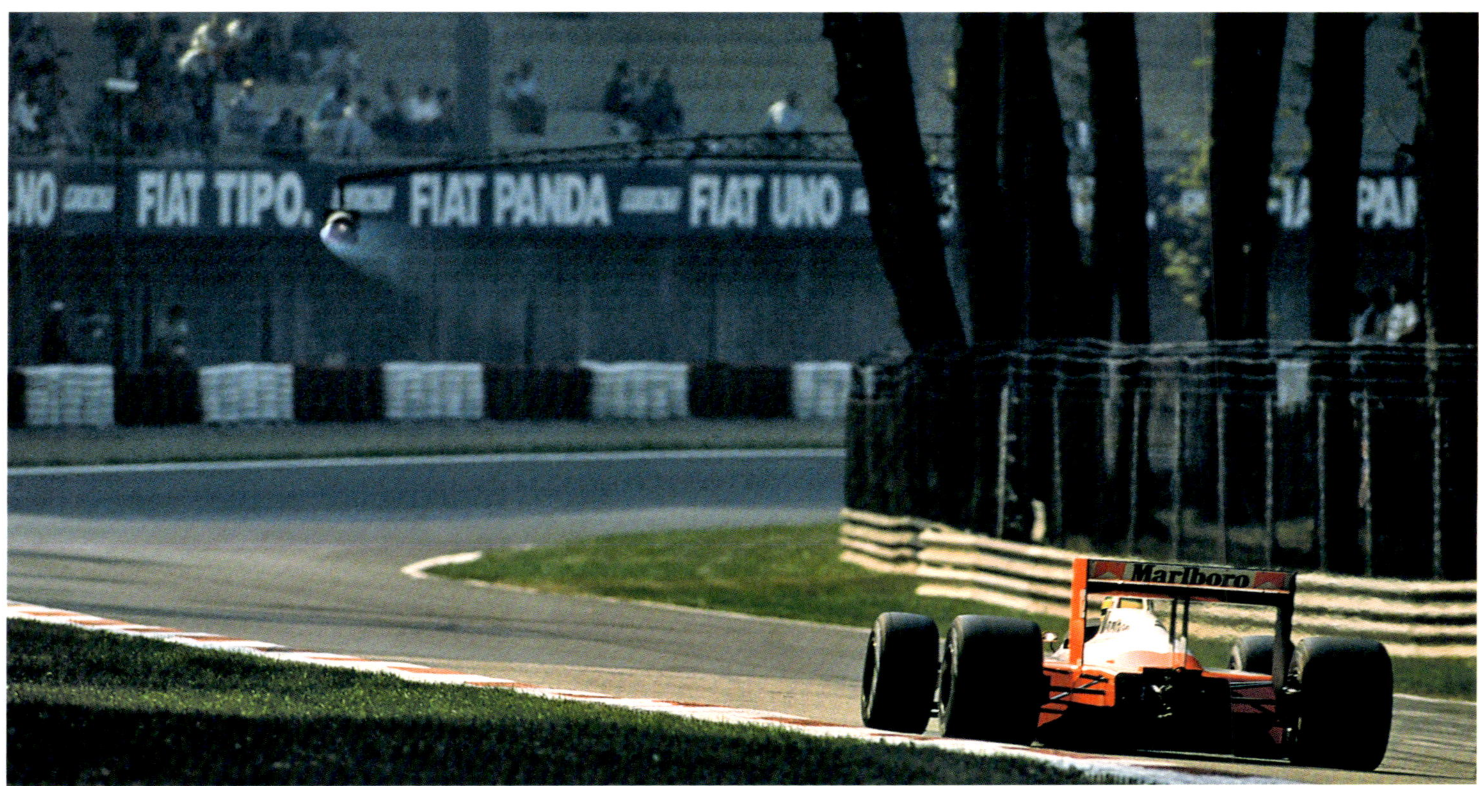

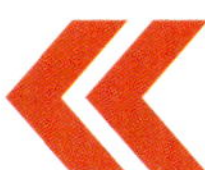

ITALY GRAND PRIX: THE MISSED GRAND CHELEM

When Senna and Prost arrived in Monza for the Italian Grand Prix, nothing had been decided yet. Senna had a 3-point lead over Prost on the heels of an eighth one-two finish in 11 races at Spa-Francorchamps. But at the venerable Italian track, where F1 cars go very fast and consume a lot of fuel, the beautiful machine jammed; Jean-Louis Schlesser, temporarily replacing Nigel Mansell at Williams, collided with Senna on the penultimate lap.

Ferrari won its only Grand Prix of the year in front of the tifosi. Meanwhile, that was the only time in the 1988 season that McLaren failed to score any points, missing the Grand Chelem by just one Grand Prix. It wasn't until Ferrari in the Michael Schumacher era, Red Bull with Sebastian Vettel and then Max Verstappen, and Mercedes with Lewis Hamilton and Nico Rosberg that we saw such domination by one team over an F1 season.

Left: In the rain, Ayrton Senna easily surpassed his rivals, including Gerhard Berger (Ferrari) and Alain Prost (McLaren), followed by a Benetton.

Top: Senna's unique driving style in the curves allowed him to gain valuable fractions of seconds on his competitors.

JEAN-LOUIS SCHLESSER

Three decades later, Schlesser still remembers everything. He recounts every detail:

The McLaren were driving above their fuel limit; Alain told me later. Ayrton absolutely wanted to overtake me entering the chicane. I went on the right of the track and braked as long as I could, straight. That's what we see on TV: I'm finishing my braking, I block my wheel because instead of taking my usual trajectory, I leave him as much space as I can. But Ayrton, that was some incredible guy, a fantastic driver. He was just a few centimeters behind me. I told myself: "If I slow down in a place where we are supposed to be flat out, maybe there will be a crash." Ayrton climbed onto my wheel and, after a spin, landed on the sidewalk. I kept going and finished my race. When I saw Ayrton again in Monaco, we had a chat. He said to me: "Jean-Louis, it's not that serious, that's how life goes." The guy who was the most upset about this story was Ron Dennis. He thought they could win all the races in that season. But Alain also had a problem earlier in the race. He told me that, in any case, the car wouldn't finish, because of its consumption. So, during the last two laps, they couldn't have done anything. When Ayrton touched my car, there was still three-quarters of a lap to go, plus another lap...

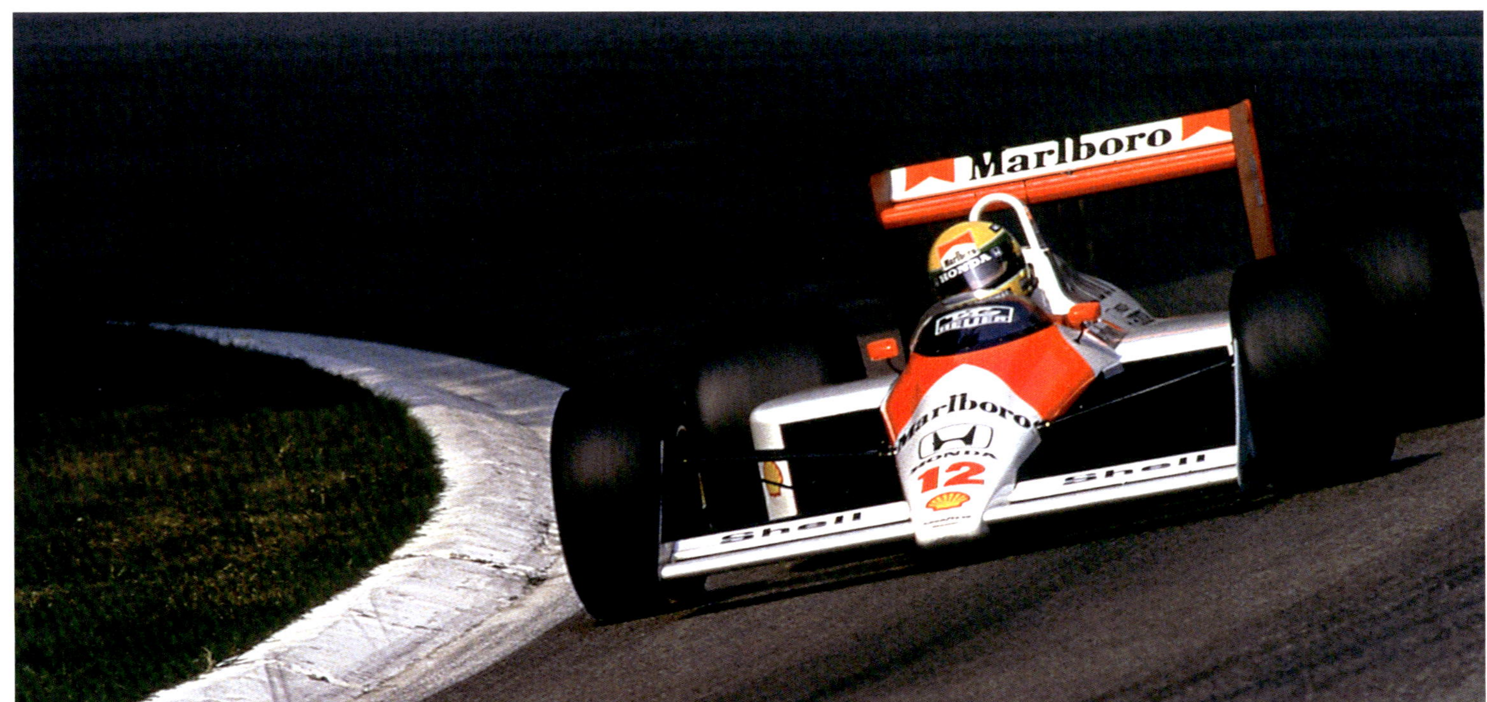

Senna's talent immortalizes the McLaren MP4/4 in F1 history.

RON DENNIS, THE MASTER OF WOKING

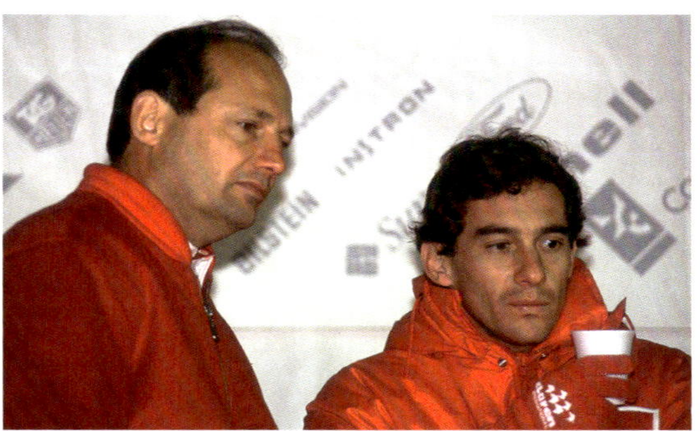

When Ron Dennis became the team manager of McLaren in 1980, the prize list of the Woking racing team was very, very thin, just like cigarette paper from its historic sponsor Marlboro. Since its creation by Bruce McLaren in 1966, the team only won three world champion titles: two in 1974 (driver and team championships) with Emerson Fittipaldi and a driver's title in 1976, thanks to James Hunt. That's all. But with Ron Dennis managing the team, it drastically changed. First, Niki Lauda was crowned in 1984, then Alain Prost in 1985. It was during these years that Williams-Honda started dominating the grid, and that Ron Dennis decided to associate Senna and Prost. He had the audacious idea to fight Mansell and Piquet and grabbed the Honda engine, the best in the world, to start dominating F1 like never before.

The contract between McLaren and Senna was signed in late 1987, at the end of a day that Ron Dennis would never forget. As the negotiations were ending, Senna and McLaren's boss couldn't agree on the monetary aspect of the contract. "We were discussing about half a million dollars. So, I decided to toss a coin," writes Dennis on the website of the McLaren-Mercedes team. "I thus threw the coin and it fell like a rocket in the curtains. I picked it up and I was the winner!" This marked the start of a long relationship, punctuated at times by quarrels and disagreements but mainly by victories and shared joy. During his time at McLaren, Senna won 35 of the 96 Grands Prix he started. That's more than a third of the total!

Dennis also played a key role in the Senna-Prost duel. This rivalry came to a climax the following year, in 1990, when Senna deliberately crashed into the Frenchman's Ferrari on the first lap of the Japanese Grand Prix to secure a second world title. Ron Dennis was deeply disappointed. "I remember looking at all the marks – the brake pedal, the gas pedal, the tires. You didn't need to be called Einstein to understand what had happened. When Ayrton came back into the pits, I told him I was disappointed in him." Dennis also recounted how Senna devoted his life to his art. "He was the first to collect all the telemetry reports and study them in his hotel room, late into the night. [...] He played the team game, cared about the mechanics. He also admitted when he was wrong. These are unusual qualities for an F1 driver."

SPAIN GRAND PRIX: FIRST TROUBLE, FUEL PROBLEMS

As they arrived in Jerez de la Frontera for the 14th race of the season, Senna and Prost were very close in the standings. There was only a 5-point margin in favor of Prost (76 to 81). McLaren kept beating every other team easily, but some rumors in the paddock said that the relationship between Senna and Prost was getting worse every week. In Estoril the Sunday prior, Senna pushed Prost into the railings in an aggressive manner, displaying an attitude despised by everyone in Woking. "They had destroyed the barrier between them and now, it's back up again. Ayrton went crazy in Estoril while Alain remained correct from start to finish. Things are getting complicated," admitted a source close to Ron Dennis. As if alone in the world, the two drivers seemed to be playing a game of liar's poker in the pits. Each driver tried to surprise his rival, for example, by changing his set-up at the last moment to create doubt. Thus, when Senna took the provisional pole position 11 minutes before the end of qualifying, he unexpectedly decided to return to the pits and not return to the track, just as Prost had done in qualifying for the Portugal Grand Prix a week earlier. He explained, "The tires were losing performance, and it wasn't worth it."

Prost took a better start than Senna, who was even overtaken by Mansell, and ended up winning ahead of Mansell (Williams) and Nannini (Benetton). During the race (like in Portugal), Senna suffered from a problem with his on-board computer; its sensors told him that he was over-consuming fuel. As a result, he ended up in 4th place, just short of the podium, which was a painful pill to swallow, especially as his McLaren MP4/4 ran out of fuel as he crossed the finish line. Exiting his car, he dodged the journalists and had a one-hour long meeting with his mechanics and engineers. At the end of the briefing, he said, "It's hard to explain why, as Alain and I had identic fuel consumption for the 12 races of the season, it changed during the last 2." Senna doubted like never before and felt a great deal of anger inside. At the Madrid airport, the driver in the blue Nacional cap was contemplating. Before he took off for Brazil, he was seen in a private lounge frantically consulting pages containing the complete telemetry data of the two McLarens.

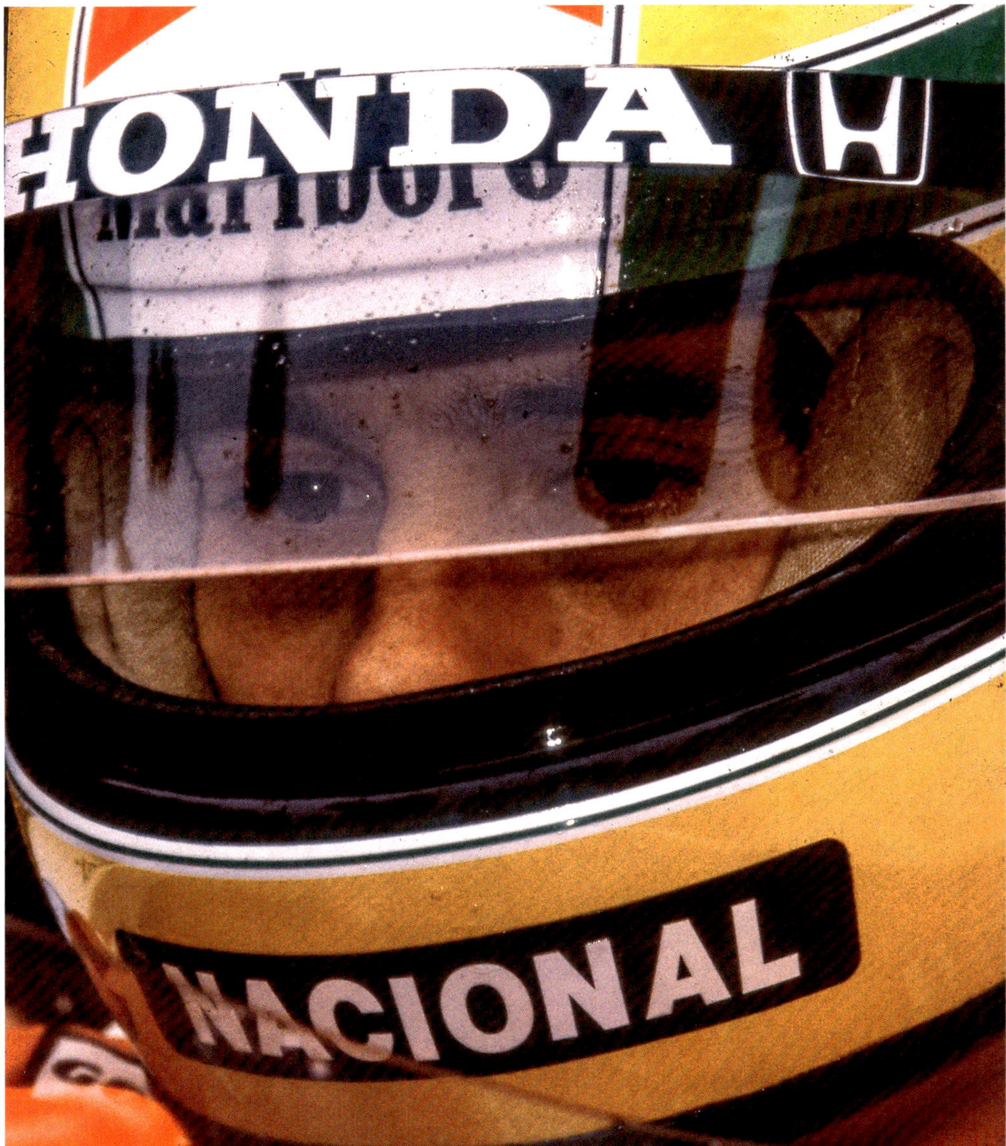

A slightly wet visor indicating rain. Conditions where Senna will excel throughout his career.

ON TRACK FOR THE TITLE 1988

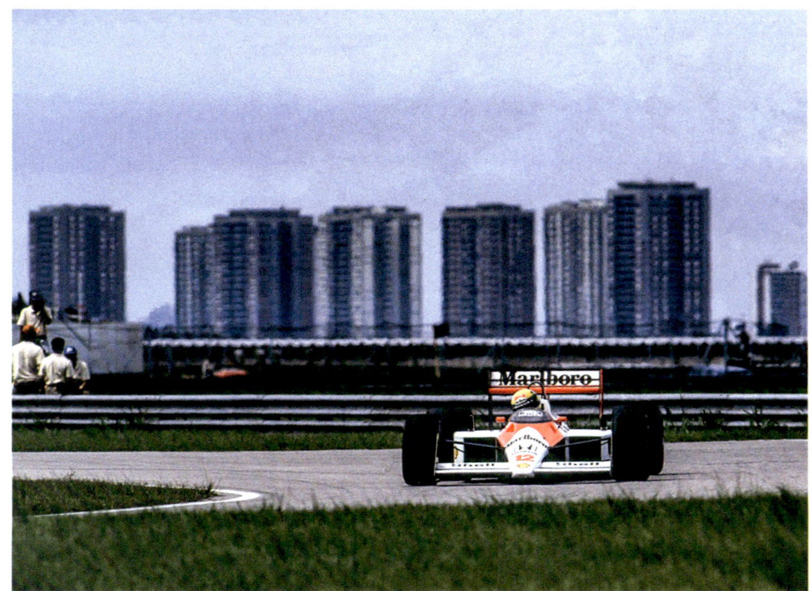

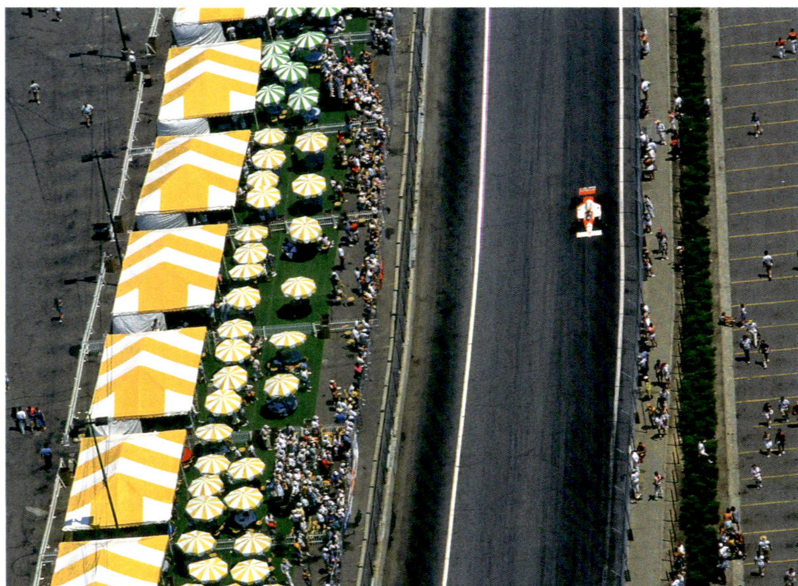

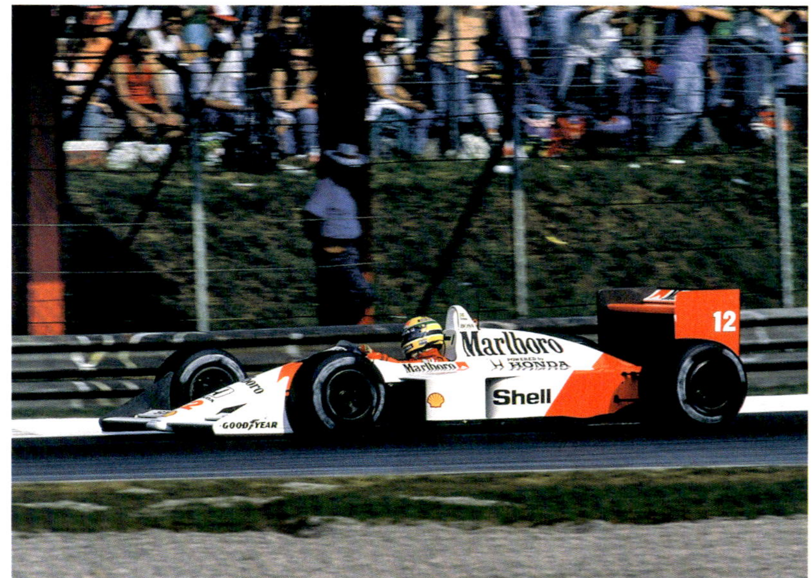

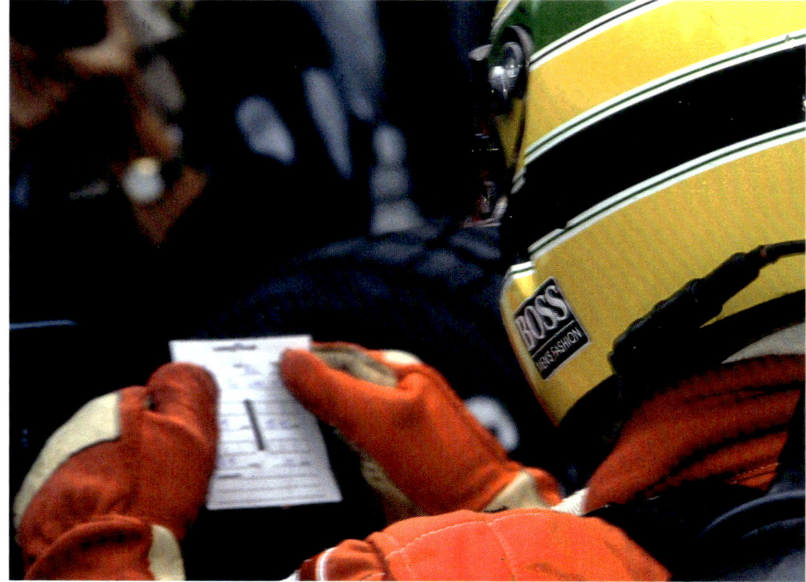

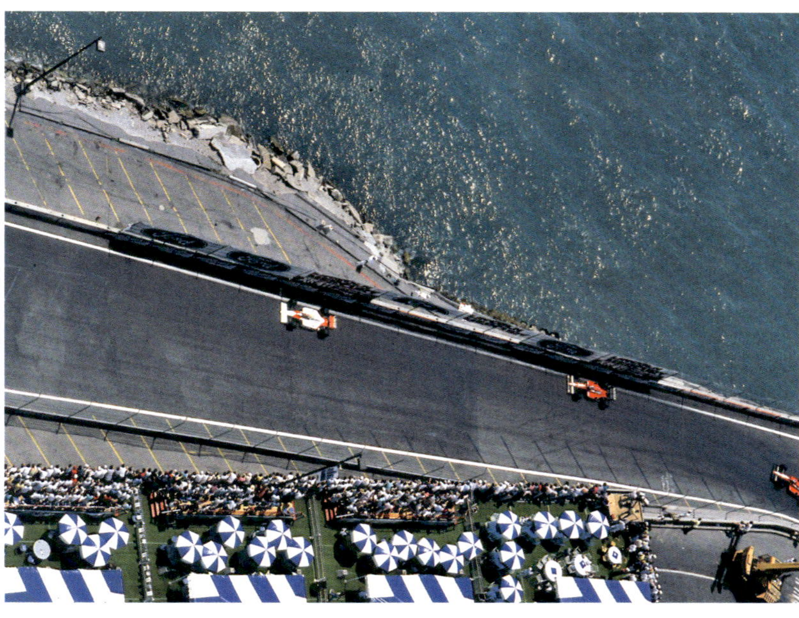

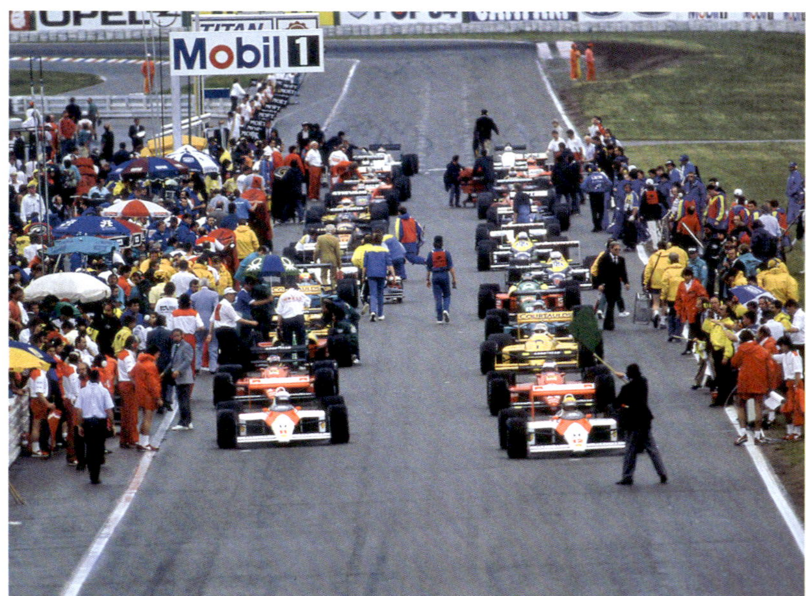

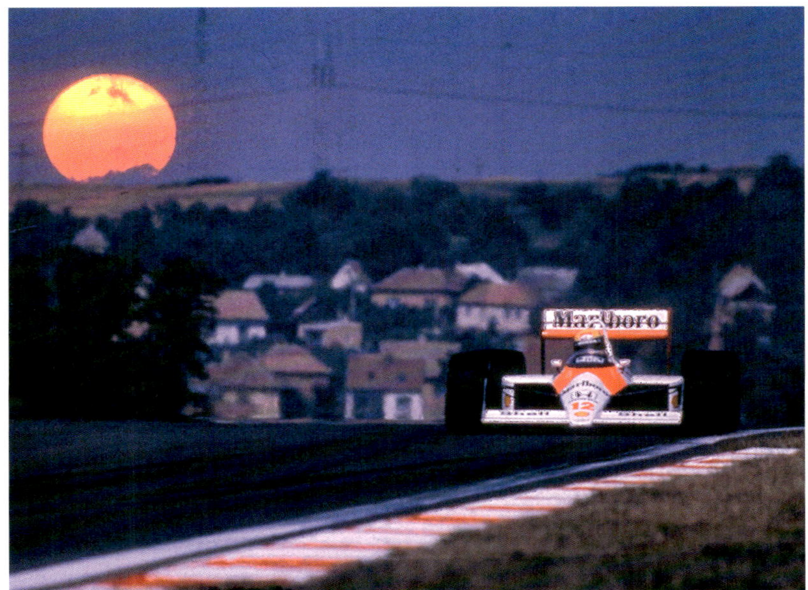

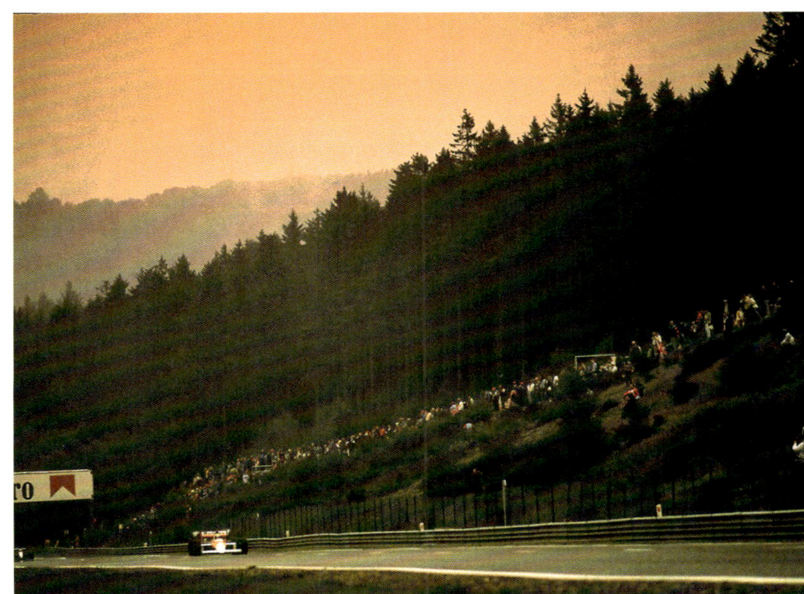

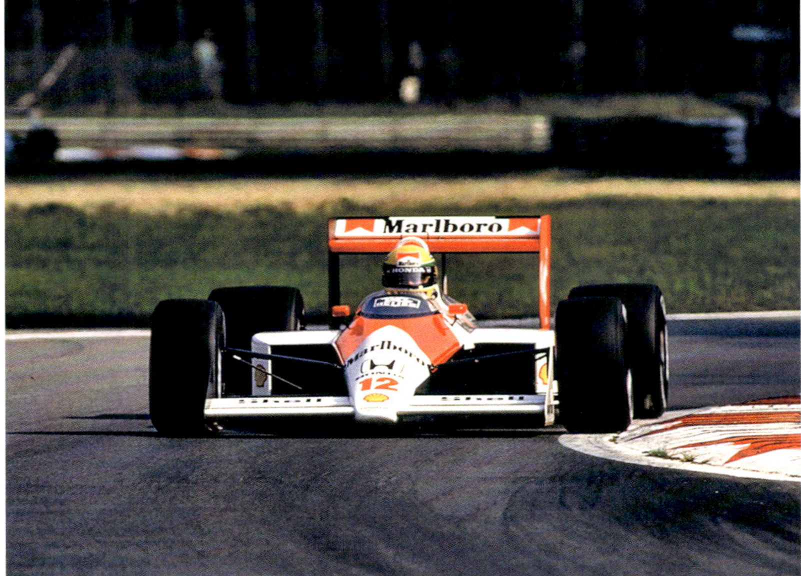

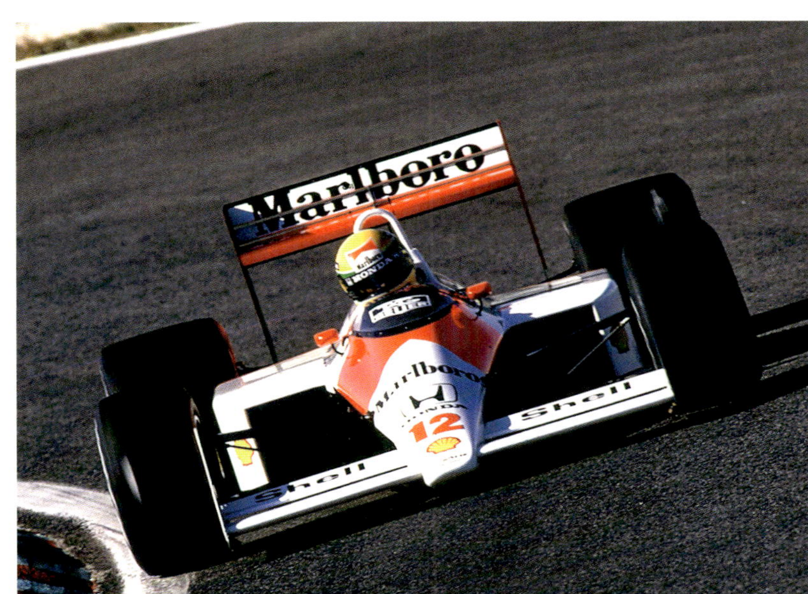

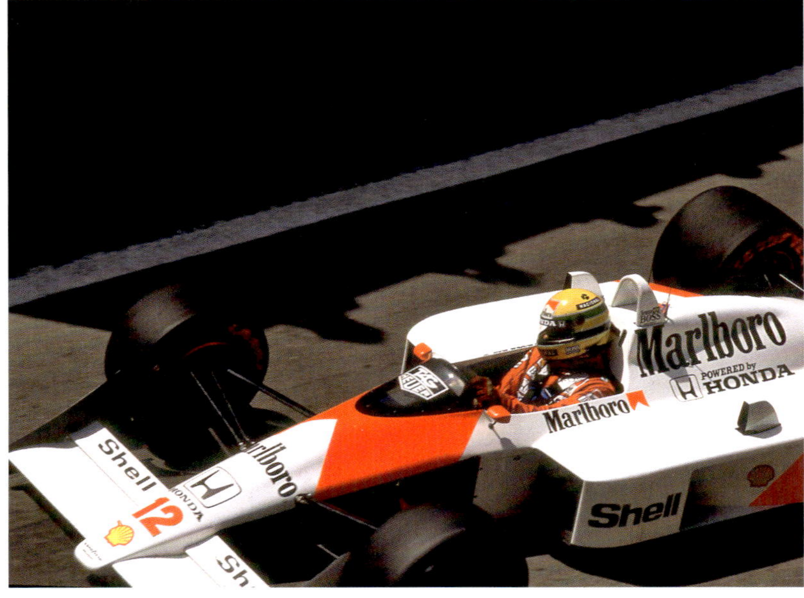

Senna's first season with McLaren is marked by numerous successes, culminating in winning the world championship in Japan. The yellow helmet and the red and white race car are set to endure.

JAPAN GRAND PRIX: THE ROAD TO HEAVEN

Ayrton Senna had his first opportunity to be crowned World Champion at the Japan Grand Prix, one race before the end of the season in Australia. And it's fairly easy to understand how; he had to win, whatever his teammate's result was. When the Honda team arrived in Suzuka, they were watched closely. Rumors of a difference in treatment between Senna and Prost from the Japanese worried the FISA. Thus, the Japanese team was asked to manage the pilots the same way. It was in that tense atmosphere that another baffling rumor started to spread—that Senna might stop driving at the end of the 1989 season. Strange things are said when the media goes crazy.

During qualifying, Senna took the pole, and Prost was next to him on the first line. Therefore, the duel would take place. The tension rose. The night before the race, at 3:15 a.m., Senna woke up in his Suzuka hotel room. It was impossible for him to fall asleep again. Adrenaline paralyzed him: he was close to his dream, to his goal, and he knew that all Brazilians would be watching him. A few hours later, he got up in his cockpit. The race started, and then all the Brazilians were deadly worried, as Senna was not moving. He had clutch problems, followed by a mistake from the pilot. Prost thus took the lead. Senna stalled and, thankfully, was able to restart the car, but the whole grid nearly overtook him. At the end of the first corner, he was 16th. Whether he would make it to Australia to finish it all was not on Senna's mind. At the end of lap 1, he was already 8th. And on lap 2, he was 6th, then 5th on lap 3. It was history in the making. As if on cue, a light drizzle began to fall on the circuit. The Brazilian excelled in these conditions. On lap 20, he found himself in Prost's gearbox; the hunt for the Frenchman had begun. On lap 28, Mauricio Gugelmin and René Arnoux, who had been delayed, held up Prost. On the pit straight, Senna took advantage of the McLaren's slipstream to overtake him on the inside. At 3:30 a.m. Brazilian time, Senna entered the final lap in the lead. He still had 5.859 kilometers to go to become world champion. And in the final sector, he had a strange flash of vision. "I entered a hairpin when Jesus appeared to me. It was indescribable," Senna told Playboy magazine two years later. After the Casio chicane, his McLaren MP4/4 made its final dash down the pit straight. The checkered flag waved. Senna was the World Champion. "I was screaming as I crossed the finish line. I hit my head, I couldn't believe it, and then I started crying," he later revealed. Honda's Osamu Goto added, "After the race, he was very tense. He couldn't even speak for a while. He was just crying in the car." After the podium, Senna met up with his entourage at their hotel in Suzuka. Jo Ramírez and Galvão Bueno joined the party. Then, he asked his TV Globo friend for a tape of the race to watch before going to sleep. At breakfast, Galvão Bueno asked him, "So, how does it feel to wake up as the world champion?" With a dazzling smile, Senna replied, "I don't know. I haven't slept yet."

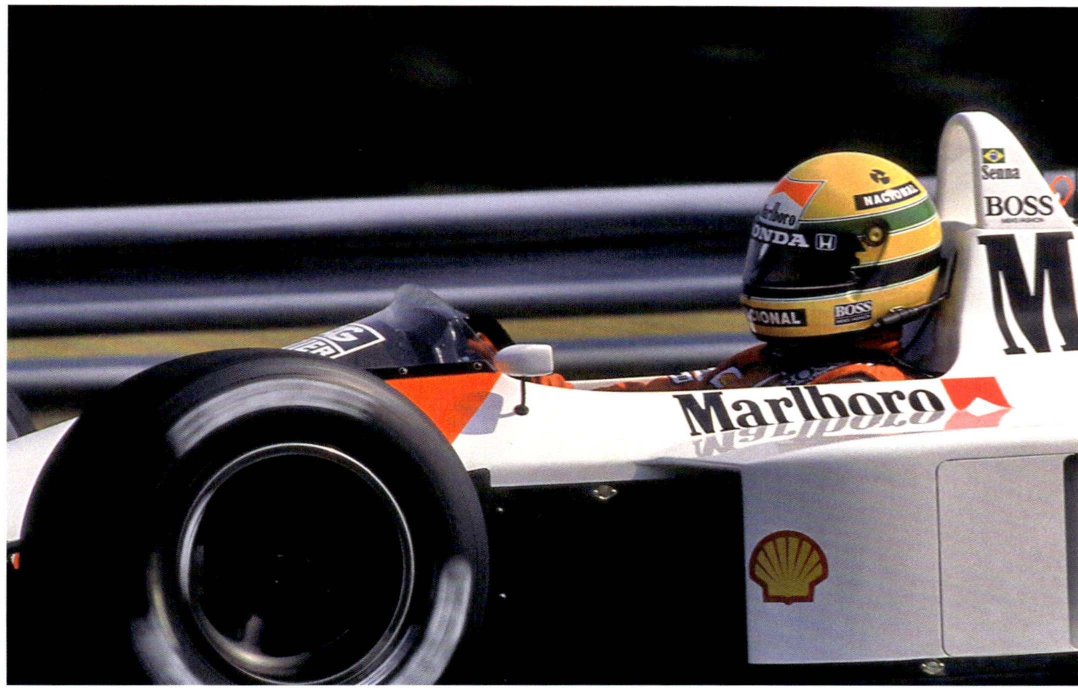

At the end of the 1988 Japanese Grand Prix, Ayrton Senna clinched his first World Championship title. A well-deserved and eagerly awaited triumph for the Brazilian.

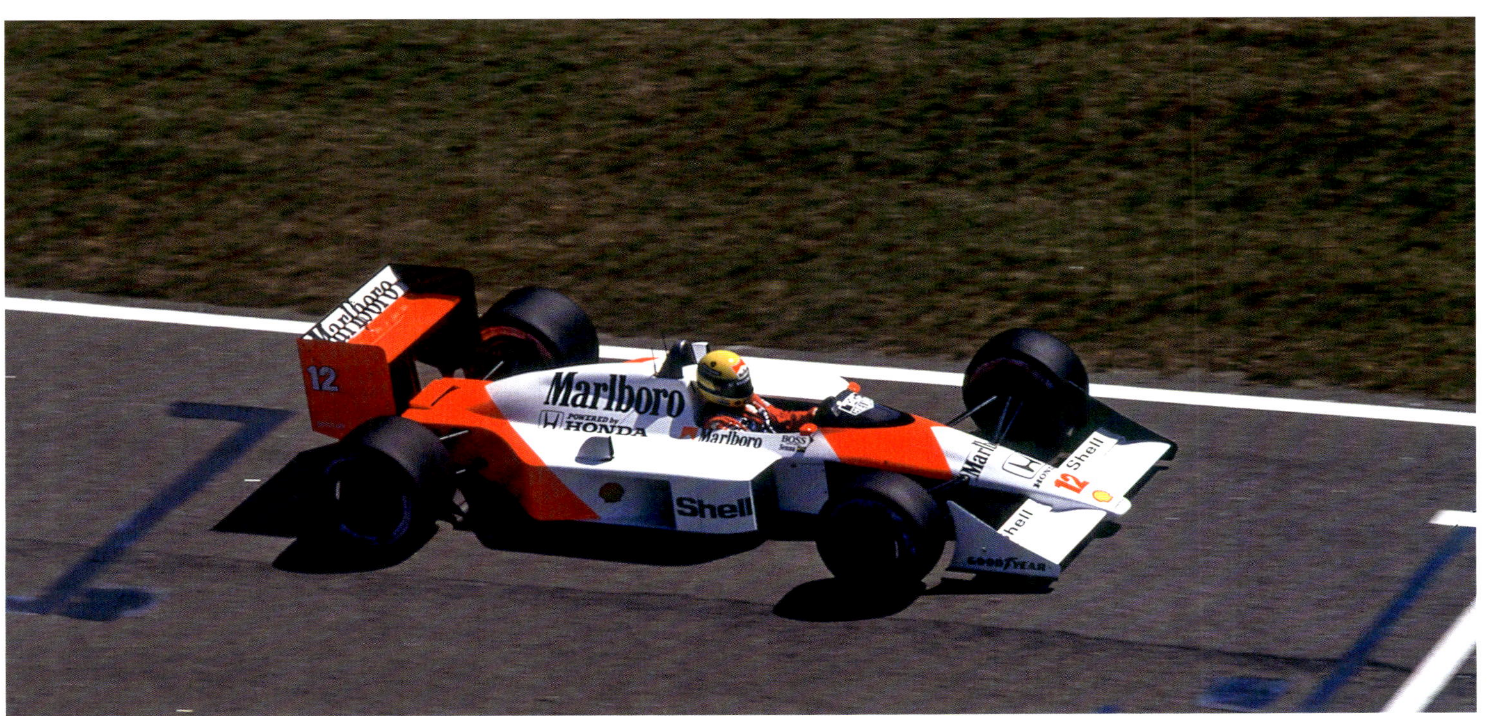

The McLaren MP4/4 driven by Ayrton Senna is one of the motorized gems in the history of Formula 1.

THE 1988 SEASON IN FIGURES

GRAND PRIX	QUALIFIERS	RACE
BRAZIL	POLE POSITION 17	DSQ (CAR REPLACEMENT)
SAN MARINO	POLE POSITION 18	VICTORY 7
MONACO	POLE POSITION 19	DNF (CRASH)
MEXICO	POLE POSITION 20	2ND
CANADA	POLE POSITION 21	VICTORY 8
UNITED STATES	POLE POSITION 22	VICTORY 9
FRANCE	2ND	2ND
GREAT BRITAIN	3RD	VICTORY 10
GERMANY	POLE POSITION 23	VICTORY 11
HUNGARY	POLE POSITION 24	VICTORY 12
BELGIUM	POLE POSITION 25	VICTORY 13
ITALY	POLE POSITION 26	10TH (CRASH)
PORTUGAL	2ND	6TH
SPAIN	POLE POSITION 27	4TH
JAPAN	POLE POSITION 28	VICTORY 14
AUSTRALIA	POLE POSITION 29	2ND

WORLD CHAMPION IN F1
(90 POINTS, 11 BEST RESULTS, 8 VICTORIES, 11 PODIUMS, 13 POLE POSITIONS, 3 BEST LAPS)

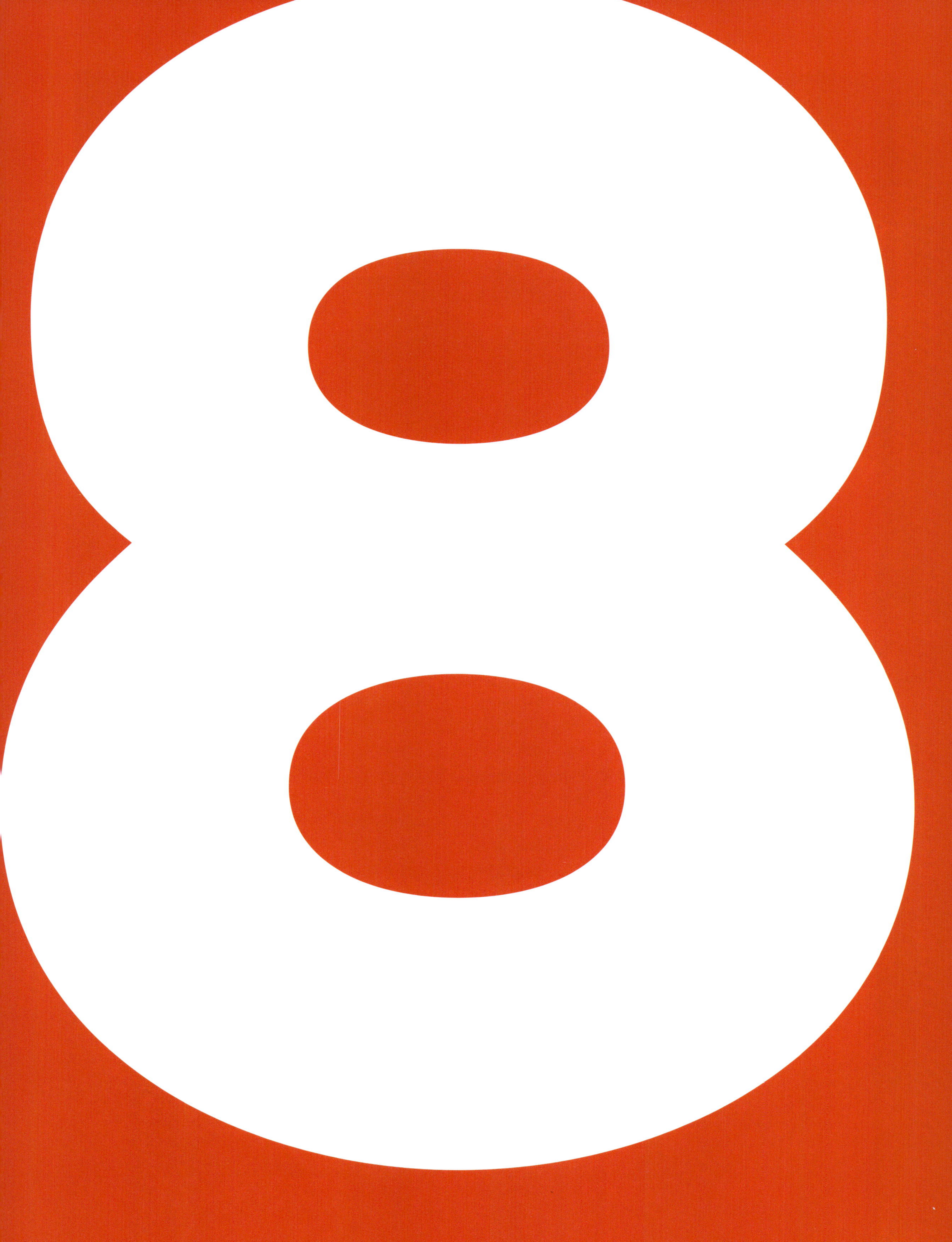
8

9

PROST'S REVENGE

THE "PROFESSOR'S" LESSON

SENNA'S SOPHOMORE SEASON WITH MCLAREN–HONDA GOT OFF TO JUST AS BAD A START AS THE PREVIOUS ONE, WITH A COLLISION WITH GERHARD BERGER'S FERRARI IN BRAZIL THAT RESULTED IN AN ELEVENTH-PLACE FINISH, NOWHERE NEAR EARNING ANY POINTS.

Everything went as well as it could for the next three races (pole position and victory in San Marino, Monaco, and Mexico). But then, something jammed: three withdrawals (and a seventh-place finish) in four races due to mechanical or electronic problems. This was enough to boost the chances of his great French rival who, during this dry spell, racked up the points with wins in the USA, France, and Great Britain. As a direct result, when the two drivers arrived in Germany halfway through the season, Prost had a 20-point lead over Senna, with 47 points to Senna's 27. The Brazilian won two out of three races (in Germany and Belgium) but Prost continued to collect second places, thus justifying his nickname of "Professor." The Frenchman didn't like this nickname, but it perfectly reflected his love of mathematics. Senna's season then took a new turn for the worse, with two consecutive withdrawals in Italy and Portugal, allowing Prost to regain the lead (victory and second place, another 15 points scored). Senna's victory in Spain, his sixth in 1989 (compared to four for Prost), did nothing to change the situation. The Frenchman could be crowned champion in Japan, and he was going to do whatever it took to get there.

The collision between the two McLaren boys on lap 47 at the chicane went down in the history of F1. It left a lasting impression on the Brazilian, who was convinced that the French President of FISA, Jean-Marie Balestre, had played into his compatriot's hands by favoring Prost in the final result. It was the third world title for Prost, who finished 13 out of 16 races in the points, but his last with McLaren. He no longer wanted to compete directly with his teammate and left for Ferrari. As for the English team's overall record, it was not as spectacular as the previous season: six victories for Senna and four for Prost, totaling ten out of 16. The crumbs from the feast were shared between Ferrari (with three wins for Mansell and Berger), Williams (two wins for Boutsen), and even Benetton (when Nannini won in Japan following Senna's disqualification).

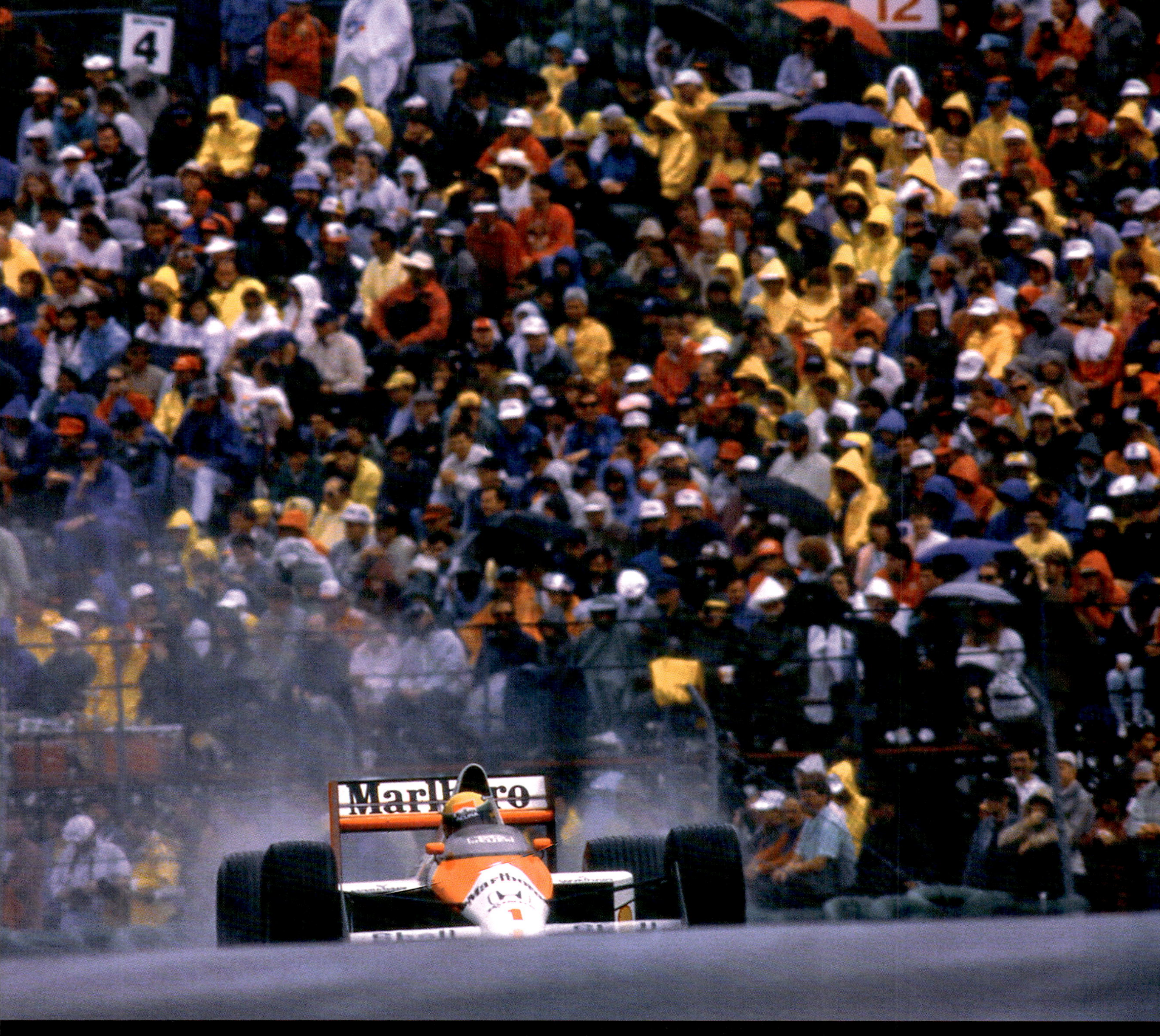

As the reigning world champion, Ayrton Senna sported the number 1 on his McLaren MP4/5 throughout the 1989 season. However, he did not retain this title at the end of the 1989 season, and it is Alain Prost who took the prestigious number 1 to Ferrari.

Following double page: In the late 1980s, F1 starts constituted a sumptuous blend of sparks, smoke, noise, and fury, enough to leave a lasting impression on the spectators.

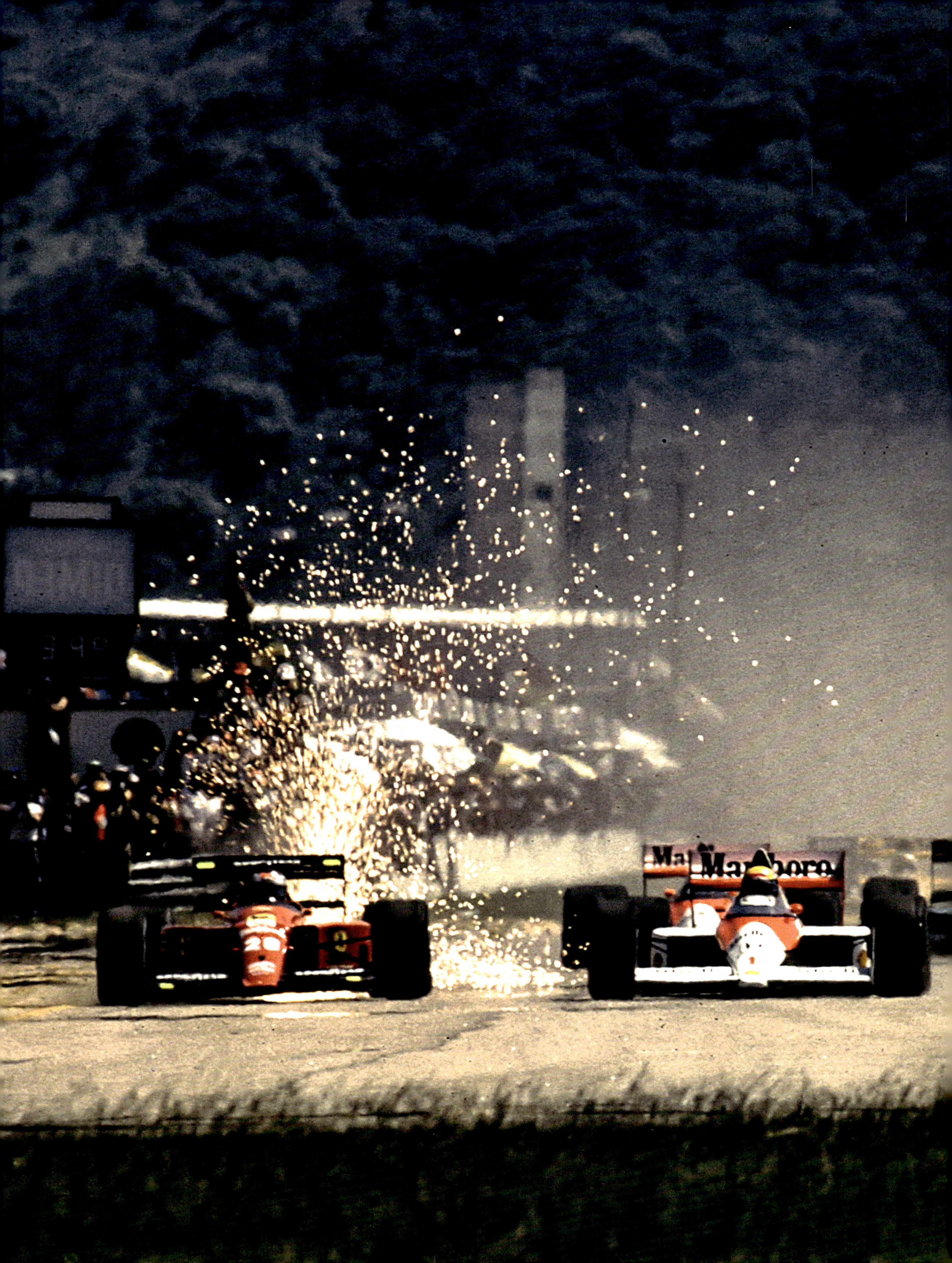

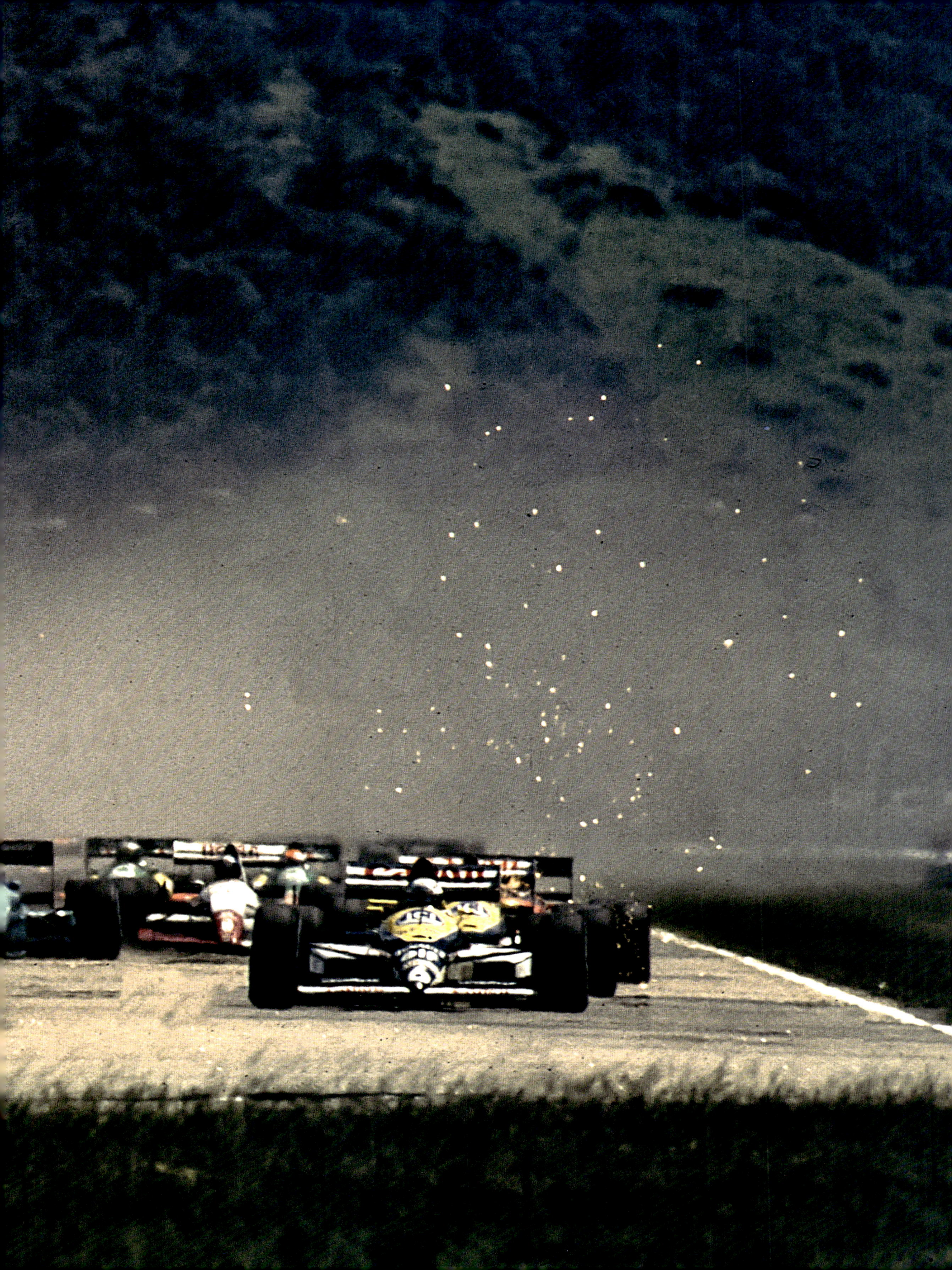

RACE AFTER RACE

1989

SAN MARINO GRAND PRIX: THE PACT IS ALREADY BROKEN

After the astonishing victory of the Ferrari of Mansell at the Brazilian GP, McLaren set to work during several practice sessions to improve the handling of the McLaren MP4/5. However, Prost was not happy that Senna had called in sick during the tests at Silverstone. He seemed nervous and tense at the start of the season. He suspected Honda wanted to favor Senna, who represented "youth and enthusiasm," according to a Japanese executive. Ron Dennis tried to reassure him, but Prost had lost faith in his boss. Hoping to avoid the worst, Senna requested a gentlemen's agreement before Imola: on the first lap, whoever started in the lead would not be attacked by the other driver before the first stop. In Saturday's sunny qualifying session, McLaren–Honda destroyed its rivals, as expected. Senna was two-tenths ahead of Prost, while the Ferrari 640s of Mansell (third) and Berger (fifth) were in the mix. On Sunday, Senna and Prost took off in the lead, one behind the other, respecting the pact. On lap four, at the entrance to the Tamburello curve, Berger likely lost a piece of wing, sending the Ferrari into the wall at nearly 270 km/h. The fire was extinguished in 15 seconds, and the Austrian driver was shocked but conscious with burns to his hands. Red flag.

A second start was given. This time it was Prost who took the lead from Senna. Senna immediately drove into Prost's slipstream, took the initiative, and overtook him at Tosa. In so doing, he violated the "non-aggression pact" according to his teammate. Prost was furious. On lap 49, he put his foot down as he was already a long way from the Brazilian and resigned himself to taking the six points for second place. Senna took his 15th F1 victory, 40 seconds ahead of Prost. Third-placed Nannini finished a lap behind in his Benetton—a virtual abyss.

On the podium, the atmosphere was tense. Prost refused the champagne, fled the journalists, and locked himself in the Marlboro motor home. "Ayrton didn't respect the pact we made on the first lap," he told Ron Dennis. He indulged in a long indictment of the Brazilian, accusing him of disloyalty and deceit. Prost also accused his boss of not having enough authority. The latter could no longer deny it: the crisis was now in full swing.

With Prost out of the way, Senna barely spoke to the media: "I have nothing to say about Alain!" he insisted. Then, under pressure from reporters, he admitted that "contrary to what Alain maintains, I didn't attack him on the first lap. We were on the fourth..." Because the race was stopped on the fourth lap following Berger's terrifying accident, Senna seemed to know that he had made a mistake and was prepared to apologize if Prost would concede his errors as well. The Frenchman was convinced that everyone was ganging up on him: Ron Dennis, Honda, the journalists, and, of course, Senna. For Prost, it was the final straw, after only two races out of 16. The next day, he canceled a meeting with Mansour Ojjeh, owner of TAG and a major shareholder in McLaren, where they were to discuss the extension of his contract.

SENNA AND PROST

ON EQUAL TERMS AT MCLAREN

During their two seasons racing together at McLaren, Senna and Prost lived up to all the predictions made by the experts when they announced their pairing. In the end, the results were balanced: a world title each and a 2-2 draw in the most significant statistics. Ayrton was often the fastest in qualifying and won three more races, while Alain, the "Professor," was more often on the podium, while setting twice as many fastest laps in the race.

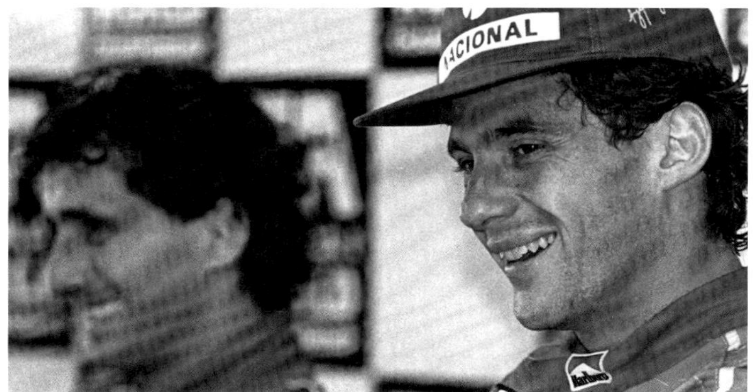

1988-1989	VICTORIES	PODIUMS	POLE POSITIONS	BEST LAPS	TITLES
SENNA	14	18	26	6	1 (1988)
PROST	11	25	4	12	1 (1989)

With his gaze lifted to the sky, Ayrton Senna could only rely on himself to try and win a second world title with McLaren. However, he was unsuccessful.

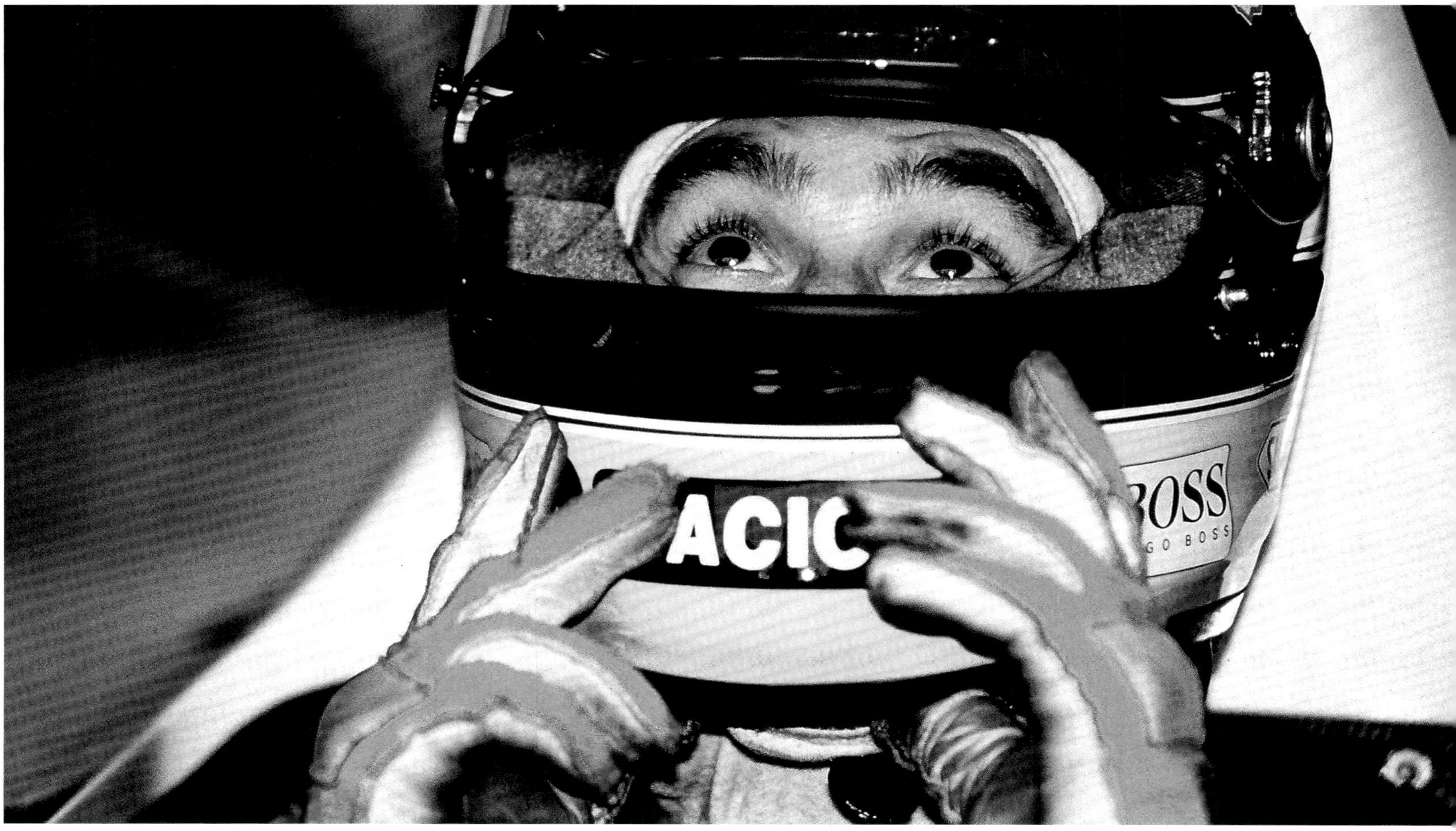

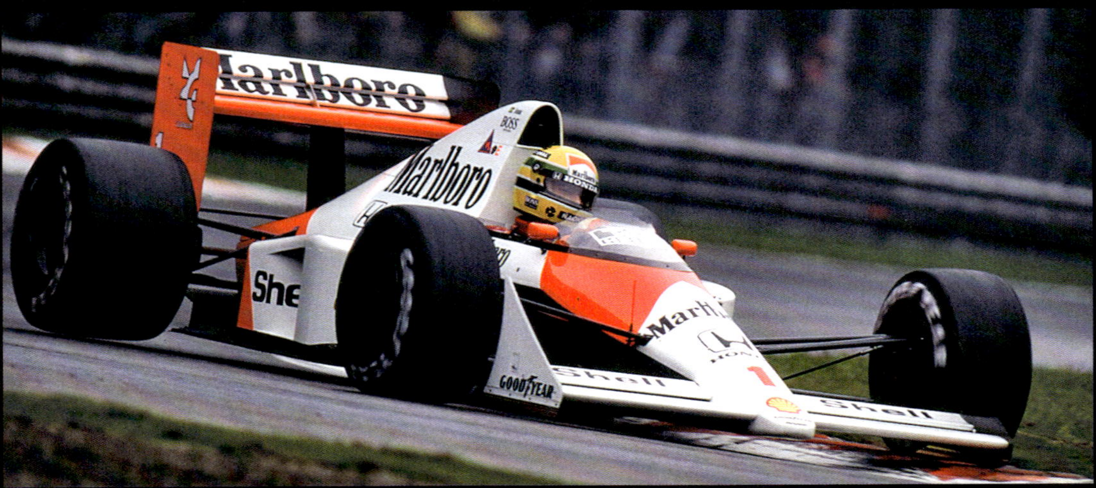

THE CAR: MCLAREN MP4/5

After observing the domination of the McLaren MP4/4, F1 experts eagerly awaited the 1989 model designed by Neil Oatley, the mastermind behind the car. With turbocharged engines now banned, Honda had to change its method and for a long time worked on a naturally aspirated V10 engine. The Honda RA109E delivered 675 horsepower at a maximum speed of 13,000 rpm. The Japanese engineers had been working on these ten cylinders since mid-season 1987 and were hoping for results to match their efforts. The monocoque and the suspension were both completely new. This was no coincidence: before designing the MP4/5, the Minato and Woking teams carried out a complete check-up on the previous season's car, which led them to rework the overall aerodynamics. Because of these changes, the appearance of the new McLaren was quite distinct from that of the MP4/4.

At the opening of the 1989 season in Rio de Janeiro, Prost and Senna complained about the lack of acceleration in the car designed by Neil Oatley and his team. Fortunately, McLaren knew how to develop and improve a car. At Woking, the teams had been working hard to improve the car's acceleration for the second race in San Marino. Over the course of the season, the McLaren MP4/5 would benefit from numerous improvements. It was fitted with new Brembo brakes—designed to make the car lighter—as well as a transverse gearbox that appeared at Silverstone, but which nonetheless made a complicated start. Although this car was not as dominant as the legendary MP4/4, it nevertheless enabled the Senna–Prost rivalry to reach new heights.

MONACO GRAND PRIX: WINNING WITH XUXA

The situation was tense by the time McLaren arrived in Monaco. The domination of the British cars was overshadowed by the rift between the two drivers. Upon arriving in Monaco, Prost spoke of the "broken pact" with Senna at Imola: "Ron Dennis must have put pressure on him to tell the truth," the Frenchman said to the Brazilian press. Senna had the support of Jean-Marie Balestre, the President of FISA, who was more than hostile to team orders, stating, "It goes against all sportsmanship."

At McLaren, Jo Ramírez was stalling. The battle was due solely to the two drivers' fierce desire to win. Senna took the 32nd pole position of his career, just one short of the great Jim Clark. Prost, his top rival, was second. Despite the confrontational atmosphere between the two men, Senna did not respond to Prost's comments in the press. He preferred to avoid aggressive statements and concentrate on two things: his race and the presence of Xuxa, his girlfriend. At this stage in his career, Ayrton had only won once in Monaco, in 1987, and Prost had won four times. This disparity was not enough to keep him awake at night: "Experience is very important, but for me it doesn't mean anything. I've already won once [in Monaco] and I could have won last year if I hadn't made a mistake," the Sao Paulo native said.

On race day, the grandstands were full. Many came to cheer for Senna, waving Brazilian flags. True to his personality, Ayrton waved shyly to the crowd, but his partner Xuxa did not approve of his reserved nature. The woman who called herself the rainha dos baixinhos ("queen of the little ones") gave Senna a lesson in public relations. Grabbing the reigning world champion's hand, she forced him to wave it in the direction of the spectators, while insisting he blow them kisses.

As an artist at work, Senna works wonders with the McLaren MP4/5, even though Prost ultimately won the championship title.

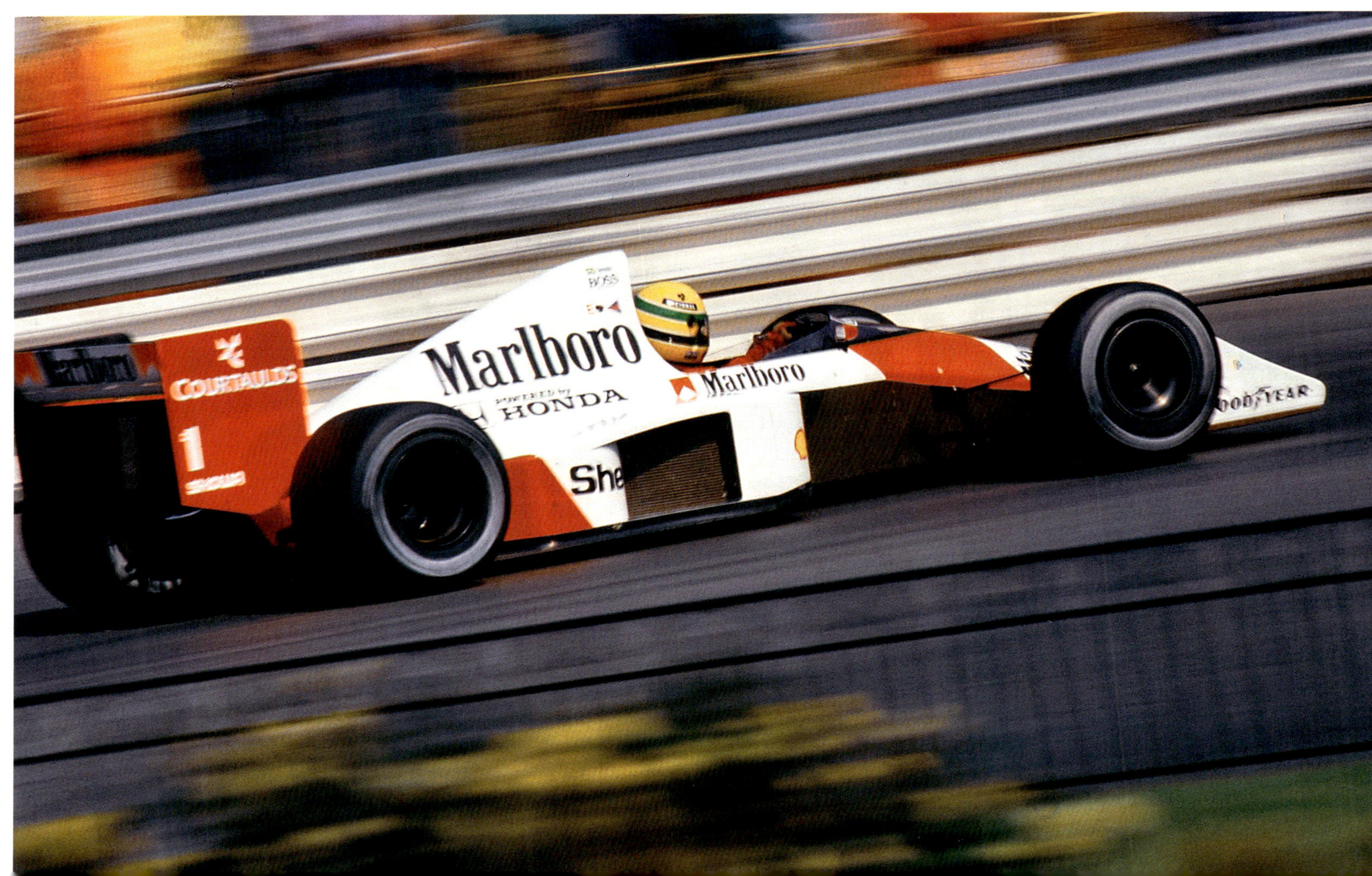

After this "spectators break," the start was given. The Monaco Grand Prix turned out in favor of Senna's McLaren, as Prost was hampered by his gearbox during the first half of the race. However, Senna suffered from transmission problems and lost both his first and second gears over the course of five laps. He managed to maintain his 40-second lead over Prost, but his mind was buzzing. Monaco was the track where the most gear changes were made on each lap. The Brazilian was still thinking about his mistake in 1988 and giving up another victory to the Frenchman would have been unbearable. A year later, he made up for his mistake through his determination and driving talent, claiming his second victory in Monaco after 1987, his first with McLaren.

On the podium, Prost and Senna shook hands warmly. Ayrton couldn't contain his joy, and showered Prince Rainier and Princess Caroline with champagne. This gesture constituted a breach of the very special—and legendary—protocol of the Monaco Grand Prix. After the traditional gala ceremony on Sunday evening, Ayrton and Xuxa climbed into a friend's boat and sailed out into the bay. The fastest of all Brazilians proudly carried his beloved flag on his shoulders. Legend has it that he carefully deposited it in the waters of Monaco, leaving it to bathe forever in the principality.

Out of Massenet and heading towards the Casino, Ayrton Senna and Alain Prost lead their way to first and second places at the Grand Prix de Monaco.

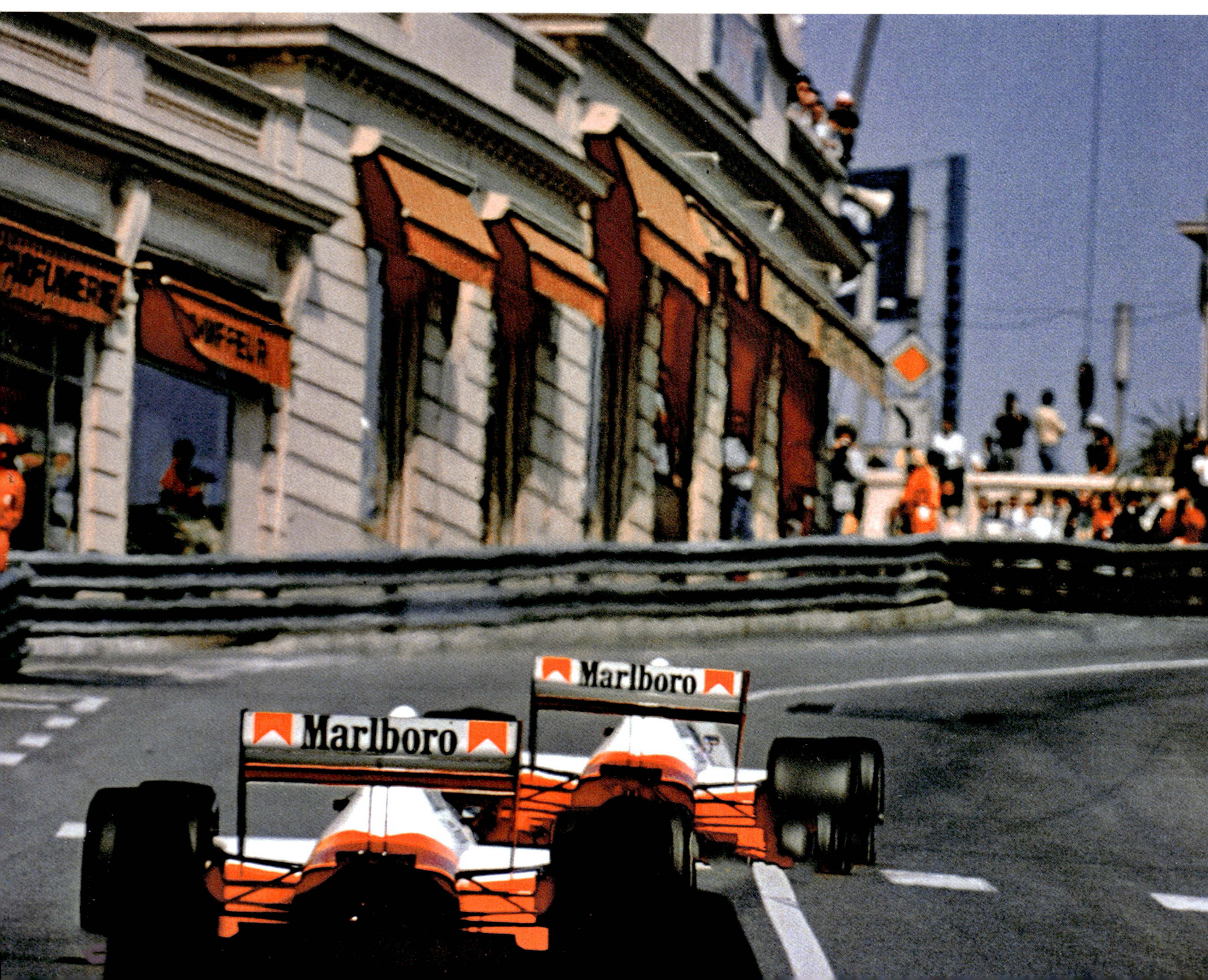

THE MAIN CHARACTERS

JULIAN JAKOBI, THE SMART MANAGER

The cast of the Senna saga also included a highly influential agent named Julian Jakobi. Born in London and raised near Silverstone, he graduated from Oxford University, where he studied philosophy, politics, and economics. He joined IMG at an early age, when the agency was the top choice for many of Europe's top sportsmen and women, including tennis players Björn Borg and Mats Wilander, and golfers Bernhard Langer and Nick Faldo. In 1984, when he joined McLaren alongside Niki Lauda, Jakobi became Alain Prost's agent, then Ayrton Senna's in 1985, again on behalf of IMG. He therefore had a front row seat to witness the rivalry between the two men in Ron Dennis's racing team. When Prost took a year off in 1992, Senna offered Jakobi the chance to work for him exclusively. Jakobi left IMG, and together they created the Ayrton Senna Group to manage and market merchandising products. After the tragedy at Imola, Jakobi helped set up the Instituto Ayrton Senna with the Brazilian champion's sister. He then considered setting up an F1 team bearing Senna's name, but eventually founded his own agency instead, the Stellar Management Group, through which Jakobi advised the new British American Racing (BAR) team. He reunited with Prost during the Prost Grand Prix adventure (ex-Ligier) and went on to advise Juan Pablo Montoya and, more recently, Sergio Pérez.

A quarter of a century after Imola, Julian Jakobi spoke to the Beyond the Grid podcast about the legendary rivalry between Prost and Senna, which he believed had been exaggerated: "I don't think the animosity between them was real. They knew that to win the world title you had to have the best car. And they did. So, each had to beat the other. And they were prepared to do anything to achieve that, on the track. Off the track, they were intelligent enough to understand that they were earning astronomical sums of money. In fact, Jakobi expressly requested that confidentiality be maintained between the two drivers regarding their respective salaries, even if they were team-mates. Only once did Ayrton and Alain ask me. They never tried again."

The Senna–Prost relationship changed once again when the Frenchman joined Scuderia Ferrari at the end of 1989. When he retired at the end of 1993 after winning his fourth world title at Williams, he was replaced by Senna. Jakobi had one last word to say: "Ayrton had immense respect for Alain because he knew that he was as good as he was and that you had to pull out all the stops to beat him. When your greatest rival retires, it changes everything."

Ayrton had immense respect for Alain because he knew that he was as good as he was and that you had to pull out all the stops to beat him.

JULIAN JAKOBI

MIKE WILSON

The 1989 FIA Gala and the reunion with Mike Wilson

At the end of each season, the Formula One community gathers in Paris for the FIA awards gala. Ayrton Senna was invited as runner-up in the world championship. During the event, he saw a familiar face: Mike Wilson, considered the most Italian of Englishmen, as he received his sixth World Karting Championship trophy. In 2023, he still had a vivid memory of the ceremony: As soon as I got off the stage, he left his table and came up to me to give me a hug, saying: "It's absolutely incredible what you've just done, winning the World Karting Championship six times!" I tell him that even if it doesn't have the same prestige as winning F1, it's a fantastic achievement. Do you know what he replied? "The difference is that in F1 I'm racing against my team-mate and two other teams, i.e. five cars, because the other F1 cars aren't competitive. Whereas in karting, just getting to the final shows that you've done a fabulous job–not to mention winning the final! And to win it six times is absolutely incredible." I was so overwhelmed. I never expected him to say something like that.

In 1993, the two men met again, this time at the Paris–Bercy karting Masters. Senna drove an all-white kart, which his rivals suspected was a bit special. The now three-time F1 World Champion was keen to please his former rival from his karting days: In the drivers' changing room, he told me to bring my children, and he took three hats out of his cupboard: one for my son, one for my daughter and one for me. He also gave me a very special key ring, with an S in the center. It's one of the most priceless things I own. Since then, Mike Wilson has turned his hand to pilot training. He has given invaluable advice to the young Fernando Alonso, Felipe Massa, and many others. "We discussed Senna several times," he said. "I remember the stars in the drivers' eyes when I told them about Ayrton. It was as if I was talking about God for them, especially for the Brazilians."

I remember the stars in the drivers' eyes when I told them about Ayrton. It was as if I was talking about God for them, especially for the Brazilians.

MIKE WILSON

Ayrton Senna left nothing to chance during the final preparations, before the start of an F1 Grand Prix.

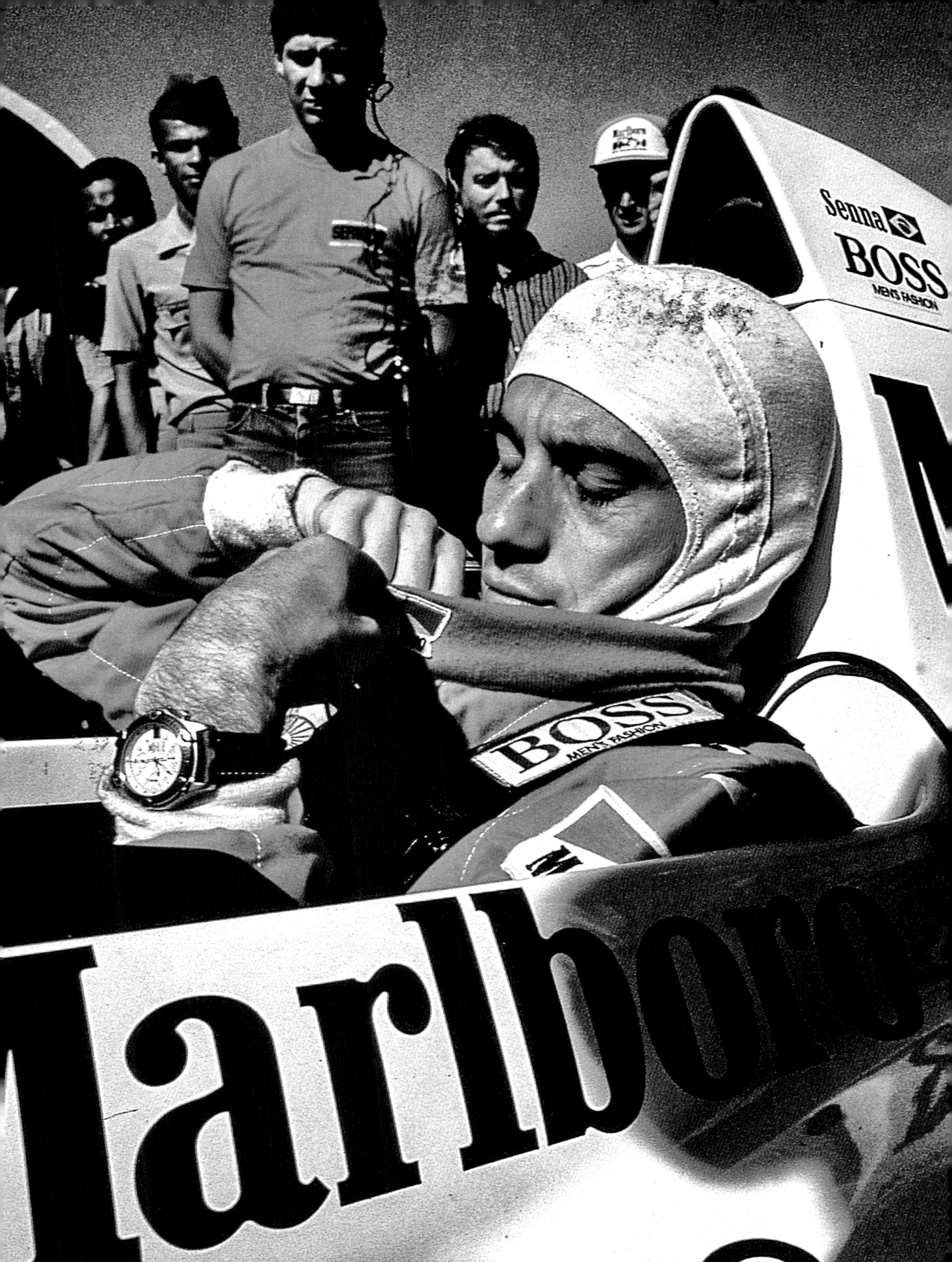
Senna
BOSS
MEN'S FASHION
BOSS
MEN'S FASHION

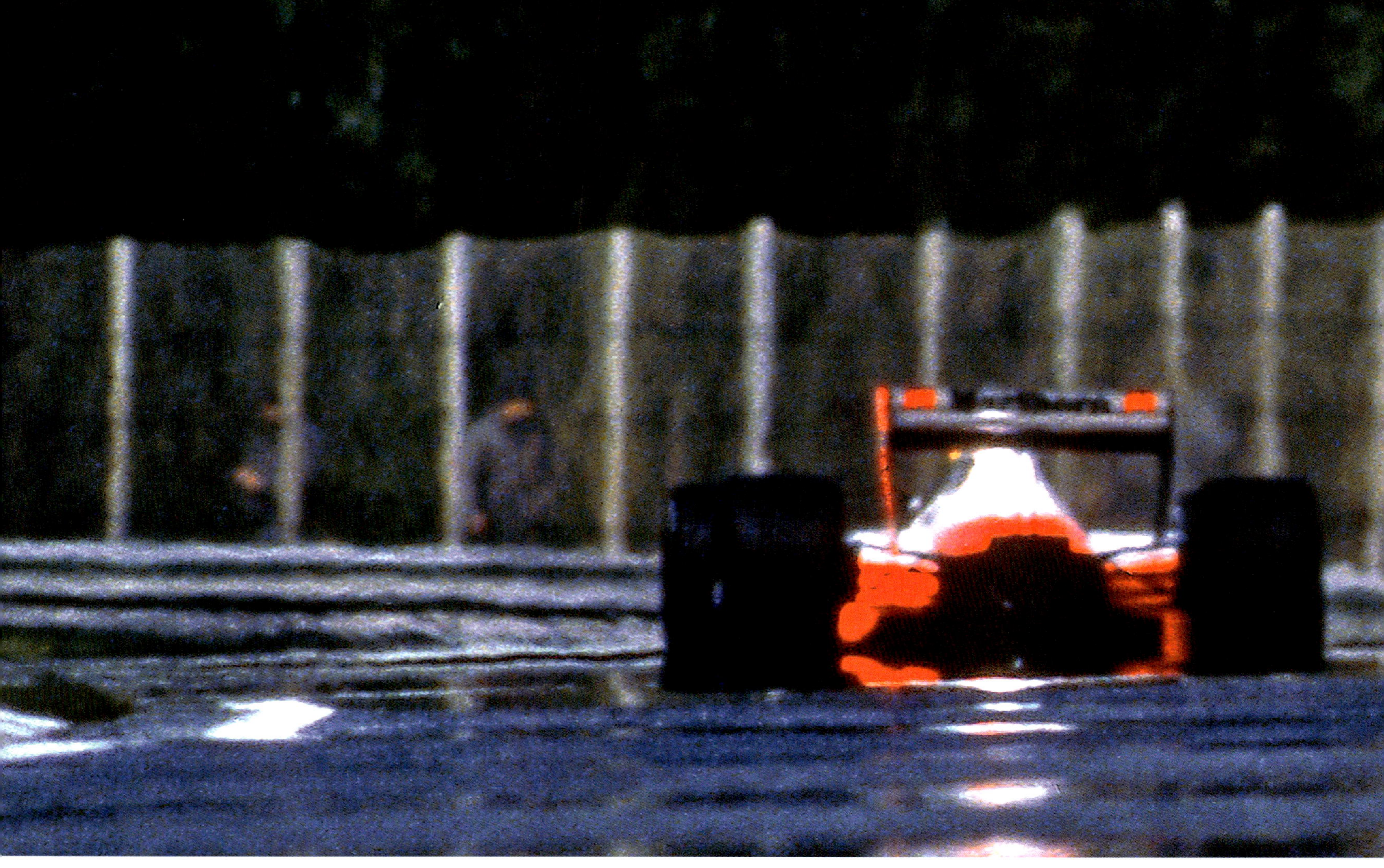

GERMANY GRAND PRIX: FOR ARMANDO

Four withdrawals. From his victory in Mexico at the end of May to the beginning of the race in Germany at the end of July, Senna did not finish a single one of the four Grand Prix he took part in. He was 20 points behind Prost. At Hockenheim, the journalists speculated that he had lost some weight. Senna waves them off, laughing: "I haven't seen my love in 30 days." He was, of course, referring to the Brazilian superstar Xuxa. Unfortunately, his smile was just a facade. His manager Armando Botelho had been suffering from heart problems since March and was hospitalized in Sao Paulo. Knowing how Senna missed his presence, his sister Viviane came to the rescue to support her champion brother. After an accident on Friday, Senna drove with the mule in qualifying but still secured his 36th pole position (ahead of Prost) on a circuit where, as it plunged into the forest, he reached 330 km/h. Senna described the track to a curious Brazilian journalist: "Here, it's just you, the car, the sound of the engine, and the screen with the car numbers. There's a bit of greenery and the trees are so tall. It's something that touches me and that only happens here." Feeling tired, he skipped the post-qualifying press conference, attracting the ire of F1 master Bernie Ecclestone.

The race soon gave way to the now-traditional Senna–Prost duel. Prost first played the role of the hare before being overtaken by his rival in the yellow helmet. On lap 20, Senna came in the pits at 28.3 seconds ahead. The Brazilian halted and, just as he was about to set off again, was told to wait. A mechanic was unsure whether he had tightened the wheel properly, sending Senna out of the pits 3.2 seconds behind Prost. Another duel began and seemed to be going in Prost's favor. But with just three laps to go, the Frenchman's McLaren snapped its sixth gear. Senna took advantage of the situation, setting the fastest lap and taking an unexpected victory seemingly out of the blue. On the podium, it seemed to be a contest of who would smile the least as the two drivers resolved to ignore each other. After the press conference, the Brazilian was talking to French television representatives when he was interrupted by Mansour Ojjeh, one of McLaren's main shareholders. They went to the team's motorhome and, surrounded by his family and friends, Ayrton learned that Armando Botelho had died at the age of 50. Senna dedicated one of his luckiest victories to him.

Top: At the end of the 1980s, the competition failed to stop the undisputed dominance of the McLaren team.

Right: At the 1989 Mexican Grand Prix, Ayrton Senna secures his 17th victory, his third consecutive in 1989.

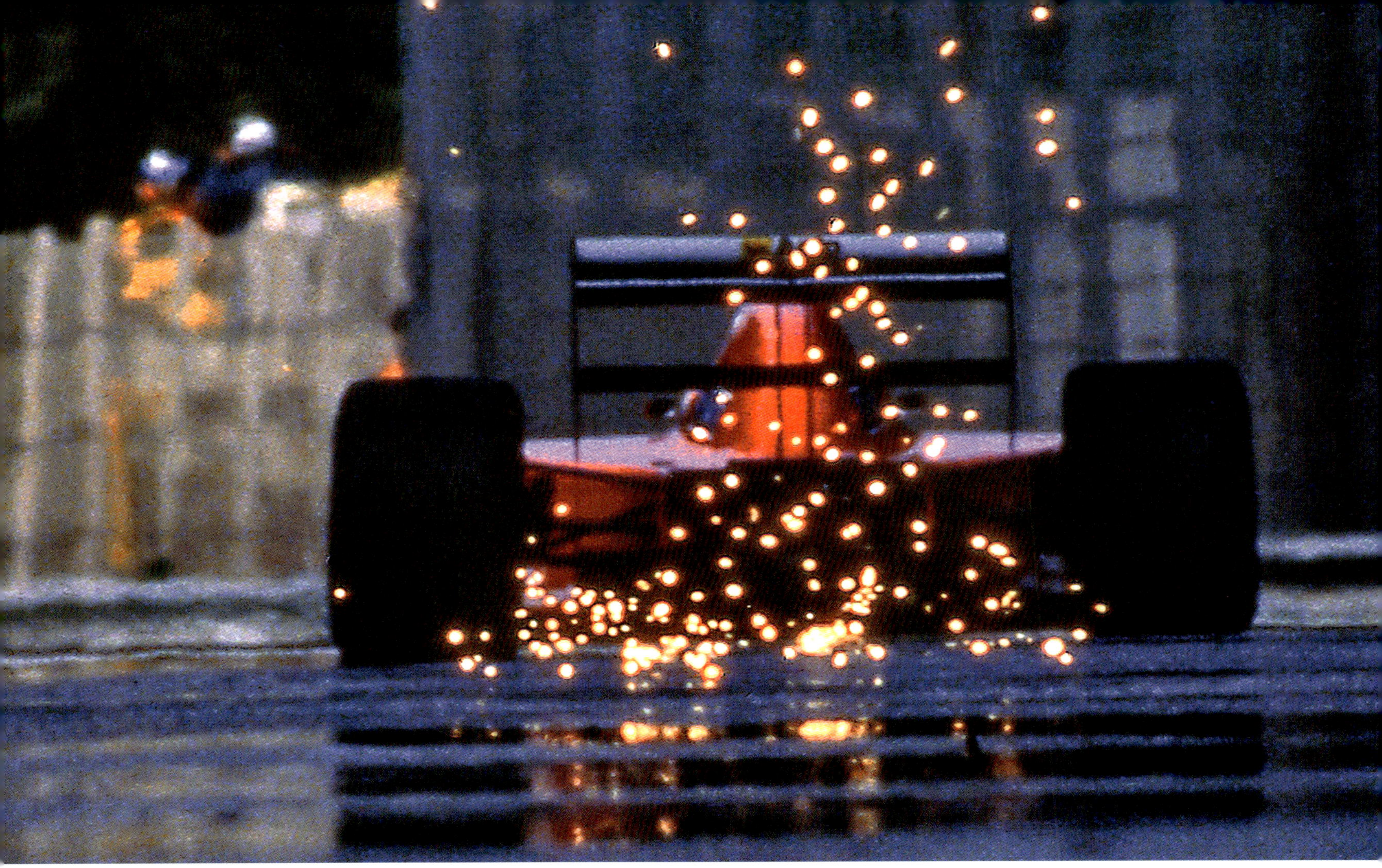

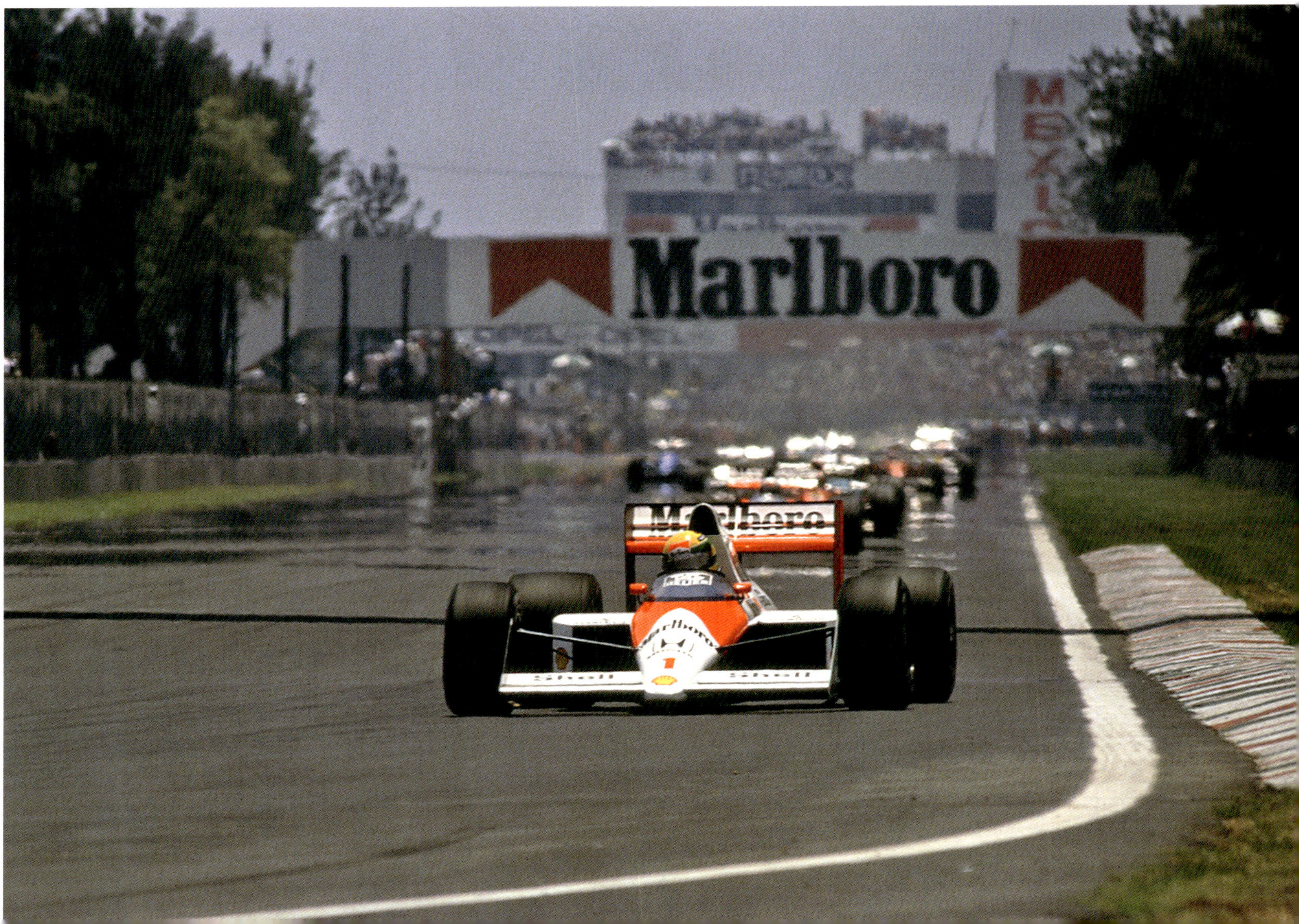

JAPAN GRAND PRIX: A FORESEEN CRASH AND A MEMORABLE CROWNING

At Suzuka, Prost held a 16-point lead over Senna (76 to 60). It was therefore Prost's priority to beat Senna in Japan, ending their competition. FIA President Jean-Marie Balestre asked Honda to treat its drivers fairly, prompting Senna to think that he was plotting in Prost's favor. The two rivals avoided each other, ignoring one another whenever they were forced to be together. Ron Dennis canceled the press conference planned by Marlboro, and Prost only spoke to his engineers, Neil Oatley and Tim Wright. He, like Senna, had a new chassis, but it was only his second of the season, compared to six for the Brazilian. He warned his rival in the press: if Senna wanted to force his way through, as he did at Estoril last year, or at Silverstone this summer, Prost won't open the door.

Senna took his 12th pole position of the season (1'38"041), 1.7 seconds ahead of Prost, who was concentrating on setting up for the race. The Ferraris of Berger (third) and Mansell (fourth) were more than two seconds behind. The two McLaren drivers chose version 4 of the Honda V10, which guaranteed extremely high revs. There were more than 130,000 spectators in the stands to watch what promised to be a fierce duel.

Prost started ahead of Senna, Berger, Nannini, Patrese, Mansell, and Boutsen. Senna's engine malfunctioned at low revs, and he lost one second per lap to the Frenchman, who he needed to catch if he was to have any chance of winning the world title. On lap 37, he increased his pace and set the fastest lap of the race with a time of 1'43"035. By lap 39, he was just 1.7 seconds behind Prost. On lap 40, Prost was blocked by Cheever in the chicane. Senna was barely behind and spent a few laps assessing his options for overtaking his rival. The Casio chicane seemed to be the ideal place for this battle of the leaders. On lap 47, at the entrance to the chicane, Senna dived inside to surprise Prost, using the wider track at the entrance of the pits. He was head-to-head with his rival as the track narrowed. Finding himself trapped, Senna was forced to brake. Prost, unperturbed, drove

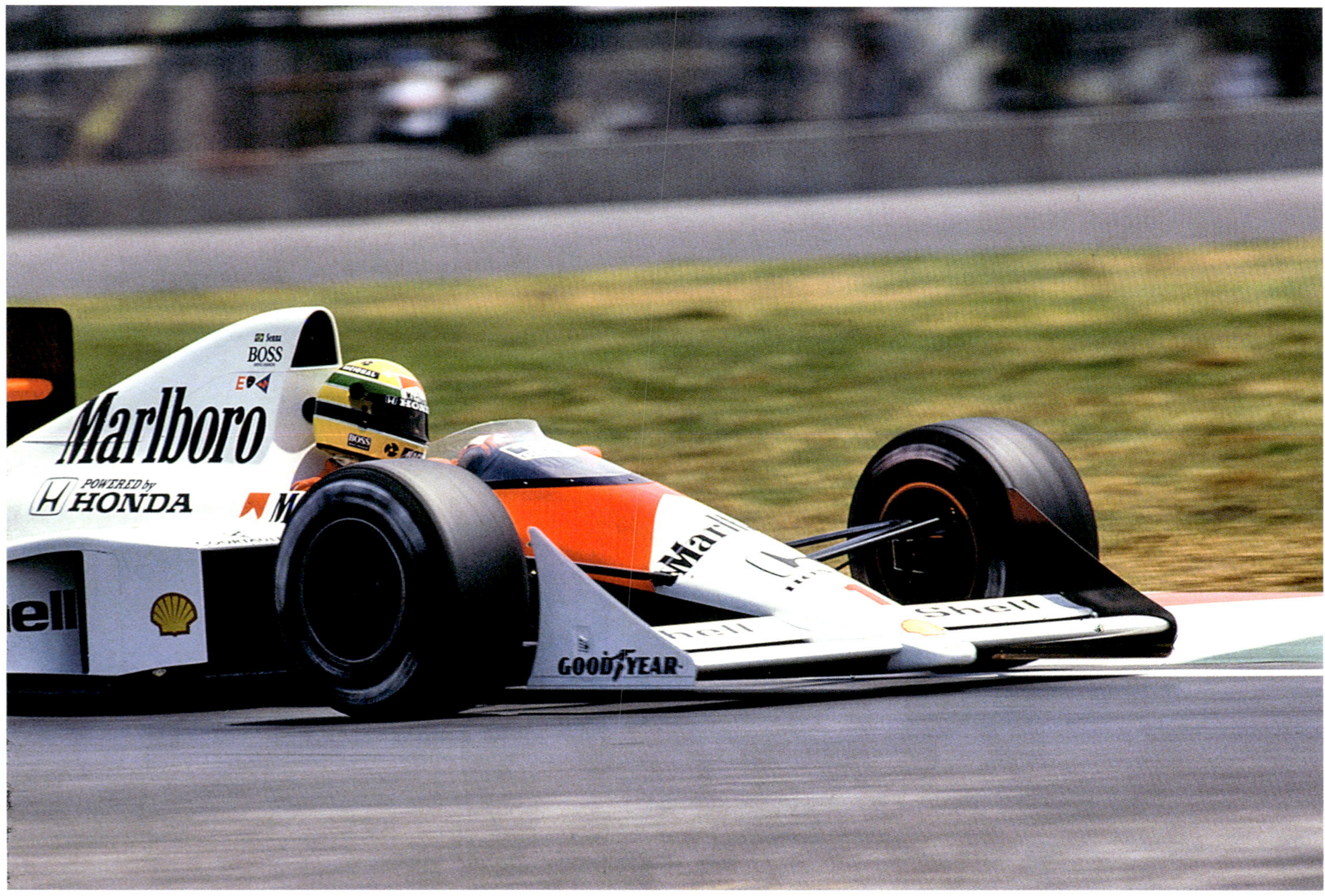

through his ideal trajectory and turned right. The Brazilian's left front wheel hit the Frenchman's right. Both came to a halt on the edge of the escape route, wheel-to-wheel.

After giving an ironic "bravo" to Prost, who had stalled his engine, Senna became tense and starting gesturing wildly, asking the stewards to push him. His engine came back to life and he reentered the track with some trouble on his front wing. He lost the wing on the next lap, returning to the pits to change his nose and fit a set of new tires. The operation took 18 seconds. Magic Senna restarted ten seconds behind Nannini's Benetton, the new leader, and started a mad chase totally in vain. He had short-circuited the chicane, and the stewards thus disqualified him. Prost returned to the pits, confident that he had won a new crown. Senna, who had finally overtaken Nannini, was first under the checkered flag and parked his car. Ron Dennis immediately informed him of his disqualification for three reasons: the deceleration zone at the entrance to the pits was not part of the track; he had restarted with outside help; and he had short-circuited the chicane. As a result, the race for the championship was finished and Prost was going to win his third world title.

Then, against all expectations, Ron Dennis announced his intention to appeal Senna's disqualification. Prost was outraged and disgusted. Senna added: I consider this result to be provisional. The ball is now in the court of the law. What I did was the right thing. I won this race on the track, but I didn't get on the podium to celebrate this success in front of the public, my biggest fan club outside Brazil. It's a shame for the sport. As for the accident itself, I had no other way of overtaking, and someone closed the door on me. That's all there is to it. If it had been any other driver than Prost, he would have let me through.

On Sunday evening, Ayrton met with Ron Dennis, Bernie Ecclestone, and Max Mosley, Vice-President of FIA, to prepare his defense before the FIA appeal tribunal. Convinced he was right, Prost savored the feeling of cold revenge, denying any responsibility: I didn't have to let Senna pass, quite simply because I was faster than him and there wasn't enough room at that point. I was on my line; he was behind me. Taking advantage of the side of the road was too easy. With Ron Dennis, of course, it wasn't very friendly. But I don't care anymore. For me, the season is over. I'm no longer interested in human relationships. After having worked as hard as I have for this team, I'm not happy to see the reward given out today in this way... This third world title left a bitter taste in his mouth.

The FIA appeal tribunal prepared to hear the case, but there was no doubt about the outcome. Senna's case was indefensible, even if his Brazilian friends saw things differently. As for Prost, his defense was quite confusing (to say the least) "I took a slightly more right-hand trajectory," Prost stated, "but at the speed he was going, I couldn't avoid him. Ayrton was in agony behind me. I wanted to let him come back a little and then accelerate again to break his morale." The videos show that the Frenchman had not kept his word: he had warned that he would not open the door to Senna, yet he did, even if it meant eliminating himself. Prost believed that he had been mistreated by McLaren and Honda since 1988, and his resentment and bitterness kept him on target to avoid the red and white torpedo that was bearing down on him.

I consider this result to be provisional. The ball is now in the court of the law.

AYRTON SENNA

The red and white McLarens dominate the end of the eighties, but in 1989 Ayrton Senna will finish second in the championship, behind the new world champion, Alain Prost.

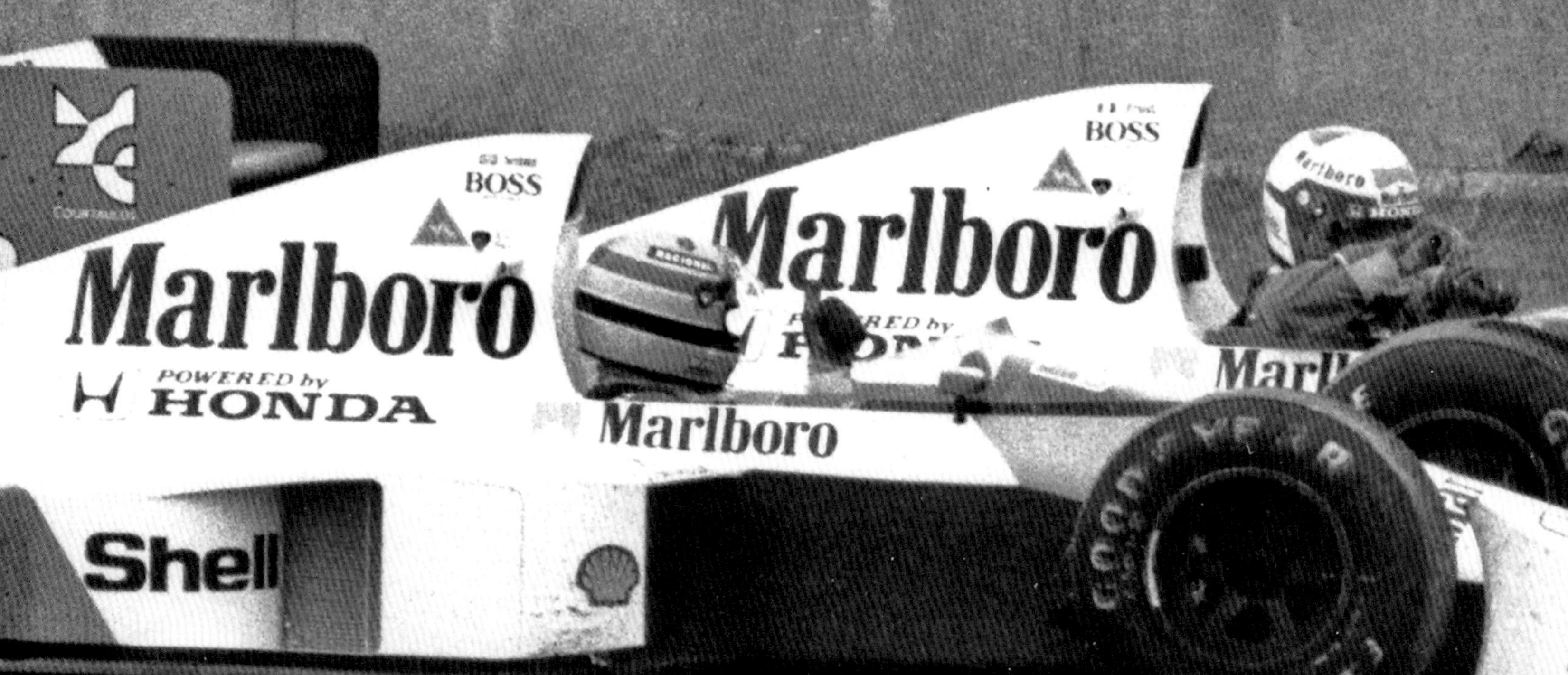
Marlboro
BOSS
POWERED by
HONDA
Marlboro
BOSS
Marlboro
Shell
GOOD

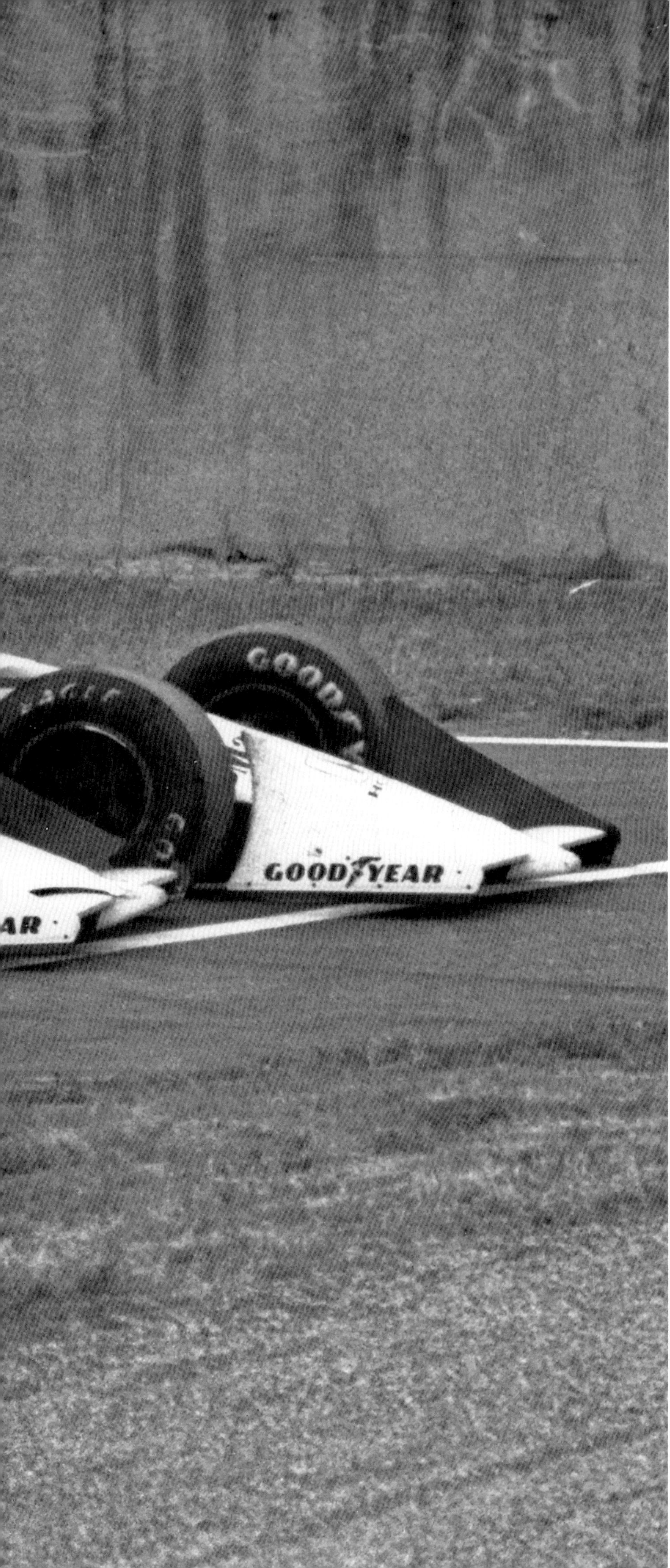

I didn't have to let Senna pass, quite simply because I was faster than him and there wasn't enough room at that point.

ALAIN PROST

The collision between Alain Prost and Ayrton Senna during the 1989 Japanese Grand Prix was one of the strongest moments of their exacerbated rivalry.

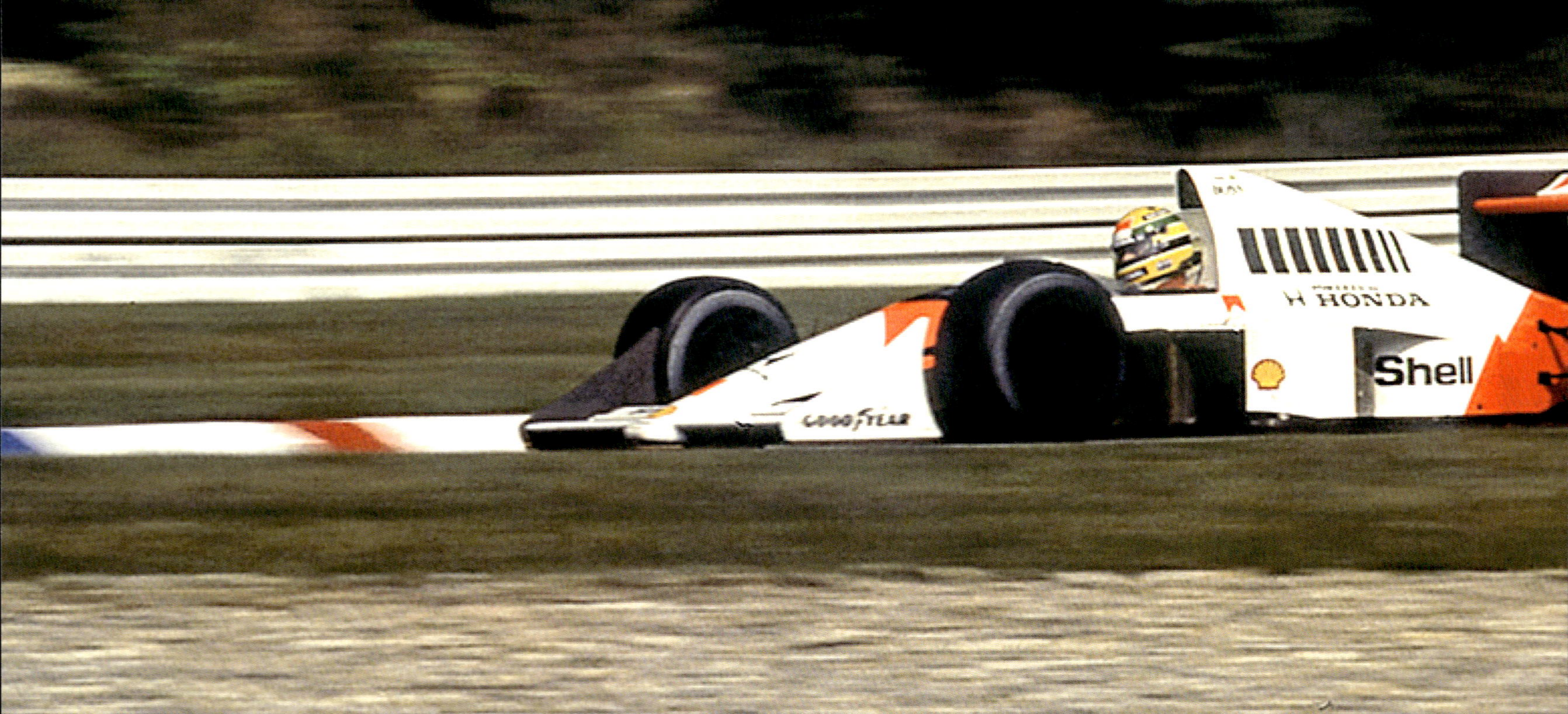
HONDA
Shell
GOODYEAR

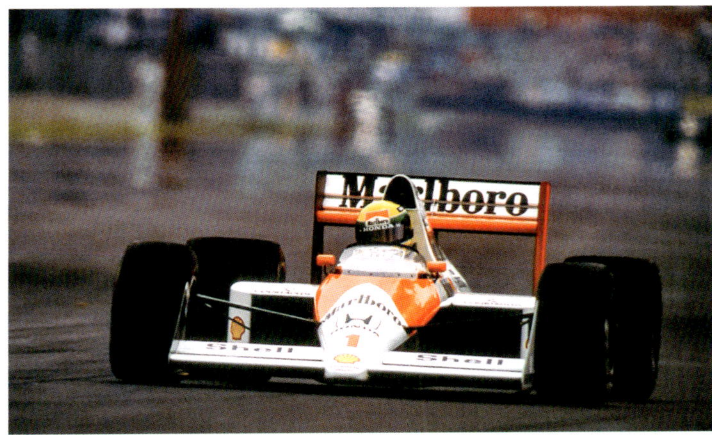

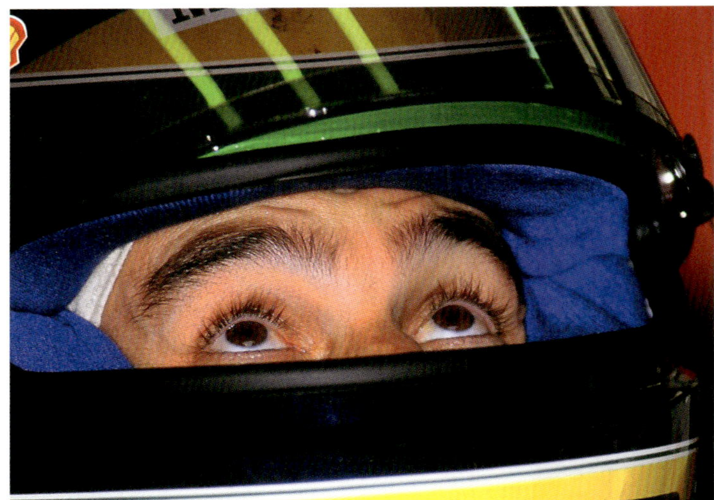

Above and left : between 1988 and 1993, Ayrton Senna and McLaren leave an indelible imprint on the history of Formula 1. In 1989, Senna will notch up a title of world vice-champion on his impressive Formula 1 results.

Bottom: Before each start, the deeply religious Ayrton Senna briefly raised his eyes to the sky in a symbolic manner.

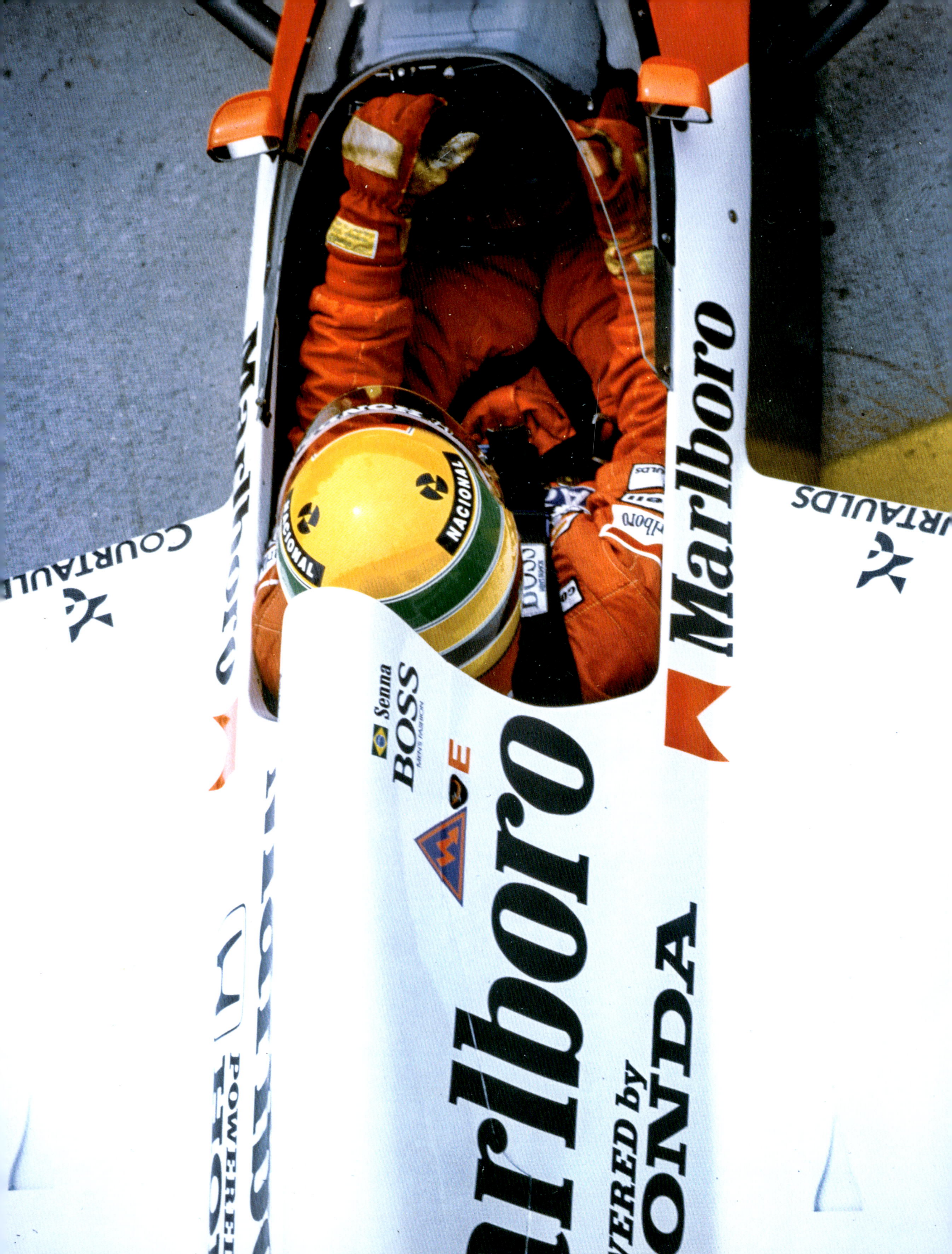
Marlboro
NACIONAL
Senna
BOSS
Marlboro

THE 1989 SEASON IN FIGURES

GRAND PRIX	QUALIFIERS	RACE
BRAZIL	POLE POSITION 30	11TH (CRASH AT START)
SAN MARINO	POLE POSITION 31	VICTORY 15
MONACO	POLE POSITION 32	VICTORY 16
MEXICO	POLE POSITION 33	VICTORY 17
UNITED STATES	POLE POSITION 34	DNF (ELECTRONICS)
CANADA	2ND	7TH (ENGINE PROBLEMS)
FRANCE	2ND	DNF (DIFFERENTIAL)
GREAT BRITAIN	POLE POSITION 35	DNF (SPIN)
GERMANY	POLE POSITION 36	VICTORY 18
HUNGARY	2ND	2ND
BELGIUM	POLE POSITION 37	VICTORY 19
ITALY	POLE POSITION 38	DNF (ENGINE)
PORTUGAL	POLE POSITION 39	DNF (CRASH)
SPAIN	POLE POSITION 40	VICTORY 20
JAPAN	POLE POSITION 41	DSQ (TRACK LIMITS)
AUSTRALIA	POLE POSITION 42	DNF (CRASH)

RUNNER-UP IN F1 WORLD CHAMPIONSHIP
(60 POINTS, 11 BEST RESULTS, 6 VICTORIES, 7 PODIUMS, 13 POLE POSITIONS, 3 BEST LAPS)

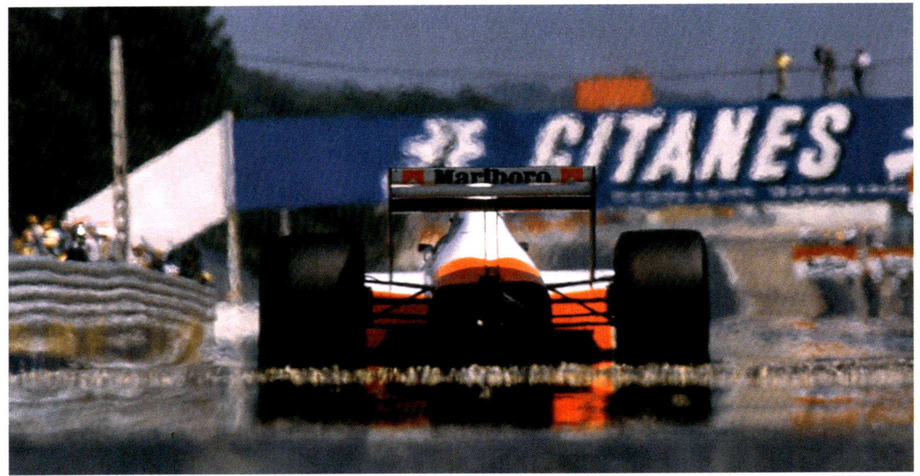

Top : during his second season with McLaren in 1989, Ayrton Senna took 6 wins and 13 pole positions.

Senna's maximum concentration before embarking on a timed lap allows him to secure six consecutive pole positions in the last six rounds of the 1989 season.

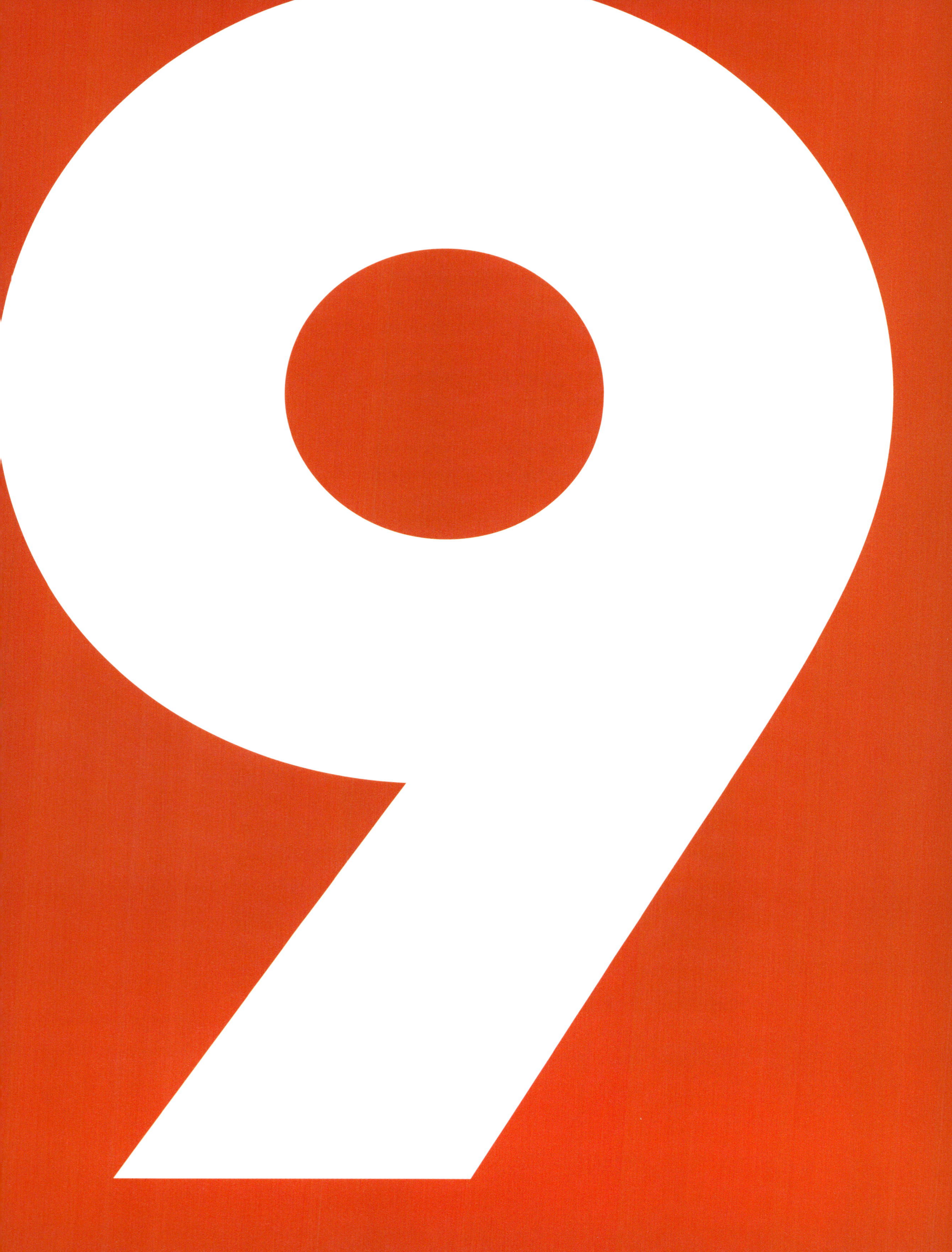
9

SECOND WORLD CHAMPIONSHIP TITLE

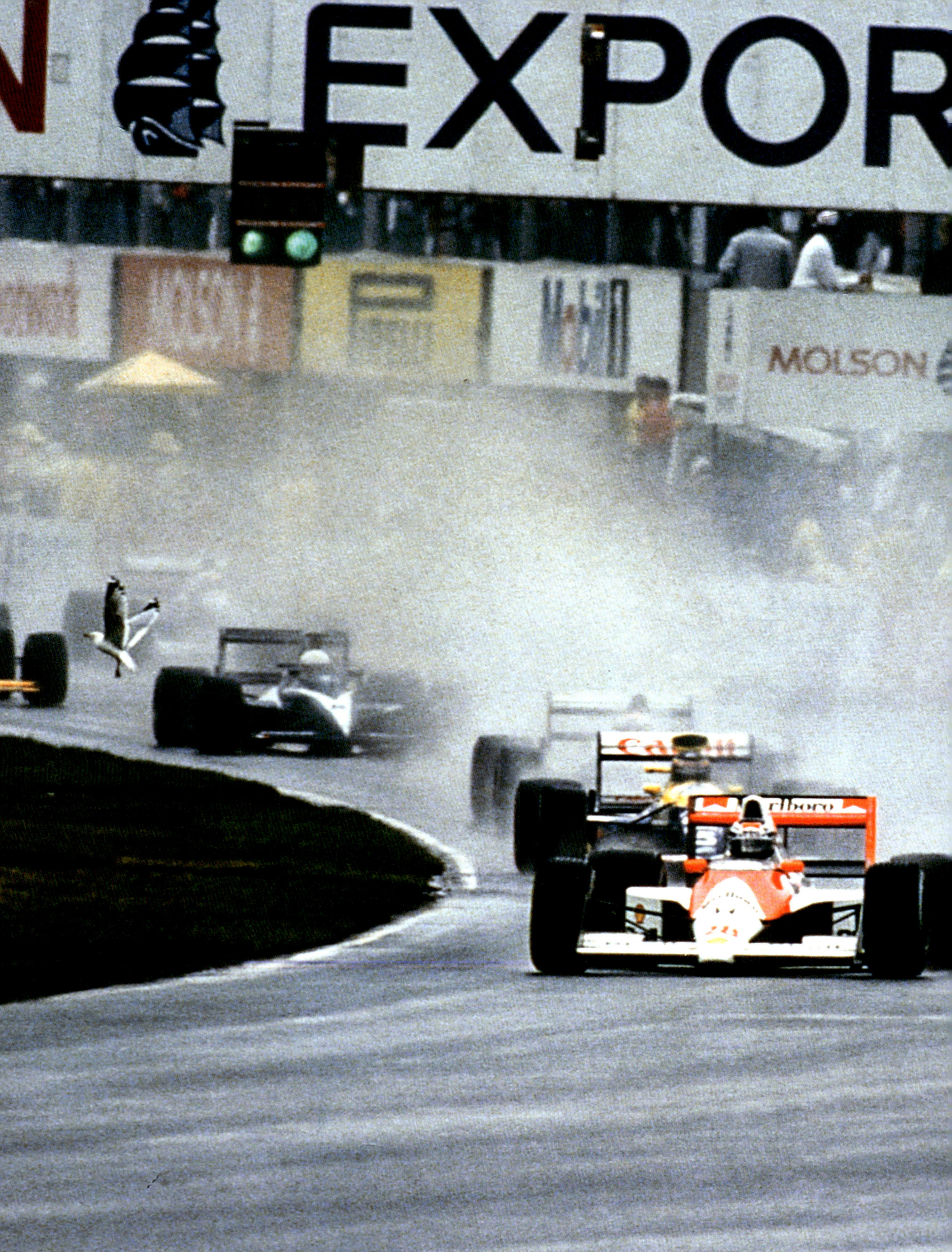
EXPOR
MOLSON

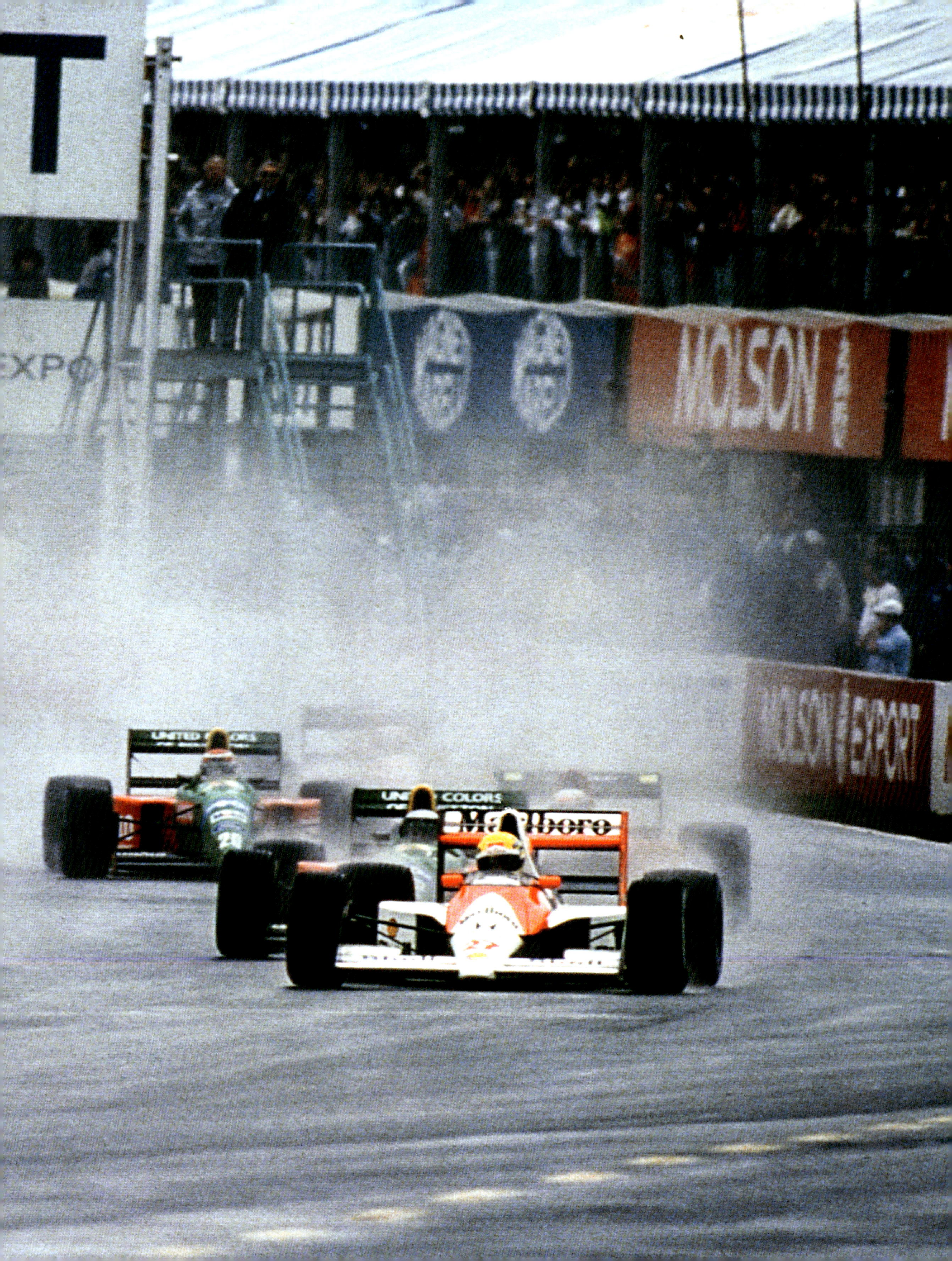
MOLSON
MOLSON EXPORT
UNITED COLORS

CARDS FOLDED AT MCLAREN-HONDA

THINGS CHANGED FOR SENNA'S THIRD SEASON WITH MCLAREN–HONDA. FIRST, ALAIN PROST LEFT FOR FERRARI AFTER SWAPPING SEATS WITH GERHARD BERGER. BERGER BECAME THE BRAZILIAN'S SECOND DRIVER AT WOKING AND CAUSED HIM FAR FEWER PROBLEMS.

Second, Ferrari worked well over the winter, following the departure of engineer John Barnard. The new 641 was ready to win it all. Roles were cleverly assigned within the Scuderia: Nigel Mansell was the showman, and Alain Prost wanted above all to win the world title against his great rival in the clean, efficient style (except at Suzuka at the end of 1989) that had already won him three world titles. This duel kept F1 fans on the edge of their seats as the two former teammates got the season off to a flying start. They won ten of the first 12 races. The McLaren MP4/5B was not as dominant as the two cars that preceded it, but Ayrton won three of the first five Grands Prix on the calendar (Phoenix, Monaco, Montreal). Prost then enjoyed a fine run of three victories (Mexico, France, Silverstone) only to be thwarted by the Brazilian in Germany. After a break in Hungary (2nd), Senna won again (Belgium, Italy) and arrived in Japan doubly armed: a nine-point lead over the Frenchman

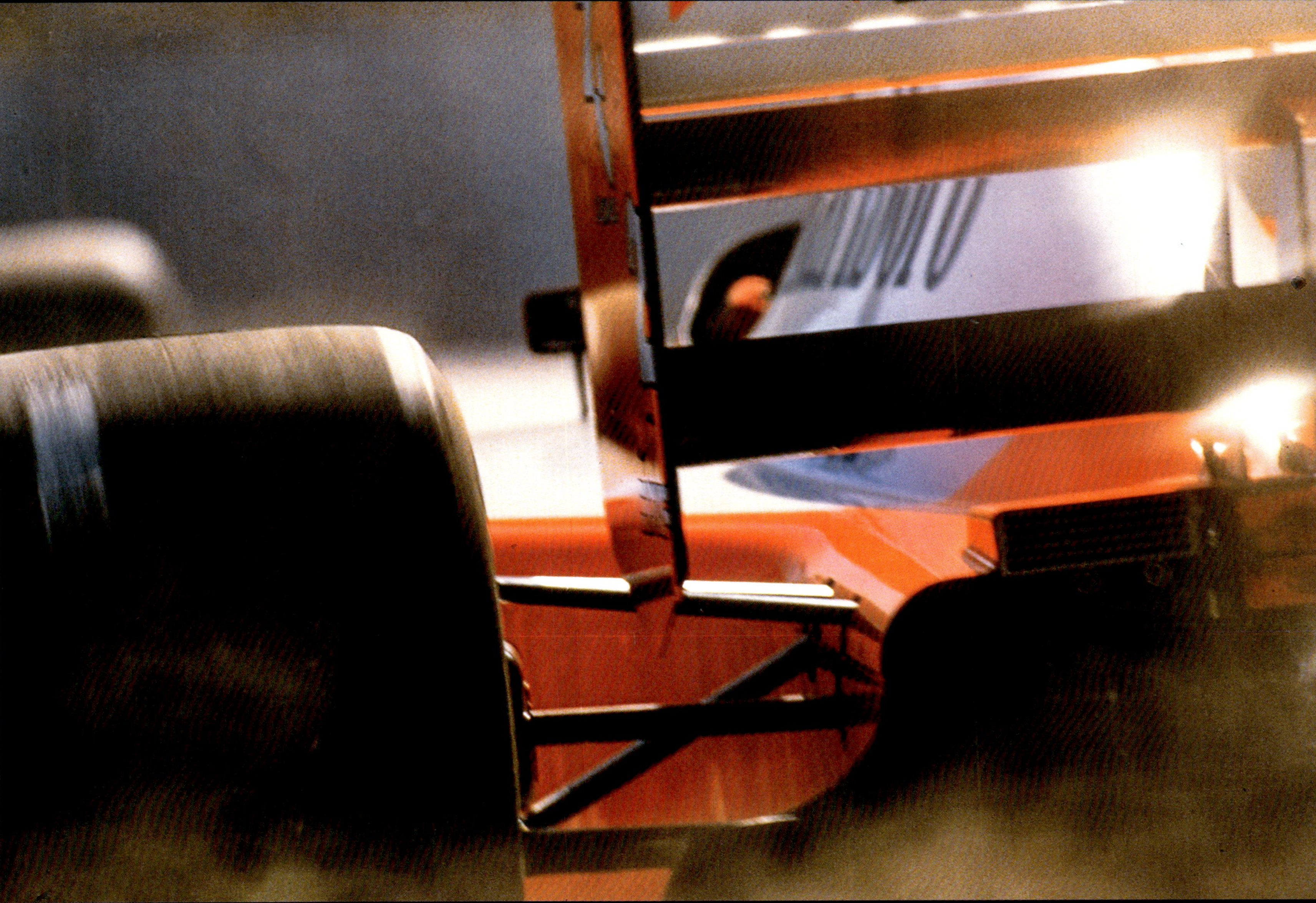

(78 to 69), who had just given himself another chance by winning in Spain, and, above all, a desire for revenge still burning one year after Suzuka 1989. The suspense didn't last long: Prost started out in front, and, on the very first lap, Senna charged at him to harpoon the Ferrari. Both cars were in the gravel trap, and the Brazilian was crowned world champion with the 11 best results of the season because Prost would have two points deducted in Australia if he won. No one at Ferrari lodged a complaint, and the race stewards validated the result and, thus, Senna's second world title. His French rival preferred to remain silent. A silence that honors him, as everyone witnessed this premeditated settling of accounts live one year after Suzuka 1989.

Previus double page: The 1990 Canadian Grand Prix takes place in heavy rain. Not a problem for Senna, who delivers a stellar performance with both the pole position and the victory.

Top: Senna's McLaren is seen from the rear—a common image the Brazilian's subdued rivals see throughout the season.

RACE AFTER RACE

1990

USA GRAND PRIX: AYRTON VS. JEAN D'AVIGNON

For once, the 1990 season begins in the United States, with the second Phoenix GP brought forward to March. The weather is gray and cool, and the driver who starts from pole position has to be in a McLaren, but it is not Ayrton Senna; it's Gerhard Berger, his new teammate, who swapped seats with Alain Prost at Ferrari. There are two other surprises as qualifying takes place on a wet track: a Minardi also on top of the grid—the car of Pierluigi Martini—and a young Frenchman on the second row, Jean Alesi, in a Tyrrell owned by "Uncle" Ken. Alesi has only eight Grands Prix to his name, but he has great driving skills, and the Phoenix track gives him the chance to shine even though Tyrrell has not been a top team for a long time.

Right from the start, Alesi makes his presence felt by taking advantage of the hesitations of Berger, who started from pole position, zigzagging around the track and getting in Senna's way. Alesi takes advantage of this to change trajectory and, thanks to some daring braking, overtakes the Austrian on the inside. He's in the lead, ahead of Berger, De Cesaris, Senna, and Martini. And he escapes, as Berger is unable to get his hard tires up to temperature. Alesi soon has Senna behind him but holds on to the lead. On lap 9, Berger misses his braking and damages his tires. He returns to the pits and sets off again, his McLaren intact. The duel between Alesi and Senna can now begin. On lap 20, the Brazilian catches up with the Frenchman, hampered by traffic and his Pirelli tires slowly degrading. On lap 34, Ayrton comes close to overtaking him at a corner, but Alesi fends off that attack with great skill. On lap 35, the Brazilian succeeds in his maneuver and begins to get some air behind him, as the Frenchman decides to go easy on his tires. The gap widens, and Senna ultimately wins, but everyone would remember this lovely mid-race duel between the champion and the young driver. On lap 72, Senna is first under the checkered flag, eight seconds ahead of Alesi, who climbs on his first F1 podium. There would be 31 more, at Tyrrell, Ferrari, and Benetton.

Jean Alesi impressed everyone with his virtuosity and fighting spirit. His lengthy battle with Senna would go down in history. "Senna had a sense of the race; he could sense when he was going to be overtaken. He didn't insist more than that, or he insisted correctly. So, if there was an opening, we knew we could jump in, and it would happen," recalls the young hero of the day. He was delighted with his 2nd place. For Jean Alesi, there was only one downside to a very successful day in Arizona: Uncle Ken (Tyrrell) wanted to keep the trophy! It was the second in less than a year, following Michele Alboreto's 3rd place in Mexico in May 1989, who, at that time, ended a six-year drought.

Driving for Tyrrell Racing, Jean Alesi passionately animates the Phoenix Grand Prix, the inaugural race of the 1990 season.

SENNA'S PASSION FOR CORINTHIANS

Ayrton Senna was only a soccer player for one friendly game in Bali. And to say he wasn't any good is an understatement. Yet, it's impossible to dissociate Brazil and soccer.

As a child, Ayrton Senna had a black-and-white flag in his bedroom: that of Corinthians, São Paulo's flagship team and one of the most closely followed on the planet, with over 30 million fans worldwide at the time, including Senna. In the 1980s, in F3, a famous photograph shows him pointing to the logo of his favorite club on his T-shirt, under his racing suit. It was the height of what is known as "Corinthian democracy." The "people's club" had in fact established a radical model, going against the country's military dictatorship. Club decisions were taken collectively, and self-management was orchestrated by an ultra-charismatic spokesman, midfielder Sócrates, a doctor by profession and captain of the Seleção. Senna has never hidden his love for the Paulista club, even though he was also a member of the Belenenses supporters' club, south-west of Lisbon. Naturally, he celebrated his favorite team's first Brazilian league title in December 1990.

Twenty years after his death, Corinthians showed their affection for him by entering the pitch wearing a replica of his helmet. Four years later, the players wore a special jersey featuring Senna's 1985–1986 Lotus colors. Finally, in a park next to the Corinthians' headquarters, a helmet of the Brazilian rests under glass, accompanied by a plaque reading: "In the chest of the cold and courageous pilot beats a Corinthian heart."

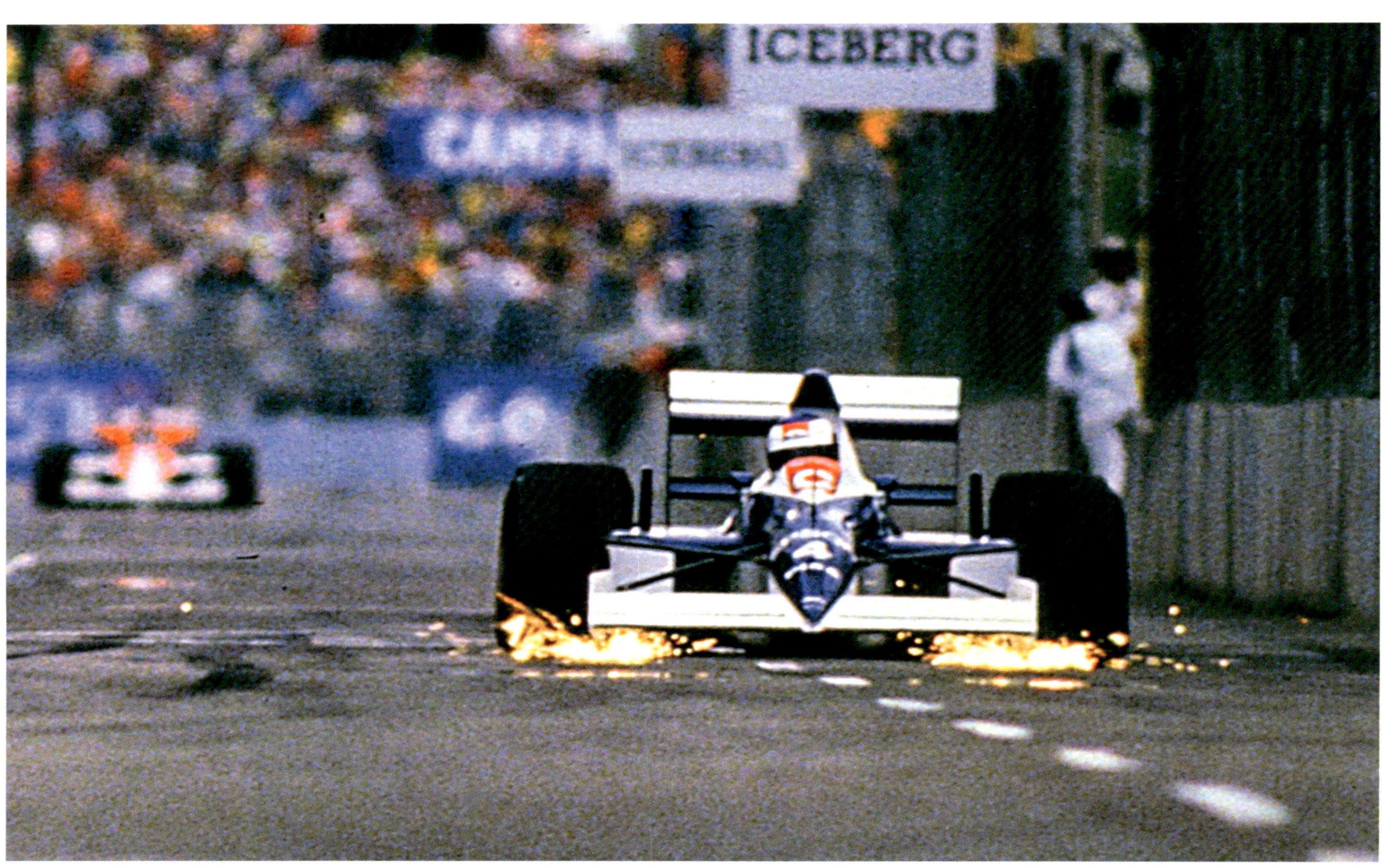

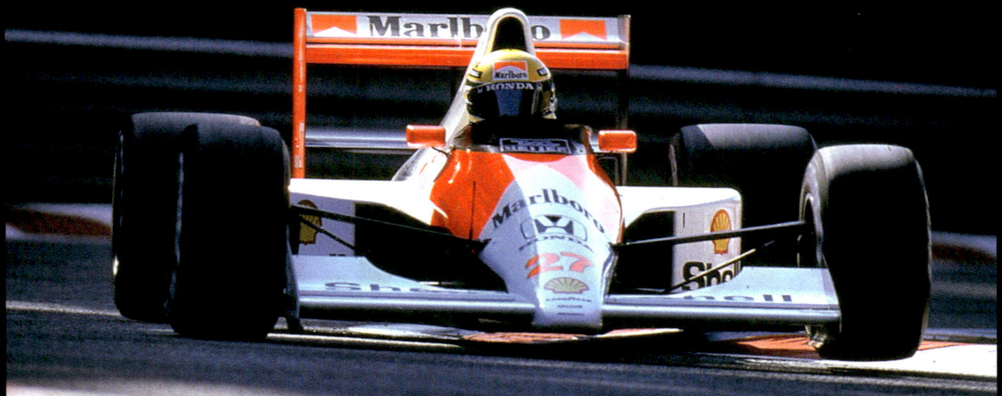

THE CAR: MCLAREN MP4/5B

The McLaren MP4/5B doesn't set the F1 world on fire. In fact, it's merely an evolution of last season's MP4/5, which won 10 out of 16 races. Why change a winning recipe when technical regulations have changed so little? The naturally-aspirated engines were fully developed, so British engineer Neil Oatley and his colleagues concentrated on aerodynamics, making a number of corrections to the pontoons, radiators, and gearbox. At the dawn of the decade, they also began work on a rear diffuser to generate more downforce. The results were encouraging in the wind tunnel. On the track, however, the car appeared to be very unstable. This technical solution was abandoned at the Germany Grand Prix. Other corrections were made in the middle of the season, concerning the flat floor, power, and weight, much to the delight of Senna and Berger, who had long been frustrated by having to drive such a nervous and uncomfortable car. The most obvious example: Berger's long legs led McLaren to redesign the cockpit of the McLaren MP4/5B so that the Austrian could enjoy a semblance of comfort.

On the technical side, the chassis of this car is stronger because the type of carbon used has changed. The 700 hp engine, the 3.5-liter Honda RA100E, is ideal for propelling the car, although some are concerned about the progress made by their opponents. Not least Ferrari, which now benefits from Alain Prost's meticulous driving and the proven skills of McLaren alumnus Steve Nichols, who left with the Frenchman. Senna works with Honda to limit the reliability problems of the Japanese engine. The Brazilian workaholic is listened to. And fortunately so: with this car flanked by the number 27, he won his second world title and established his reputation as an outstanding driver, even if the McLaren MP4/5B won't exactly go down in history.

CANADA GRAND PRIX: PERFECT MANAGEMENT

Ayrton Senna is anxious at the beginning of the Canadian GP. In Monaco, two weeks earlier, he heard a strange sound coming from his Honda engine. And even though his victory soothed him, he was worried. Ron Dennis summed up the situation: "Senna swears the noise was coming from the engine, but Honda, apparently, disagrees." Senna is also disturbed by a supposed flirtation with Ferrari, who are trying to lure the Brazilian to the Scuderia for 1991. But Ron Dennis would have none of it: "We can show him the difference between winning and losing," he told Brazilian newspapers. The two McLarens dominate the competition throughout the weekend. King of the qualifying, Senna adds a pole position to his collection, on a dry track. But the start on Sunday is given in the rain. Disrupted by the conditions, Gerhard Berger flies by him and overtakes his teammate. As a result, the new McLaren driver is given a one-minute penalty. Senna resumes his initial position, followed by Berger, on a dry track. Senna leaves his teammate in front after the pit-stop waltz, well aware that victory is promised to him. But he is not serene. As he exits a corner, he shifts into first gear and would later report, "a loud, agonizing noise." First gear is temporarily out, just like it was in warm-up. He immediately adapts his driving style to avoid forcing the transmission and only uses second gear on corner entry and exit. He wins anyway, ahead of Piquet and Mansell. For Brazil, it is a day of celebration, as the Brazilians' one–two finish comes shortly before the start of Brazil–Sweden at the 1990 World Cup. The Seleção would win 2–1 in Turin.

Later, at around 8:00 p.m., Dr. Jacques Dallaire, who had closely followed Senna's physical and mental preparation, witnesses a funny scene. As he walks along the circuit, he catches sight of a slow-moving normal car. As night falls, the car pulls up alongside him. The driver gets out:

It was Ayrton! He said to me: 'I wasn't happy with the way I'd driven in a few corners. I wanted to drive some more to spot the little things I could do to go faster.' It was incredible: This boy who had reached the pinnacle of his sport was still driving around the circuit, in a rental car, when everyone had left and the race was over. Just to get better for next year's race.

Amidst a dispute with Honda, Senna dominates the 1990 Canadian Grand Prix with ease.

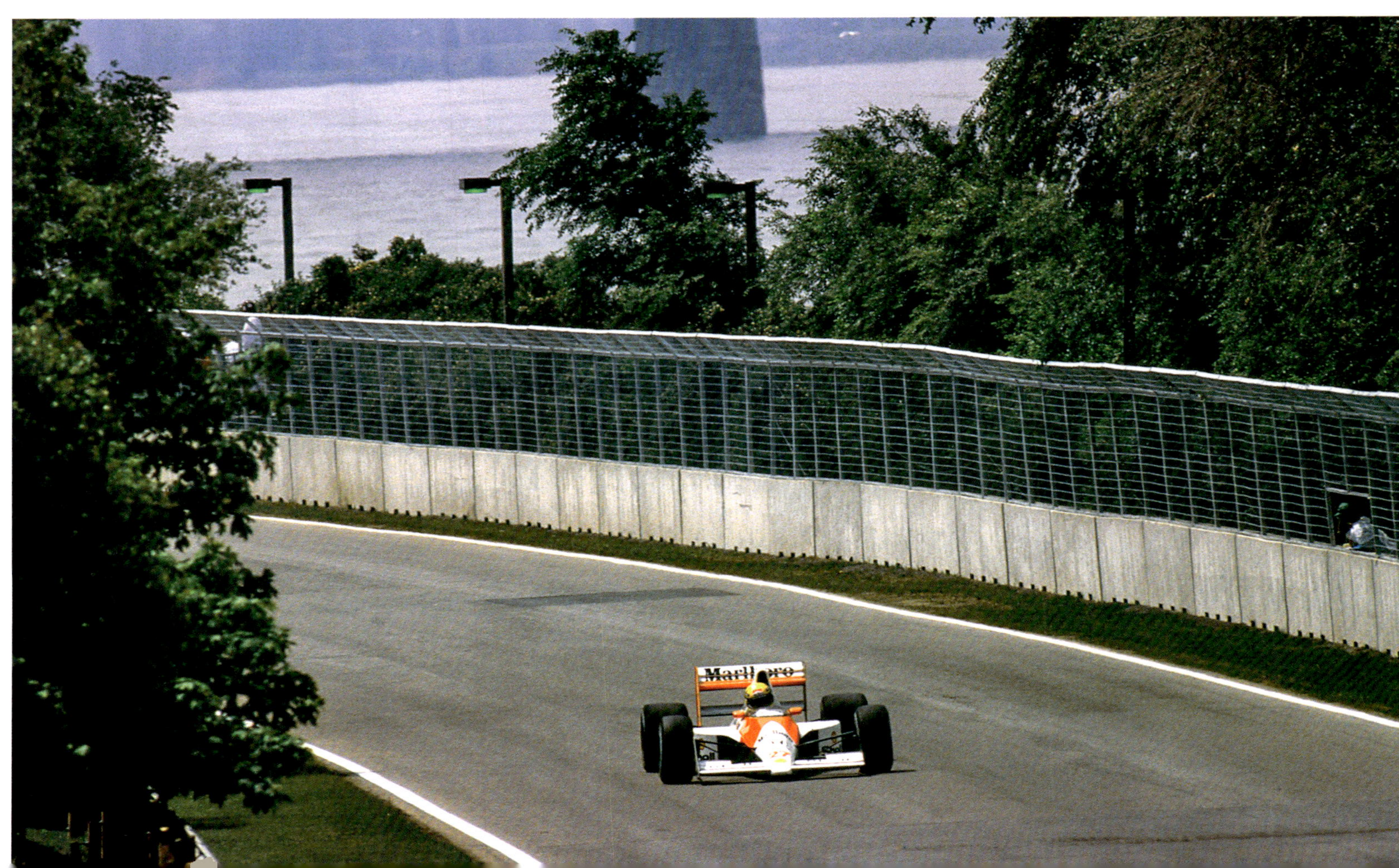

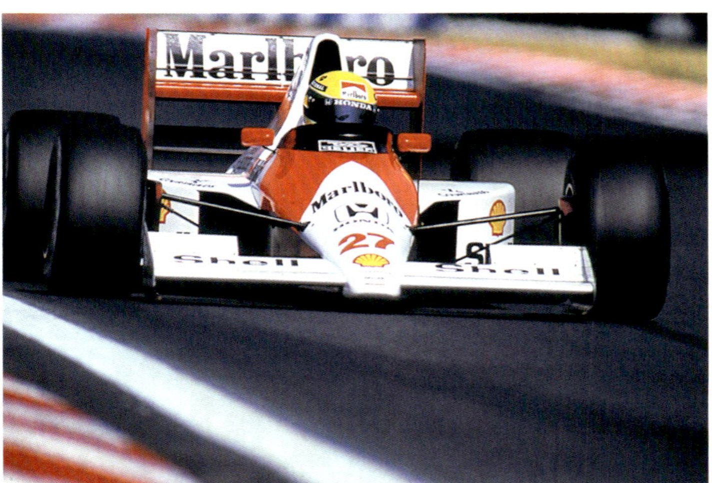

Senna leaves his mark on the 1990 F1 season.

ITALY GRAND PRIX: FAKE TRUCE

At Monza, the Tifosi's hearts beat only for Ferrari. But some fans don't hesitate to cheer for the Brazilian, who is not insensitive: "Do you hear how the stands applaud and support me? One day, when I'll be racing for Ferrari, their enthusiasm will know no bounds," Senna confides to a local journalist. It looks like he's got something up his sleeve... In the media, Ferrari is going all out for the Italian round. Improvements are being made with the promise of a more powerful engine to beat the McLarens in the temple of speed. Senna responds in his own way, taking pole as he did in 1989 and breaking the circuit record. At lights out, his McLaren takes off perfectly, while Prost is overtaken by Berger and then Alesi. The race then comes to a halt at the end of the first lap, as Derek Warwick's Lotus goes off at the Parabolica. A new start, then, with "Jean d'Avignon"—as some journalists call Jean Alesi—who has Italian origins and seems capable of upsetting the McLaren drivers.

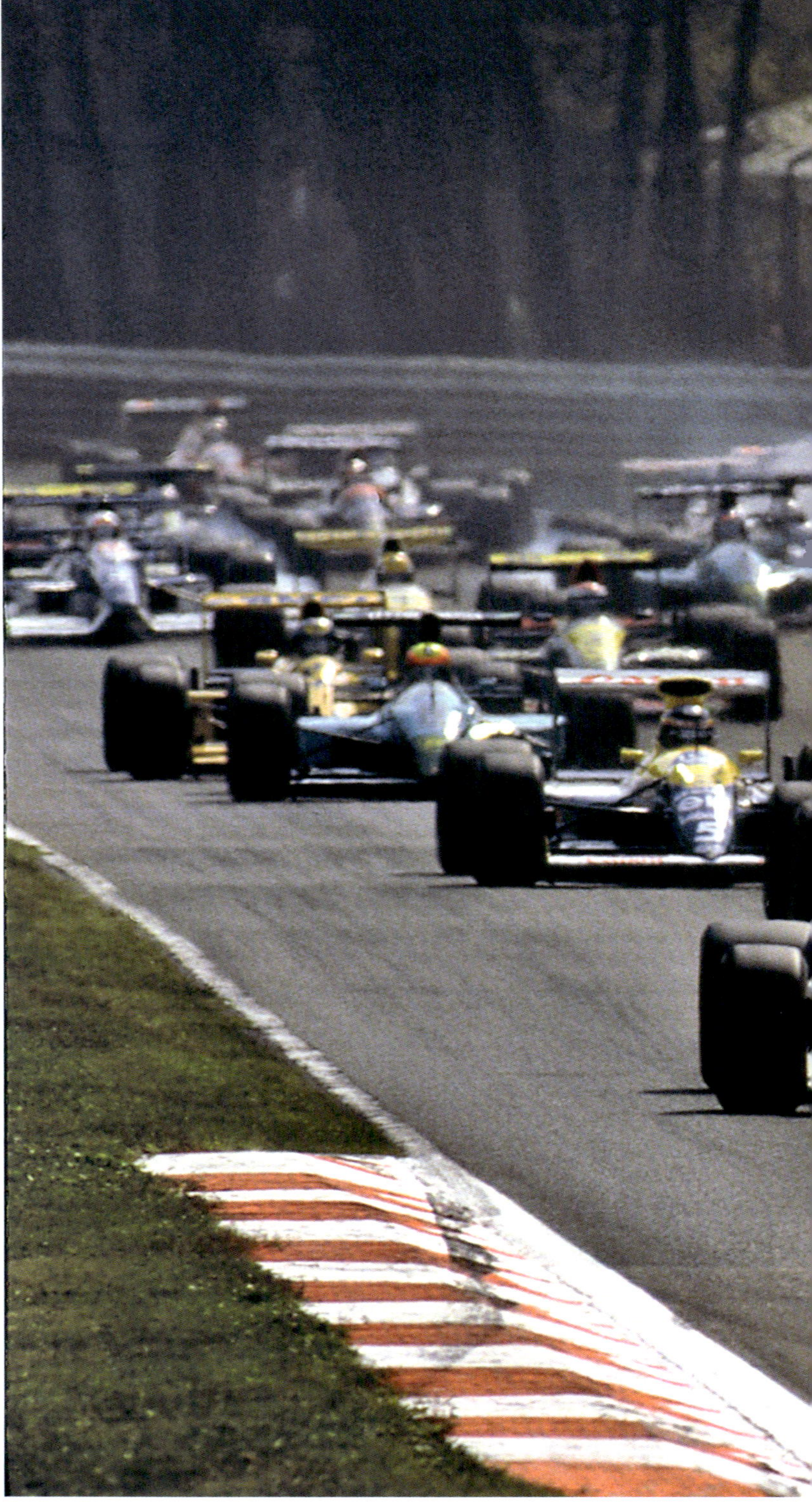

Helped by his teammate, Senna breaks away, but Prost manages to get back to 2nd place. What follows is a race in which the two drivers battle it out for the fastest laps. But in the end, it is Senna who takes the victory he has been waiting for since 1987. Some in the media spoke of the "curse of Monza." It is now broken even if the proud Ayrton never believed it: "The Ferrari people laughed at us, said they were going to be the fastest in practice, that we wouldn't win the race. I really wanted to win," he tells reporters. The Tifosi could console themselves with Prost's 2nd place.

During the press conference, a surprising event takes place. Carlo Marincovich, a journalist from the daily newspaper La Repubblica, asks Prost and Senna directly in Italian, a language both drivers have mastered: "Since we're in Italy, the land of love, [...] why don't you make a beautiful gesture of peace here, in front of us all? Why don't you shake hands?" The assembly is dumbfounded, especially as the official language at FIA press conferences is English. Prost throws his hand in the Brazilian's direction... who can't refuse it; in front of the world's media, the effect would be catastrophic. The symbolism is beautiful, even if some journalists have slight doubts. A few days later, Italian

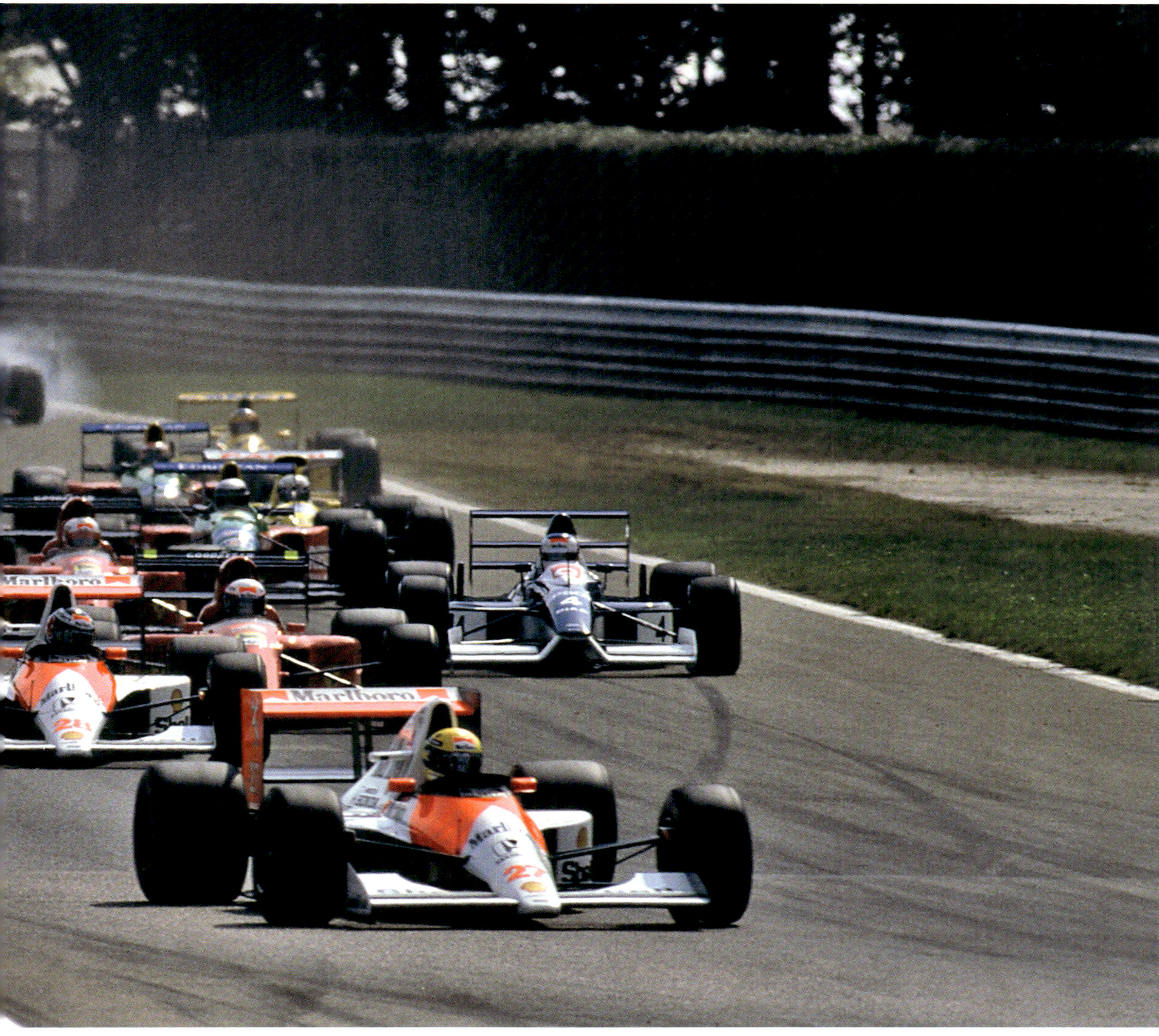

journalist Leo Turrini meets Ayrton Senna and his father Milton at Lisbon airport. He reported Senna's curious statement: “He told me: 'It was a fake truce. I don't trust Prost, and if, to win the championship, I have to take him off the track, I will.’ I wrote this story in my diary the next day, but nobody believed it.” A month and a half later, at Suzuka, Leo Turrini would put pictures to this premonitory sentence.

Senna is shown in front with others behind—a succinct summary of the 1990 F1 season.

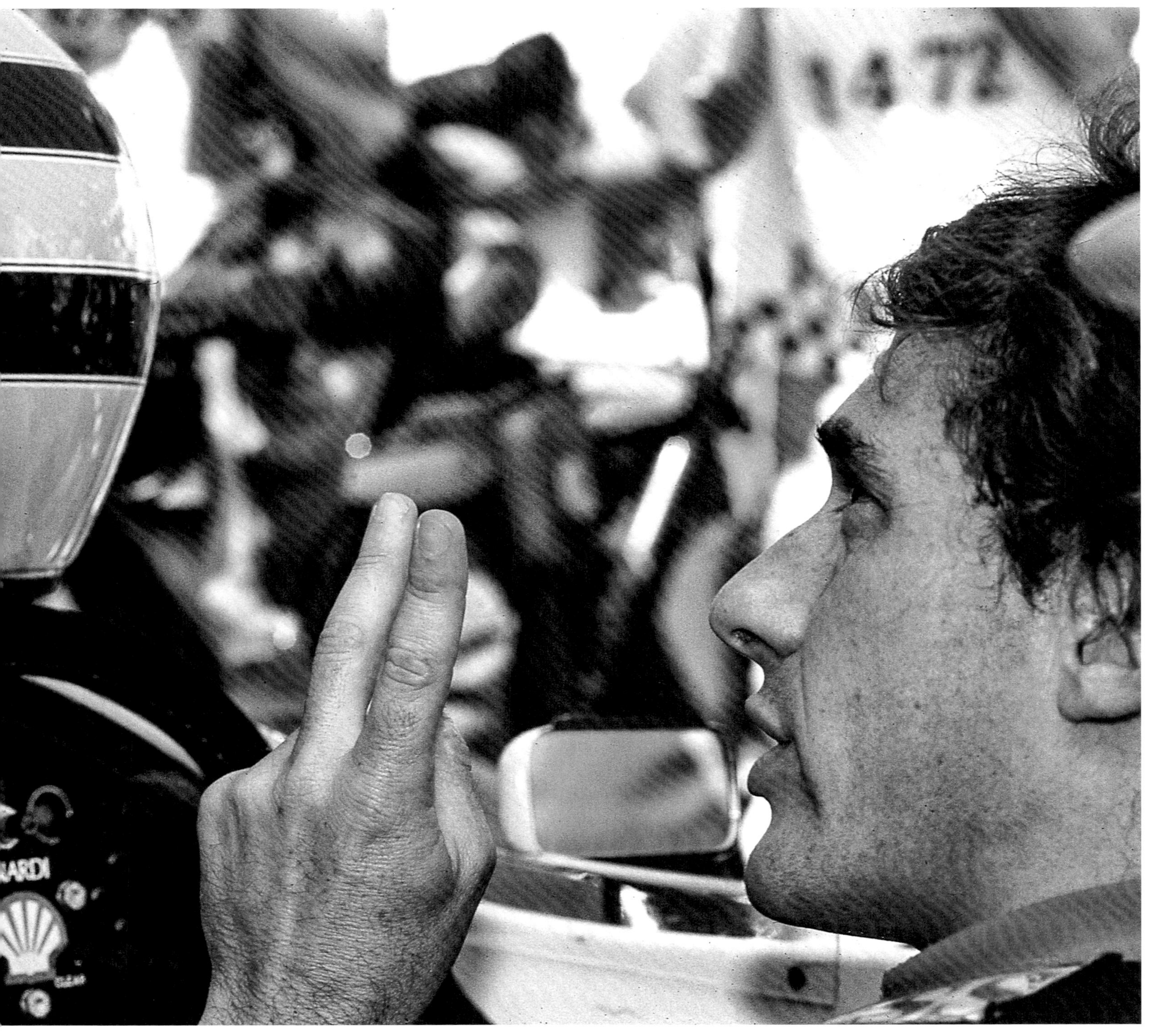

I've always thought that Ayrton was the best driver in the history of F1.

GERHARD BERGER

With his engineers, Senna—driven by his relentless pursuit of ultimate speed—meticulously examines every piece of information as it relates to his car's behavior.

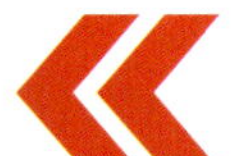

GERHARD BERGER, THE ECLECTIC JOKER

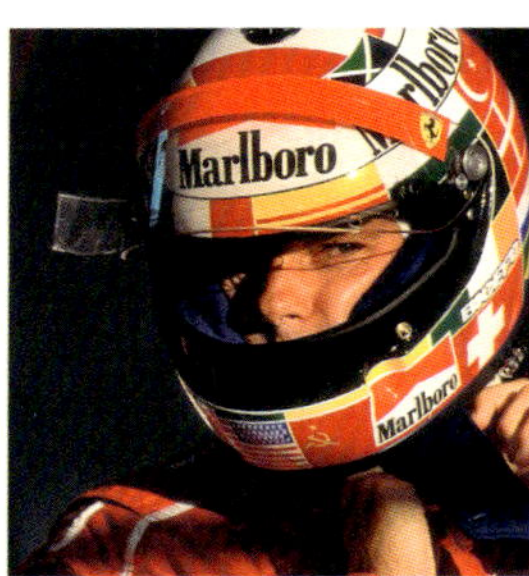

Gerhard Berger was a highly gifted driver, as evidenced by the fact that he won 10 of the 210 F1 Grands Prix he started between 1985 and 1997. He drove for ATS and Arrows at first, then for three top teams: Ferrari, McLaren, and Benetton. He twice finished on the final podium of the F1 World Championship. Above all, he raced at a time when the field was particularly tough. His rivals included Alain Prost, Ayrton Senna, Nelson Piquet, Nigel Mansell, and Michael Schumacher.

When he arrived at McLaren, it was to succeed Prost, who had left for Ferrari after two seasons of fierce rivalry with the Brazilian. As a result, things became calmer at McLaren, and Berger accepted his status as the number two driver. Gerhard Berger told photographer Dominique Leroy the following:

Honestly, I think Ayrton was so tired and damaged by his painful period with Alain, by all the fighting, all the controversy. So, after Alain, Ayrton didn't really care who his next teammate would be. He didn't give his opinion; he just wanted things to change. For my part, I studied him in detail because I wanted to beat him, and I learned that there were very few areas, perhaps even none, in which it was possible to beat him. He was almost perfect—disciplined, focused, very intelligent, and very talented. He had a lot of F1 experience and he had no weaknesses. A bit like Prost. When I arrived in F1, I thought I was going to be able to beat everyone. But I learned later, when we were both at McLaren, that we weren't in the same category. He was evolving in another dimension. He drove in a very intense, extreme way. His concentration was fantastic.

So, who was better, Senna or Prost?

I've always thought that Ayrton was the best driver in the history of F1. I can't compare him with Fangio and Jim Clark because that was a different era. But Senna fought against a lot of very strong drivers, like Prost, Piquet, Mansell, and so on. My judgment is also a little emotional because he was my friend. And when I spoke with Bernie Ecclestone, we agreed: The title of best of all was between Ayrton or Alain. Because Alain had to fight so hard to get where he was. He won four world titles. And he often finished 2nd in the championship.

That said, there was one area in which Berger was the number one driver in Ron Dennis's team: making jokes. One example serves to highlight this. One day, leaving a palace, the two drivers boarded a helicopter on the shores of Lake Como. As always, Ayrton took with him his perfectly organized carbon case, which never left his side. How could he have imagined that Gerhard would dare to throw it out of the door of the helicopter as it took off, to "test its sturdiness?" This first episode marked the beginning of a comic escalation between the two men, with the insertion of cheese into Berger's bedroom air-conditioning and the introduction of frogs into Senna's in Australia. The two guys got on like a house on fire, and nothing ever disturbed their complicity. Indeed, there was a royal gift at the 1991 Japanese GP, when Senna, assured of his third world title, thanked his loyal lieutenant by offering him victory, on a plate, on the last lap. The Austrian looks back on this complicity:

We had a lot of fun together, but I don't like to talk about it too much because I prefer to talk about the races: It was very hard; we were often at the limit, very professional; it was intense. When we talk about the jokes, people think we were just having fun, but in fact it was to chill, to take our minds off things. Because racing against Ayrton, in the same car, was the biggest challenge you could face at the time, and all the drivers who were his teammates can say so. I always joked with him because he liked to read the Bible before qualifying and the races. I'd show him Playboy, it was my very own Bible. And I'd say to him, "Explain to me, you're reading the Bible and then, in the first corner, if I'm in front of you, you're going to get on top of me?" It's just that when he put on his helmet, he forgot everything. There were two Ayrtons...

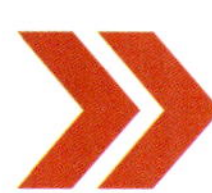

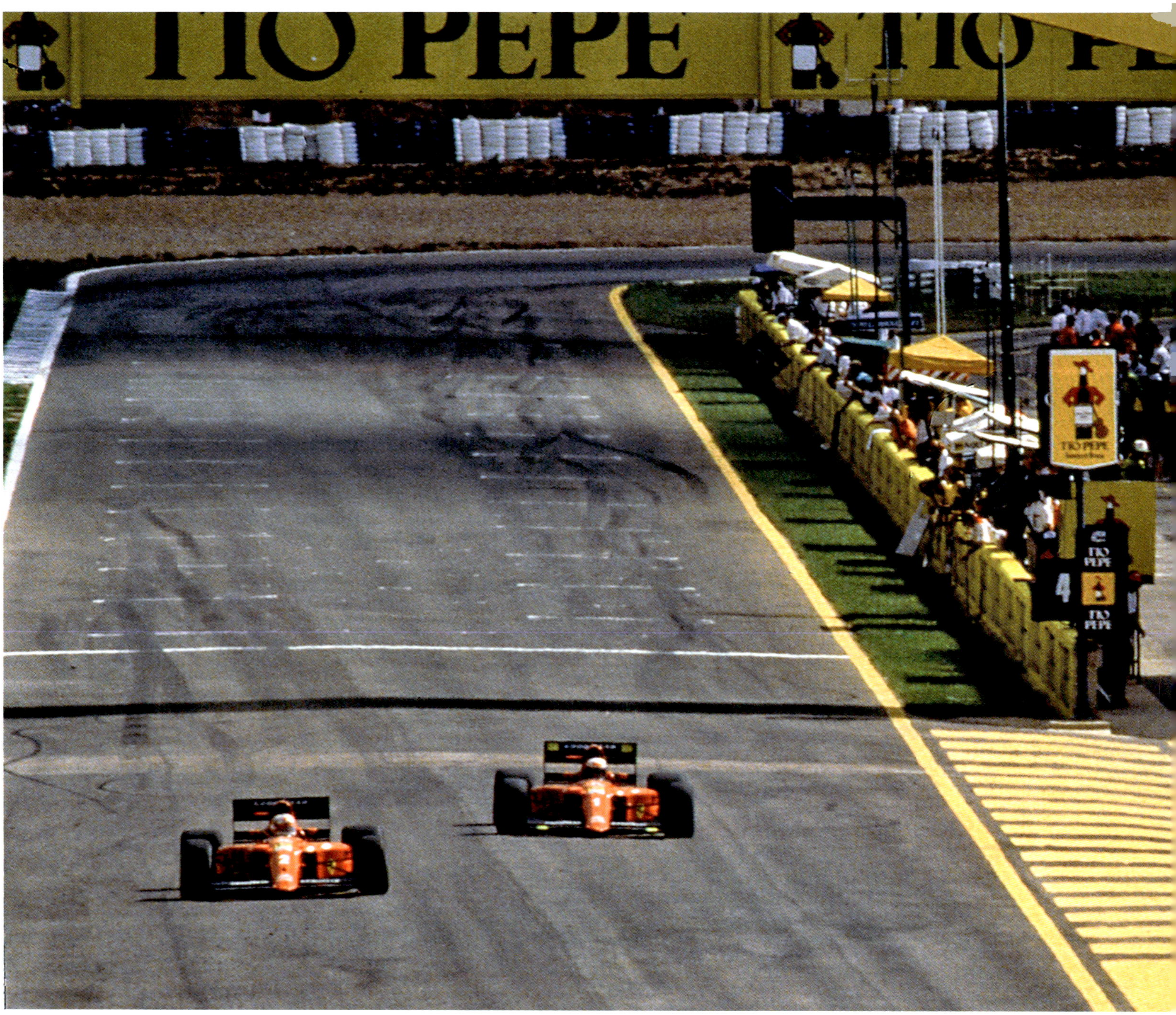

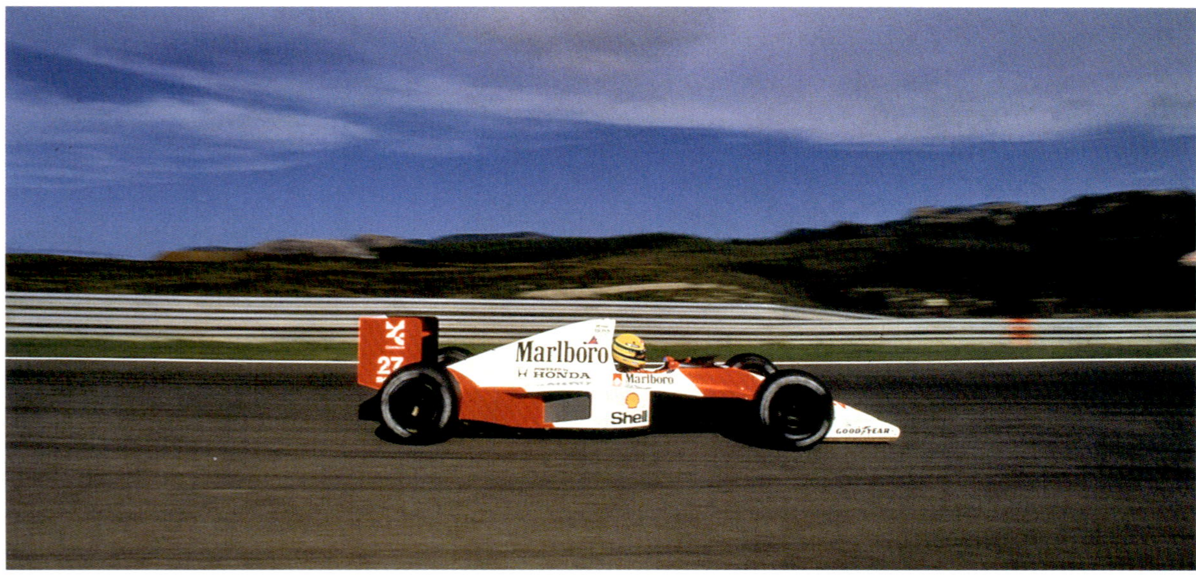
27
Marlboro
HONDA
Shell
GOODYEAR

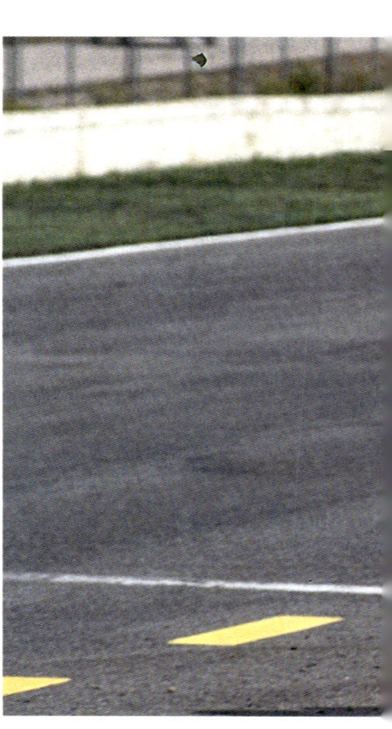

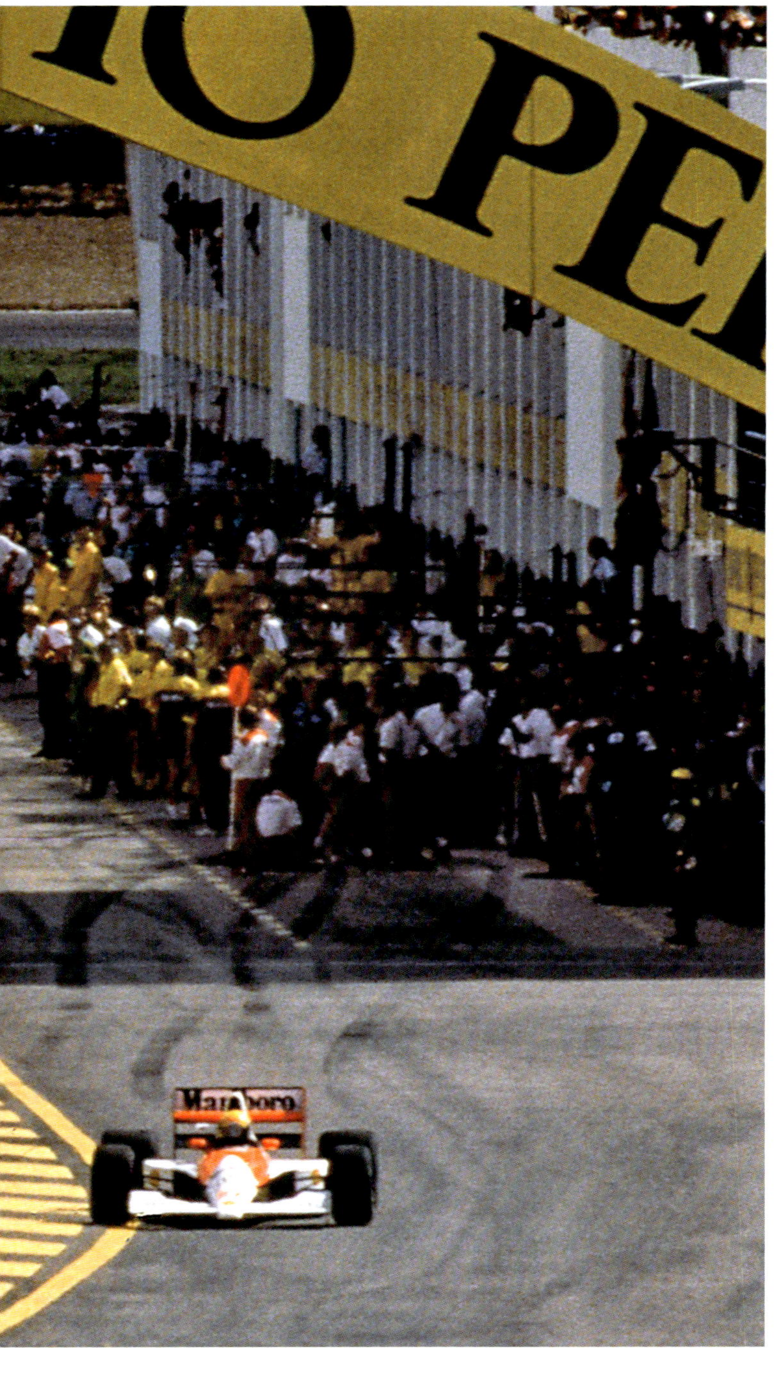

SPANISH GRAND PRIX: THE 50TH POLE, WITH MIXED EMOTIONS

It is a fine day at the Jerez de la Frontera circuit on September 28, 1990. But, fine weather notwithstanding, the Grand Prix weekend gets off to a worrying start. At 1:51 p.m., Martin Donnelly's Lotus nearly explodes in the guardrail. Under the force of the impact, the Irishman is thrown four meters from the impact zone. He is lying like a disjointed puppet. The worst is feared after this 200 km/h impact, reminiscent of the images of Gilles Villeneuve's death in 1982. Ayrton Senna is shocked by what he sees. Leo Turrini remembers the scene:

Back then, safety checks in Formula 1 were not as strict as they are today. A group of journalists, including myself, went to the scene of the accident. We met Ayrton there. He was the only driver there. Ayrton then headed for the medical center, where he closely followed what neurosurgeon Sid Watkins was doing to help the injured driver. The Brazilian knew Donnelly, having crossed paths with him in Formula 3.

According to Alberto Sabbatini, another Italian journalist, he "put his arms around Donnelly's neck as if to protect him." For a moment, he considers not racing, too affected by what he saw. The next day, however, he manages to secure his 50th pole position, but could not contain his tears in the press conference. "This pole will be unforgettable for me [...] it was difficult to understand and assimilate what had happened," he tells the media. His starting position gives Senna a chance to win the World Championship on Spanish soil. All he has to do is finish 1st. But a radiator problem forces him to withdraw, and the McLaren driver leaves victory to Alain Prost. Three weeks later, the Formula 1 grid would meet up again on the infamous Japanese track of Suzuka. And, in retrospect, little did they know what was about to happen on the Suzuka-Mie circuit.

Top left: On the Jerez de la Frontera circuit in Spain, Alain Prost and Nigel Mansell's Ferraris are too fast for Senna, securing the second double of the season.

Bottom left: The McLaren MP4/5B is extremely fast and secures Senna's 50th pole position of his career at the Spanish Grand Prix.

Bottom right: A radiator issue prevents Senna from finishing the 1990 Spanish Grand Prix, which is a stroke of luck for Riccardo Patrese, who finishes 5th in his Williams Racing car.

Top: After his collision with Prost in the first corner of the first lap at Suzuka, Senna snatches the world championship title from his French rival. The two drivers walk back to the pits without uttering a word.

Bottom: Andrea de Cesaris, the driver with 147 retirements in F1, contemplates the wreckage of Senna's McLaren and Prost's Ferrari after their collision.

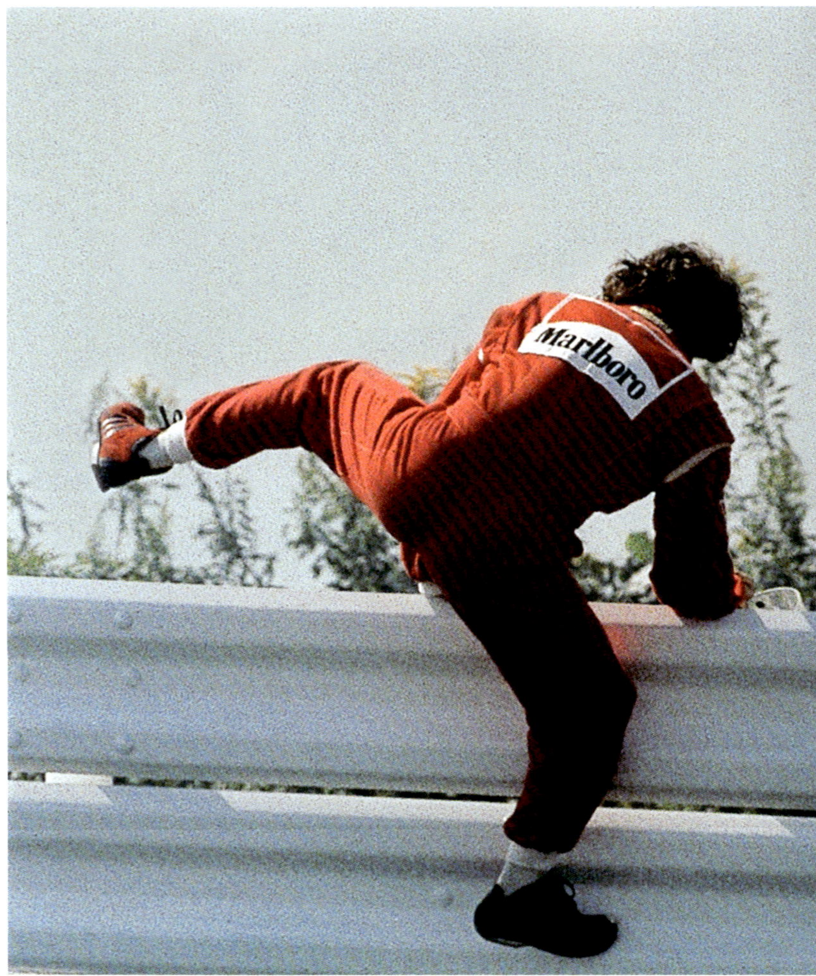

JAPAN GRAND PRIX, SUZUKA: REVENGE IS A DISH BEST SERVED COLD

Suzuka hosted another decisive round one year after the 1989 collision. In Honda's homeland, the equation is simple: If Prost doesn't finish, Senna is to be crowned champion, even before the final race in Australia. But Senna is unsettled. During testing, he spins and misses several gear changes, even though he has the latest, lighter version of the Honda engine. He has one engine for free practice, another for qualifying and yet another for the race. The tension between Prost and Senna is palpable. Many wonder if there will be another clash. As journalists discuss pole position and the first corner, Senna tells them: "It's impossible to overtake here. If Prost tries, we'll be in a difficult situation." The qualifying session gives a foretaste of the race. Senna and Prost are head-to-head, lap after lap, but Senna is once again the stronger. Well played...or maybe not. The Brazilian observes that pole position is on the right-hand side of the track, on the so-called "dirty" side. No matter how good his impulse is, it doesn't necessarily guarantee that he will remain first. Prost starts on the "clean" side. Senna insists on changing the pole position. Nothing is done. To add fuel to the fire, Piquet brings up the Casio chicane again, the one that cost Senna the title a year ago. He wants the chicane to be "open." The other drivers agree, much to Senna's annoyance. He leaves the briefing very angry. The scene is captured on Japanese television. Ayrton's nerves are on edge. He would later explain: "I've been screwed [sic] too many times by the system, so I said to myself: Today, it's not possible. I'll do it my way."

At the start, as predicted, Prost gets the better of Senna and enters the first corner. Senna, still on the inside, doesn't slow down...and crashes into the rear of the Frenchman's Ferrari. The 1990 World Championship ends nine seconds after the start of the penultimate round. The Brazilian unloads his anger and frustration on the Italian car, and both cars end up in the tire wall. They emerge from their cockpits, their eyes never meeting. Prost gives up the idea of "punching Senna in the face." His great rival returns to the pits with his head bowed after this "hara-kiri" in mondovision. Known for being sometimes flamboyant, sometimes rough, Senna has just shown his darker side in front of his adoring Japanese fans. The rest of the race remains a mere anecdote. Piquet wins and local hero Aguri Suzuki takes 3rd place on the podium. McLaren also clinches the constructors' world title, ahead of Ferrari. But on that Sunday, October 21, 1990, the whole of Formula 1 lost.

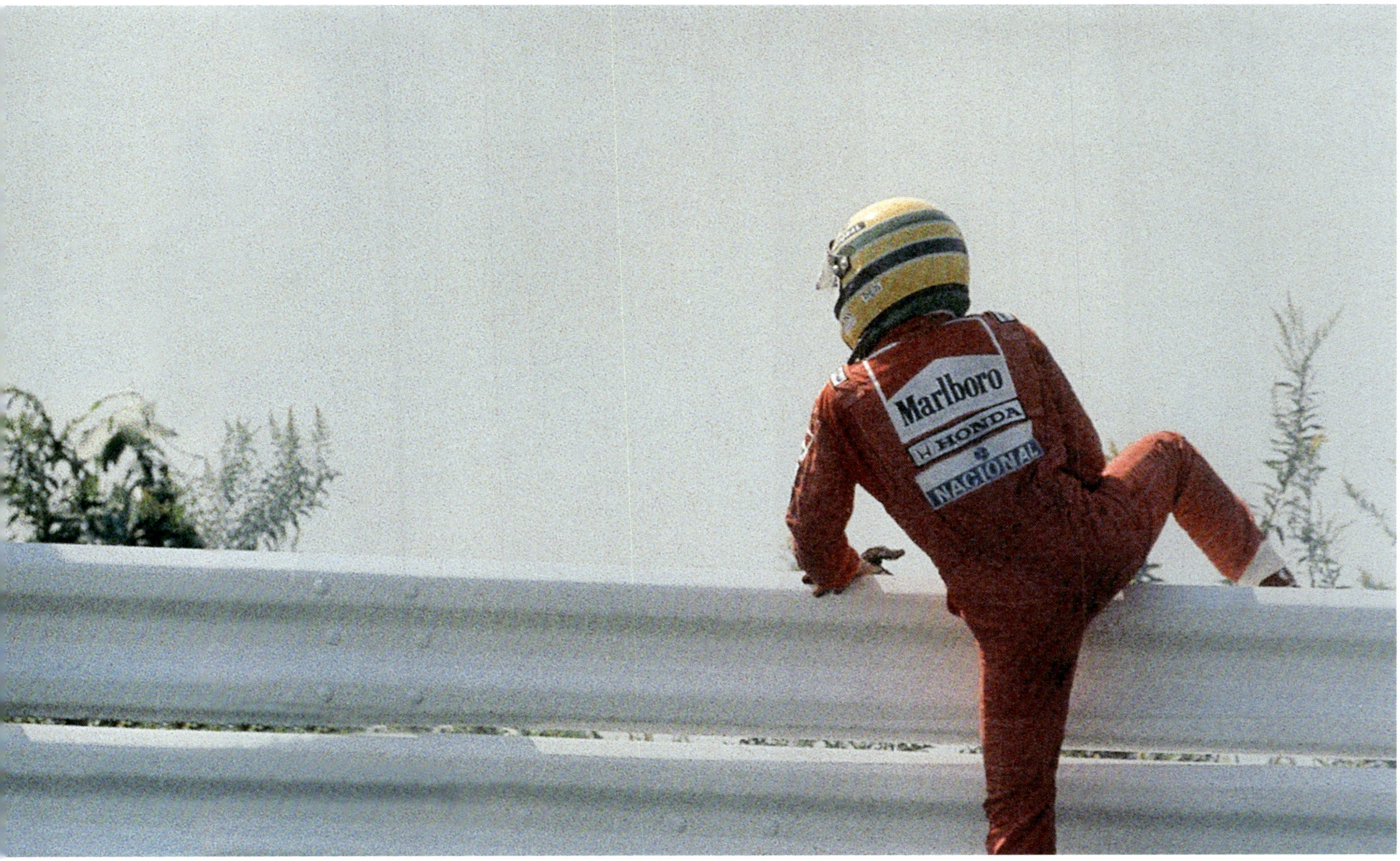
Marlboro
HONDA
NACIONAL

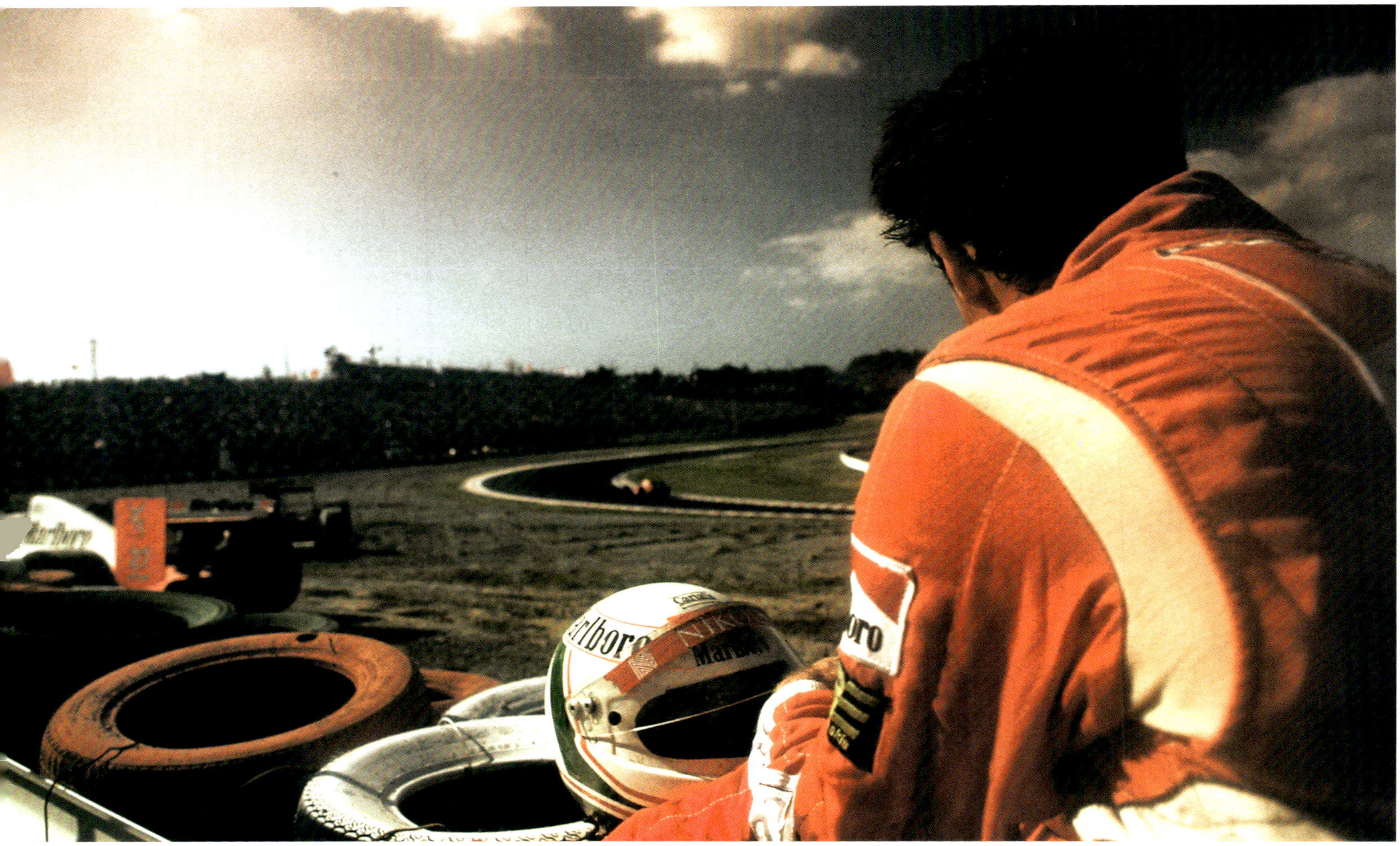

ON TRACK FOR THE TITLE **1990**

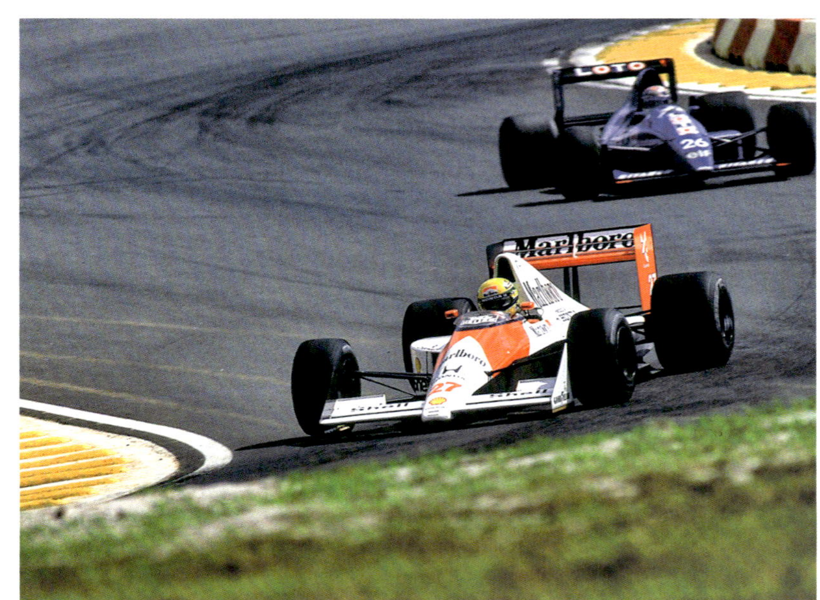

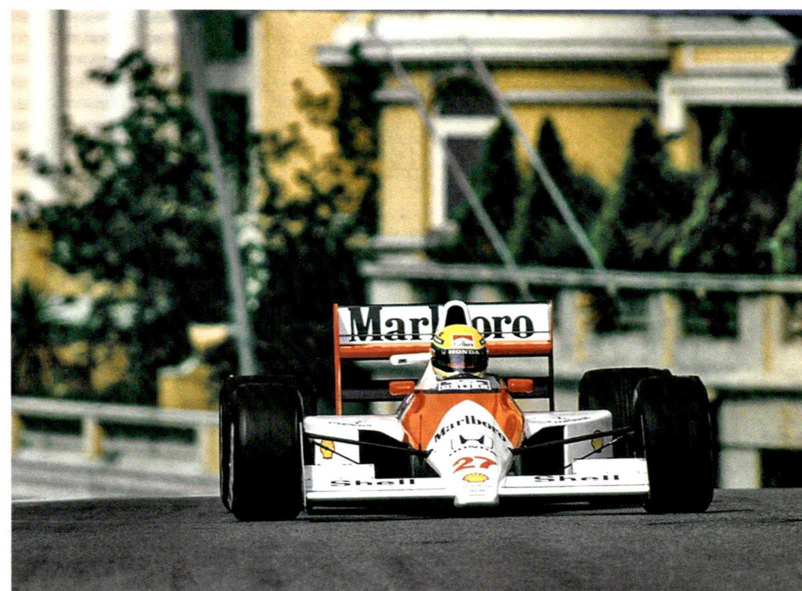

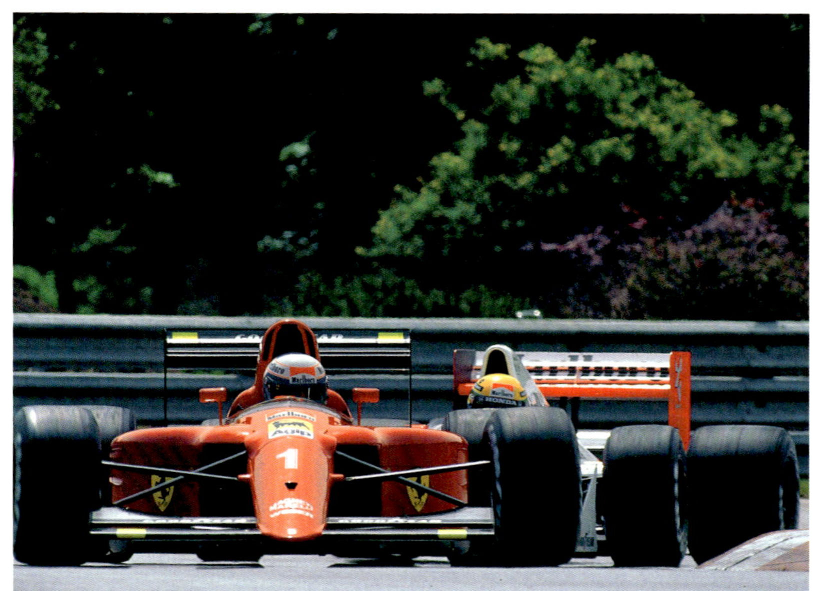

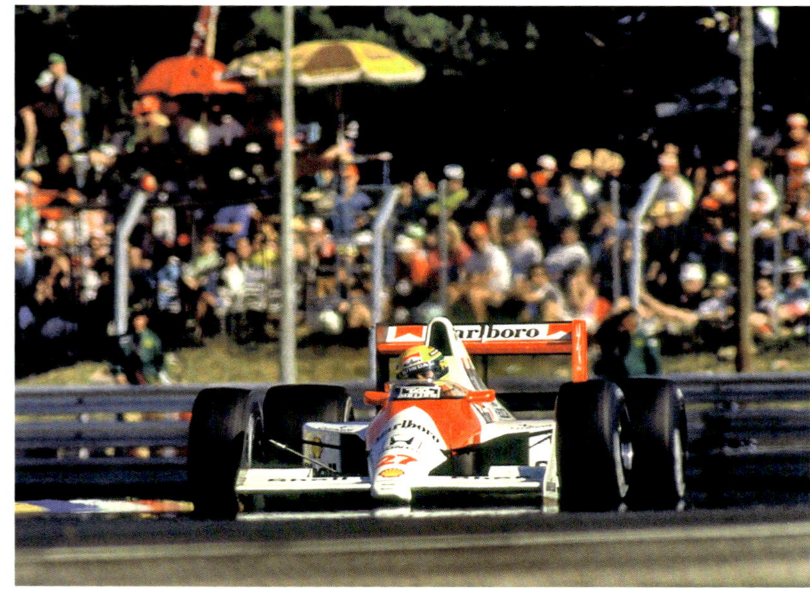

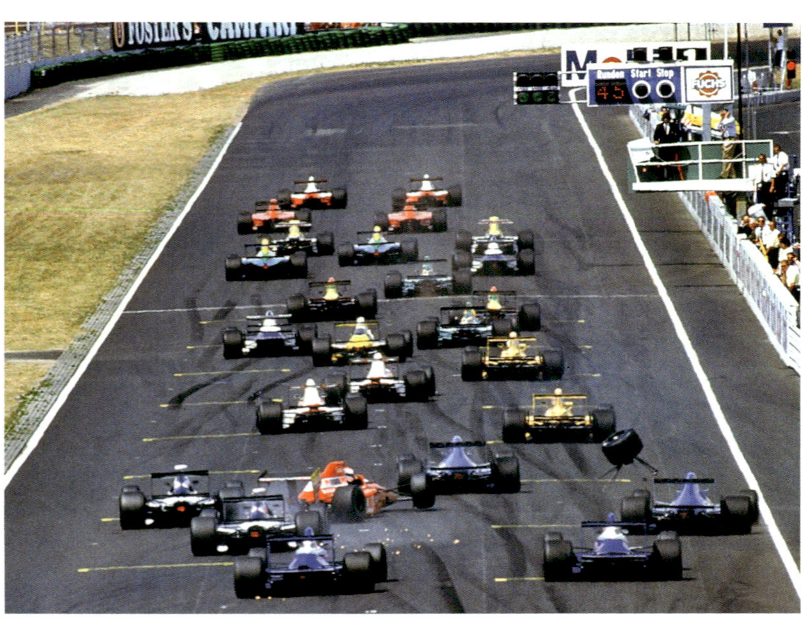

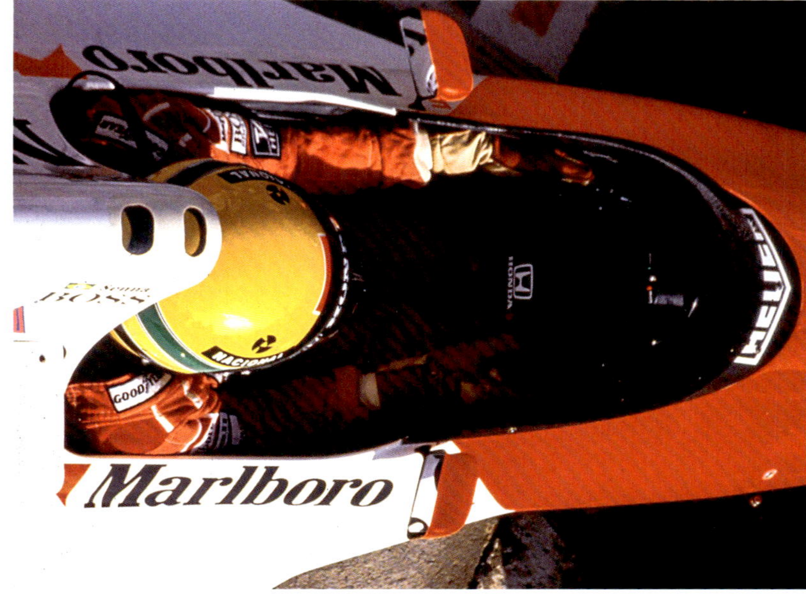

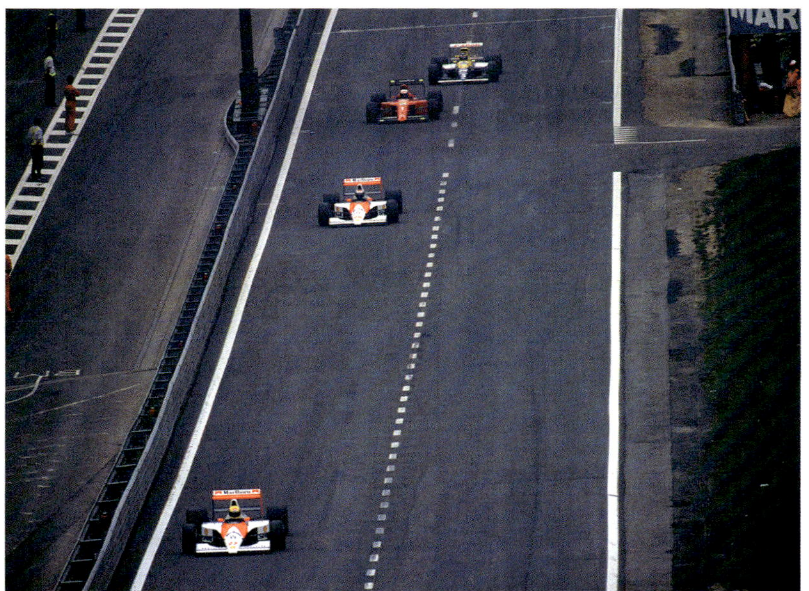

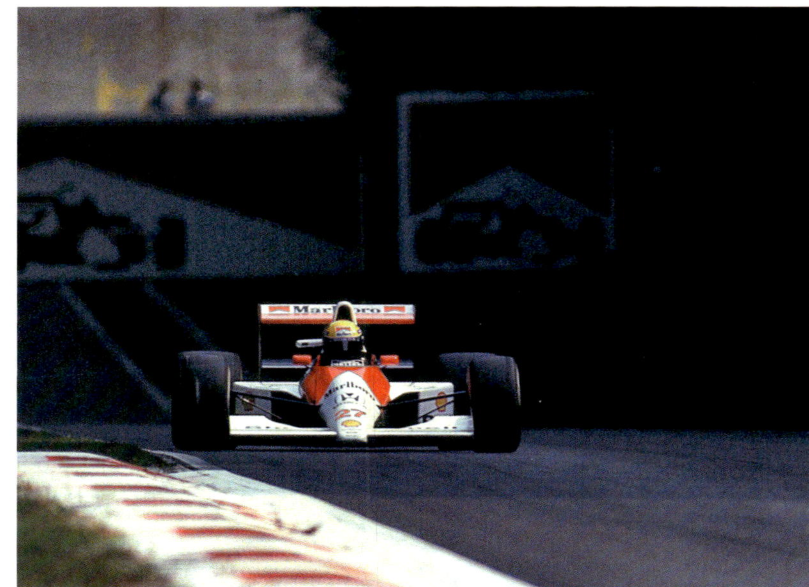

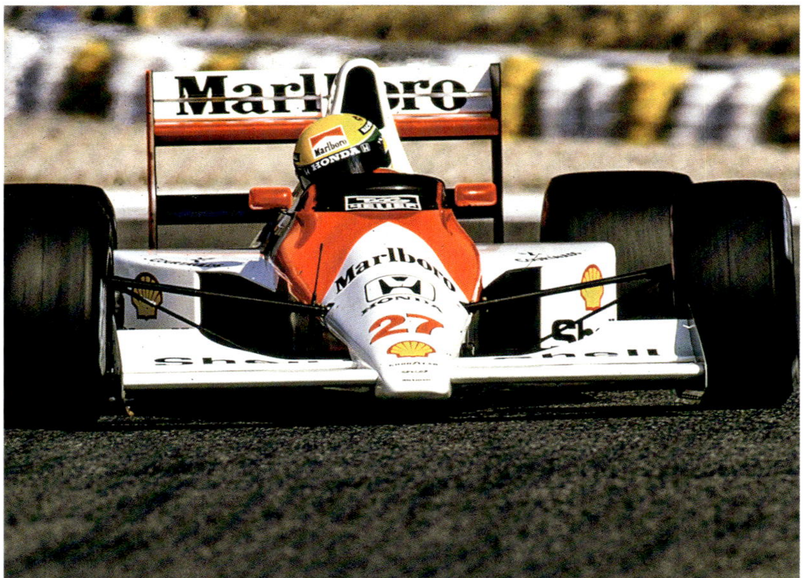

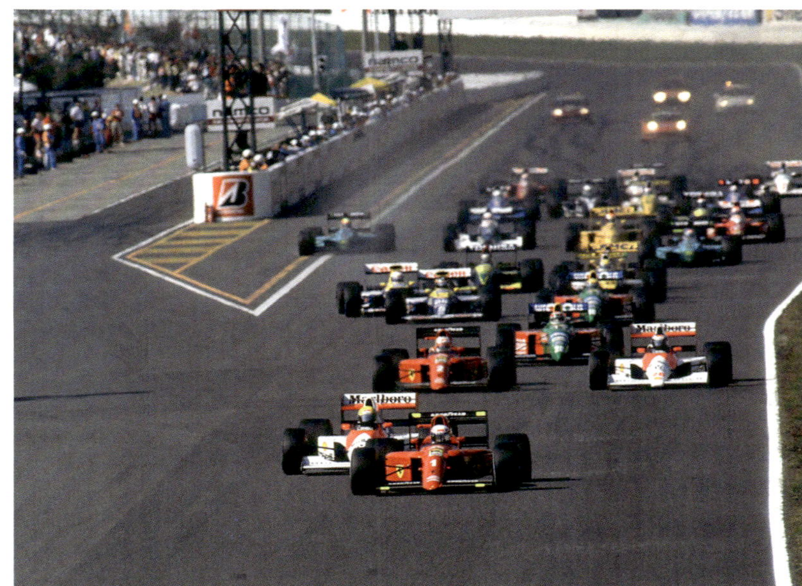

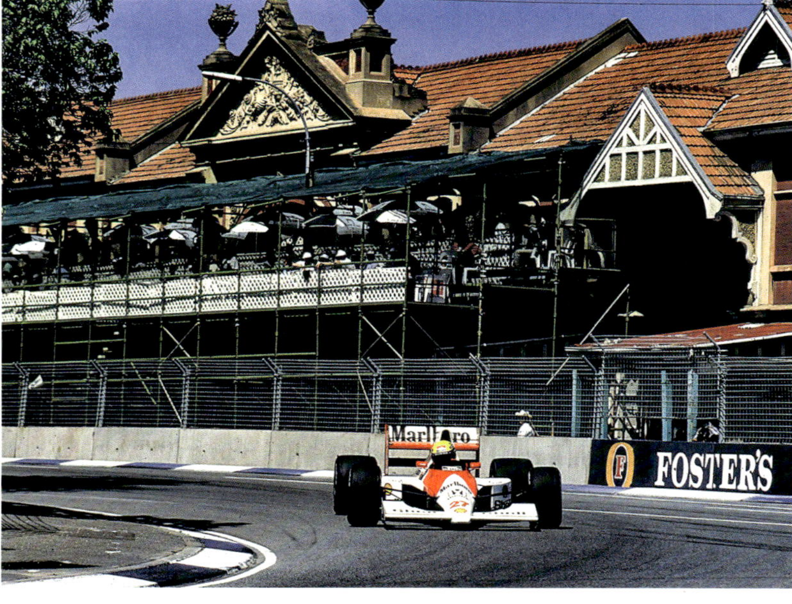

McLaren and Senna did everything in their power to beat Prost and Ferrari until the controversial conclusion of this rivalry at the 1990 Japanese Grand Prix.

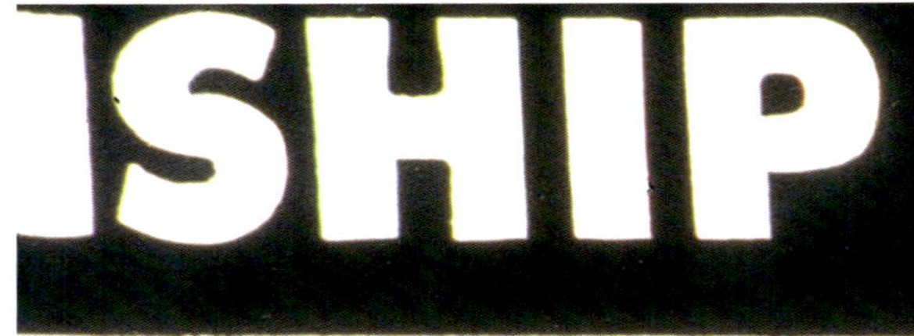

Below: In his world of speed and precision, Senna left nothing to chance. After donning his yellow helmet, the Brazilian became completely unshakeable.

Right: Despite their allegiance to Prost (2nd place, on the left), the tifosi congratulate Senna and Berger (3rd place, on the right), who also drive for Ferrari.

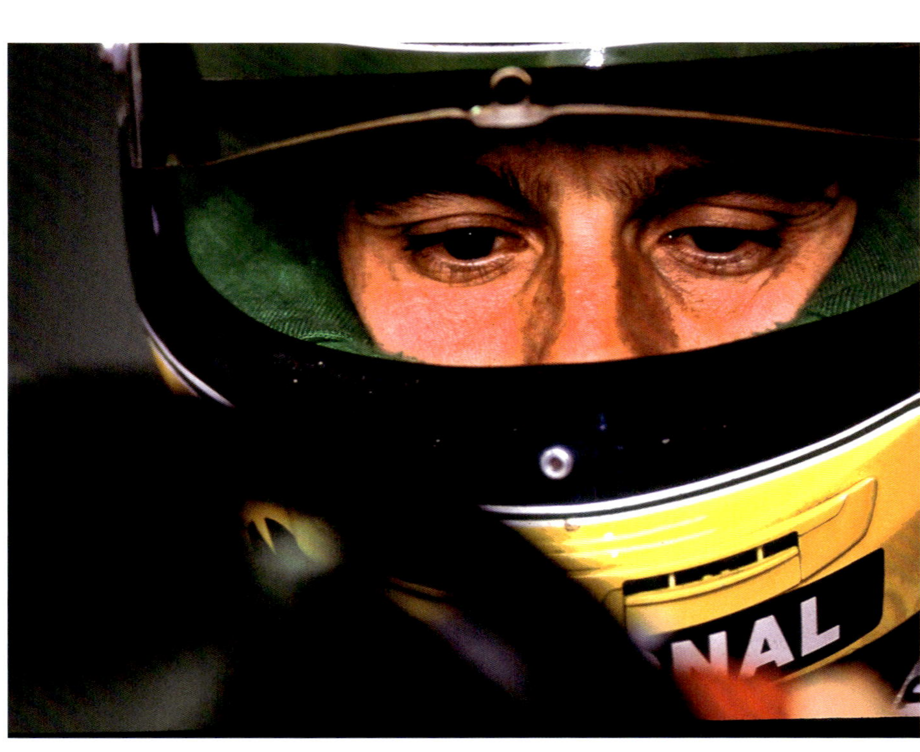

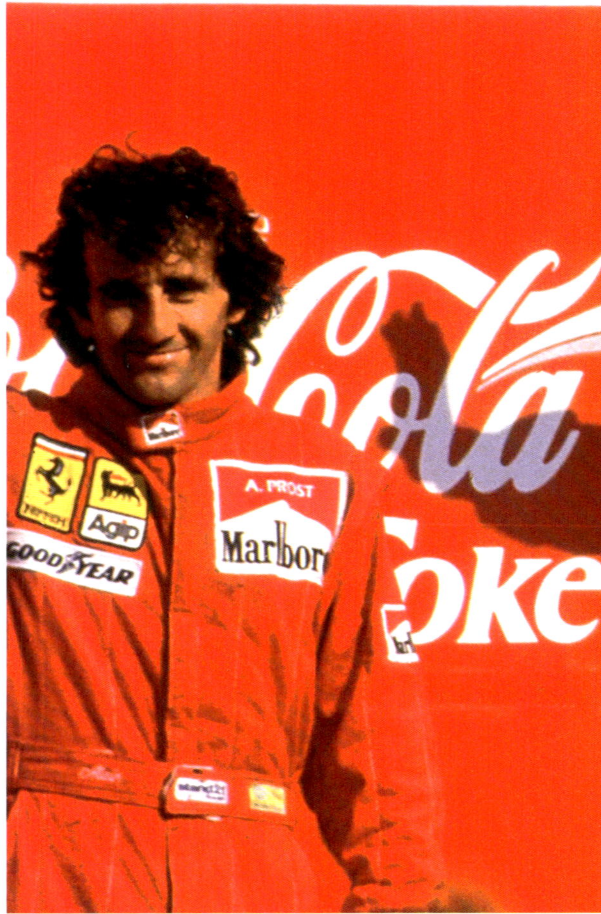

THE 1990 SEASON IN FIGURES

GRAND PRIX	QUALIFIERS	RACE
UNITED STATES	5TH	VICTORY 21
BRAZIL	POLE POSITION 43	3RD
SAN MARINO	POLE POSITION 44	DNF (WHEEL)
MONACO	POLE POSITION 45	VICTORY 22
CANADA	POLE POSITION 46	VICTORY 23
MEXICO	3RD	20TH (PUNCTURE)
FRANCE	3RD	3RD
GREAT BRITAIN	2ND	3RD
GERMANY	POLE POSITION 47	VICTORY 24
HUNGARY	4TH	2ND

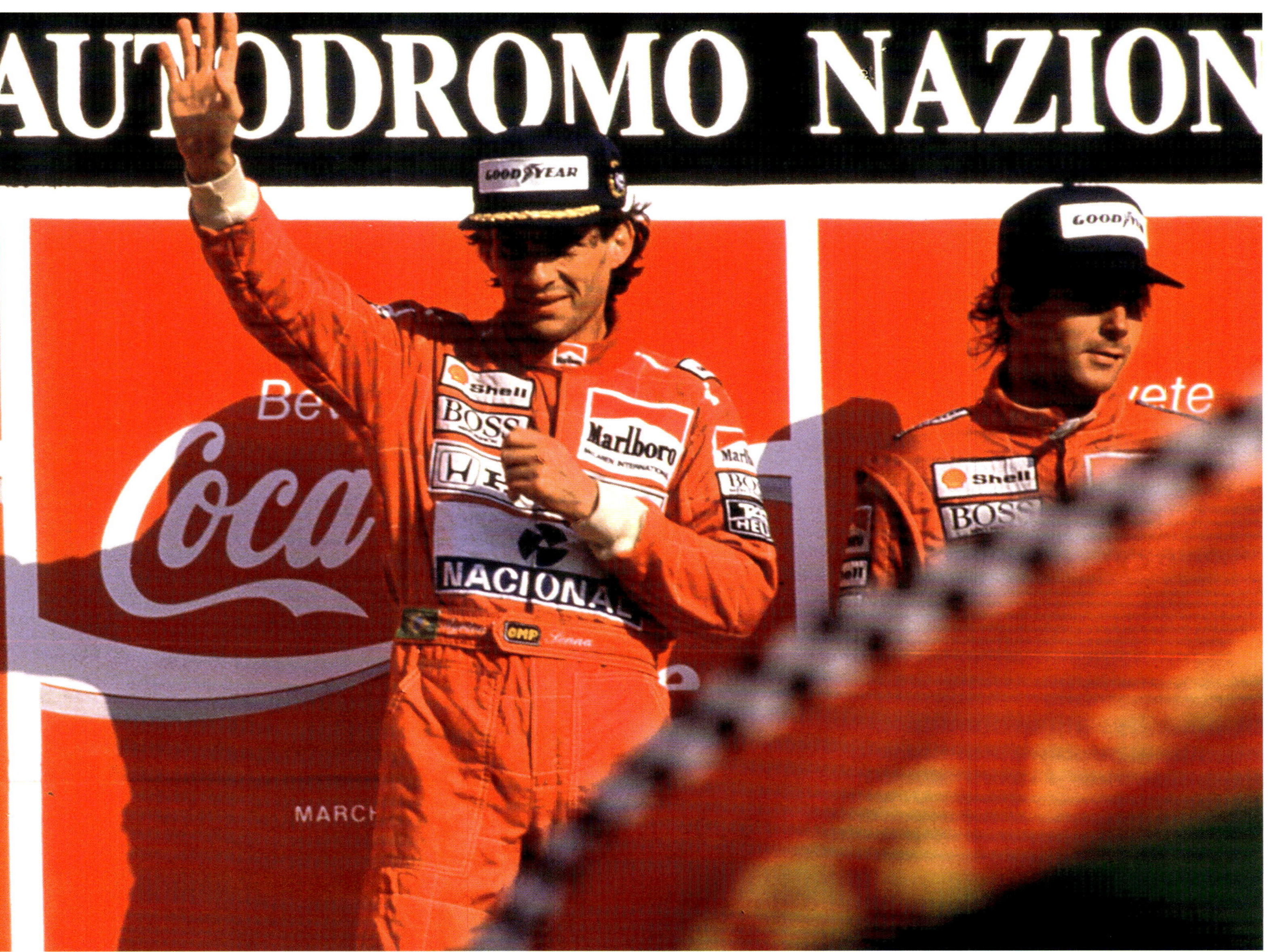

GRAND PRIX	QUALIFIERS	RACE
BELGIUM	POLE POSITION 48	VICTORY 25
ITALY	POLE POSITION 49	VICTORY 26
PORTUGAL	3RD	2ND
SPAIN	POLE POSITION 50	DNF (RADIATOR)
JAPAN	POLE POSITION 51	DNF (CRASH WITH PROST)
AUSTRALIA	POLE POSITION 52	DNF (CRASH)

FORMULA 1 WORLD CHAMPION
(78 POINTS, 11 BEST RESULTS, 6 VICTORIES, 11 PODIUMS, 10 POLE POSITIONS, 2 BEST LAPS)

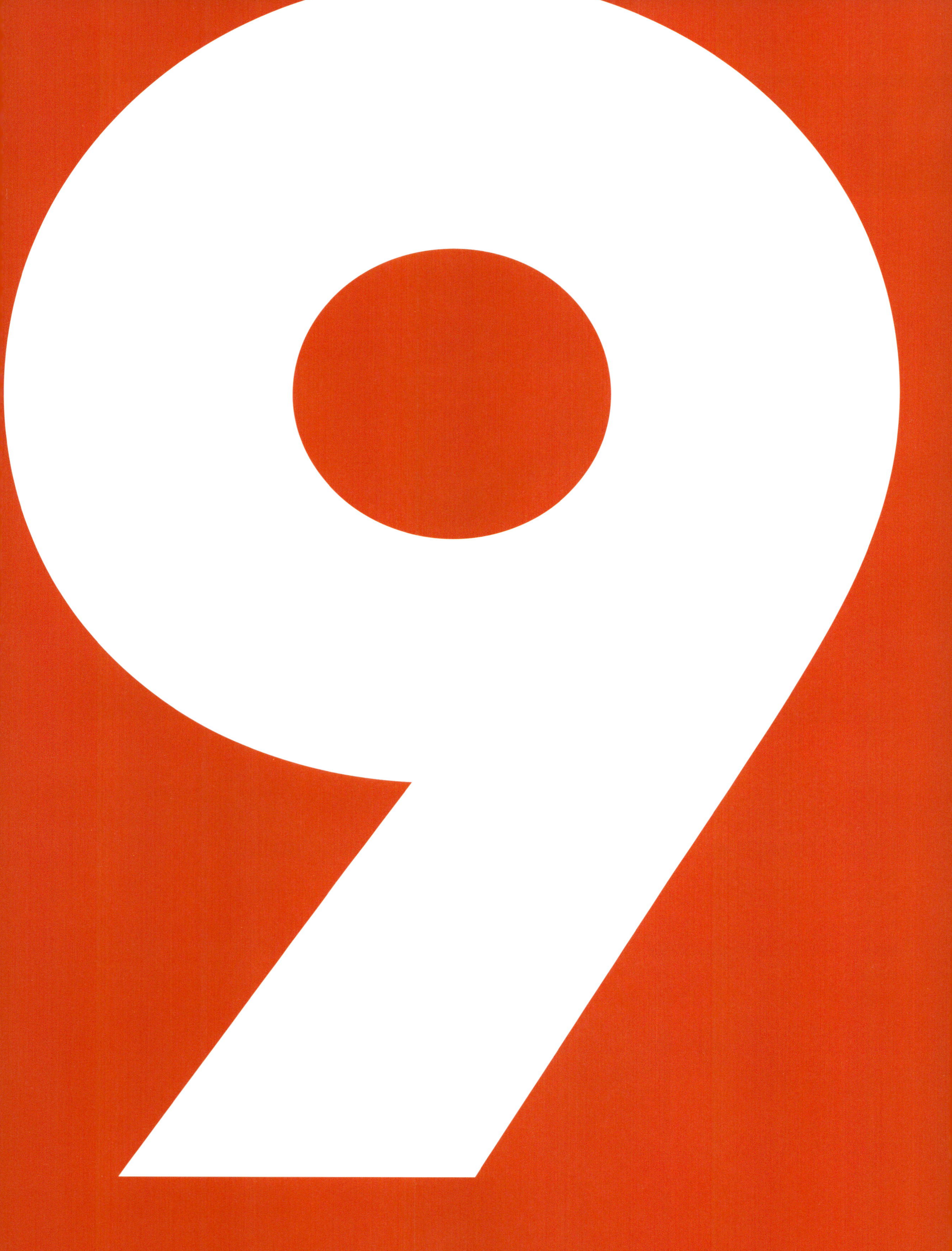

SENNA AT THE TOP

AN EASIER THIRD TITLE

THE SMALL FERRARI'S DOMINANCE WAS OVER. AT LEAST TEMPORARILY, AND ALAIN PROST COULD DO NOTHING ABOUT IT.

The Scuderia failed to achieve good results in 1991. The Suzuka collision at the end of the previous season preceded this. Neither Ferrari's two French drivers, Alain Prost (fifth in the championship, five podiums) nor Jean Alesi (seventh), managed to win a single race. The Williams-Renault team stepped up to the plate thanks to Nigel Mansell, who made life difficult for the McLaren drivers. The British won five races, including three in a row in the middle of summer (the French, British, and German Grand Prix), to come within eight points of the Brazilians, who had won the first four rounds. But he collapsed in Japan, crashing out of the gravel trap on lap 10, all on his own. This incident, which occurred one race before the end of the season in Japan, was enough to secure a third-world title for Senna. The final score was impressive in terms of points (96 to 72) but not in terms of victories (six for Senna, five for Mansell). The Brazilian's main achievement was winning this new title with a car that was anything but dominant. He fulfilled his usual specifications by securing as many pole positions (eight), victories (seven), and podiums (12) as possible, given the level of the competition. We didn't know it yet, but it was the beginning of McLaren's decline, according to the law of cycles that has always marked F1. Senna, having won three crowns in four seasons, had joined the ranks of the greats, including Alain Prost. However, Prost would regain his lead two years later.

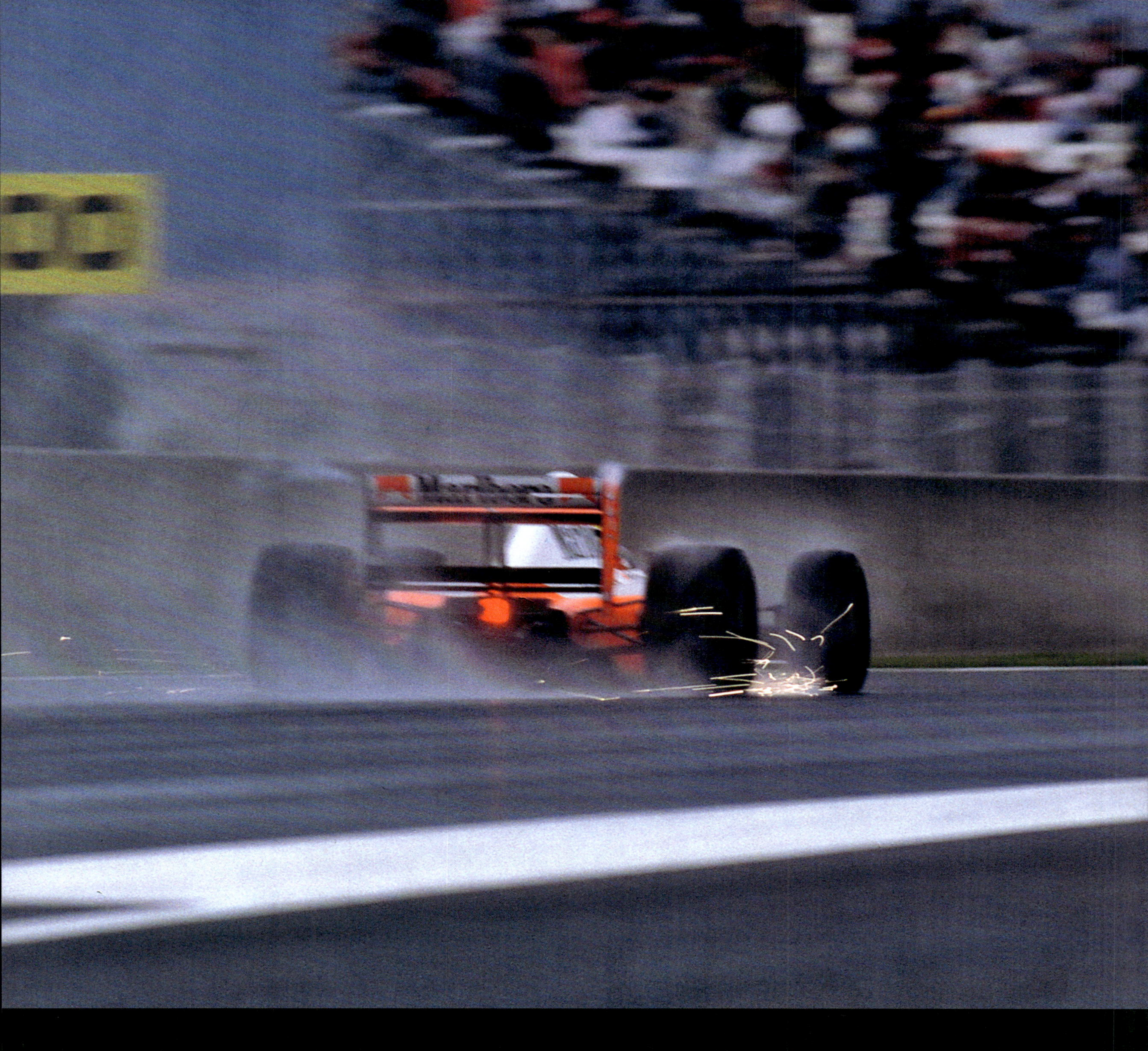

In 1991, rain will not prevent Senna from making sparks, and even in the face of adversity from Williams-Renault, he will be crowned world champion for the

RACE AFTER RACE

1991

BRAZIL GRAND PRIX: THE FIRST AND THE BEST

Winning at home has long been Senna's wish. Ever since his F1 debut in 1984, he has dreamed of winning in his homeland. The weekend began with weather conditions typical of the Brazilian GP: the characteristic, romantic rain—known as chuva in the language of Vasco de Gama—arrives. Senna was like a fish in water, even though he didn't like the weather. Nuno Cobra, his long-time physical and mental trainer, recalls: "I used to ask Ayrton, "How do you manage to drive in the rain? Can you see anything? What do you do to get such a head start in the race?" He'd say, "I hate it. All I do is follow the tire tracks, but I can't see a thing!" The Brazilian knew full well that all eyes would be on him for the next three days. And, as if touched by grace, he splashed the Interlagos circuit with his talent and courage, getting off to a flying start in practice. With just a few minutes to go in one of the sessions, he asked his mechanics to harden the rear suspensions. The strategy paid off: he improved his lap time. According to the Brazilian, this decision was based on intuition. For others, it was just a man on a mission.

On Saturday, during the qualifying round, Senna outperforms everyone else. He repeats this feat. With four minutes to go, he clocks a time of 1'16"392, almost four-tenths ahead of Riccardo Patrese. His time was almost one second slower than his teammate Gerhard Berger's time. A photo capturing Nigel Mansell's wide-eyed reaction as he glimpses Senna's time on the control screens serves as a testament to Senna's performance. In 1986, Senna finished second at Jacarepaguá, his best performance to date in his home GP, behind his great rival Nelson Piquet. His expectations were high, and his frustration was palpable, especially considering that Prost had already secured six victories on Brazilian soil.

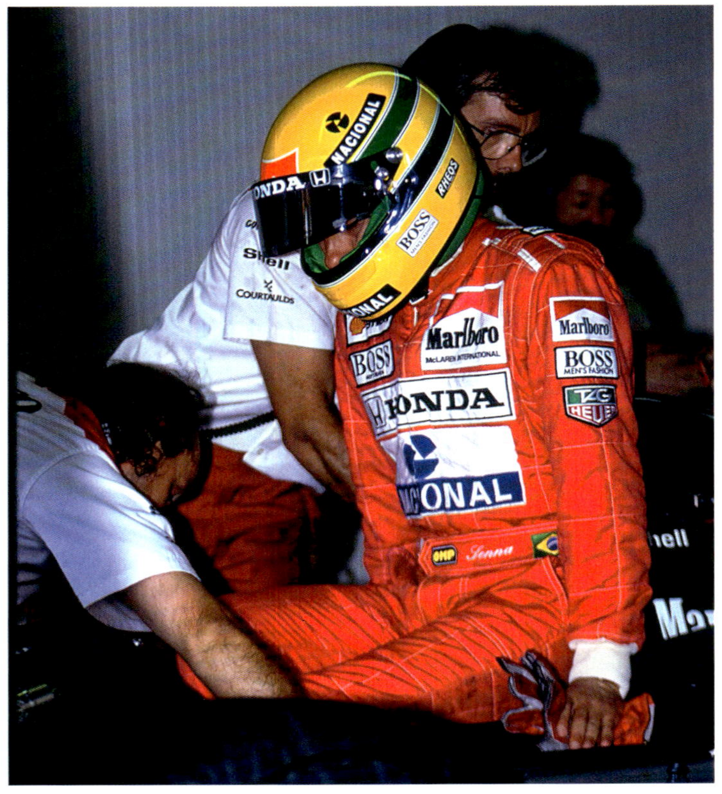

Final adjustments by teammates before getting behind the wheel for the race.

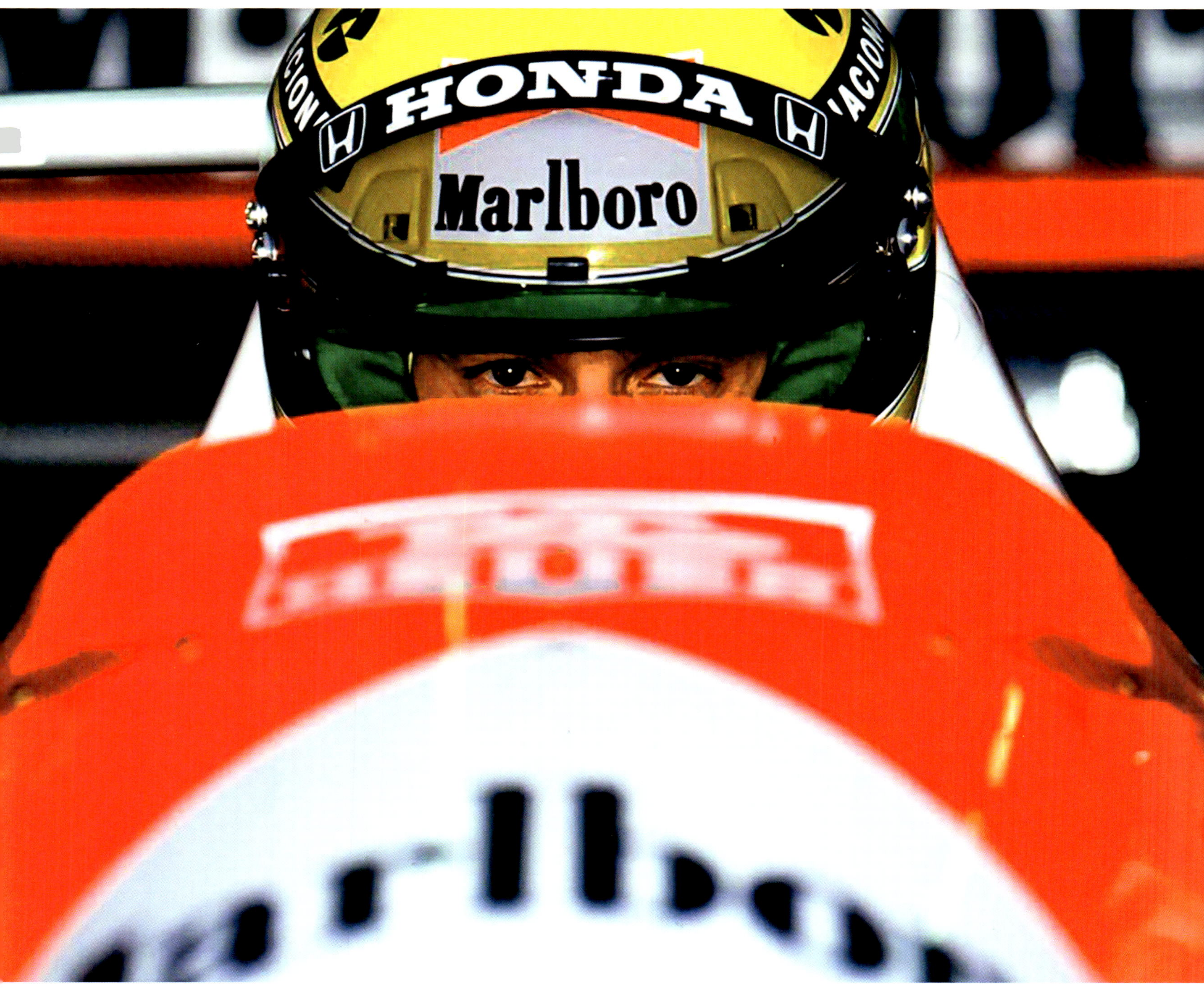

Before starting the engine of his McLaren, Senna has only one goal in mind—to win the race.

However, he was going to have to go to the very depths of his soul to achieve the victory he had longed for. With 71 laps to go, Senna starts "his" Grand Prix from pole position for the fifth time. Hoping for a happier outcome than in the past. The asphalt at Interlagos was dry at the start of the race, but meteorologists were forecasting potential rain showers that could turn the race upside down. In front of his home crowd, the Paulist had a perfect start. He quickly took command of the race and never relinquished it, even under threat from the Williams of his pursuers: Mansell and Patrese.

He lost fourth gear on his McLaren with 20 laps to go. Then, with seven laps left, he lost the second, third, and fifth gears. A nightmare just as victory was in his grasp. McLaren's engineer, Steve Hallam, was on the pit wall at Interlagos. He remembers the moment well: "He was calm at first. But on the wall, we were all anxious. We couldn't see much or understand what was going on. When a driver announces that he has this type of problem with a manual gearbox, he has some idea of what he can do. Ayrton was able to find the strength to keep the car on track. He was able to use the brakes more to try and 'save'

the gearbox. I don't think there's ever been a better driver than Ayrton in this area. For many drivers, this situation would have been the end of the world."
On Rede Globo, nobody suspected what was going on. And the channel only had eyes for the McLaren driver. At the old La Cinq channel, only Patrick Tambay and Jean-Louis Moncet managed to guess what was happening, as they noticed Senna not downshifting on the onboard cameras. FISA President Jean-Marie Balestre, who was a guest in the studio, later rewarded this observation by granting the channel exclusive rights to broadcast the drivers' briefing for the San Marino GP.

Returning to the race, Senna was struggling with his car and experiencing excruciating pain in his hand and back. This was a situation he had encountered before, and Nuno Cobra had taught him how to manage it. The Paulist's trainer recalls: "He has acquired a mental depth that few people, however athletic, achieve. He entered a unique and very powerful zone of mental control. Ayrton sought this in the depths of his soul and of his being. He was always striving to surpass himself and could continue to drive even if his arms were out of power and his breath was short."

The final laps were grueling. Senna inquired about the position of his pursuers and let out a shout. Then, as if a sign from heaven, the rain began to fall, and everyone was frozen in position. Patrese was too far behind and no longer had a chance to win. "I remember him asking for help on the radio. He was in a lot of pain. The problem for him was that he was so close to the end of the race. A lot of things seemed to be going against him winning that race, but it was a great triumph! As for his cries, there was pain, of course, but also relief and satisfaction at winning that race. He wanted so much to celebrate that victory; it was so important to him," Hallam recalls with a tremor in his voice three decades later. Cramped, Ayrton was escorted back to his pit in the medical car. "When the last few laps came around, I said to myself, 'If I make it, it will be with blood, sweat, and tears.'" I've been fighting for this victory for years. It had to happen. It was a day I'll remember for the rest of my life," said the emotional "King of Brazil," as he was dubbed by the Brazilian press the following day.

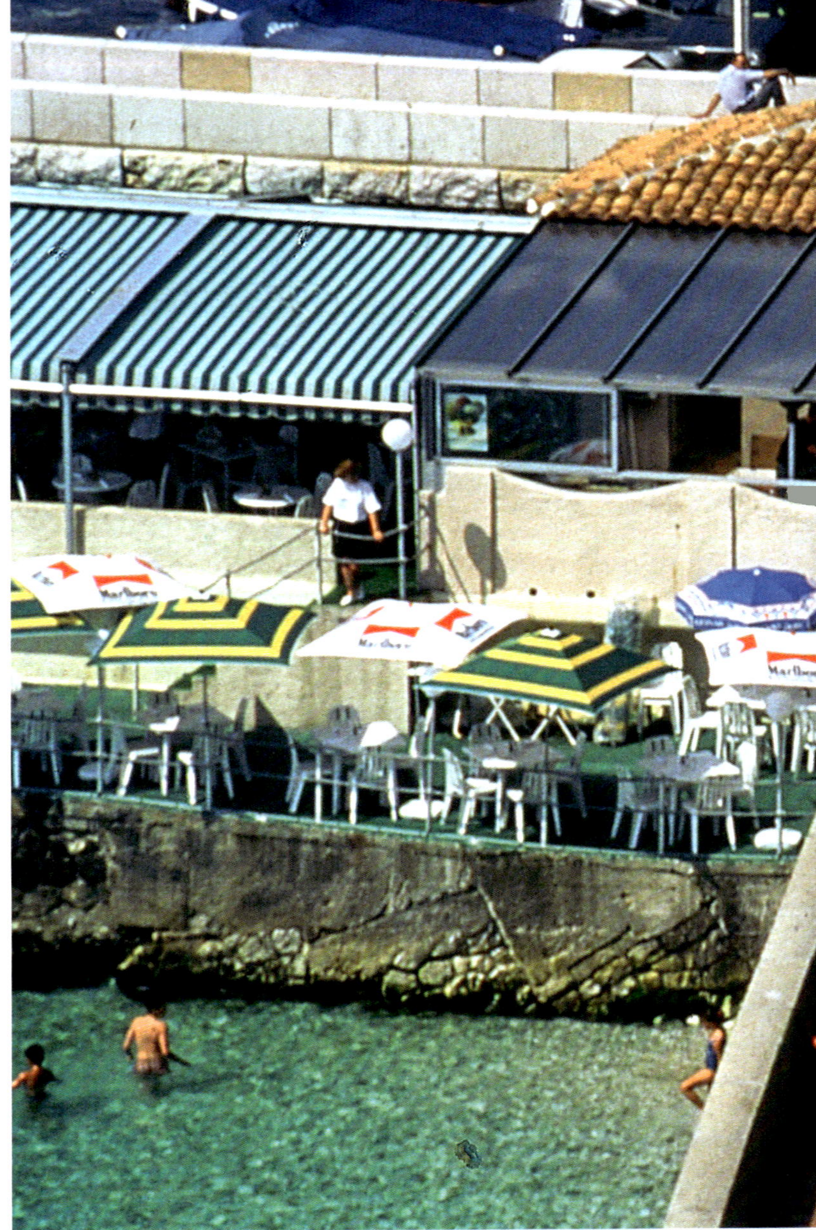

The grandstands celebrated en masse, as did the track marshals. On the podium, Patrese was second, and Berger was third. But the crowd had eyes only for its double champion. Despite his grimaces of pain, he found the strength to lift one of his finest trophies in front of a crowd completely behind him. Three days after his 31st birthday, Ayrton Senna had made his dream come true.

Top: In 1991, the streets of Monaco hold no secrets for the Brazilian world champion and allow him to win the Monaco Grand Prix for the fourth time in his career.

Bottom: Whether on a yacht or in the stands, the spectators of the principality are amazed by Senna's talent.

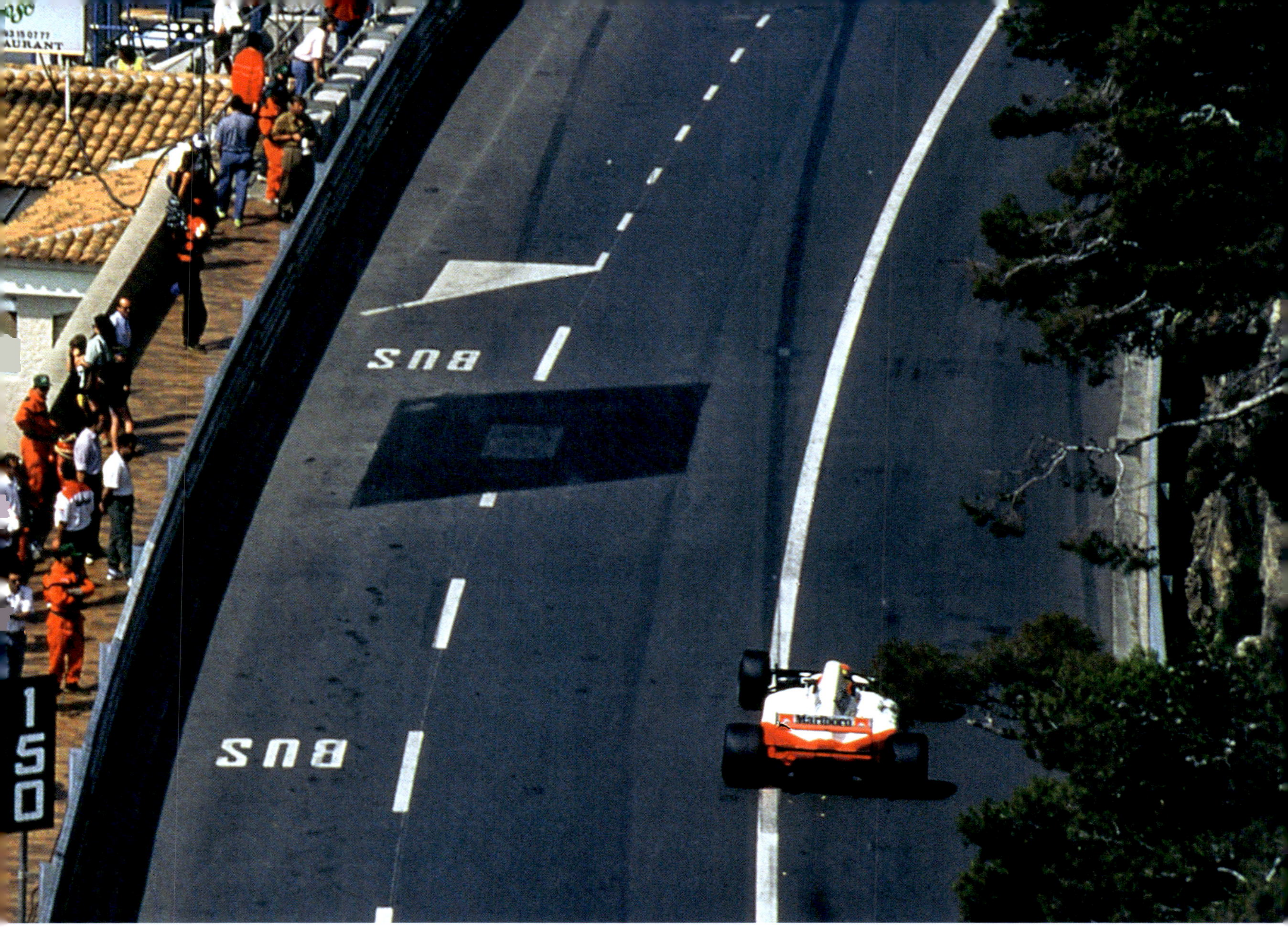

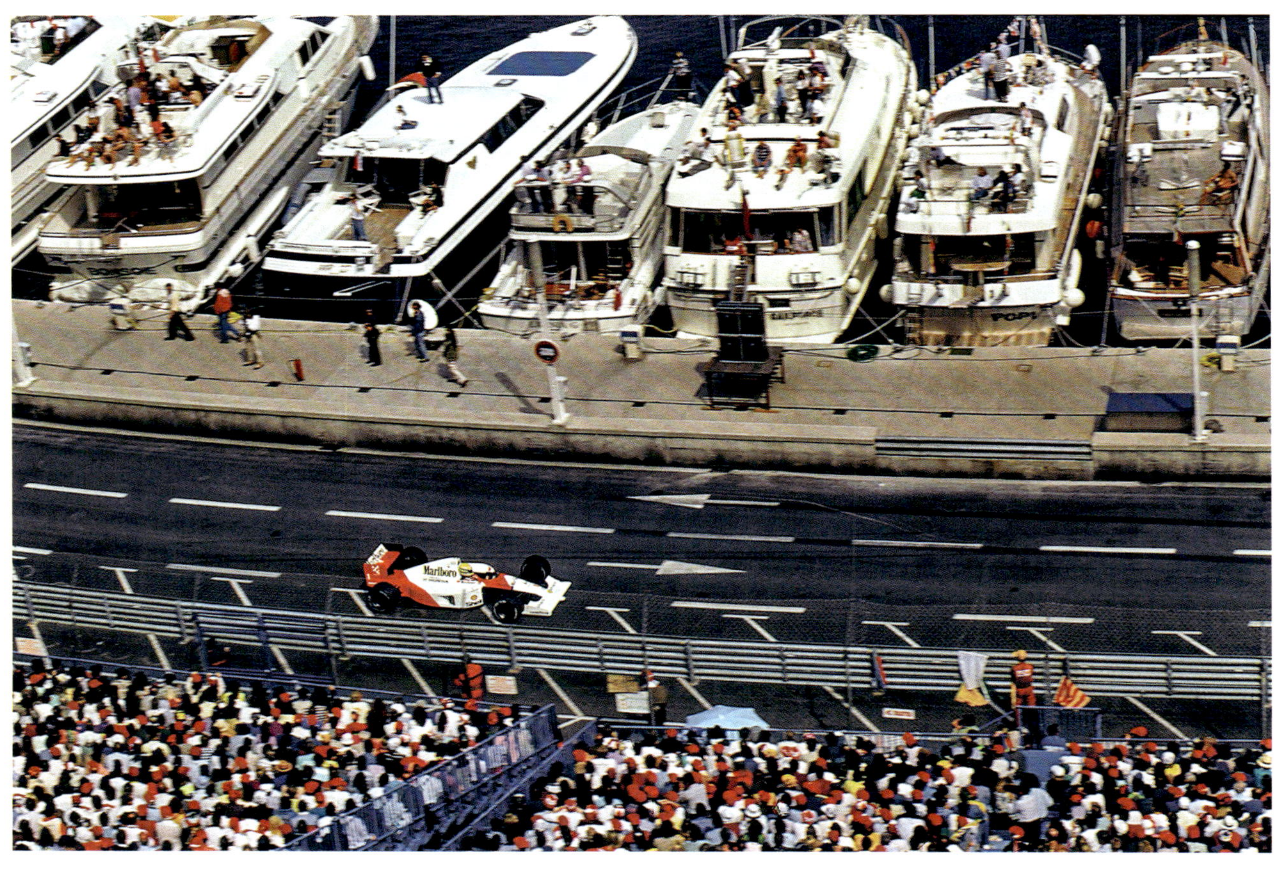

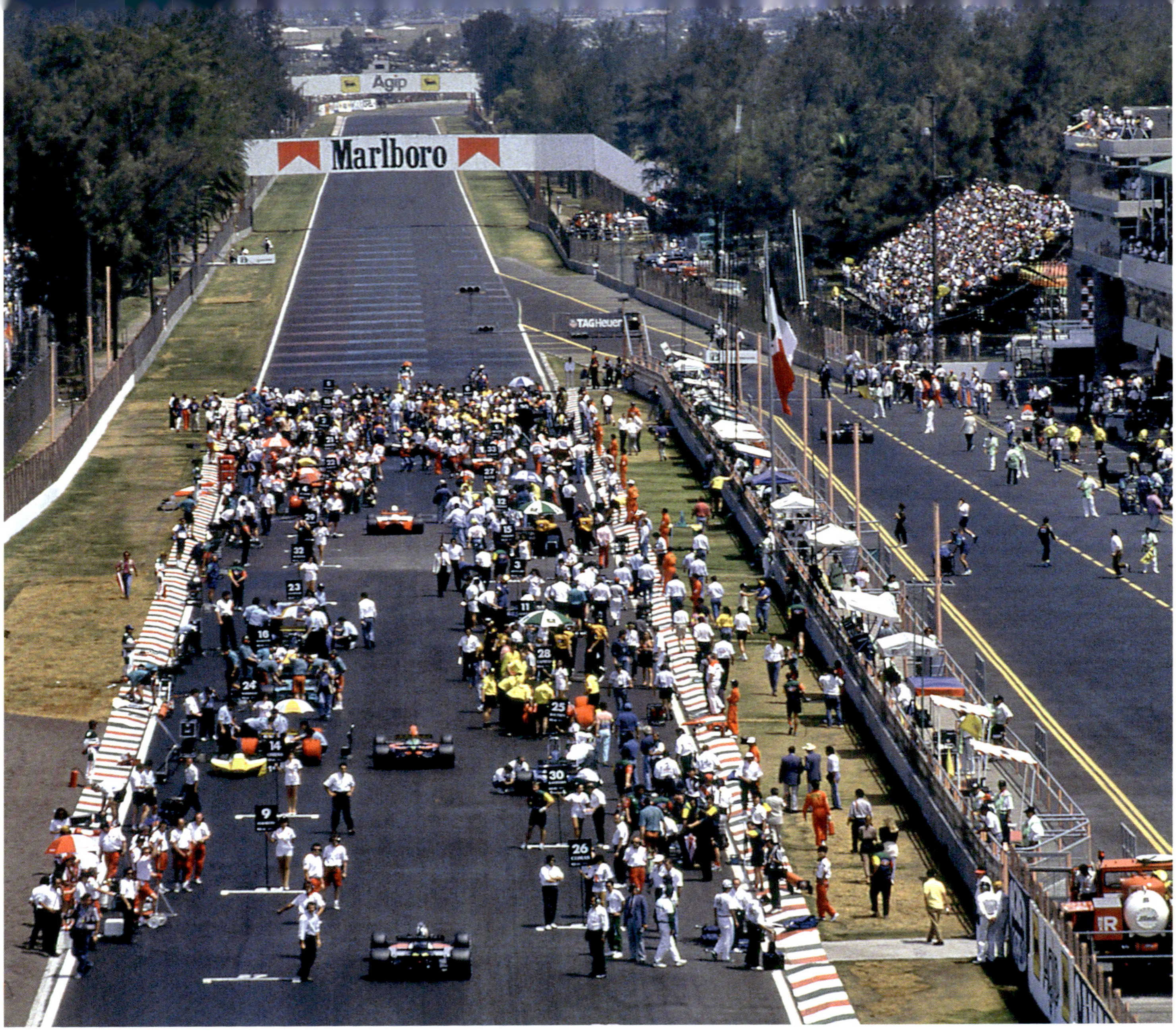

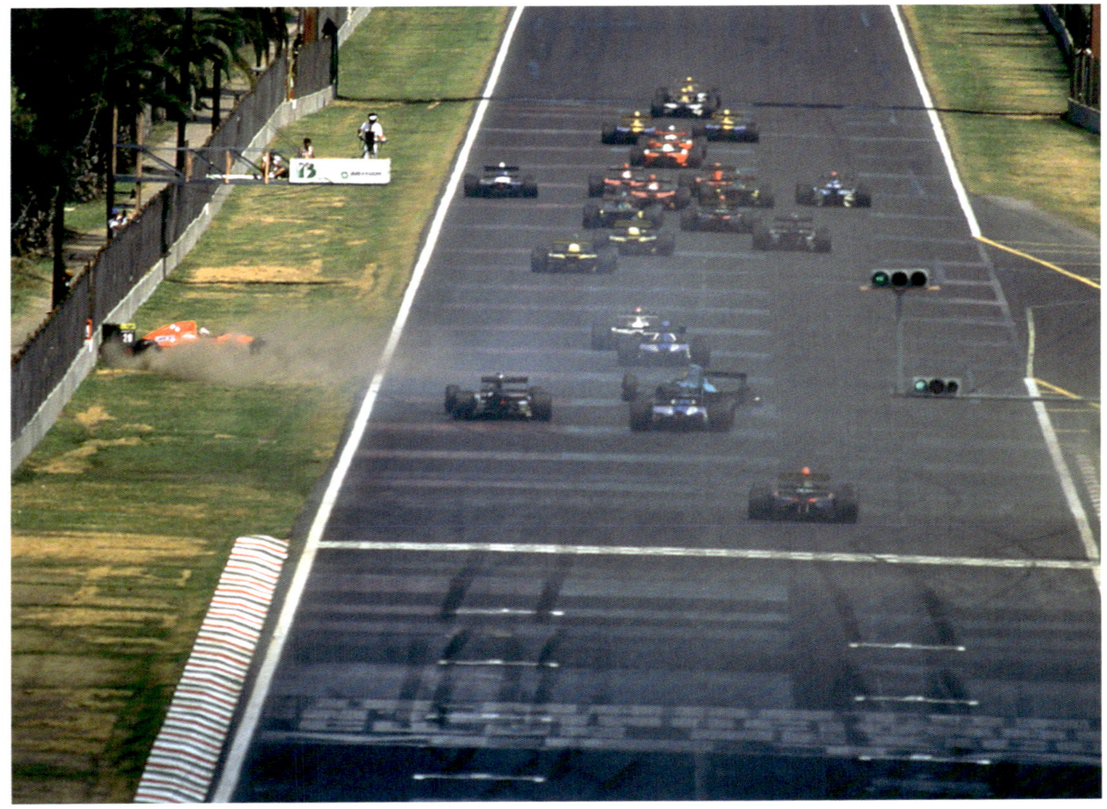

Top: As if he were above the rest, the many artists of the F1 circus religiously make way for Senna at the end of his grid formation lap at the 1991 Mexican Grand Prix.

Bottom: Jean Alesi crashes into the tire barrier during the warm-up and is unable to start the race.

Far right: Senna clinches seven more victories during the 1991 season and brings the Constructors' World Championship title to McLaren for the fourth consecutive season.

MEXICO GRAND PRIX: FRIGHT AND FEAR

Senna wore his blue Nacional cap screwed onto his head as he arrived in Mexico. It was a promotional item that his fans wore in the stands, which allowed the Brazilian to hide the ten stitches in his head. A week earlier, Ayrton had been hit by a jet ski at his home in Angra dos Reis, which was not an ideal preparation for the race. During testing, he continued to struggle. While trying to set a better time than Williams drivers Patrese and Mansell, Senna pushed his machine beyond its limits. In the curve leading to the pit straight, he spun, took off slightly, and flipped over after hitting the tire wall. Bertrand Gachot had crashed his Jordan at the same point twenty minutes earlier. Fortunately, Senna emerged unharmed from the incident. However, the event inspired some unusual headlines in the Brazilian media. The June 16 edition of O Globo had the headline: "Witch pursues Senna." During an interview on the same day, Senna shared his thoughts on fear, saying, "Fear is a part of our lives. Some people don't know how to deal with it, but others, like myself, learn to live with it and don't see it as a negative thing."

Throughout the weekend, Senna's McLaren was no match for the Williams drivers. Moreover, the high temperatures in Mexico were not conducive to the Honda engine, causing it to overheat and underperform. This increased the risk of a breakdown, necessitating Senna to adjust his driving style. "I had to be very careful, even going so far as to reduce my speed and get out of the slipstream of the car in front of me," he explains. Despite the reliability concerns of his MP4/6, Senna maintained a strong lead in the championship with 44 points, compared to Patrese's 20. However, the sight of Gerhard Berger's engine failing on lap five, ending his race prematurely, was a cause for concern. At that moment, the initial joy of four consecutive wins at the start of the season seemed distant, and the threat from the Williams drivers was becoming increasingly apparent.

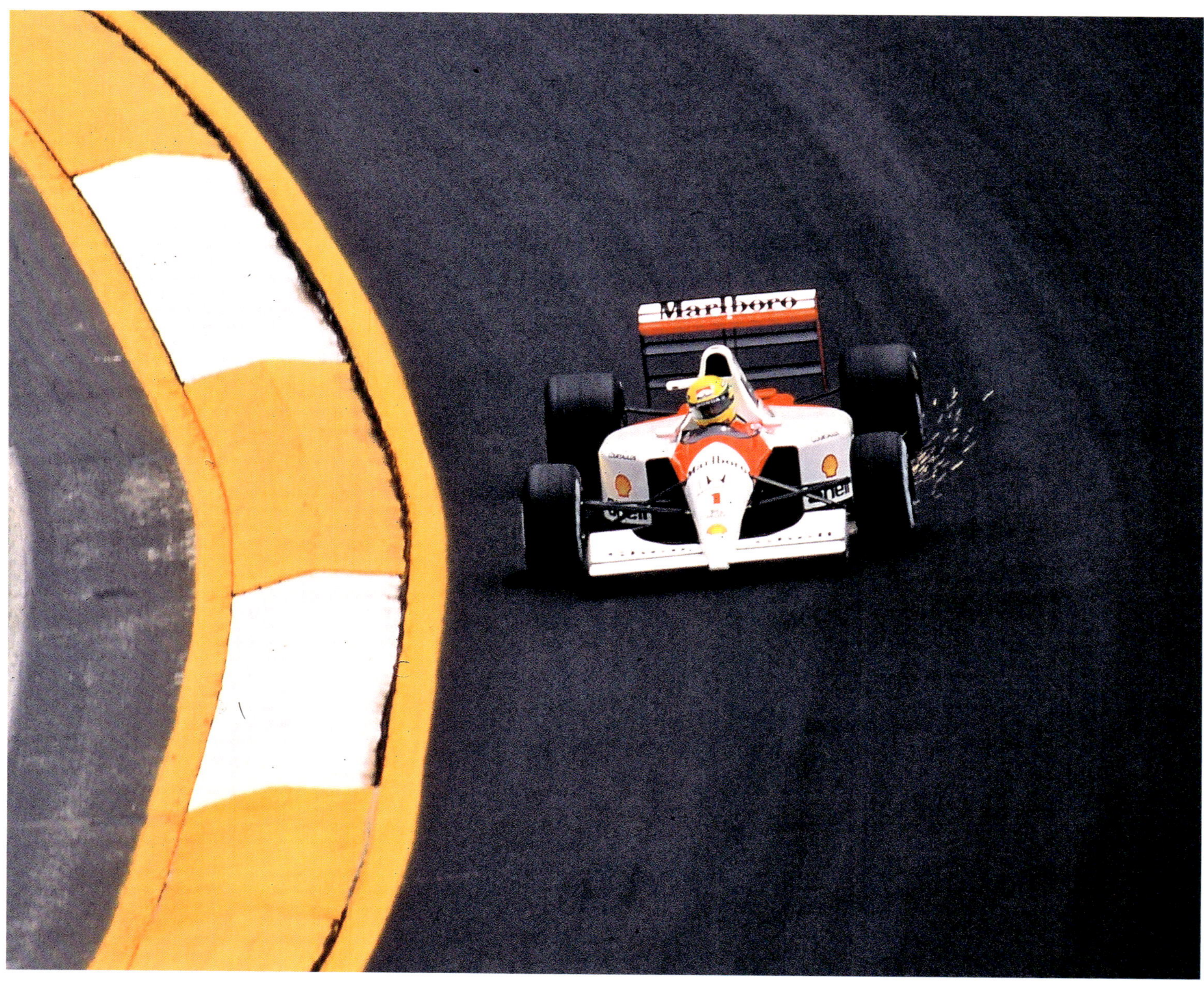

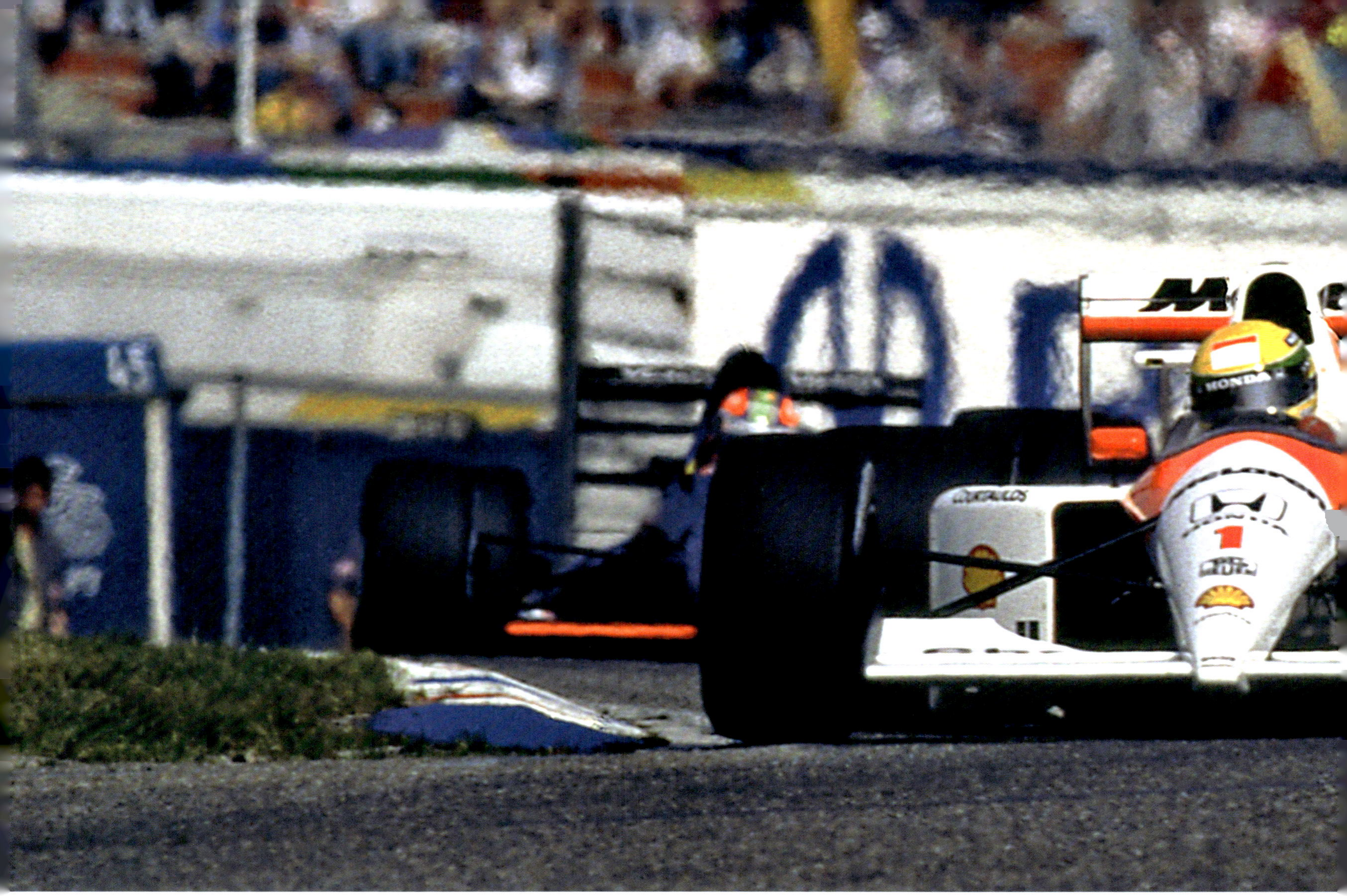

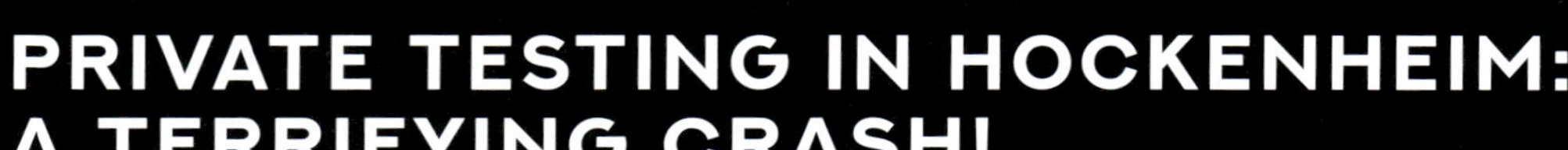

PRIVATE TESTING IN HOCKENHEIM: A TERRIFYING CRASH!

The accident in Mexico City was not the only worrying crash of the summer of 1991. On July 19, during private testing at Hockenheim, Senna was involved in a terrifying accident in the chicane leading to the German circuit's Stadium—the same circuit where, in 1984, he suffered his first major accident and experienced his first major scare. The repercussions of this July accident were such that they made the front pages of Brazilian newspapers. And with good reason: at 320 km per hour, his car hit a vibrator and took off after a puncture at the rear. The McLaren rolled several times and came to a standstill, completely destroyed. The worst was yet to come. Luckily, Senna escaped with a dislocated shoulder and a neck injury. “I was at least five meters off the ground, at tree height. And I remember how my helmet hit the asphalt several times. I know exactly what I felt and what I thought. I was sure I wasn't going to make it,” he tells German journalist Karin Sturm afterward.

The accident occurred 10 minutes before the end of a three-day test session. Observers noted that Senna had never worked as hard as he had in recent months to improve his car; indeed, the idea that Williams was outperforming McLaren in certain areas exasperated the Brazilian and his team. After a brief examination in the hospital, Ayrton left with his father, Milton, and returned home to Monte Carlo. He then calls his mother, Dona Neyde, to reassure her. But inwardly, he knows that on July 19, 1991, he came very close to the worst.

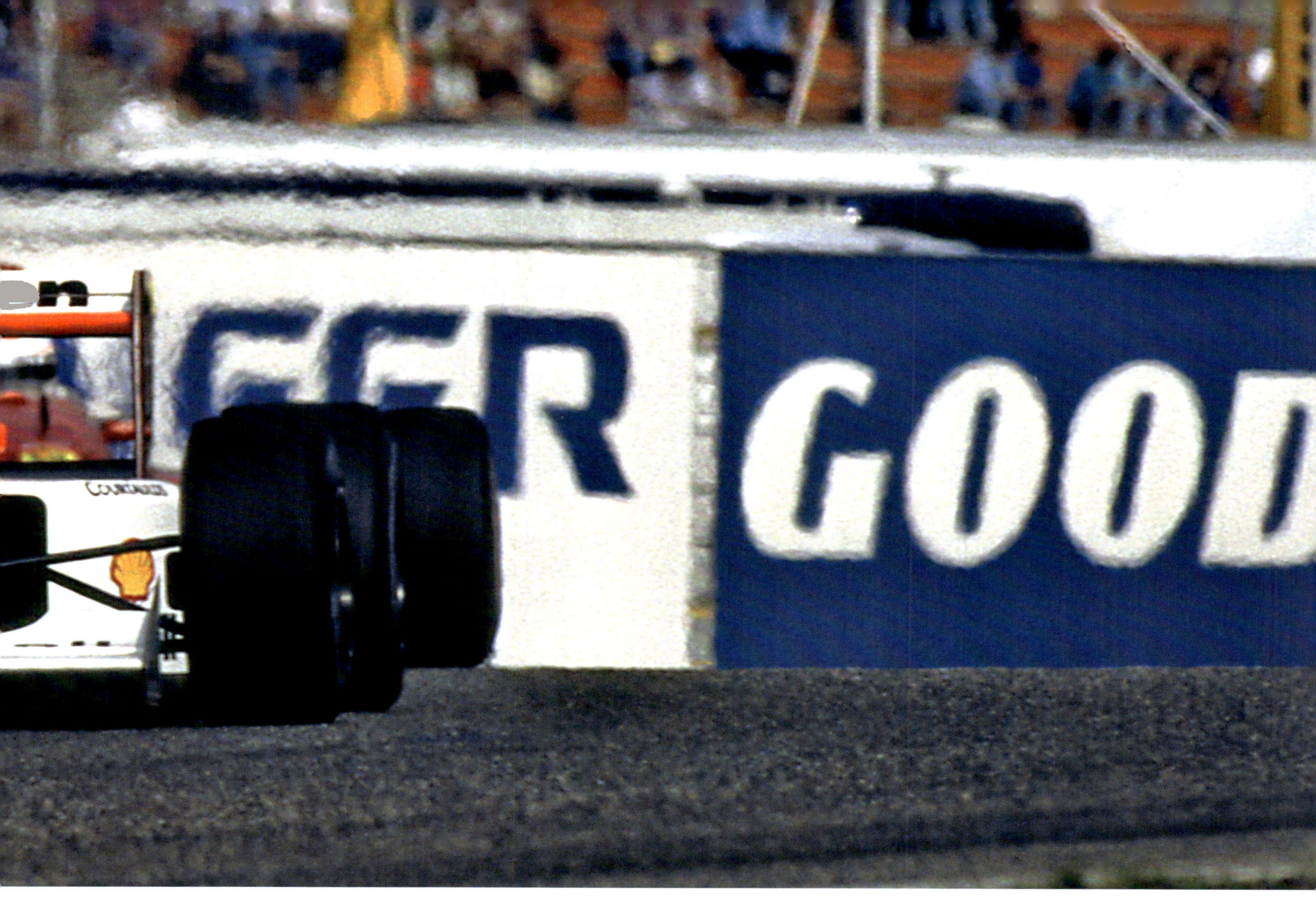

With his visor lowered and elevated concentration, Senna continues to make history in F1 in the early 1990s.

GERMANY GRAND PRIX: PROST UNDER PRESSURE, SENNA OUT

Upon his arrival at Hockenheim at the end of July, Prost found himself under significant pressure. Umberto Agnelli, the vice president of the Fiat group and the younger brother of the big boss, publicly criticized his French drivers. He stated in the press, “The best driver is Senna. I’d like to see him with us.” This was hardly the ideal morale booster for the team, who were already grappling with a disappointing season. In response, Prost retorted, “Either we return to normal working conditions, or I’m leaving Ferrari! Yes, I have a contract for 1992, but if I no longer enjoy being here, I’m prepared to leave.”

The race wasn’t going smoothly, either. On the 38th lap, Prost attempted to overtake Senna on the outside at the first chicane by following in his slipstream. However, Senna didn’t give him any space, forcing an overly optimistic Prost to jam his brakes. He ended up driving straight into the chicane and downshifting, which resulted in a clutch failure and a stalled engine. Prost, visibly upset with Senna, exited his car. Senna, on the other hand, ran out of fuel and pulled into the first chicane on the final 45th lap. Mansell secured his third consecutive win, followed by Patrese (completing a Williams one-two), Alesi, and Berger, who also ran out of fuel during the victory lap. Despite the setbacks, the British driver managed to close the gap with Senna to just eight points. Williams also surpassed McLaren in the constructors’ standings. The eventful weekend was far from over.

In front of journalists, Prost lashed out at Senna: “He played some bad tricks on me on the straights. He was braking for no reason—to force me to take my foot off the accelerator. And then, before the chicane, he didn't hesitate to obstruct me.” Senna replies, "Everyone knows Prost now. He complains about his car, his tires, his team, his fuel, the other drivers, the circuits, etc. It's never his fault! Today, he took a lot of risks and got out on his own. Prost needed a break, that was for sure. He was getting ready to take a sabbatical in 1992, but no one had heard the news yet.

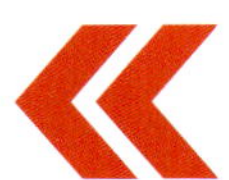

NUNO COBRA

Nuno Cobra, a renowned physiotherapist, began working with Ayrton Senna in 1984, coinciding with the start of his Formula 1 career. As a professor at the University of São Paulo, Cobra gradually became one of the individuals closest to the driver. He was constantly aware of Senna's every move and was always ready to find the best solutions. His goal was to ensure that Senna continued progressing, improving, and dominating his sport.

Almost 30 years after the Brazilian champion's death, Nuno Cobra granted us an exclusive interview for this tribute book. He remembers everything, so he talked for a long time. Selected excerpts.

THE YOUNG AYRTON SENNA

"I didn't know who Ayrton was. I didn't know him. He was about 23, very shy, and introverted, and I found it hard to make eye contact with him. He seemed very fragile. What I achieved in transforming an extremely weak, uncertain, nervous, restless, and unfocused young man into a Formula 1 phenomenon is unique in the world. It was a very rich experience. I'd never met a student like him before, with such extraordinary inner energy. No obstacle could stop him from getting what he wanted. Ayrton was unique. An energy he didn't know existed was bubbling up inside him, and he wasn't prepared for it."

THE FIRST RACES

"Ayrton's personality was very intense. I lived with him for the first three months of his life in England. After every race, he'd have a story to tell: a flat tire, an engine failure, a broken gearbox. There was always a problem. What struck me most was how exacting he was with his engineers and mechanics. I looked after the "Ayrton Senna machine" while they looked after his machine, his Formula 1. He used to surprise me by banging on the table and shouting. He was always very angry with the whole team. Sometimes, I'd leave the factory with him at 11 p.m. He wanted to know the details of every corner, every lap, and every little thing. He was extremely curious."

DR. AYRTON AND MR. SENNA

"I loved Ayrton, but I hated Senna. Senna was execrable, very demanding, and difficult, whereas Ayrton was a gentle, kind, delicate, and lovable person. The former was always very angry, irritable, nervous, sad, and upset. I don't remember the "Senna" very well. What I remember very well is Ayrton; he represented goodness and kindness in a human being. How did you go from one to the other? For example, we could be having a pleasant conversation, sitting in beautiful surroundings, with Ayrton being generous, polite, and kind. Then the phone would ring—it was always someone bothering him with suspension, tire, or engine problems. He'd hang up the phone and turn into a demon, a horrible Senna. Ayrton was, therefore, a charming person, but Senna was troubled because he had to produce results and depended on elements beyond his control. He felt under constant pressure."

LIFE OUTSIDE CIRCUITS

"I remember fondly the trips out on his yacht. In those moments, he would leave Senna behind. I'd say to him, "Ayrton, did you lock the door properly? Did you lock it properly and turn the key twice so that bloody Senna wouldn't come after us?" Then he'd drop anchor, and we'd jump off the boat to go for a swim—something I often worried about as he'd go a long way from shore. Finally, we'd prepare something to eat together. These moments were magical, delicious, and unforgettable. He also owned a tennis court in the Algarve. When Senna was restless and bothering me in the living room, I had a way of getting Ayrton back: I'd suggest a game of tennis. He was crazy about the sport. I remember running around the court like a madman and hitting the ball straight back into his racket. We'd play tennis for hours. Then he would transform, and the wonderful Ayrton would return. Tennis was our weapon to bring Ayrton back and send Senna away."

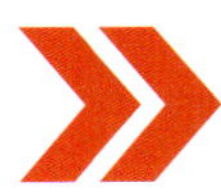

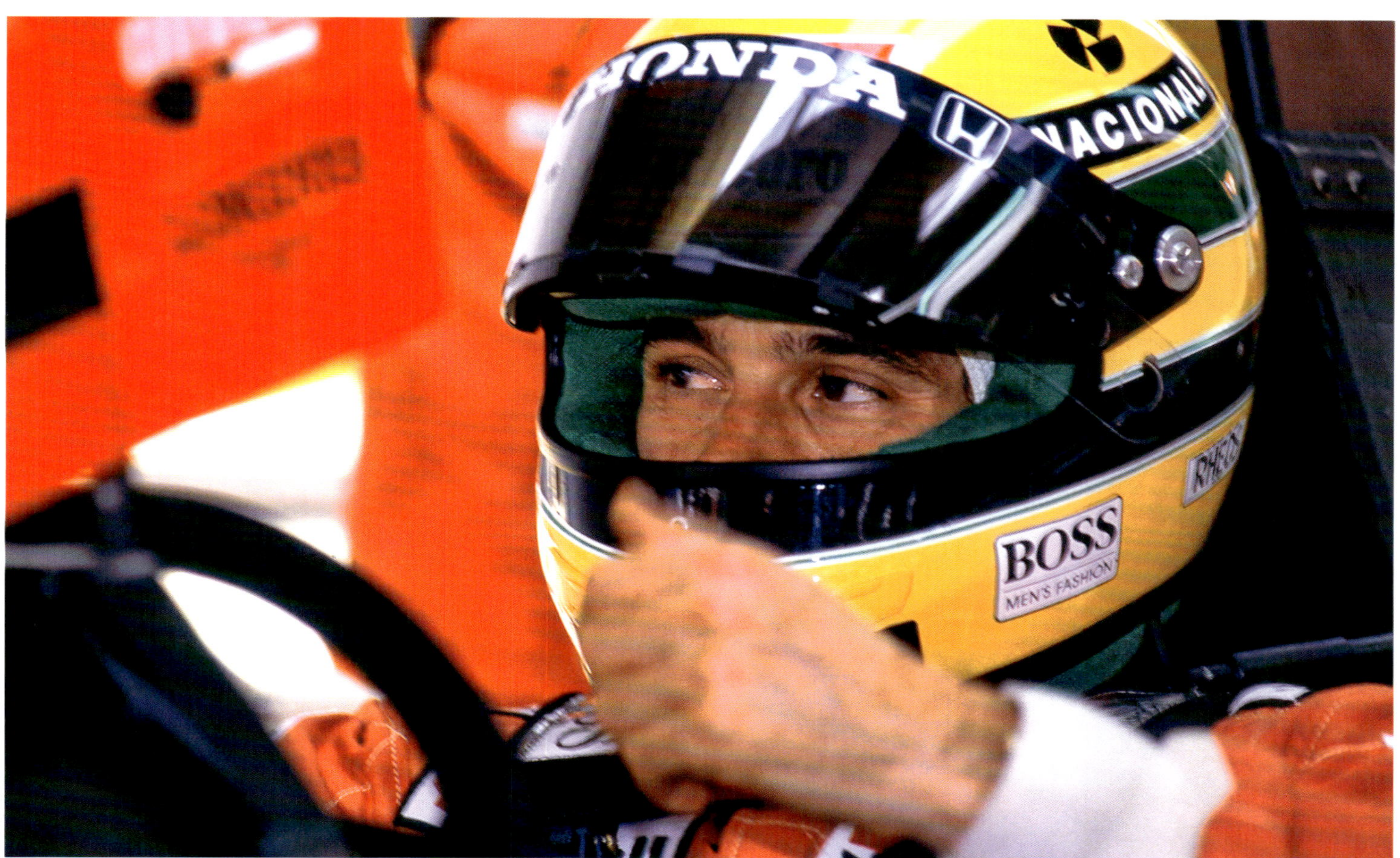

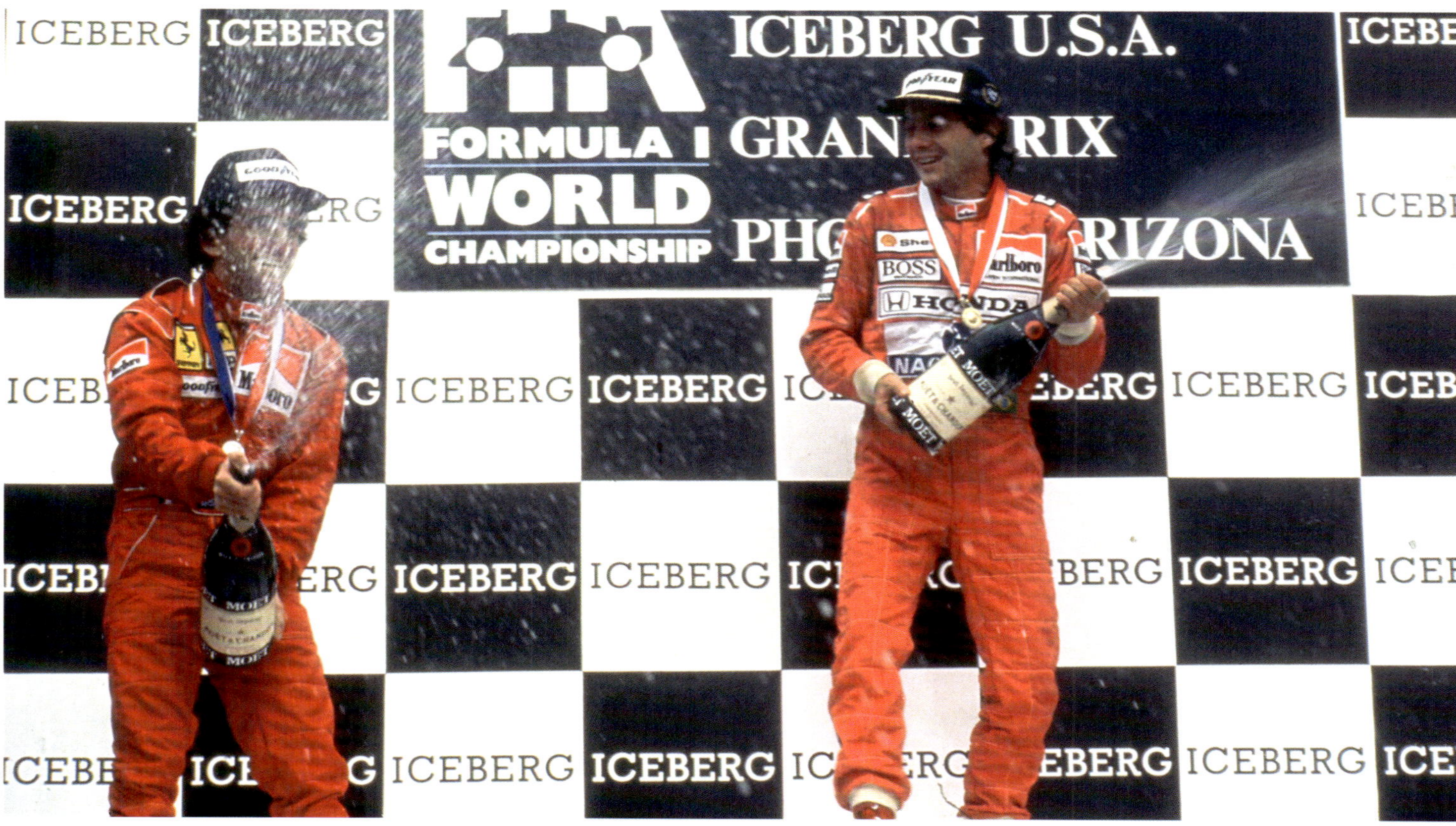

Top: The telemetry system of that time, already highly efficient, allows Senna to tirelessly request improvements from the entire McLaren team during qualifying sessions.

Bottom: Open the champagne! Senna and Prost finish 1st and 2nd at the United States Grand Prix on the Phoenix street circuit, kicking off their 1991 season in style.

JAPAN GRAND PRIX: SENNA WIN, ROYAL GIFT FOR BERGER

Senna came to Suzuka with a 16-point lead over Mansell, who only had a slim mathematical chance of securing his first world title. For the suspense to last until Australia, the Williams leader needed to win, and Senna had to finish outside the podium. On the grid, the two McLarens were leading, but Berger was on pole. Senna explained this by saying, "He's found a better set-up than me." Mansell was just behind them, having secured the third-fastest qualifying time. Thus, anything could have happened. However, on lap 10, Mansell, who was in 3rd place behind Berger and Senna, veered off the track at the first corner. He lost control of his car, slid on the dirty part of the track, and ended up in the gravel trap. Consequently, the championship was over; Senna was assured of his third title, regardless of whether he finished the Japanese GP or not.

Once again, an unexpected event took place at Suzuka. However, this time, it did not involve a collision.

GERHARD BERGER

"I'd agreed all season long to help Senna win the world championship, even without receiving any race instructions. I had always helped him, quite simply, in a sporting way. And Ayrton appreciated that, so at Suzuka, he wanted to give me something back. I'd taken the pole and was ahead of him, 10 seconds ahead, but then I had a mechanical problem: my exhaust broke, and I had to slow down. At the end of the race, I thought he had a problem too or was afraid of running out of fuel, and I said to myself, "Well, it's my lucky day." He was very hard to beat, but I honestly think I could have won that race without him offering me victory. I might have refused to win it that way if I'd had time to think, but that's how it happened."

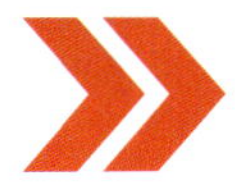

Senna takes all the risks in 1991, here showing his signature aggressive steering input on a tight kerb.

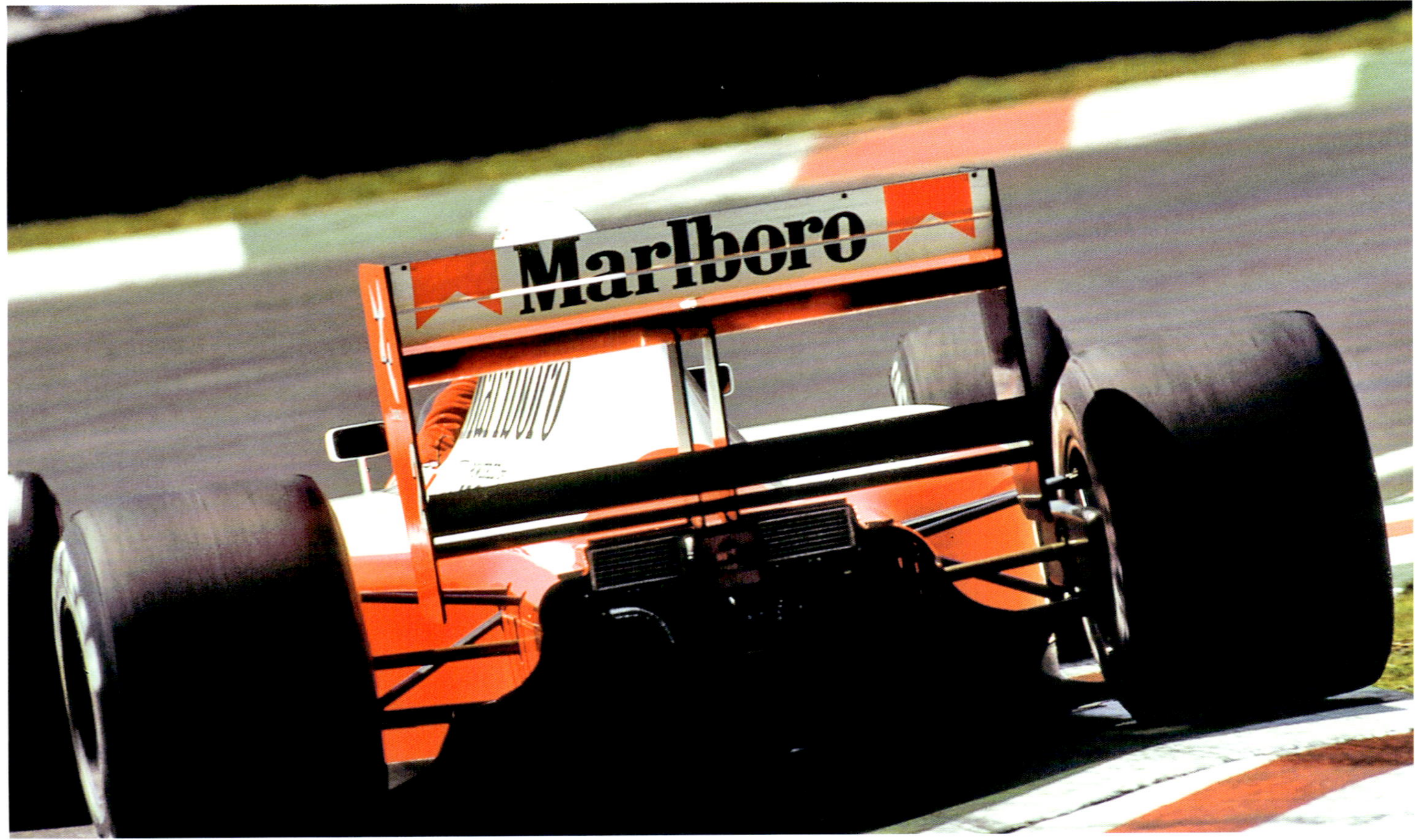

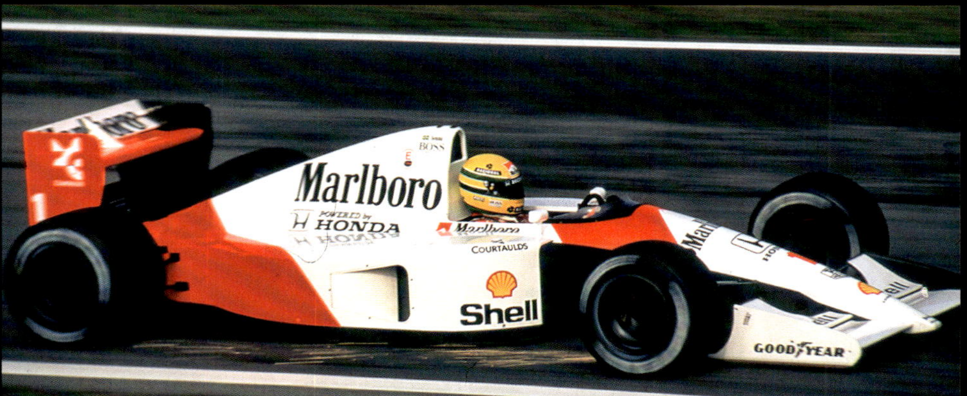

THE CAR: MCLAREN MP4/6

As Ayrton Senna tested the McLaren MP4/6 for the first time, he humorously remarked, "I can't drive a Ferrari, so McLaren made me one." This 1991 model bore a striking resemblance to the Ferrari 641, which Alain Prost had driven the previous year. The long nose and side pods of the McLaren were particularly similar to those of the Maranello car. This similarity was largely due to the arrival of Henri Durand, the former Chief Aerodynamicist of Ferrari, in mid-1990. After years of rigorous development, Honda introduced a 3.5-liter Honda RA121E V12 engine.

The engine, being heavier and more fuel-consuming, didn't impress the drivers at first. It was so heavy that the car exceeded the season's starting weight limit by 25 kg. Although the drivers felt it lacked power, the engine compensated with its reliability. Looking back, Neil Oatley confessed that switching from the V10 to the V12 was a mistake. He said, "We would have been more competitive if we had continued to develop the V10. The V12 was heavier and didn't offer much more performance." The English engineer also hinted that the engine transition contributed to Williams' dominance in 1992. Steve Hallam, who was Gerhard Berger's engineer at the time, concurred: "We all knew that once Nigel Mansell and Williams achieved a certain level of reliability, they would have a very fast car. Technically, their car was superior to the McLaren, especially since the Williams had a semi-automatic gearbox."

Despite his H-shaped gearbox, Senna still managed to win the season's first four races, and McLaren beat Didcot's team with an improved car from the Hungarian GP onwards, despite Williams' advances. Senna, driving the only V12-powered McLaren that has won a world title, managed to secure pole position eight times and achieve seven victories in a total of 16 races. With that McLaren MP4/6, he equaled, among others, Jackie Stewart, Niki Lauda, and Nelson Piquet. It was his third world championship. His last.

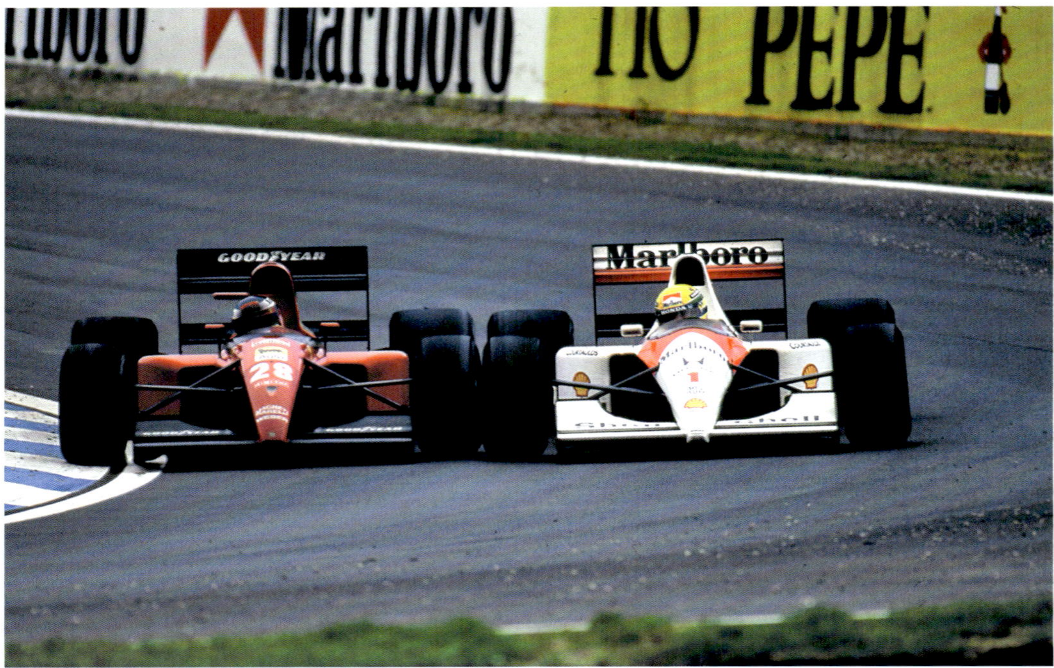

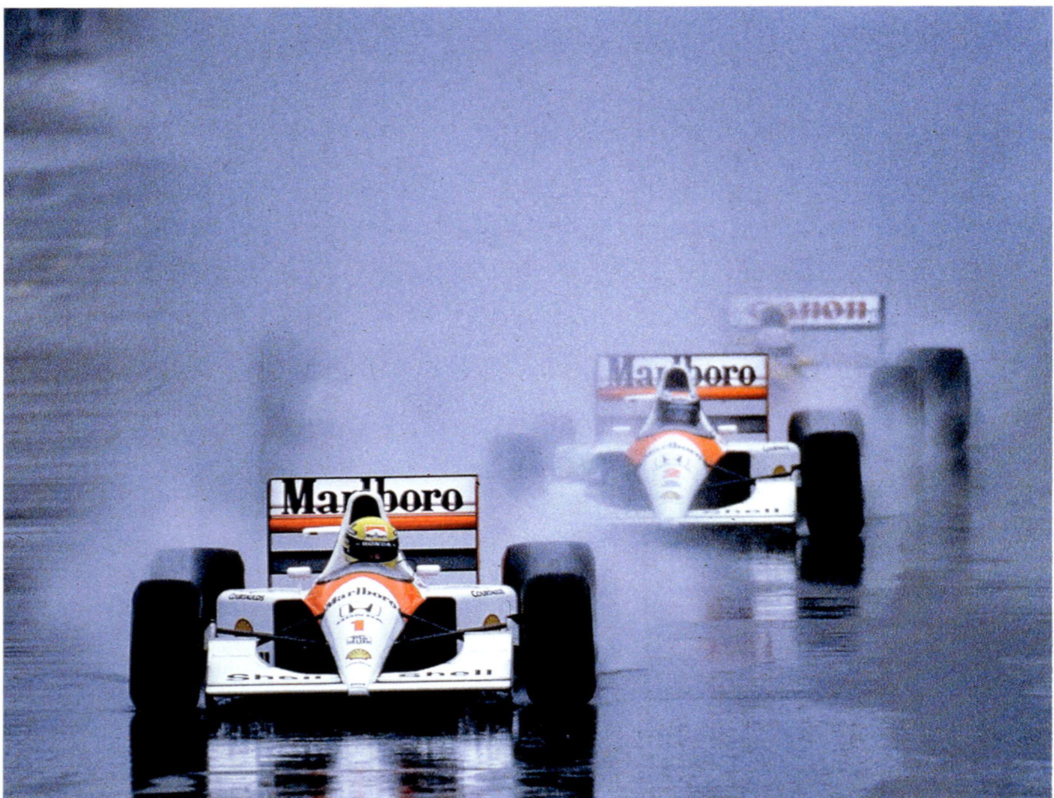

Top: Like in Phoenix in 1990, Ayrton Senna and Jean Alesi are side-by-side at the 1991 Spanish Grand Prix.

Bottom: After 16 laps, all F1 cars are forced to return to the pits due to treacherous weather conditions, making the 1991 Australian Grand Prix one of the shortest in history. Senna concludes his season with another victory.

Right: In the Barcelona circuit's main straight, Nigel Mansell and Ayrton Senna are in a fierce battle (part of a sequence that is entered into F1 history).

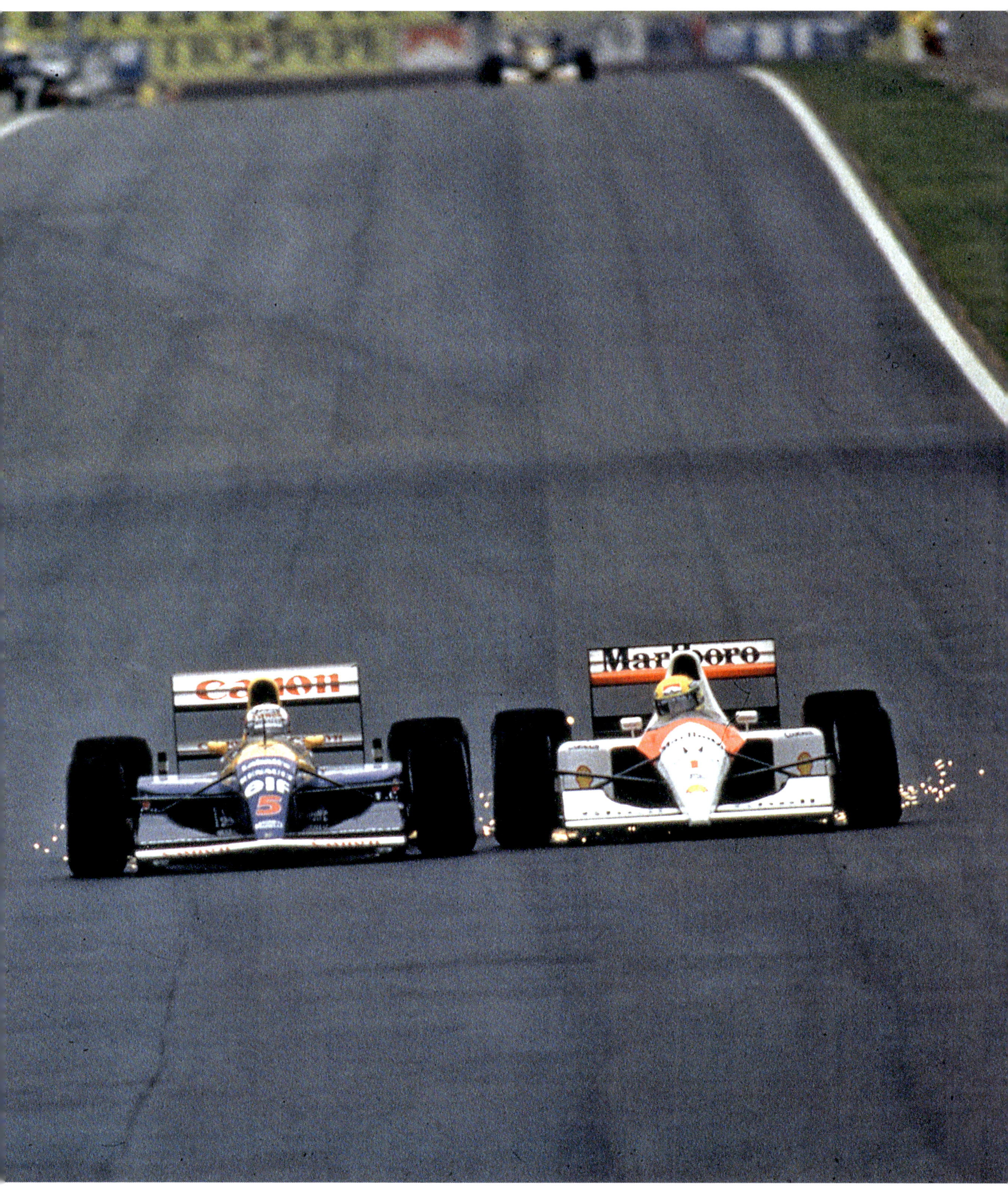
Canon
Marlboro
5

ON TRACK FOR THE TITLE 1991

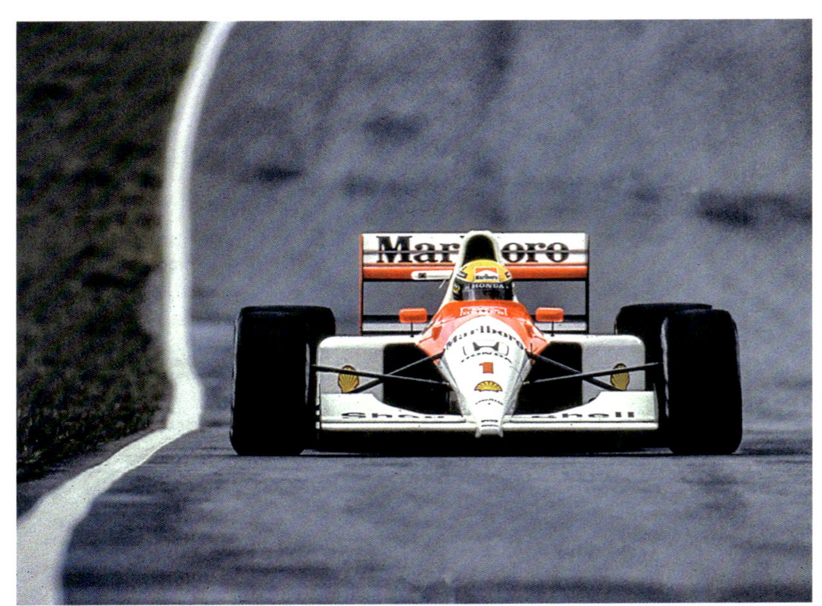

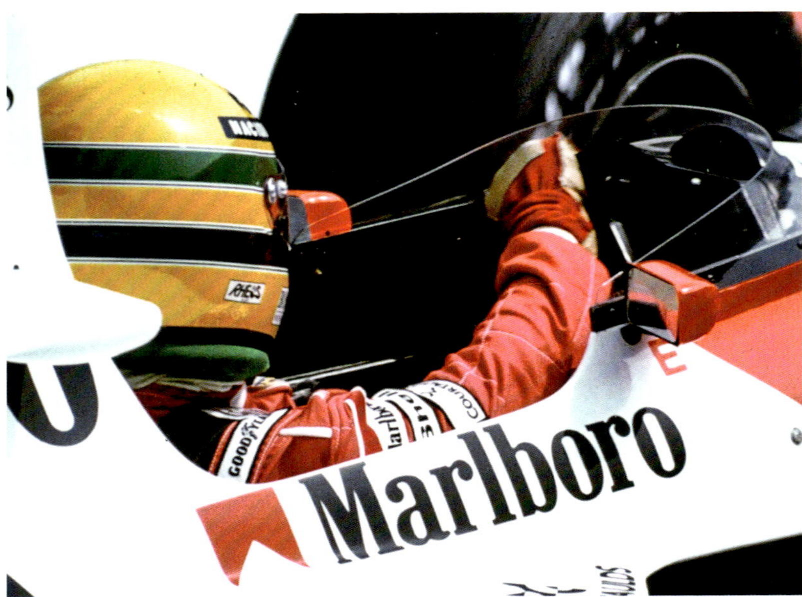

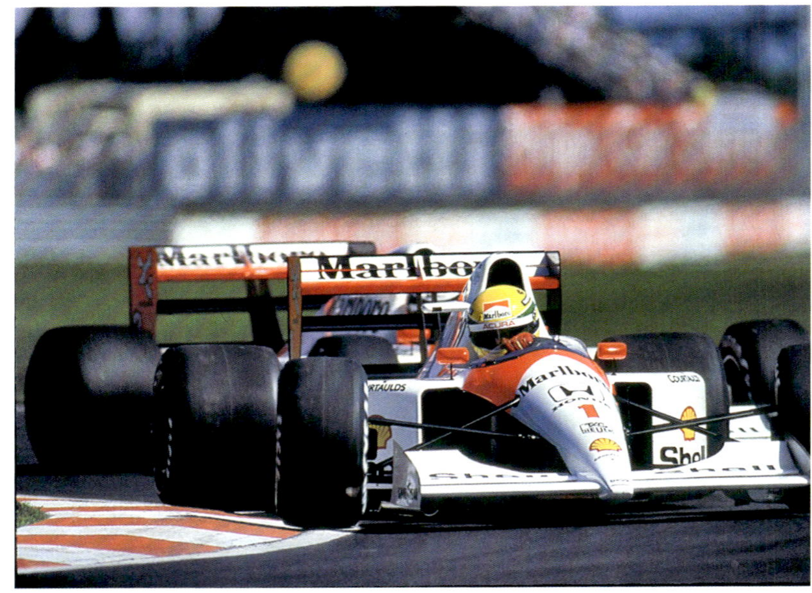

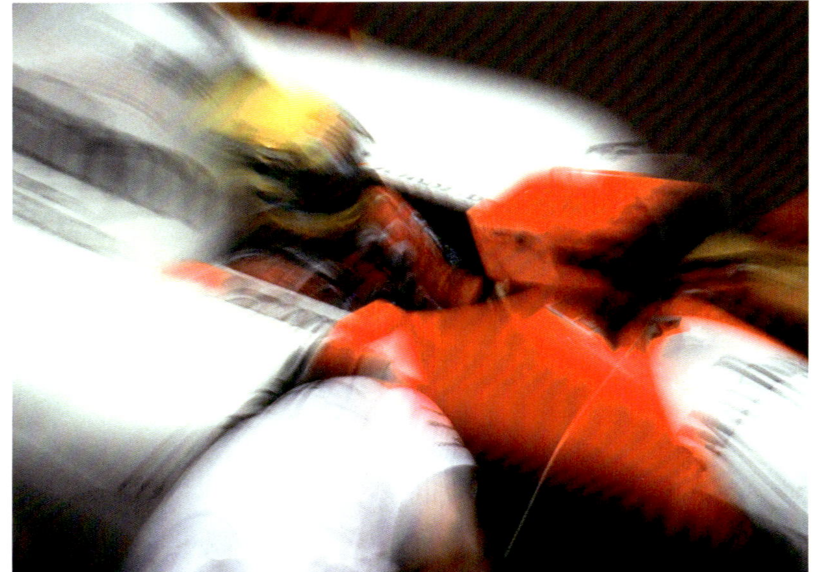

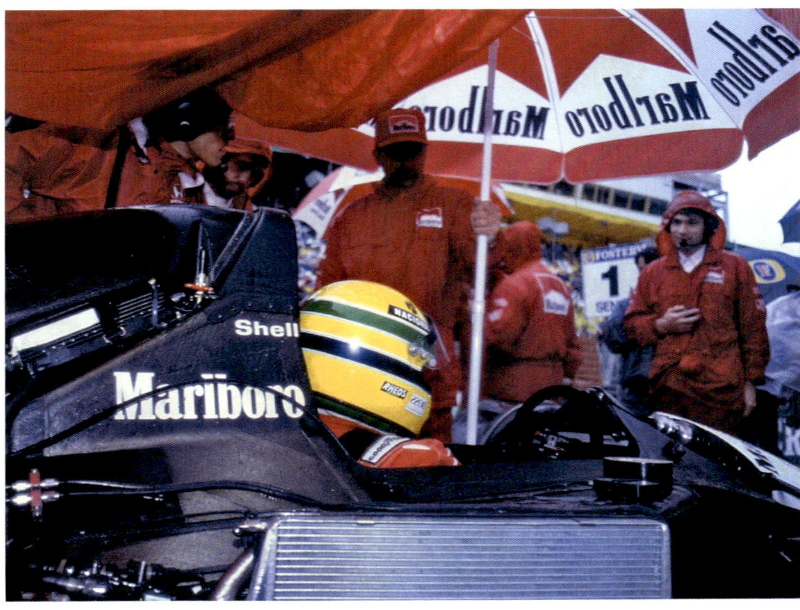

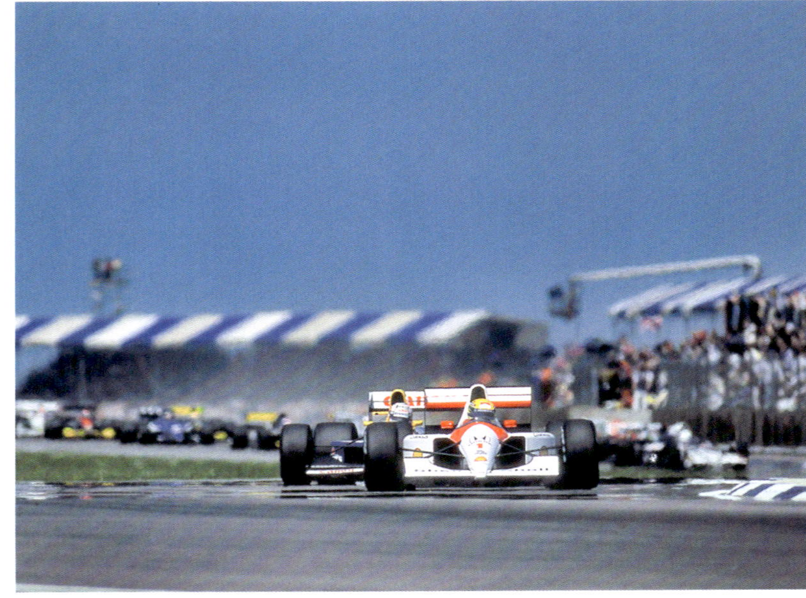

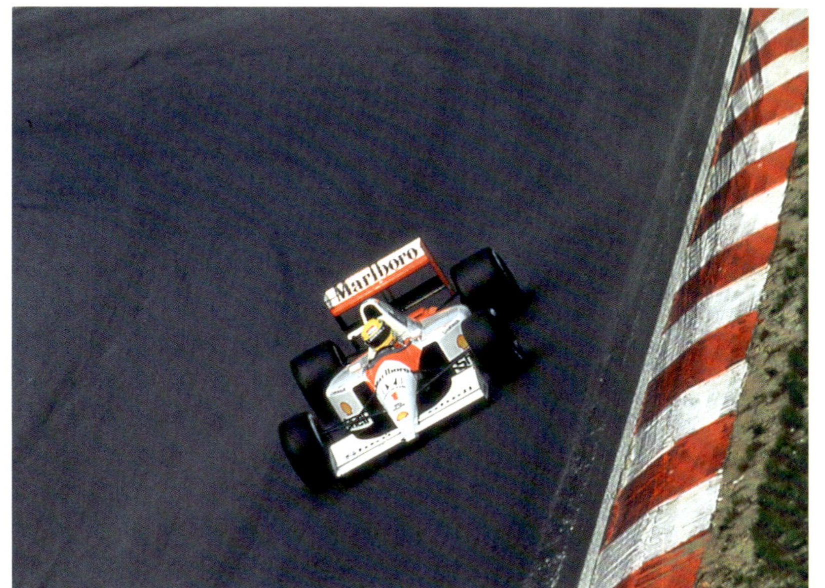

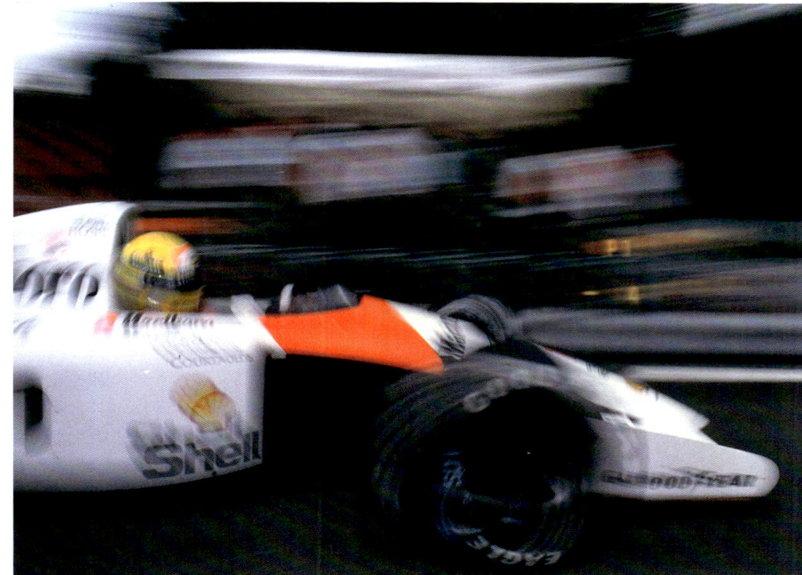

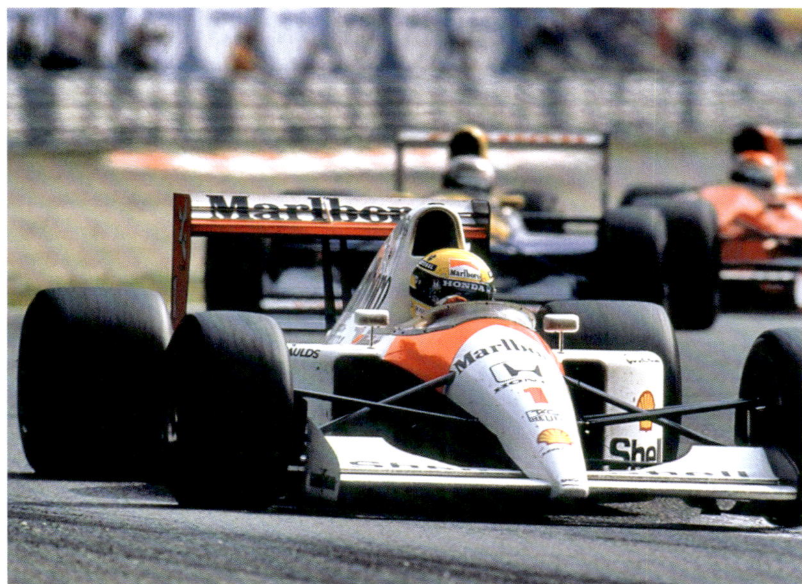

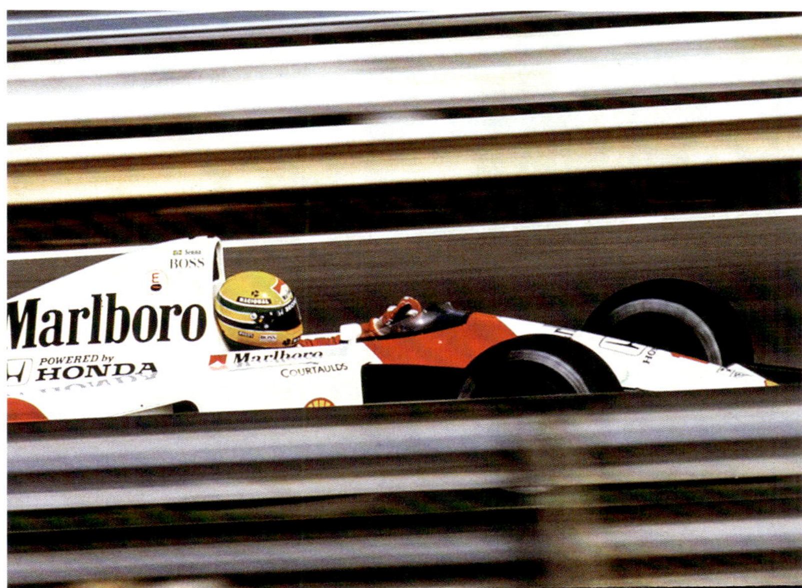

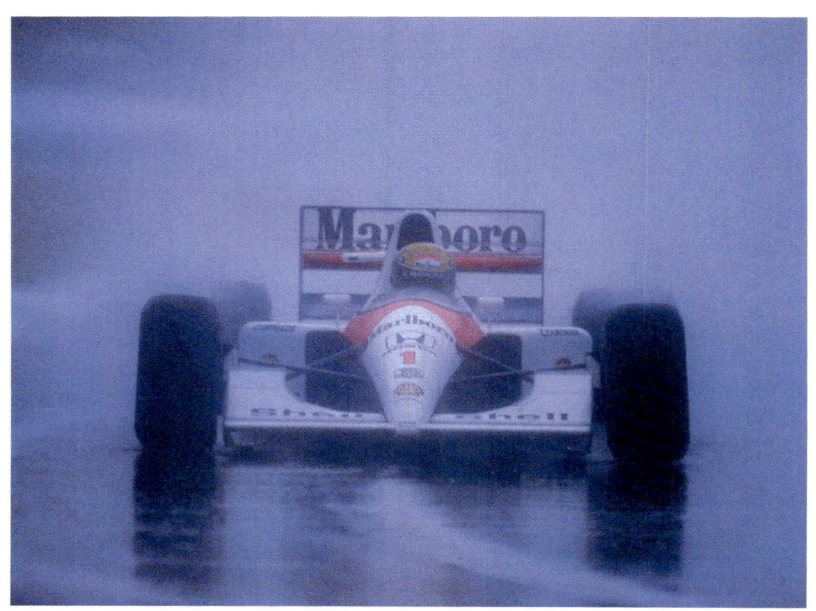

Ayrton Senna's 1991 season is a benchmark for the Brazilian driver. Between his first win in Brazil and his third World Championship title, he further cements his name in Formula 1 history.

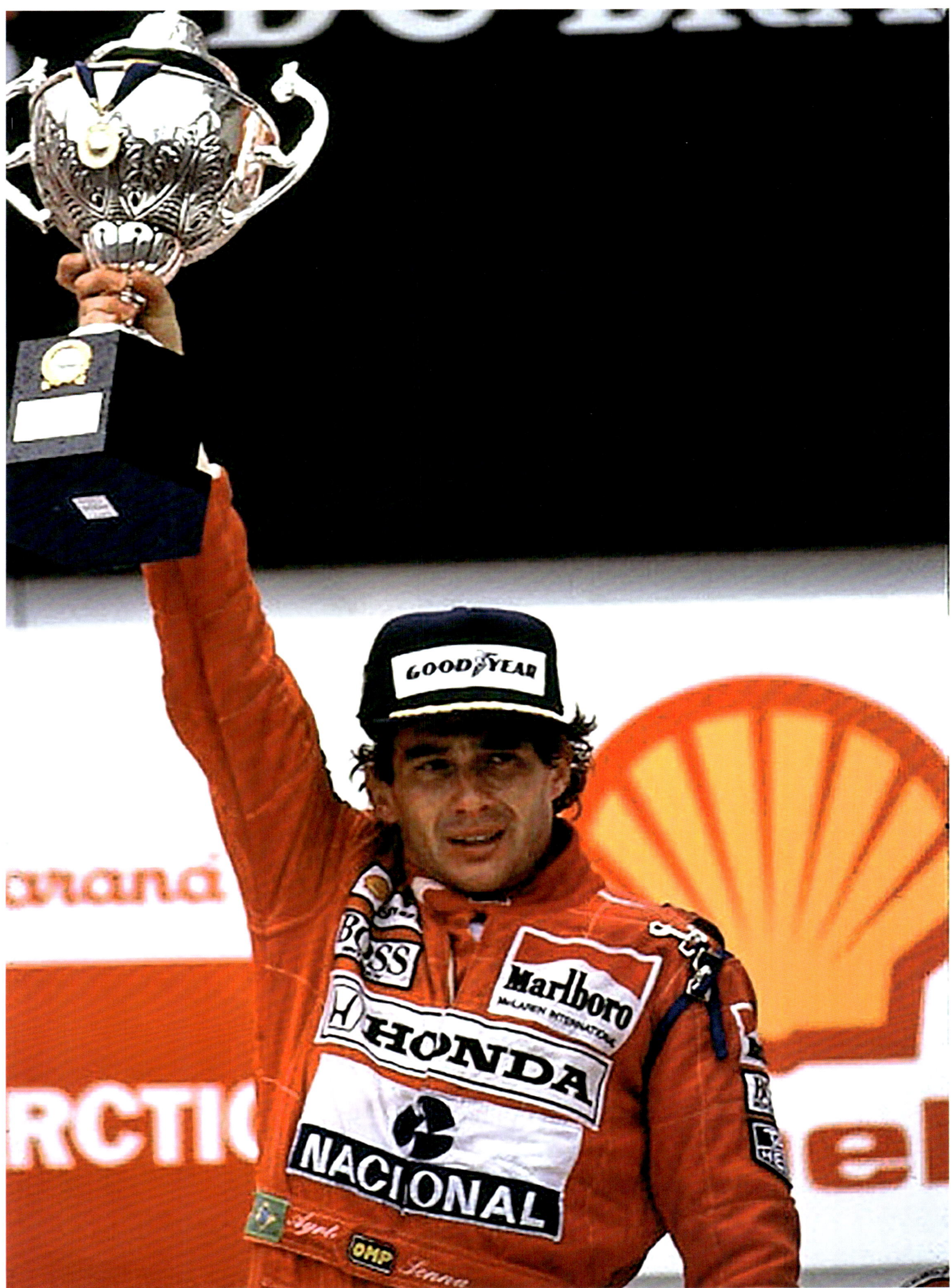
GOODYEAR
BOSS
Marlboro
McLAREN INTERNATIONAL
HONDA
NACIONAL
OHP

Left: Senna secures his first victory in Brazil at the Interlagos circuit in São Paulo in 1991 in front of a devoted crowd that cheers him on from start to finish, achieving his dream of winning in his birthplace.

Right: Ayrton Senna had a level of concentration that was far above average and visible to the naked eye, even to the common people.

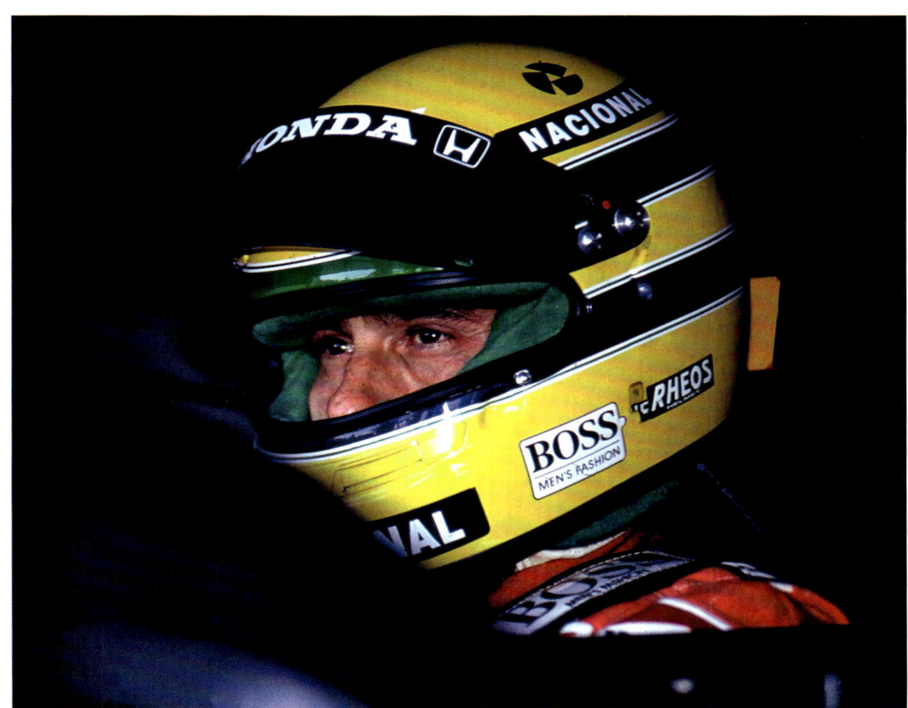

THE 1991 SEASON IN FIGURES

GRAND PRIX	QUALIFIERS	RACE
UNITED STATES	POLE POSITION 53	VICTORY 27
BRAZIL	POLE POSITION 54	VICTORY 28
SAN MARINO	POLE POSITION 55	VICTORY 29
MONACO	POLE POSITION 56	VICTORY 30
CANADA	3RD	DNF (ALTERNATOR)
MEXICO	3RD	3RD
FRANCE	3RD	3RD
GREAT BRITAIN	2ND	4TH (OUT OF FUEL)
GERMANY	2ND	7TH (OUT OF FUEL)
HUNGARY	POLE POSITION 57	VICTORY 31
BELGIUM	POLE POSITION 58	VICTORY 32
ITALY	POLE POSITION 59	2ND
PORTUGAL	3RD	2ND
SPAIN	3RD	5TH
JAPAN	2ND	2ND
AUSTRALIA	POLE POSITION 60	VICTORY 33

FORMULA 1 WORLD CHAMPION
(96 POINTS, SEVEN VICTORIES, 12 PODIUMS, EIGHT POLE POSITIONS, TWO BEST LAPS)

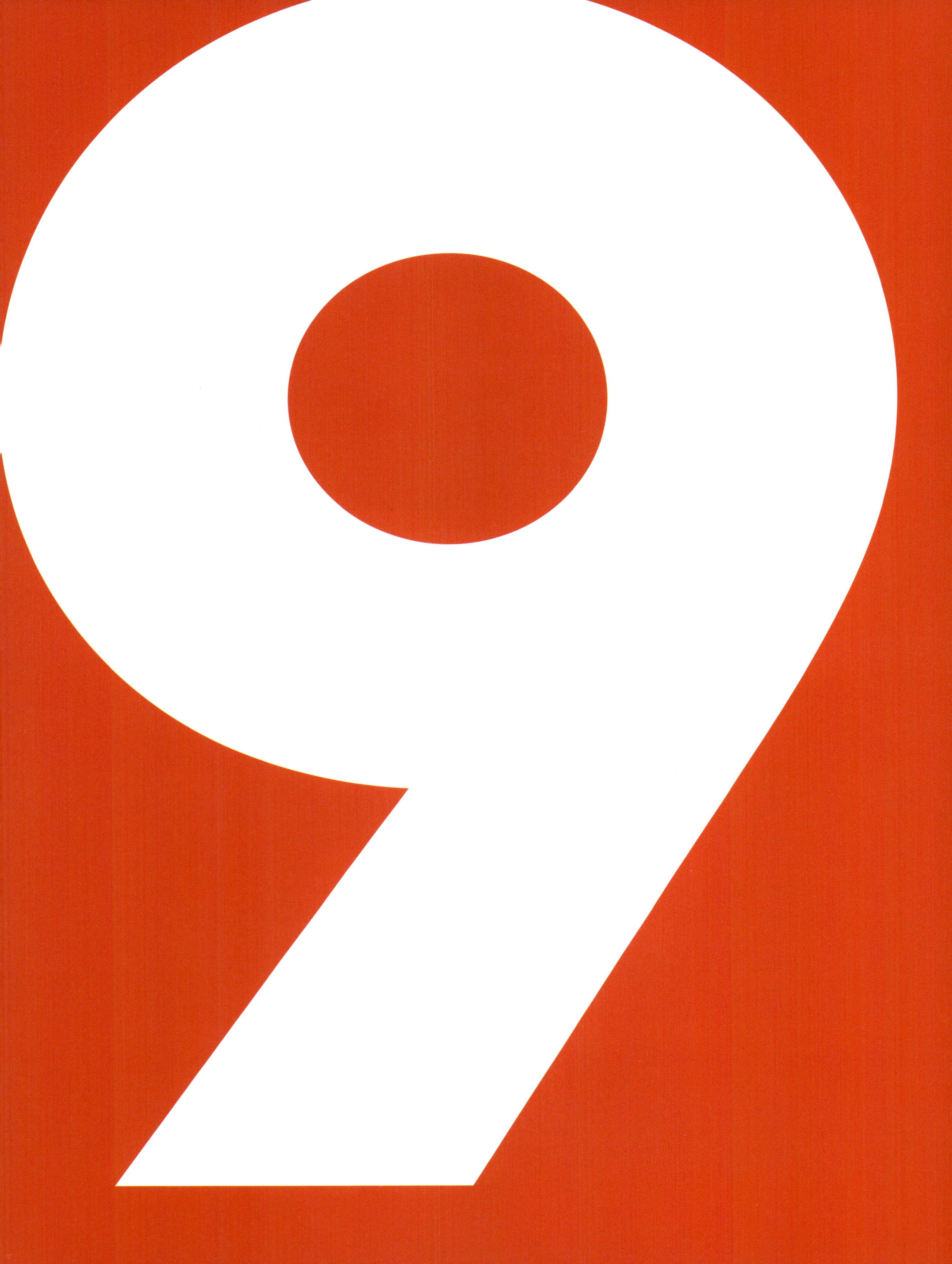
9

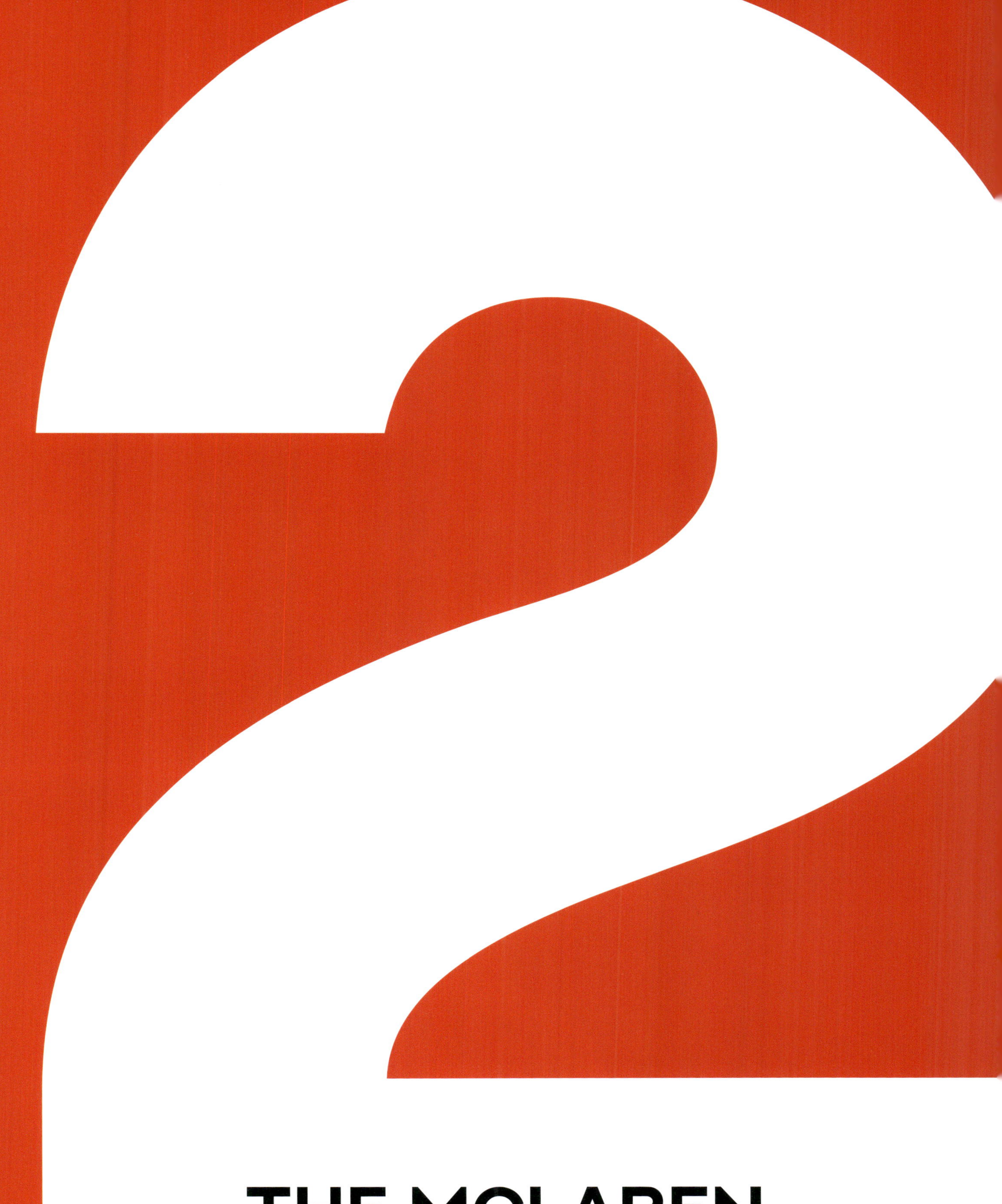

THE MCLAREN WILLIAMS DUEL

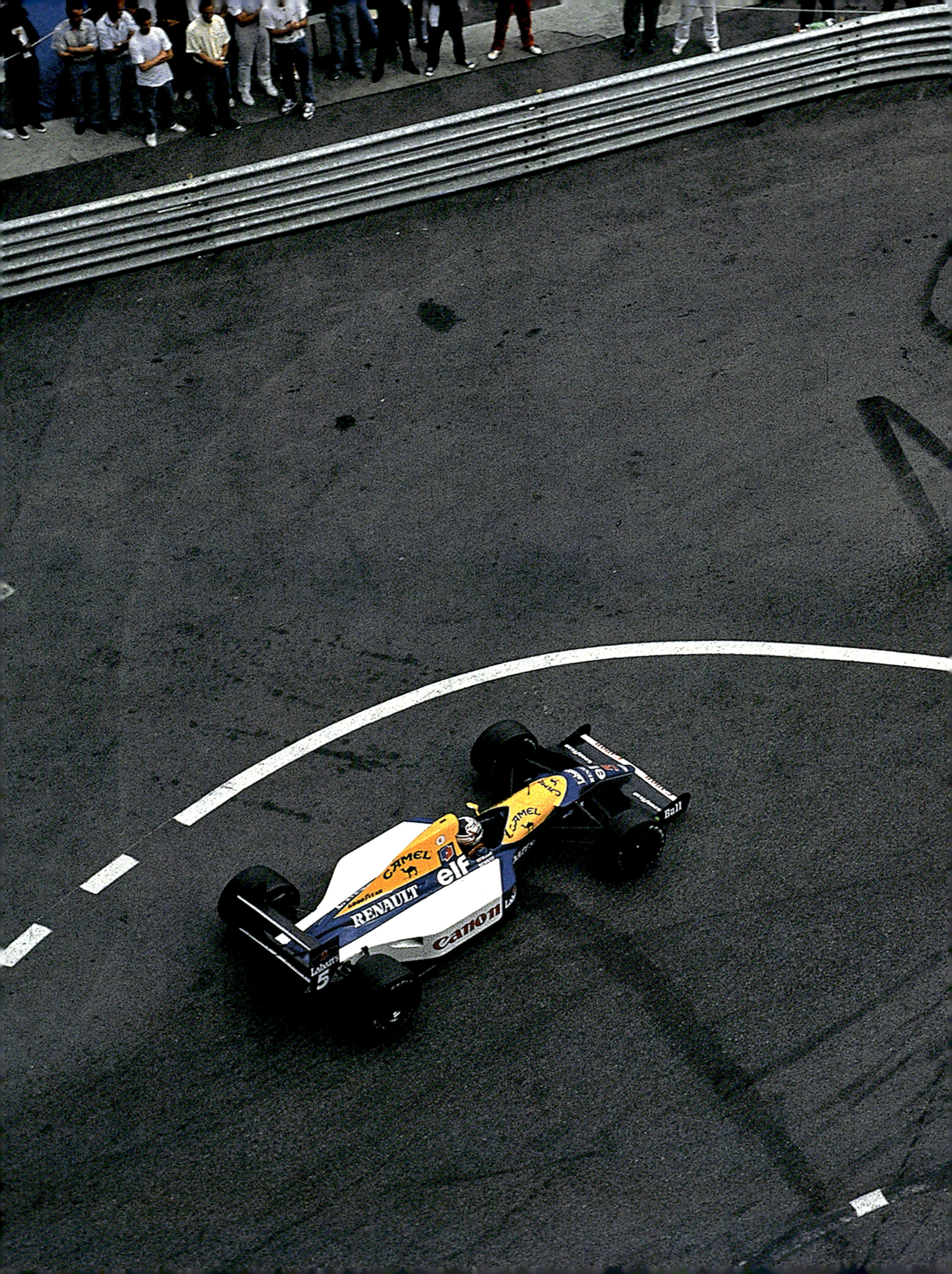
CAMEL
RENAULT
elf
Canon
CAMEL
Bull
5

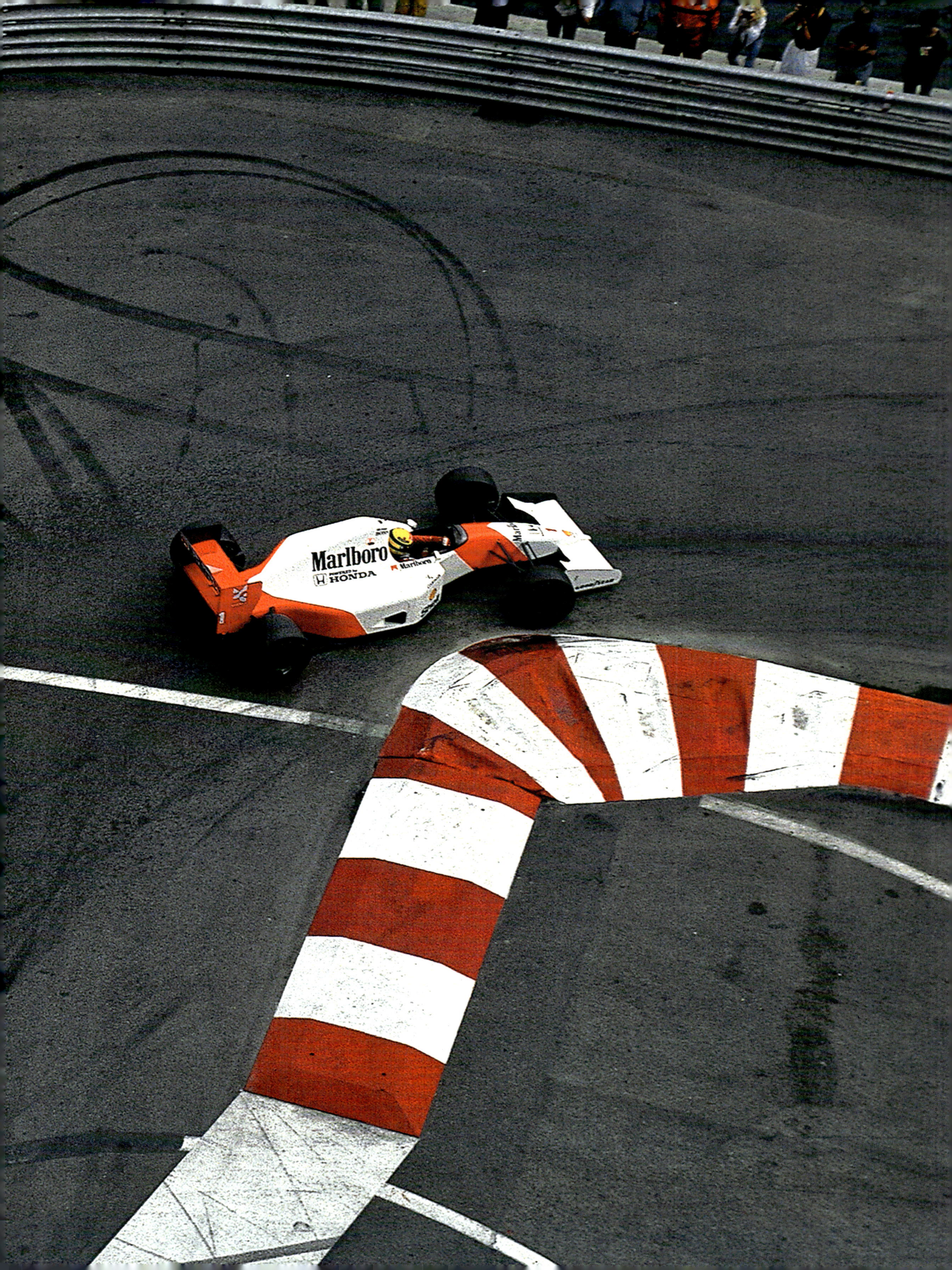
Marlboro
HONDA

IN FRONT OF MANSELL AND SCHUMACHER

WITH THE NUMBER 1 ON HIS MCLAREN, THREE-TIME REIGNING WORLD CHAMPION AYRTON SENNA WAS IN FOR A TOUGH SEASON. THE TRENDY RACING PACKAGE THAT YEAR WAS NIGEL MANSELL IN HIS WILLIAMS-RENAULT.

The Brit, who had long awaited his moment of glory, was driving the best car on the grid—and he knew how to use it. He killed the suspense from the outset by winning the season's first five races, scoring 50 points compared with just eight for the Brazilian, who suffered a serious accident in Mexico. Although his winning streak was interrupted in Monaco (Senna's fifth victory in the Principality), a summer hat-trick (France, Great Britain, and Germany) followed by a final victory in Portugal secured him the world title he had been chasing for over ten years. Mansell collected almost twice as many points as his Williams teammate, Riccardo Patrese (108 to 56), and Senna had to be content with the crumbs of the feast with just three victories: Monaco, Hungary, and Italy. Three points ahead of him in the final championship standings, a newcomer began to make his presence felt. Driving a Benetton, he won in Belgium on the Spa-Francorchamps circuit. His name was Michael Schumacher.

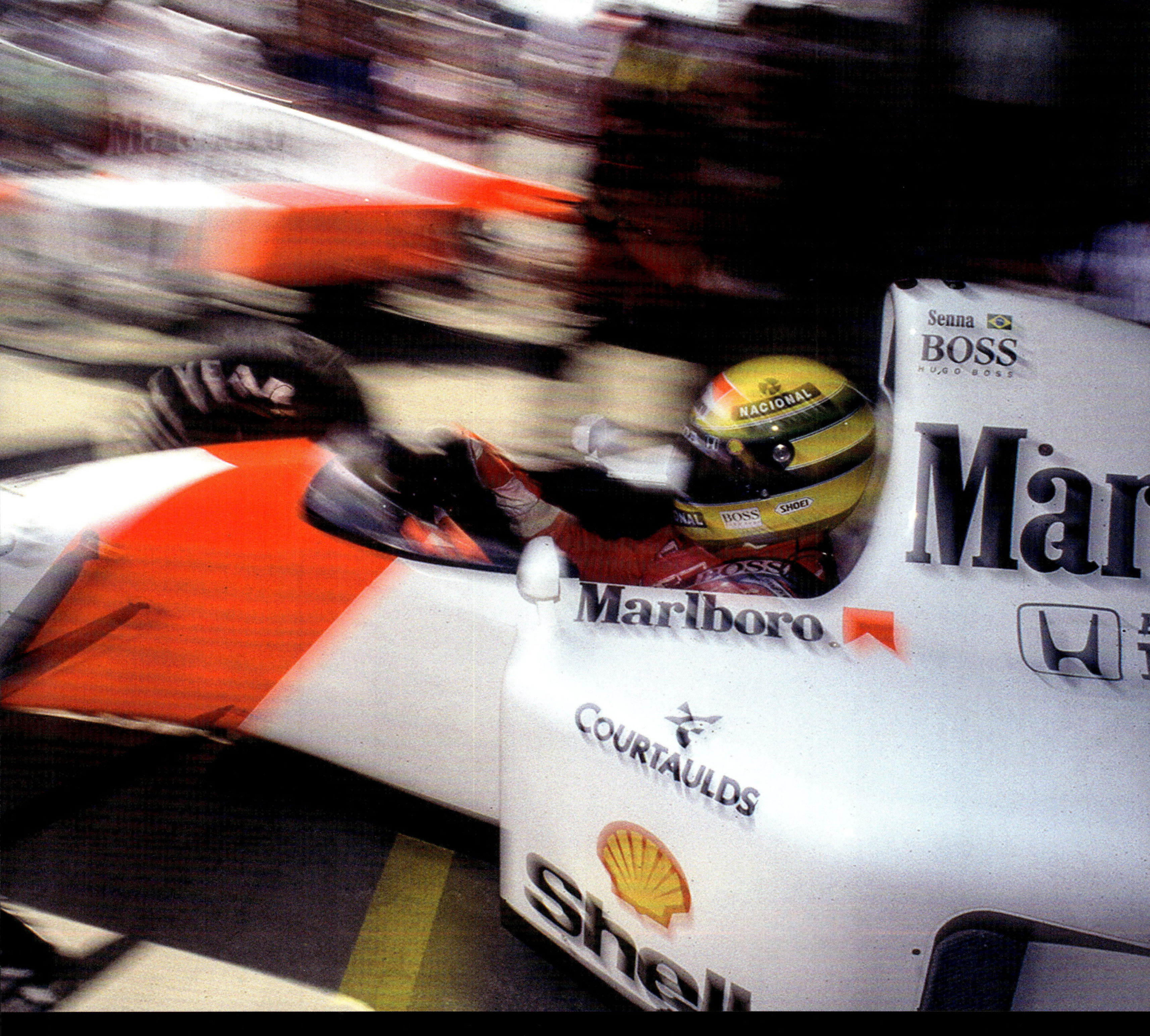

Previous pages: The duel in Monaco between Nigel Mansell and Ayrton Senna ultimately turns in favor of the Brazilian in 1992, securing his 5th victory in

RACE AFTER RACE

1992

MEXICO GRAND PRIX: A WEEKEND IN HELL

Senna suffers a violent accident during practice for the Mexico Grand Prix, the season's second round. His McLaren slams into the wall after a spin in the circuit's final chicane. Under the force of the impact, the McLaren's suspension sank into the cockpit, preventing Ayrton's left leg from being released. As a result, Senna is trapped in his McLaren. It takes the stewards and Dr. Sid Watkins, the FIA's chief medical officer, ten minutes to get him out of the cockpit—an interminable wait for the Brazilian. His body language betrayed panic and concern. "I thought I'd broken my legs," he says later. For a few hours, we wondered if he would be able to race on Sunday.

Shocked but not despondent, Senna takes the sixth place in qualifying, behind his teammate Gerhard Berger. This was on his 32nd birthday, in a car fitted with extra protection. The following

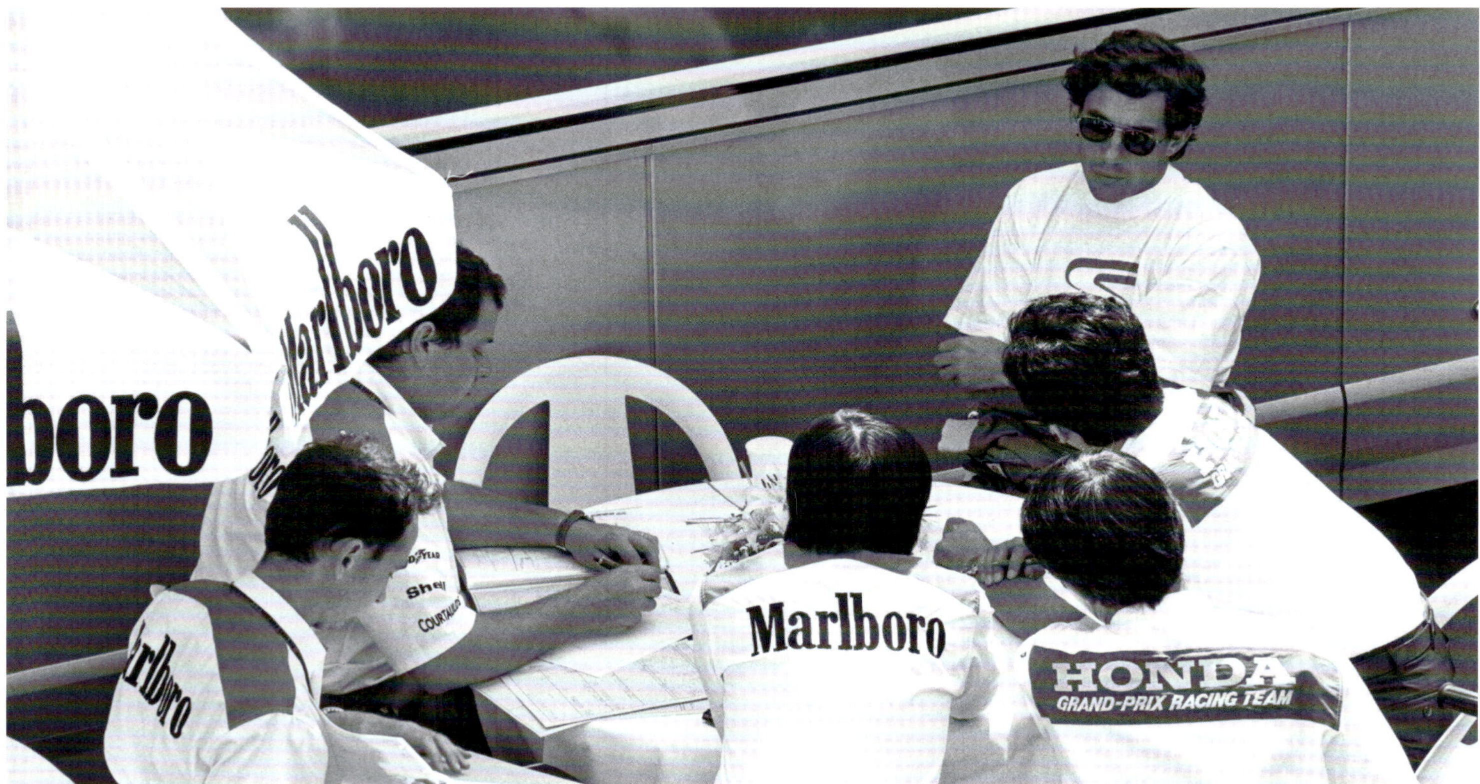

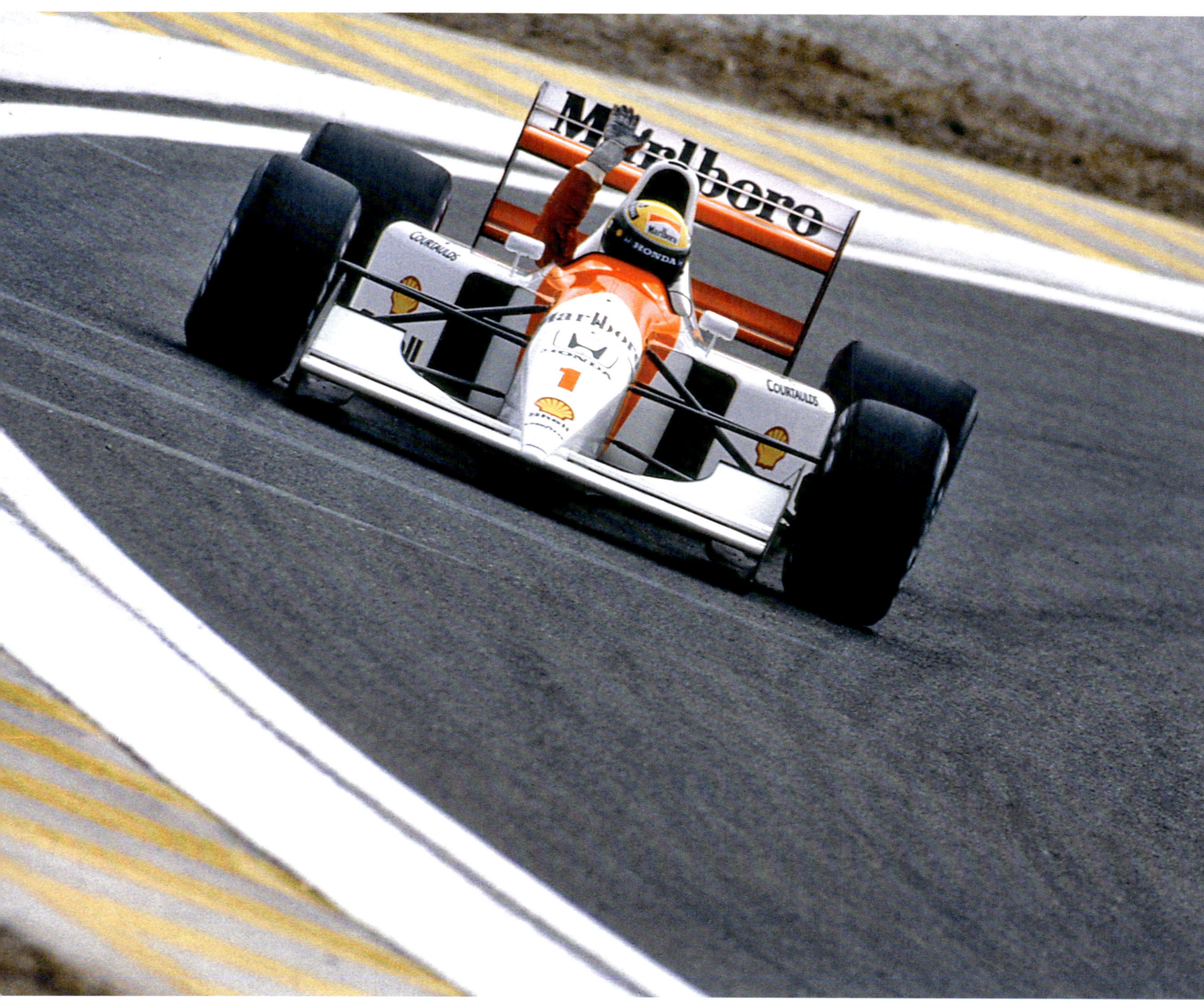

day's race was a very short one. On lap 12, his McLaren stops—the transmission is broken, while the temperature of the asphalt reaches 55°C. His Mexican run was never-ending. As you'd expect, Senna is very unhappy: "It's no longer possible with this car. The championship will start for us at Interlagos." As in South Africa, Nigel Mansell and Riccardo Patrese finish first and second. Williams and the FW14B set the tone right from the start. Therefore, the McLaren MP4/6B from 1991 was retired earlier than planned to make way for the MP4/7A at the Brazilian GP. Unfortunately, this 1992 model would not shine in terms of performance.

Left: McLaren's and Honda's engineers listen and meticulously note Senna's remarks.

Above: Senna's McLaren MP4/7A will only steer him to 4th place in the 1992 world championship, a great disappointment after his extraordinary 1991 result.

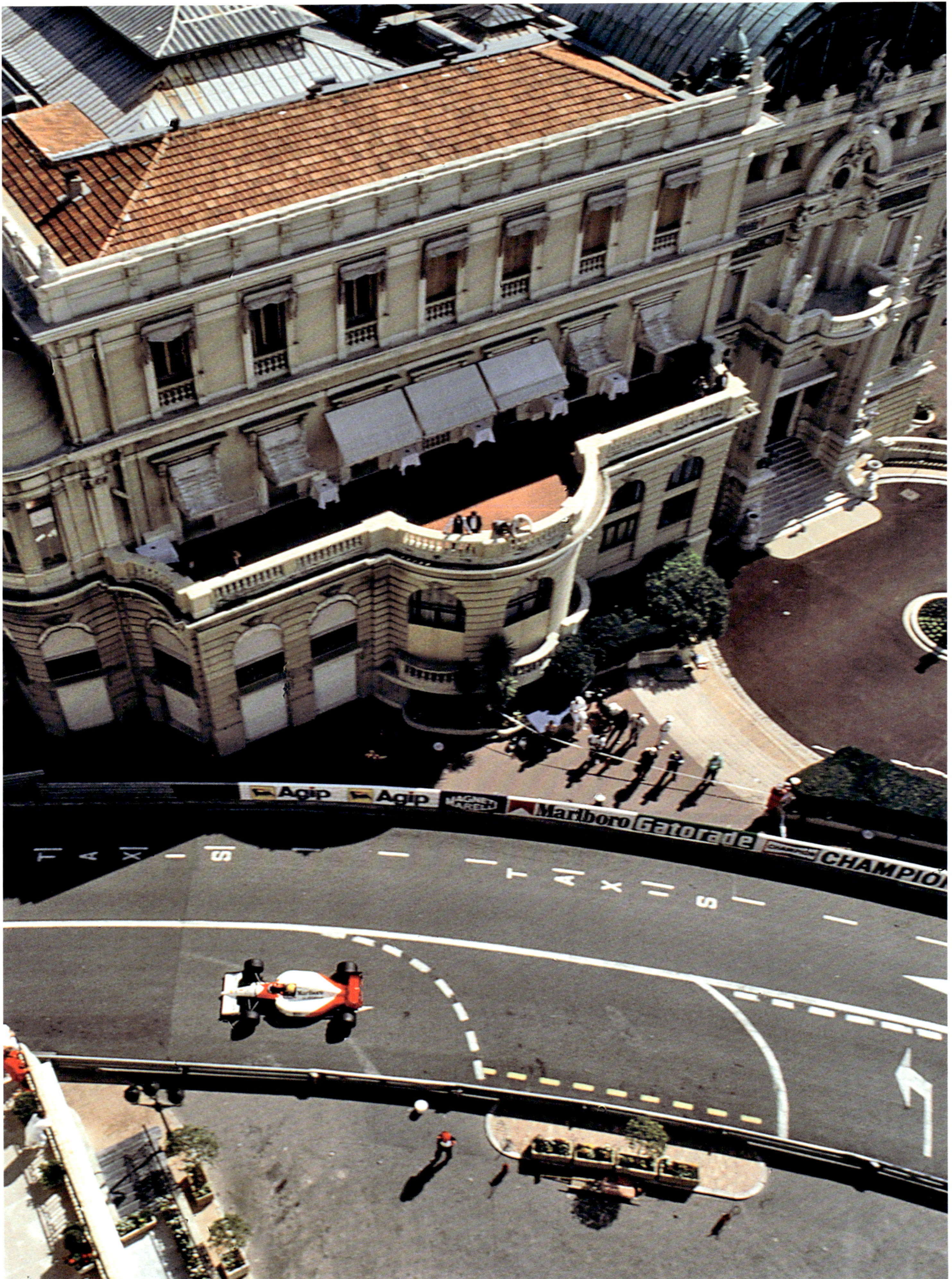
Agip
Agip
Marlboro
Gatorade
CHAMPION

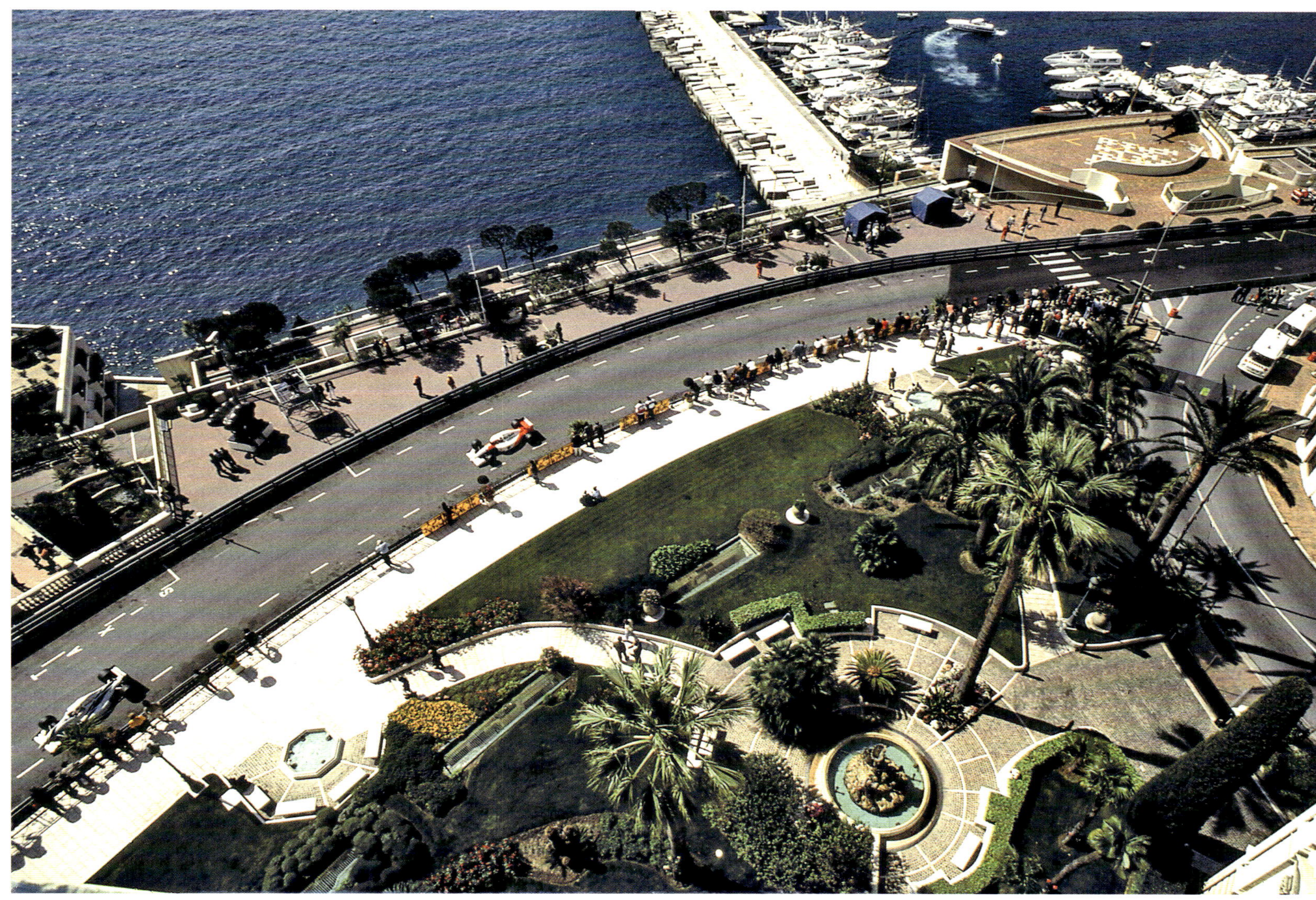

MONACO GRAND PRIX: A DUEL WITH MANSELL

For the 50th edition of the Monaco Grand Prix and the 20th anniversary of the Philip Morris Group's presence in F1, there's a lot of mundanity and personalities in the Principality, which isn't necessarily to Senna's satisfaction. Above all, there's a world championship leader, Nigel Mansell, who dreams of winning on one of the Brazilian's favorite hunting grounds for the first time. On the other hand, Ayrton Senna wants to honor Graham Hill's memory in his own way by joining him on the podium with five victories. The only other four-time winner of the Monaco Grand Prix, Alain Prost, is not here. On leave following his tumultuous divorce from Ferrari, he's aiming for a Williams seat for 1993... And he'll get it.

As you'd expect, Mansell is having a ball on the track. He breaks the circuit record (1'19"495) in qualifying and becomes the first man to drive at an average speed of 150 km/h on the Principality's streets. Senna is only third on the grid behind the two Williams and wishes on a race incident to beat them. His wish comes true with seven laps to go when he is 30 seconds behind the dominant Briton. The Williams shot straight into the chicane on lap 67 and returned to the pits on new tires—the mechanics and engineers found nothing wrong with the car. The end of the race proved to be sumptuous: Mansell is going wild, and, at the end of a fantastic comeback, he finally falls 215 thousandths short of the Brazilian, who signs his fifth victory in the Principality.

At the Sunday evening gala, another rare and unforeseeable event occurs. Senna is so happy with his victory that he offers his yellow helmet to H.S.H. Prince Rainier, who rises from his head table to thank him. It's not part of the protocol, but it is sincere and heartfelt. The Monegasque resident honors his monarch, who is moved, and the Beach Plaza room applauds the champion—a moment of grace.

Left: In the principality of Monaco, Senna was one of the most skillful in maximizing the potential of his race car.

Above: The Brazilian knows every aspect of the principality by heart due to living in Monaco for a long time.

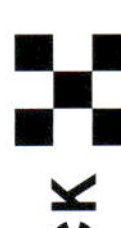

FROM THE COCKPIT TO THE JOYSTICK

In August 1992, Ayrton Senna lent his image to the video game Ayrton Senna's Super Monaco GP II. Released on the Sega consoles of the time—Mega Drive, Master System, and Game Gear—this game lets you race on the F1 circuits of 1991. The game's gameplay, a "classic" for video game industry enthusiasts, is simple and effective. With two buttons, one for acceleration and the other for braking, the aim is to sneak past your rivals and cross the finish line first. Incredibly, in 1992, Senna intervenes from time to time to give advice and information on each race to the driver behind the screen. But the main aim was obviously to beat the three-time Brazilian world champion. Released in the same year as Nigel Mansell's World Championship, this was not Senna's last appearance in a video game. In 1996 and 1998, Senna posthumously appeared on the covers of the PlayStation 1 games Ayrton Senna Kart Duel 1 and 2. More recently, the Brazilian shared the cover of the Legends edition of the F1 2019 game with Alain Prost.

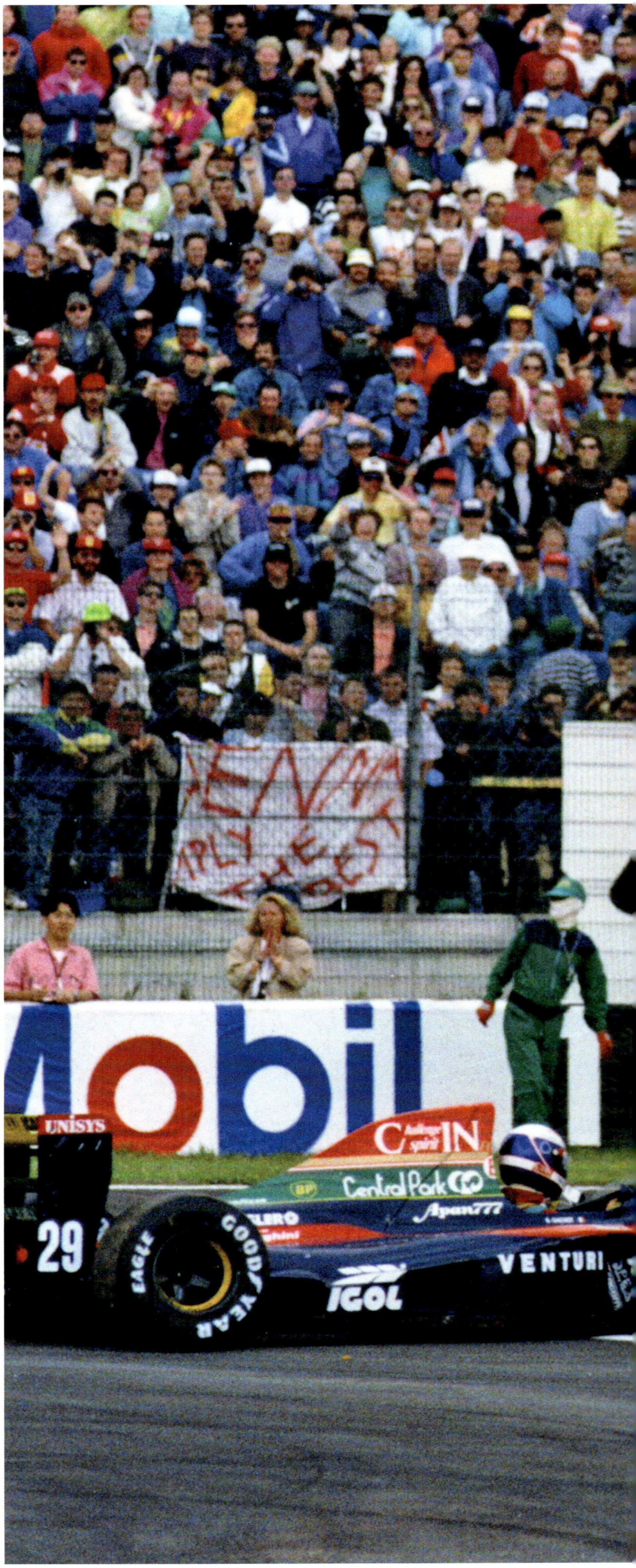

The 1992 French Grand Prix is short-lived for Senna—in the first corner of the Nevers Magny-Cours circuit, his McLaren is involved in an accident.

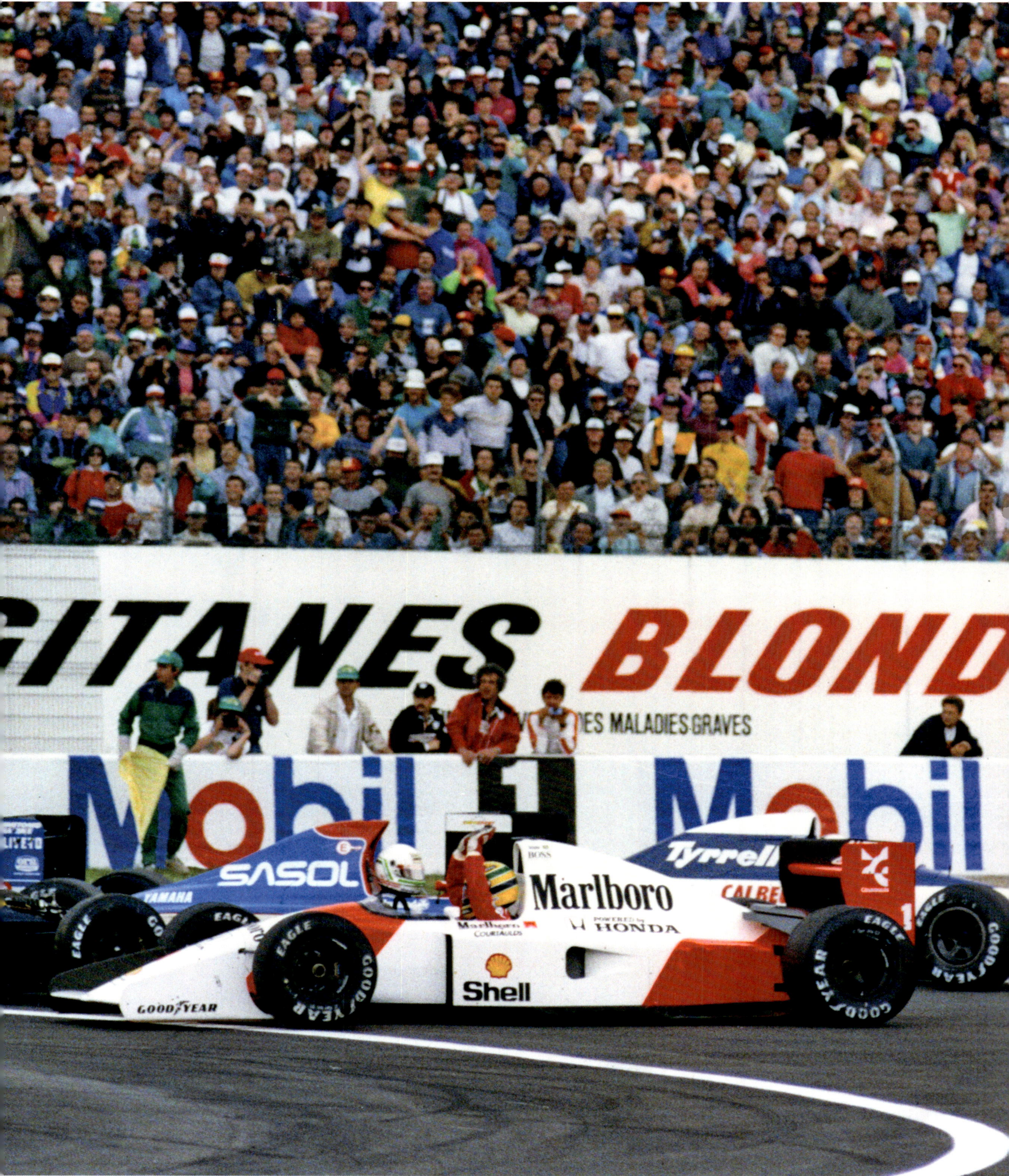
GITANES BLOND
ES MALADIES GRAVES
Mobil 1
Mobil
SASOL
YAMAHA
Tyrrell
Marlboro
HONDA
Shell
GOODYEAR
EAGLE

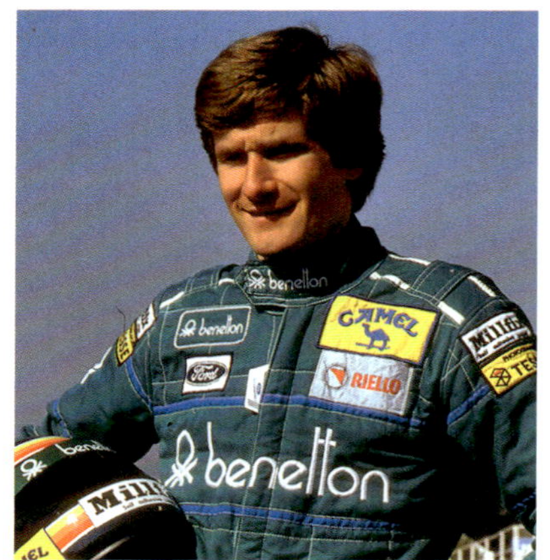

THIERRY BOUTSEN, ONE OF AYRTON'S CLOSEST FRIENDS

The Belgian raced in 163 F1 Grands Prix between 1983 and 1992 with Arrows, Benetton, Williams, Ligier, and Jordan. He had a front-row seat to witness Senna's great battles against Prost and Mansell, among others. He forged a true friendship with the Brazilian and is happy to recount it thirty years on. Here's a selection:

"I have his helmet at home, and I think of him every day. He was my best friend in F1. We could talk about anything; we often saw each other on vacation, and he should have been my son's godfather. He believed very strongly in God and talked about God when he won a Grand Prix. That certainly helped him to be so strong. He was the only one like that, and that was exceptional. [...]

Ayrton was the best of them all, but not of all times, because you can't compare eras. He fought well with everyone—Nelson, Alain, Nigel, whom I saw again last night in Monaco. We were a group of six or seven drivers who were always in the top six, but Ayrton had something extra. He dominated his era, and wherever you talk about F1 in the world, people quote Fangio because he was the first and Ayrton. He was Magic Senna on every level. [...]

We lived through an era when there were some very funny boys. Ayrton had a great sense of humor, Gerhard was quite a joker, Nigel and Nelson bickered all the time, and Ayrton's run-ins with Alain made for a lot of laughs. One year, we were doing private testing at Magny-Cours, and we were all staying at the same hotel. There were fir trees planted in big tubs in the parking lot, so we found a rope and hung all the trees on Ayrton's bumper. When he drove off the next morning, all the trees fell on his car... [...].

In Ayrton's day, when we raced in the Monaco GP, we'd make 4,500 gear changes during the race. You'd end up with your hand in tatters, with a big blister in the middle, and you couldn't drive for four or five days while the wounds healed. We didn't have power steering, the brakes weren't the same, we had very powerful turbos—over 1,200 HP of engine power—it was very different from now. Nowadays, everything is electronically controlled, just like in aviation. Technology is much more dominant than it used to be, and it's always the same people who are ahead. In that respect, it was better before, because you could catch up, whereas today, even a tenth's difference is impossible to make up. [...]

What were his plans for the future? I imagine he was tempted by the idea of going into politics, and those close to him certainly talked to him about it. But we never talked about it together. Considering the country's distress and his notoriety, it's fair to say that he was very clearly above the pack."

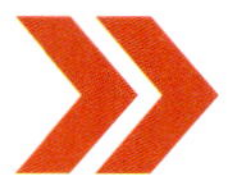

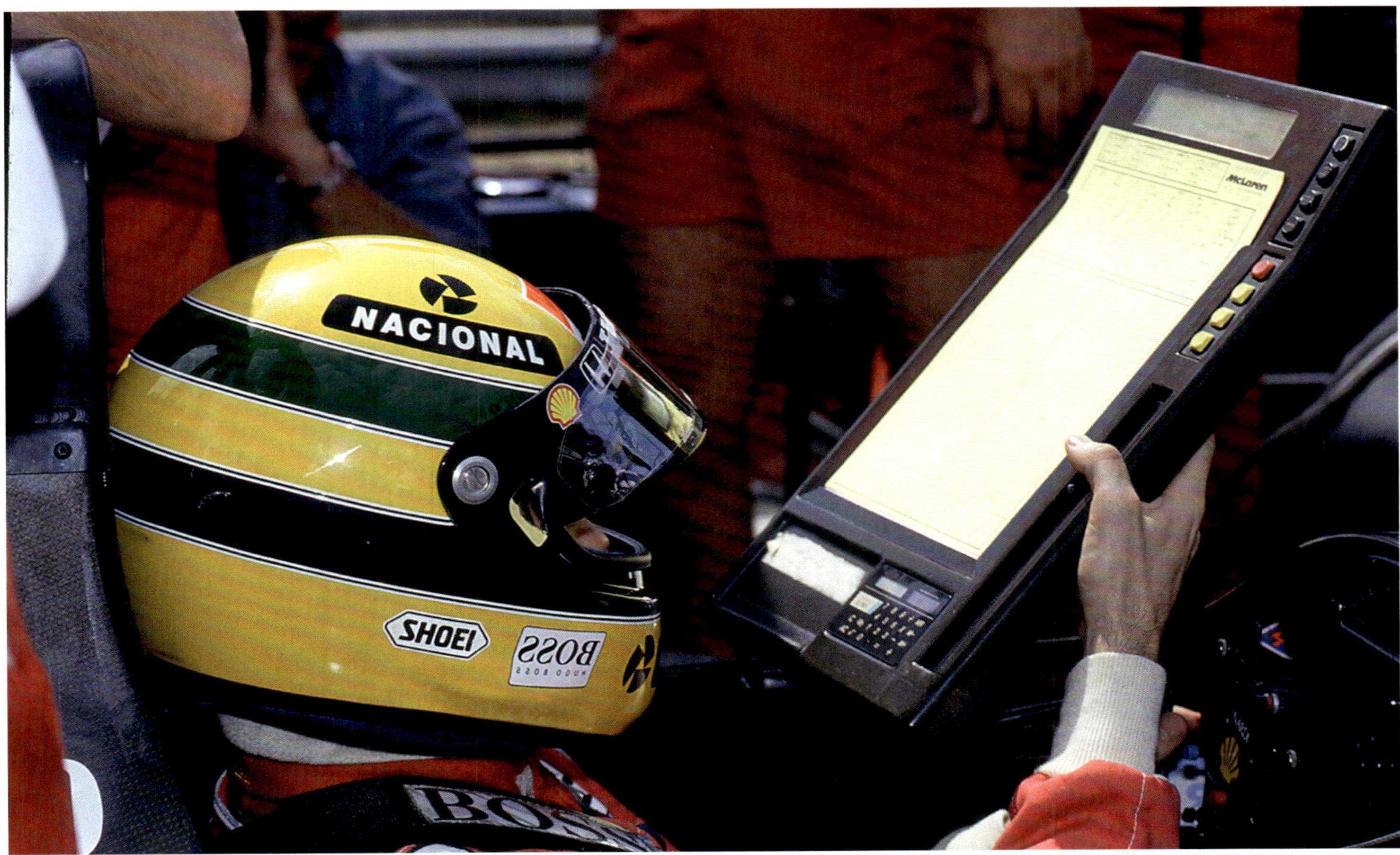

Telemetry in Formula 1 in the 1990s enabled Senna to store as much data as possible before a qualifying lap.

GERMAN GRAND PRIX, HOCKENHEIM: SCHUMACHER, THE NEW RIVAL

Young Michael Schumacher's first full season in Formula 1 allowed him to compete against the category's absolute benchmark, Ayrton Senna, and the Germany Hockenheim Grand Prix was the ideal place for the young German to make his mark. He does so at 300 km/h at the end of the long straight that leads into the stadium, braking hard in front of the Brazilian. Senna is furious and lets him know it, first on the track, driving wheel-to-wheel with him for an entire lap, then shoving the young man at the back of the Benetton stand. "Next time will be the last time," he tells him, very irritated.

McLaren coordinator Jo Ramírez comes to the rescue, and members of the Benetton team take Schumacher away for an interview with German TV. When he returns, he's accompanied by his mentor, Flavio Briatore. Senna explains that he didn't purposely embarrass him in Brazil at the beginning of April and was just suffering from engine failure. By the end of the day, Senna is calm, so he declares the end of hostilities: "Schumacher has talent, he's at the start of his career, he's under a lot of pressure, but he needs to learn how things work in F1. Someone could get hurt."

LEO TURRINI

For Italian journalist Leo Turrini, it's obvious that "Senna didn't like Schumacher. There was that row at Hockenheim and another at Magny-Cours after a collision at the start. But as a driver, Senna understood that Michael had everything it took to become a great driver. He sensed that the German was there to beat him and not just in one race. So, there was never any friendship between them, and there was certainly mutual respect."

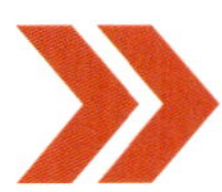

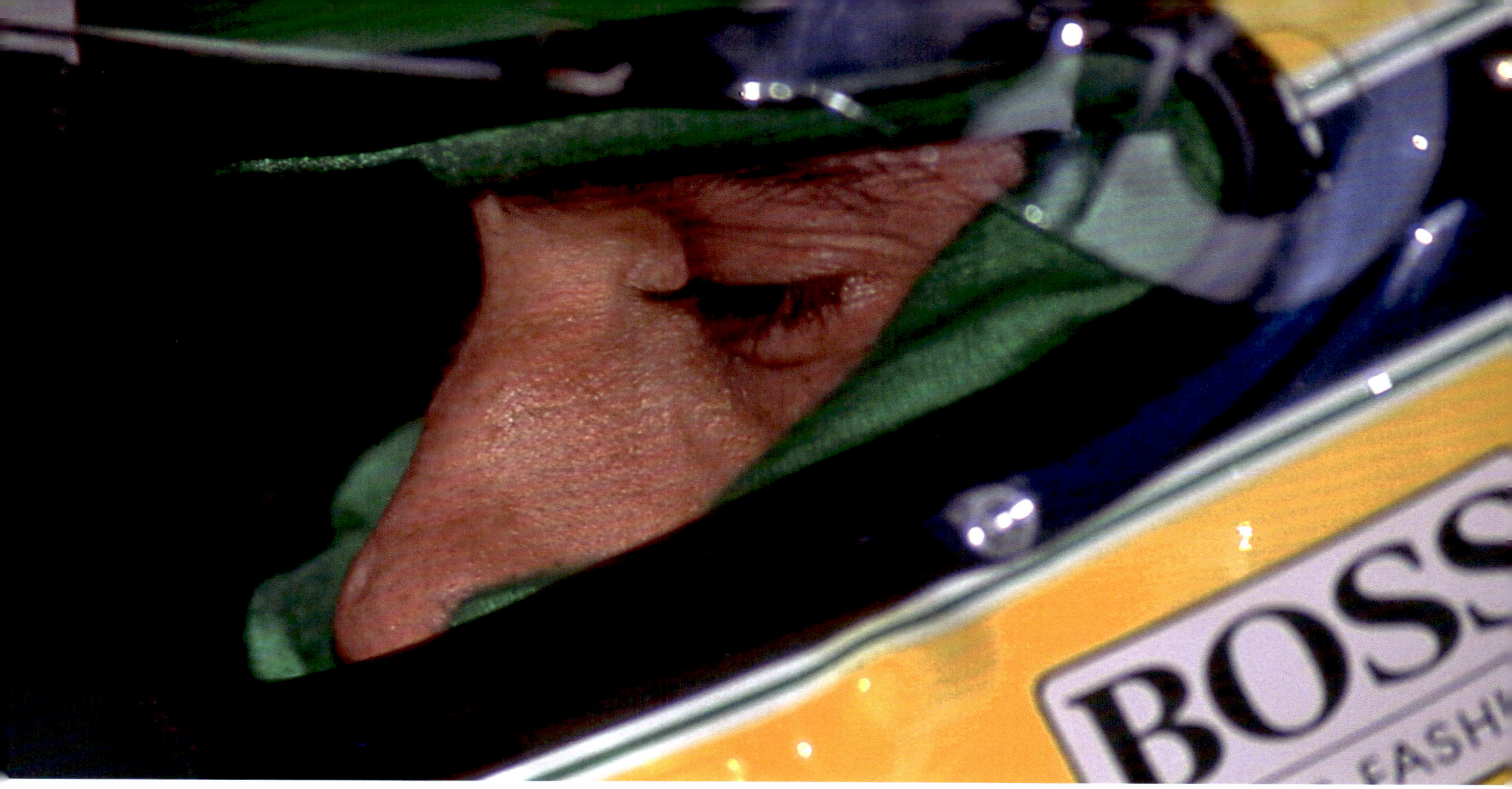

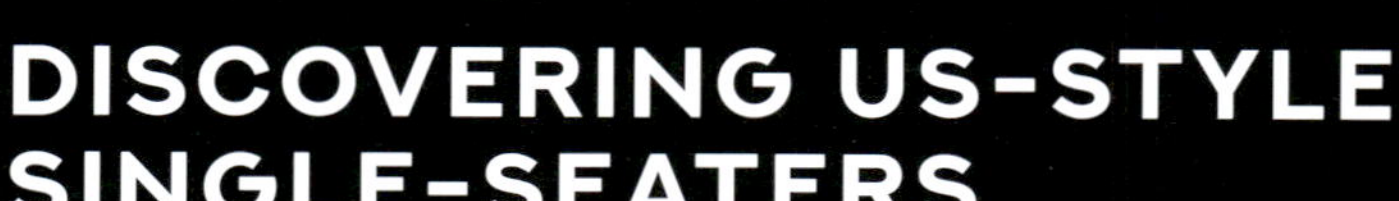

DISCOVERING US-STYLE SINGLE-SEATERS

Ayrton Senna in an American single-seater? It happened on December 20, 1992. Bored and probably tired of Williams' domination, the Brazilian wanted to taste the flavor of CART—the American single-seater championship—of which Emerson Fittipaldi, two-time F1 world champion, was one of the most illustrious ambassadors. Fittipaldi offered Senna a test drive in Phoenix with his team, the legendary American Penske team. Both drivers wore Marlboro colors, Senna for McLaren and Fittipaldi for Penske, so the agreement was a formality.

At around 10 a.m., Senna and Fittipaldi arrived in a limousine at Phoenix Firebird Raceway. Ayrton climbed aboard the Penske-Chevrolet PC-21 after Fittipaldi's test run. The car was 200 kg heavier than the McLaren MP4/7A, and it is very rudimentary in terms of electronics. Senna appreciated this return to a cockpit where only driving counted. All the more so, behind the scenes, he's taking advantage of this moment to sow doubt in the F1 paddock. After Mansell announced his departure for Newman/Haas in CART, he knew that the only star left in F1 was himself. This not-so-secret test is also an ideal way of putting pressure on McLaren to pay him a better salary.

Fittipaldi set the fastest time of 49.7 seconds. At the end of the day, having made a few adjustments, Senna was very satisfied with his best time of 49.09 seconds. In his only CART outing, the King of Brazil beat the 1989 CART champion, twice winner of the Indianapolis 500, by almost seven-tenths of a second. As he exited the cockpit, he spoke to Penske engineer Nigel Beresford. Beresford, now team manager of the DS Penske Formula E team, recalls: "He said, 'Thank you very much. I've learned what I wanted to know.' He unhooked his harness and jumped out of the car. He was just fast." Roger Penske, too, was convinced: "If Senna had been available, we would have tried to find a solution," he says, 25 years on from that ill-fated test. December 20, 1992, will forever remain a parenthesis in the career of the three-time Brazilian world champion.

SENNA VS. MANSELL THE FIGURES

During their nine-season rivalry in F1 (1984–1992), Senna and Mansell often engaged in great fights on the track, and the Englishman's record of achievements is anything but ridiculous against such a high-caliber adversary. The statistics show that he was the third man in F1's golden era, alongside Senna and Prost.

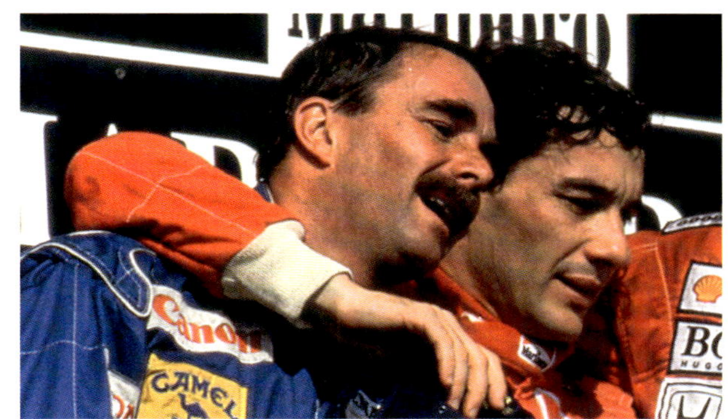

1984-1992	VICTORIES	PODIUMS	POLE POSITIONS	BEST LAPS	TITLES
SENNA	36	73	61	18	3 (1988, 1990, 1991)
MANSELL	30	55	31	29	1 (1992)

THE MAIN CHARACTERS

NIGEL MANSELL, THE THIRD MAN

It's impossible to write a book about Ayrton Senna's career without mentioning Nigel Mansell, if only because of the coincidence of dates and the final phase of their rivalry—with a happy ending for the Briton. Senna raced in F1 from 1984 to 1994, winning 41 Grands Prix. Mansell battled for 14 years, winning 31 times, and his record deserves respect. Of his 31 F1 victories, 28 came in Williams cars and only three in Ferraris. Nigel had a frustrating first period, from 1985 to 1987, often appearing as a rather sympathetic "loser," a great specialist in collisions and mechanical breakdowns, but nevertheless twice runner-up in the world championship (1986, 1987), with a Honda engine powering him. A second, much more rewarding period, thanks to the Renault V10 engine and active suspension, enabled him to finally win a world crown in 1992.

"Ayrton used to talk a lot about Prost and Mansell, and he attributed great strength to the latter. It was a sort of triangle: Ayrton, Mansell, and Prost. Ayrton said they sometimes made him angry, but they were important because they were very good and pushed him to give more of himself, to give his best. That's how he got the best results." This confidence comes from Nuno Cobra, Senna's physical and mental trainer. It sums up the importance of this second role—always essential in a good film—held by Mansell for over ten years, including two full seasons with Ferrari (1989, 1990), which was already a form of consecration for an English driver.

Mansell vividly remembers Sunday, August 16, 1992, when he became world champion with five races to go, finishing second in the Hungarian Grand Prix behind Senna. "On the podium, Ayrton turned to me and, putting an arm on my shoulder, said: 'Now you realize what a great feeling this is, right? Do you understand why I'm such a bastard on the track? Because this feeling is the best in the world.'"

Ayrton Senna is a driver with meticulous preparation that allows him to touch the peaks of racing.

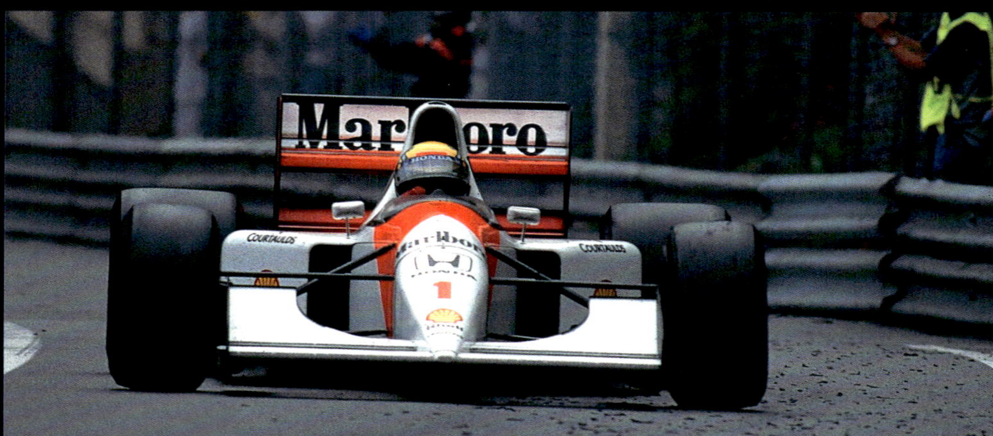

THE CAR: MCLAREN MP4/7A

The McLaren MP4/7A makes its racing debut in Brazil, the third Grand Prix of 1992. Far from being a competitive car, it struggles to keep up with the Williams FW14B and its active suspension, which ensured ten victories in 16 races. The MP4/7A was originally due to debut at the next Grand Prix in Barcelona. But Ron Dennis and his teams decided to bring forward the new model's arrival, watching helplessly as Didcot's team scored double victories in the first two rounds.

This McLaren—designed by Neil Oatley as chief designer and Henri Durand for aerodynamics—is the first to feature a semi-automatic transmission. The long nose was chosen to improve aerodynamic performance. It was powered by a Honda RA122E engine, a 75-degree V12, whereas the previous year's engine was installed at 60 degrees. It also benefits from a further innovation, the first-ever "fly-by-wire" system. This technology allows McLaren drivers to keep their foot on the gas pedal even while shifting gears. These innovations are made possible by an old "friend" of McLaren, Techniques d'Avant-Garde (TAG). Mansour Ojjeh's group, famous—among other things—for having helped the British team with its Porsche engine in the 1980s, made a huge effort to close the gap on the Mansell-Patrese duo. However, these attempts were unsuccessful in the face of the omnipotence of Frank Williams' team. It was the end of a cycle, and engine-maker Honda withdrew from F1 at the end of the season with five more victories (three for Senna, two for Berger). The McLaren-Honda alliance's record would remain phenomenal: 44 victories in five seasons between 1988 and 1992, including 11 for Prost, three for Berger... and 30 for Senna! No comment.

BELGIUM GRAND PRIX: SAVING ERIK COMAS

During the Belgium Grand Prix on August 28, Erik Comas is involved in a terrible accident. While he is unconscious in his car, one driver stops immediately to come to his aid: Ayrton Senna. Flash back almost thirty-one years later with the former Larrousse and Ligier team driver: "It was free practice, and I was on my third lap. I slipped on gravel scattered a few moments earlier by Finnish driver JJ Lehto and couldn't avoid hitting the guardrails at Blanchimont at high speed. This corner is like the one at Tamburello in Imola: It's at full speed, a blind corner. I was knocked unconscious by one of my wheels. Afterwards, I don't remember a thing: The stewards told me."

A few seconds later, Senna arrives at the scene, even before the emergency services. He hears the engine still running. Erik is unconscious, his right foot crushing the gas pedal. Senna runs towards the wrecked car and manages to activate the circuit breaker. "He knew something was wrong, so he braved the danger and zigzagged between the F1 cars, which were arriving at full speed," says Comas. The three-time world champion saved his life, no more, no less. "For us, Ayrton was God. He was the one who pulled me out of extremely serious consequences," explains the former Ligier driver, before continuing, not without emotion: "He was a generous person with others. He saw me in danger, he didn't question me, he didn't think. He put his life in danger to save me. Ayrton was like that. Helping his fellow man was his main concern!"

Later, Sid Watkins would detail that Ayrton "held Erik Comas's neck the whole way, making sure the Ligier driver could breathe properly." The following day, the former Formula 3000 champion had the opportunity to see his savior again: "When I came back to the track to thank Ayrton, he was still worried about me. And he was right. I had to wait two months before I was fully recovered," recalls the Frenchman.

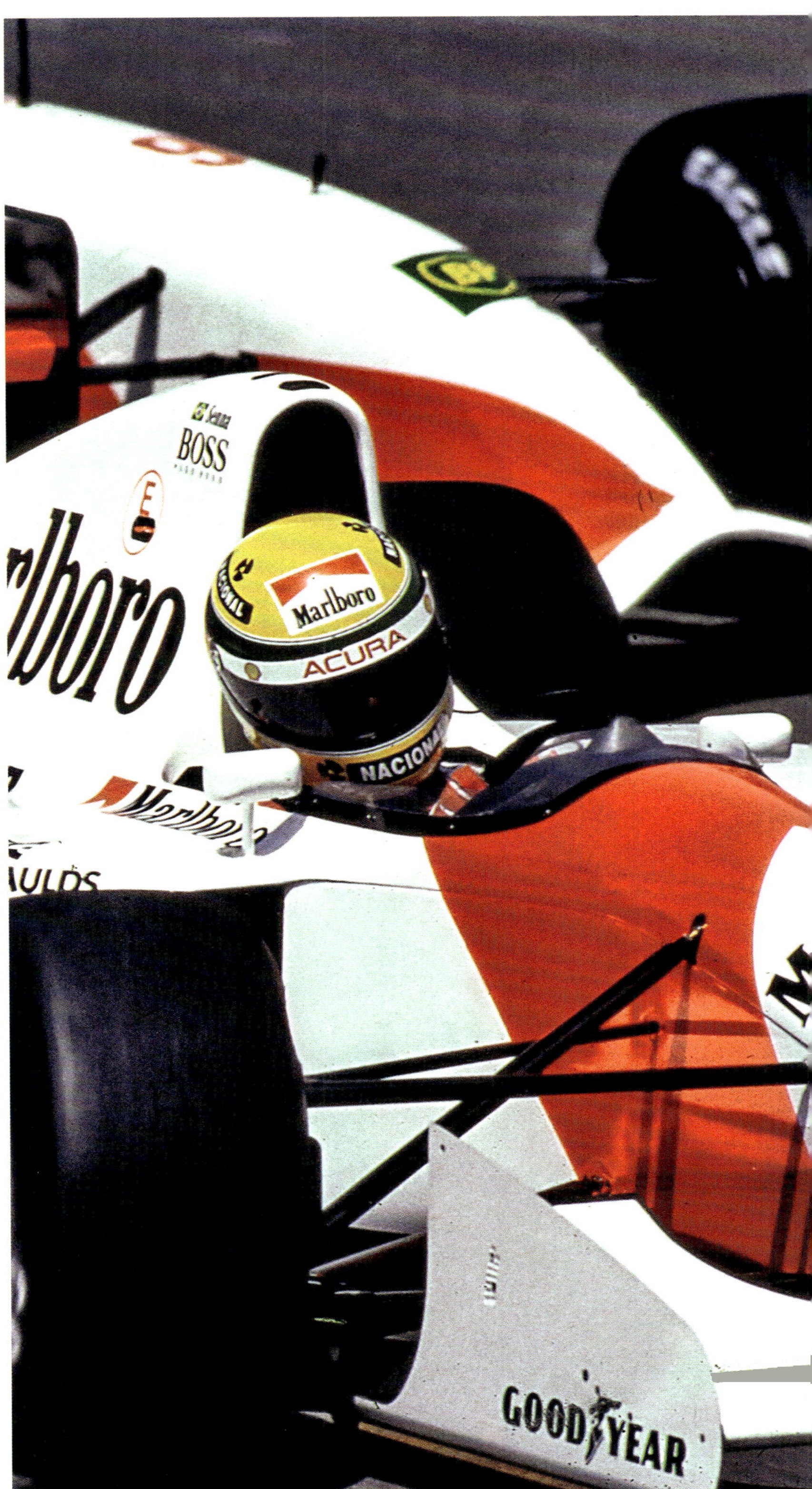

Senna's driving is of surgical precision. Each turn is calculated, anticipated, negotiated, and mastered at the highest possible speed.

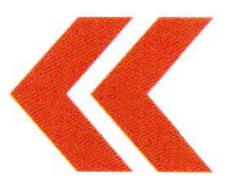

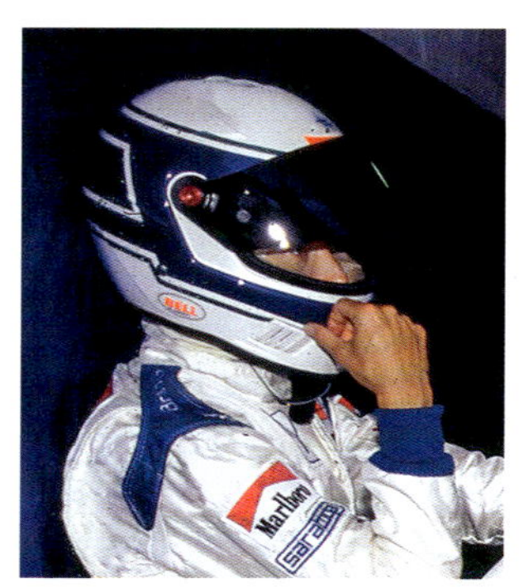

GIOVANNA AMATI AND SENNA, THE GENTLEMAN

Giovanna Amati, the last woman to drive an F1 car during the practice sessions for three Grands Prix—in 1992, in a Judd-powered Brabham—remembers the only driver to greet her on her arrival in the paddock: Ayrton Senna.

"I'd already met him in Monaco in 1985 when he was Elio De Angelis' teammate at Lotus, and I'd even asked Elio to introduce me to him. After the Monaco GP, a friend who knew I wanted to meet him said to me, 'If you want, I'll take him to the heliport in Monaco on Monday morning. Would you like to come?' I replied, 'Yes, yes, yes, I'd be happy to keep you company.' And then, when we got to the heliport [laughs], I said 'Goodbye Ayrton, bon voyage' and kept looking at him—because for me, he was an idol, a myth—and took two steps back, not realizing that a suitcase was lying right behind me. I just had time to see the expression on Ayrton's face, and then I fell backwards. I swore I'd never have an idol in my life again if I lost control like that [smile]."

"[When I joined Brabham in 1992,] the only one who came to say hello was Ayrton. The Brabham team was 'in the Bronx,' at the other end of the pit lane, while McLaren was in front, very close to the exit. So, he drove up the whole pit lane and back to Brabham. All the mechanics and engineers were stunned! One mechanic came up to me and asked, 'What did you do to him?' I replied that I hadn't done anything. He insisted, 'Did you squeeze him on a curve?' But I hadn't done anything: I'm very attentive to others, I'm a professional. In the box, they were stunned and didn't know what to expect. In fact, he simply came over and shook my hand, saying, 'Welcome, I'm glad you've arrived in Formula 1, and I'd like to congratulate you.' I didn't know what to say. For him to come and greet me was unique. He was special and he felt the best. That's why he could welcome someone like me, who was nothing, who was just a beginner."

In fact, he simply came over and shook my hand, saying, 'Welcome, I'm glad you've arrived in Formula 1, and I'd like to congratulate you.'

GIOVANNA AMATI

At every Grand Prix weekend, Senna, a fierce competitor at heart, considers all factors that can make him better.

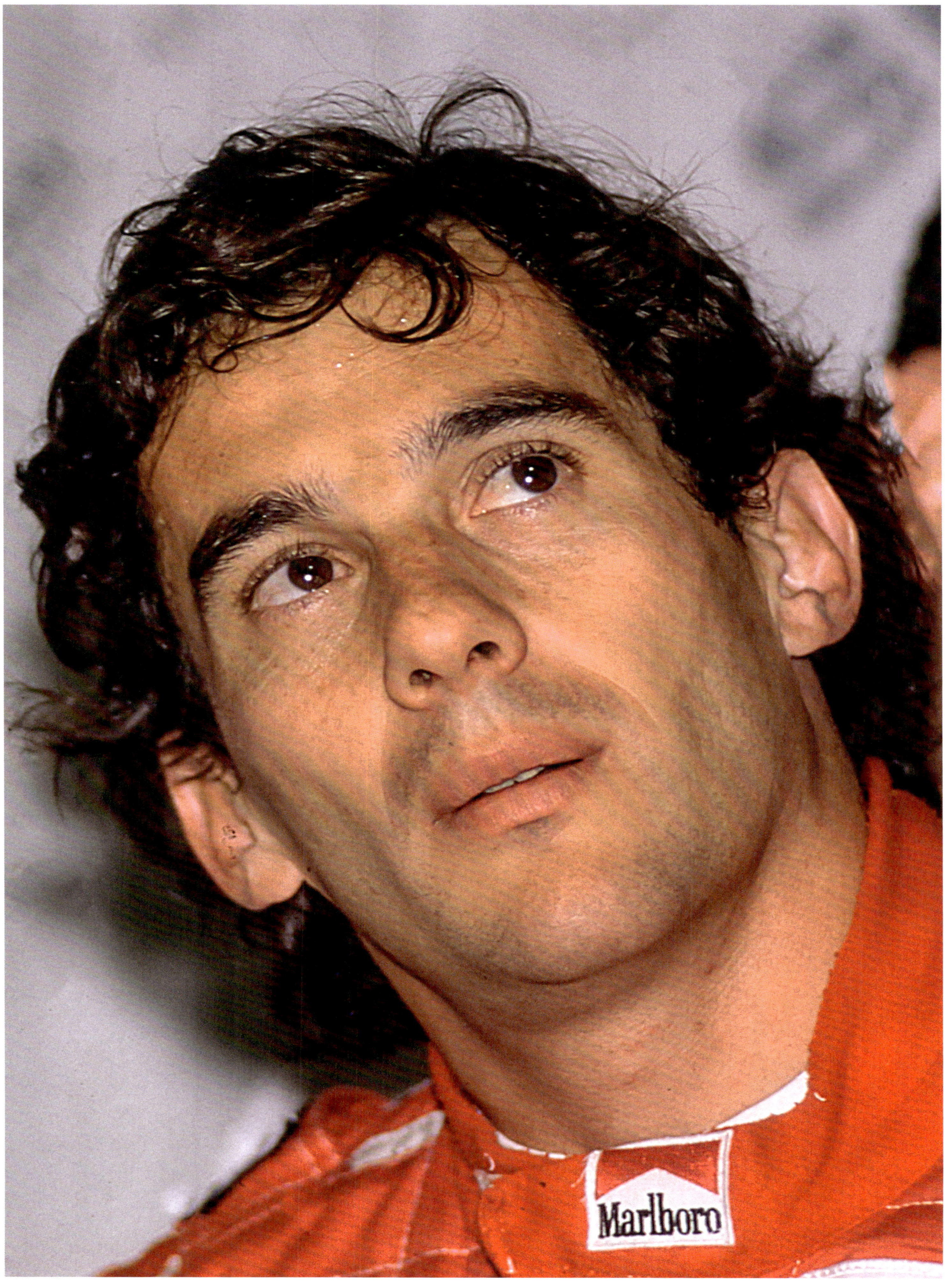
Marlboro

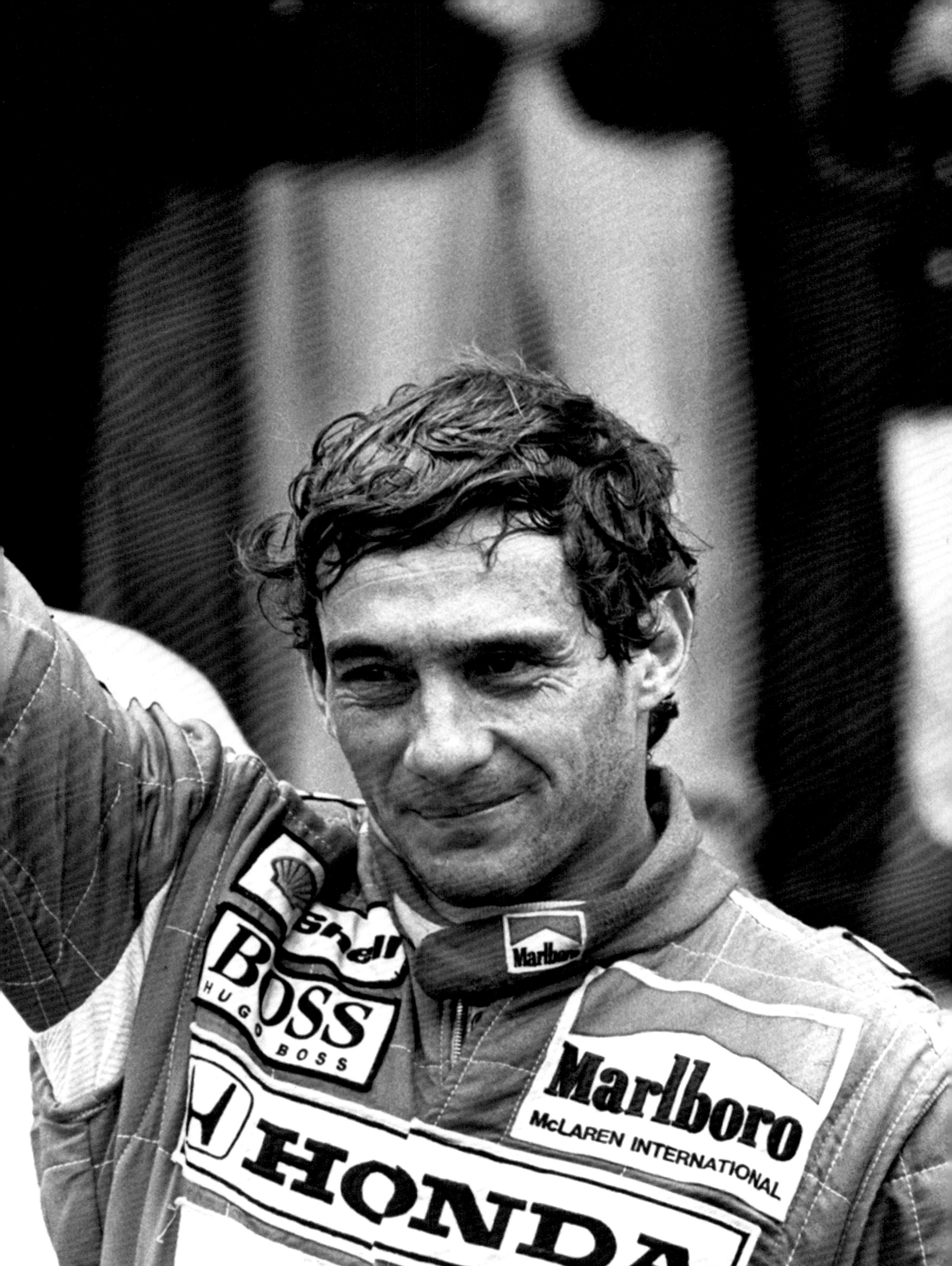
Shell
BOSS
HUGO BOSS
Marlboro
Marlboro
McLAREN INTERNATIONAL
HONDA

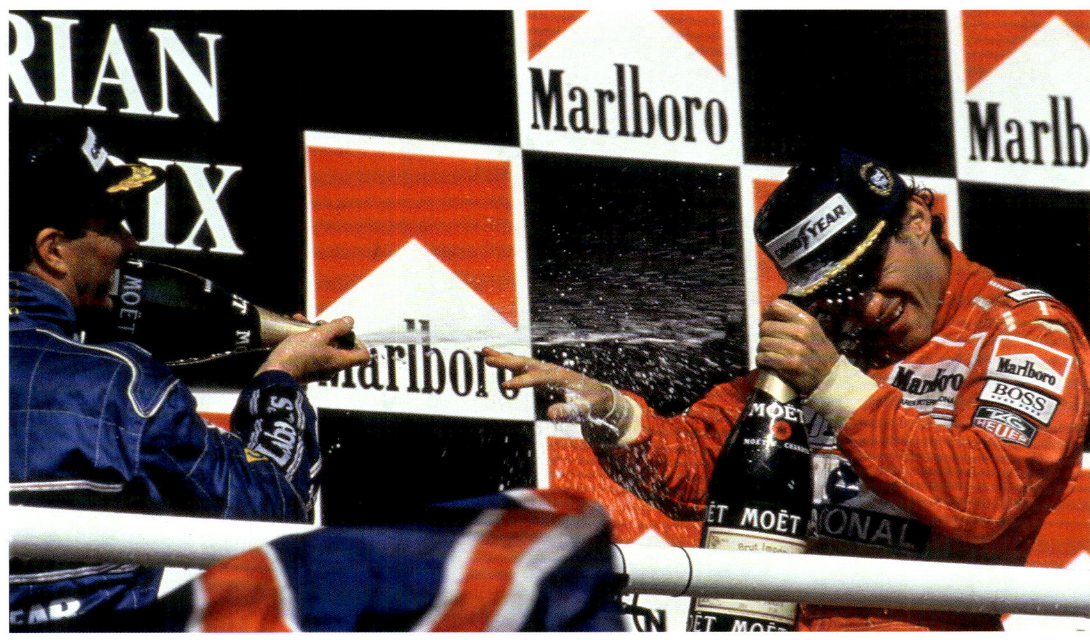

THE 1992 SEASON IN FIGURES

GRAND PRIX	QUALIFIERS	RACE
SOUTH AFRICA	2ND	3RD
MEXICO	6TH	DNF (TRANSMISSION)
BRAZIL	3RD	DNF (ELECTRICAL PROBLEM)
SPAIN	3RD	9TH (SPIN)
SAN MARINO	3RD	3RD
MONACO	3RD	VICTORY 34
CANADA	POLE POSITION 61	DNF (ELECTRICAL PROBLEM)
FRANCE	3RD	DNF (CRASH)
GREAT BRITAIN	3RD	DNF (GEARBOX)
GERMANY	3RD	2ND
HUNGARY	3RD	VICTORY 35
BELGIUM	2ND	5TH
ITALY	2ND	VICTORY 36
PORTUGAL	3RD	3RD
JAPAN	3RD	DNF (ENGINE)
AUSTRALIA	2ND	DNF (CRASH)

4TH IN THE FORMULA 1 WORLD CHAMPIONSHIP
(50 POINTS, THREE VICTORIES, SEVEN PODIUMS, ONE POLE POSITION, ONE BEST LAP)

Left: In Monaco, Senna relishes yet another victory to beat Williams Racing's Renault in the riviera principality.

Above: The 1992 Hungarian Grand Prix is the stage for and beautiful victory by Ayrton Senna but also the Grand Prix that crowns Nigel Mansell as the 1992 world champion.

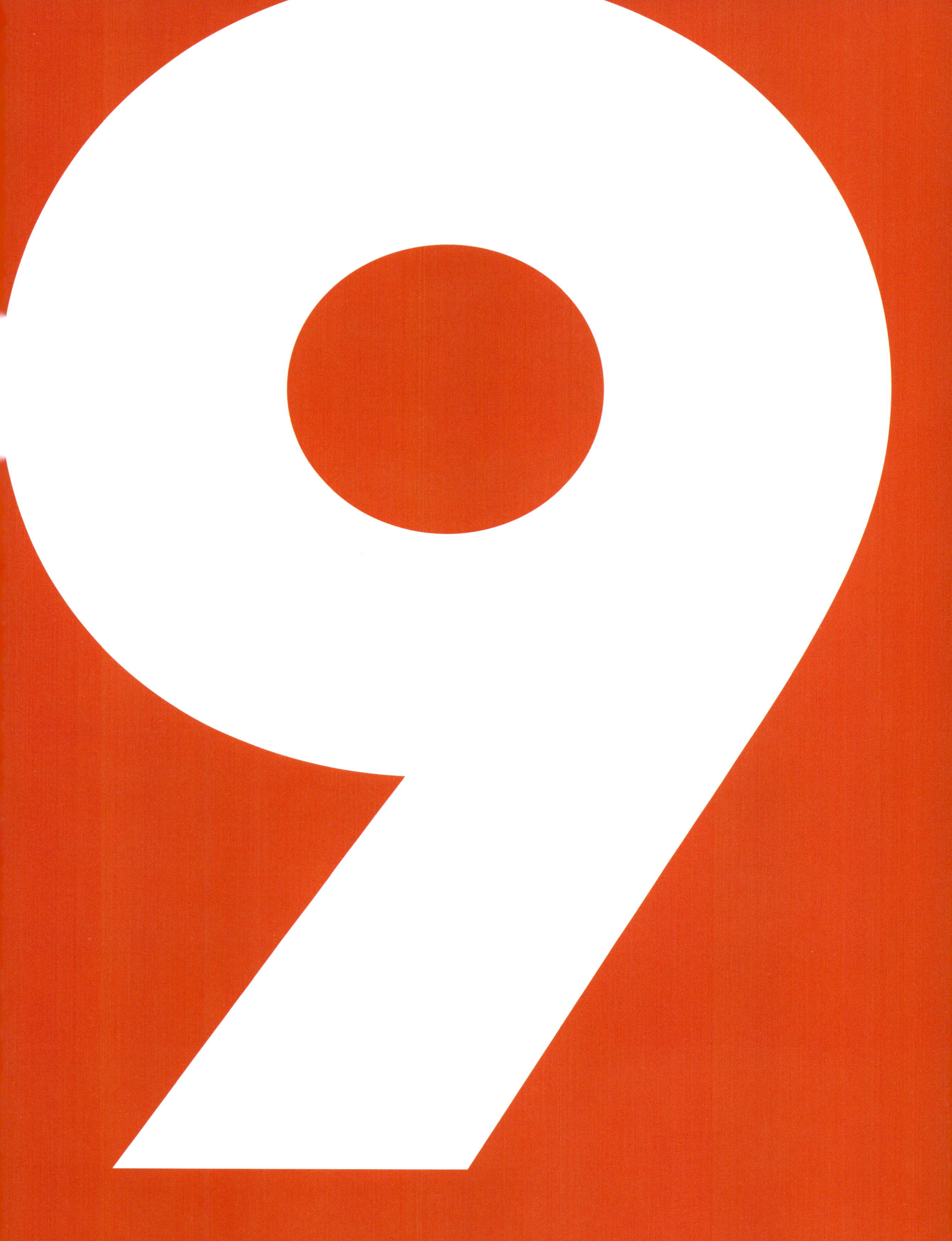
9

3

THE REUNION WITH PROST

WILLIAMS: THE WINNING TICKET

AT THE BEGINNING OF 1993, ALAIN PROST EMERGED FROM HIS SABBATICAL AND TOOK THE SEAT HE'D BEEN AIMING AT FOR SEVERAL MONTHS IN FRANK WILLIAMS' TEAM: THAT OF NIGEL MANSELL, WHO HAD SET OUT TO CONQUER AMERICA IN INDYCAR, IN THE CART CHAMPIONSHIP. IT SUITED HIS MUSCULAR, NO-NONSENSE DRIVING STYLE PERFECTLY, AND HE WON IT HANDS DOWN ON HIS FIRST ATTEMPT.

Prost's move to Williams—the best team at the time—was obviously a good one; otherwise, the Frenchman wouldn't have done everything in his power to get behind the wheel. The 1993 season confirmed that it was the ideal package, with the added bonus of a certain Damon Hill as the second driver, son of Graham and Prost's perfect lieutenant in a team above the rest, as in 1992. The statistics are crystal-clear: seven wins for Prost in the first ten rounds, then three more for Hill at the end of the season.

Overall: 10 wins for Williams-Renault in 16 rounds, compared with five for Senna (including Brazil and Monaco) and just one for Schumacher. Prost, freewheeling, finished with three 2nd places in a row, including two behind Senna in Japan and Australia. The score was indisputable: 99 points to 73 for the Brazilian, who narrowly avoided a Williams drivers' double in the World Championship, with a 4-point lead over Hill. Last but not least: Prost now leads Senna 4–3 in the number of world titles, but he's about to retire for good. The road is open for the Brazilian, who will succeed him at Didcot.

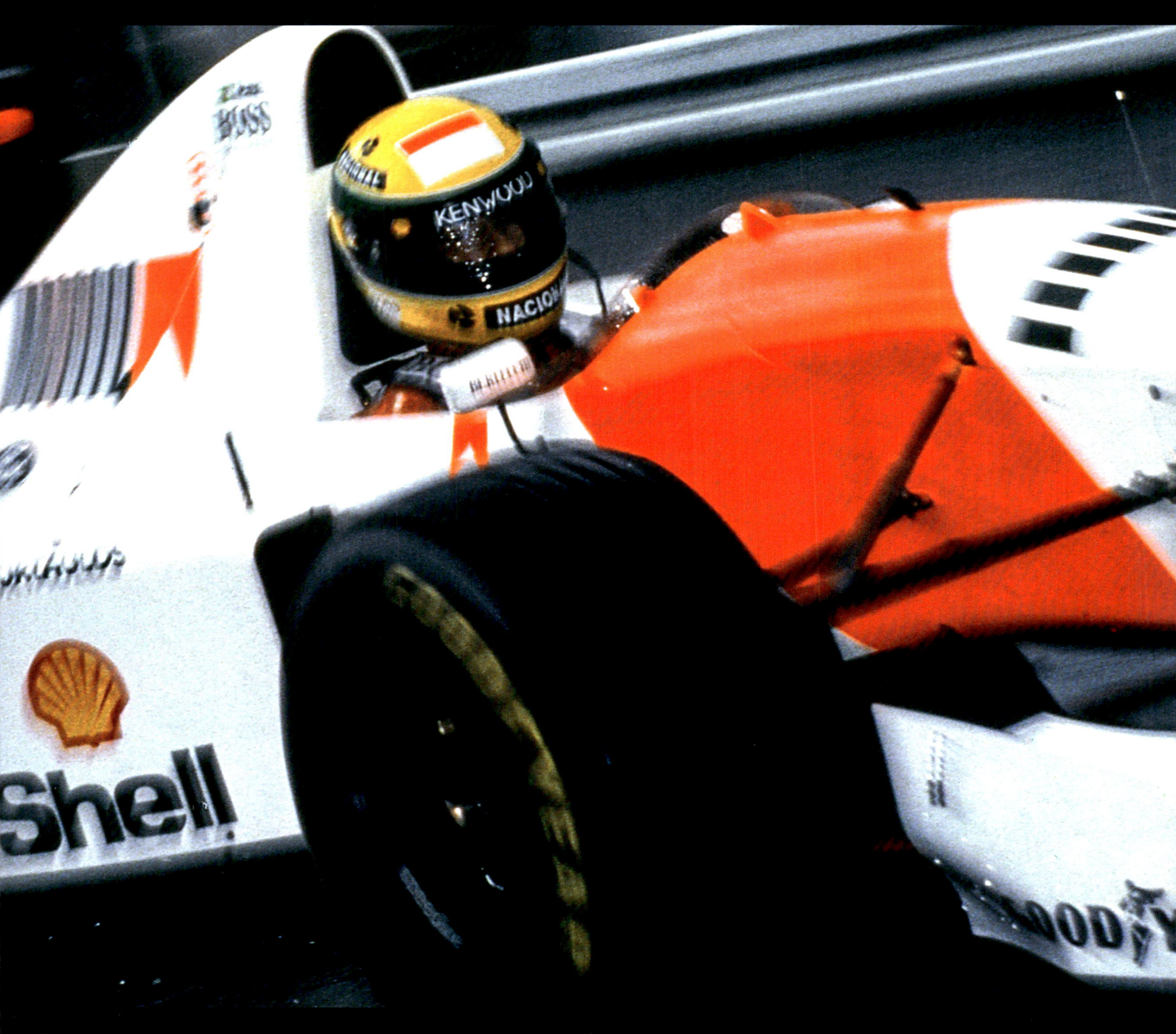

Senna hates driving in the rain but proves formidable when the weather is atrocious.

RACE AFTER RACE

1993

BRAZIL GRAND PRIX: INTERLAGOS' MIRACLE

Two years after the "victory of his life," Senna is back on home turf at Interlagos. However, his McLaren doesn't reassure him at the start of the weekend. The sensors that control the hydraulic suspension are doing their own thing. Not the best possible start, given that he's not hoping for anything better than a podium finish. In qualifying, the Williams of Alain Prost and Damon Hill are predictably in front. Senna, driven by his torcidas, snatches 3rd place, just ahead of Michael Schumacher. However, the Brazilian is pessimistic before the race: "With the engine we have, we can't think about winning," he predicts.

For the first quarter of the race, the Williams are in front, and Senna struggles to keep Schumacher at bay. As he battles with the German, Senna receives a penalty for overtaking Erik Comas under yellow flag conditions. On lap 24, he is subjected to a 10-second stop-and-go and emerges in 4th place, with only a slim chance of victory. However, sometimes fortunes are made. On lap 26, torrential rain begins to fall at Interlagos. Senna is one of the first to put on rain tires, followed a lap later by Hill... but not by Prost. Communication with his engineers is suddenly interrupted when his radio fails. He stays on track, but in these conditions, disaster can strike quickly. One spin later, the most frequently victorious driver in Brazil ends up in the gravel.

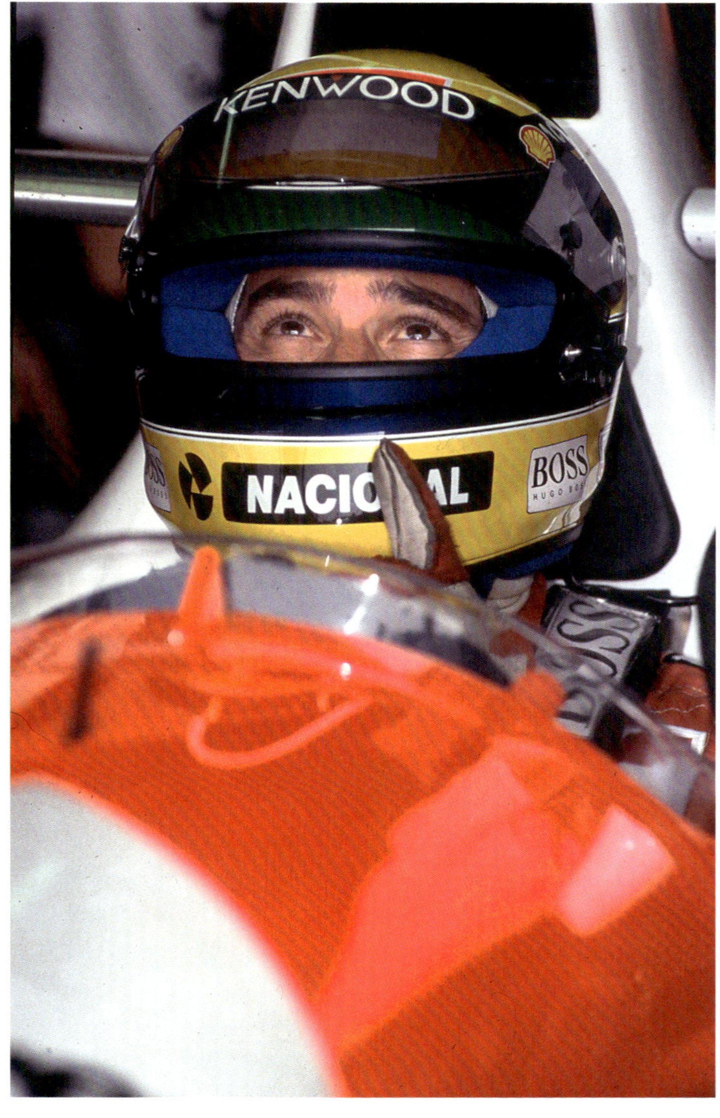

Senna takes a fleeting glance toward the sky before letting his talent unfold on the track.

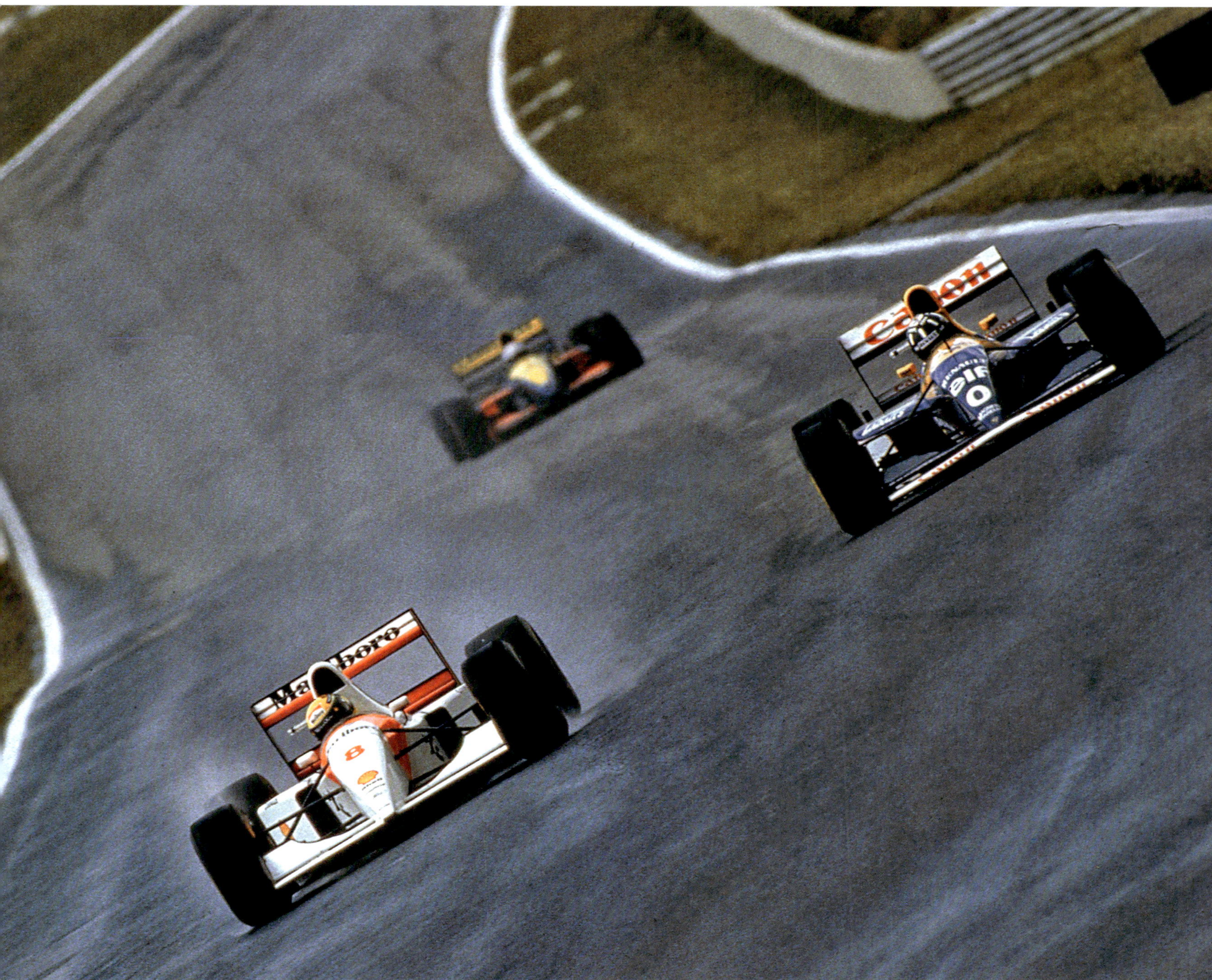

In 1993, Senna overtakes Damon Hill (the son of the great Graham Hill), who is in his debut season with Williams Racing.

In view of the cataclysmic conditions, the safety car is deployed. With the drivers regrouped, they resumed their race pace on lap 37, the track having become dry again. Preceded by Hill, Senna stops in the pits on the same lap as Schumacher to put on slicks. The German ceases to be a threat: his jack jams, and he loses precious seconds. Senna sets off in pursuit of Hill, 2nd, and Alesi, leading in his Ferrari. He succeeds in his mission and takes the lead. But, as in 1991, it is a victory he draws from deep within himself. TV Globo installs a heart sensor on him, to give international spectators the local hero's heart rate: 190 beats per minute. The Brazilian hangs on and hopes until the end. On the penultimate lap, it wasn't his gearbox that faltered but an LED that lit up, indicating an oil pressure problem. Miraculously, the Ford V8 held firm, giving McLaren its 100th F1 victory. The crowd invades the track, preventing the beautiful red-and-white single-seater of the nation's favorite from taking a lap of honor. No big deal: it dropped just after passing under the checkered flag. "When God really wants you to win, he really makes you win," smiled Senna, appeased. The next day, O Globo ran the headline: "Senna works miracles at Interlagos."

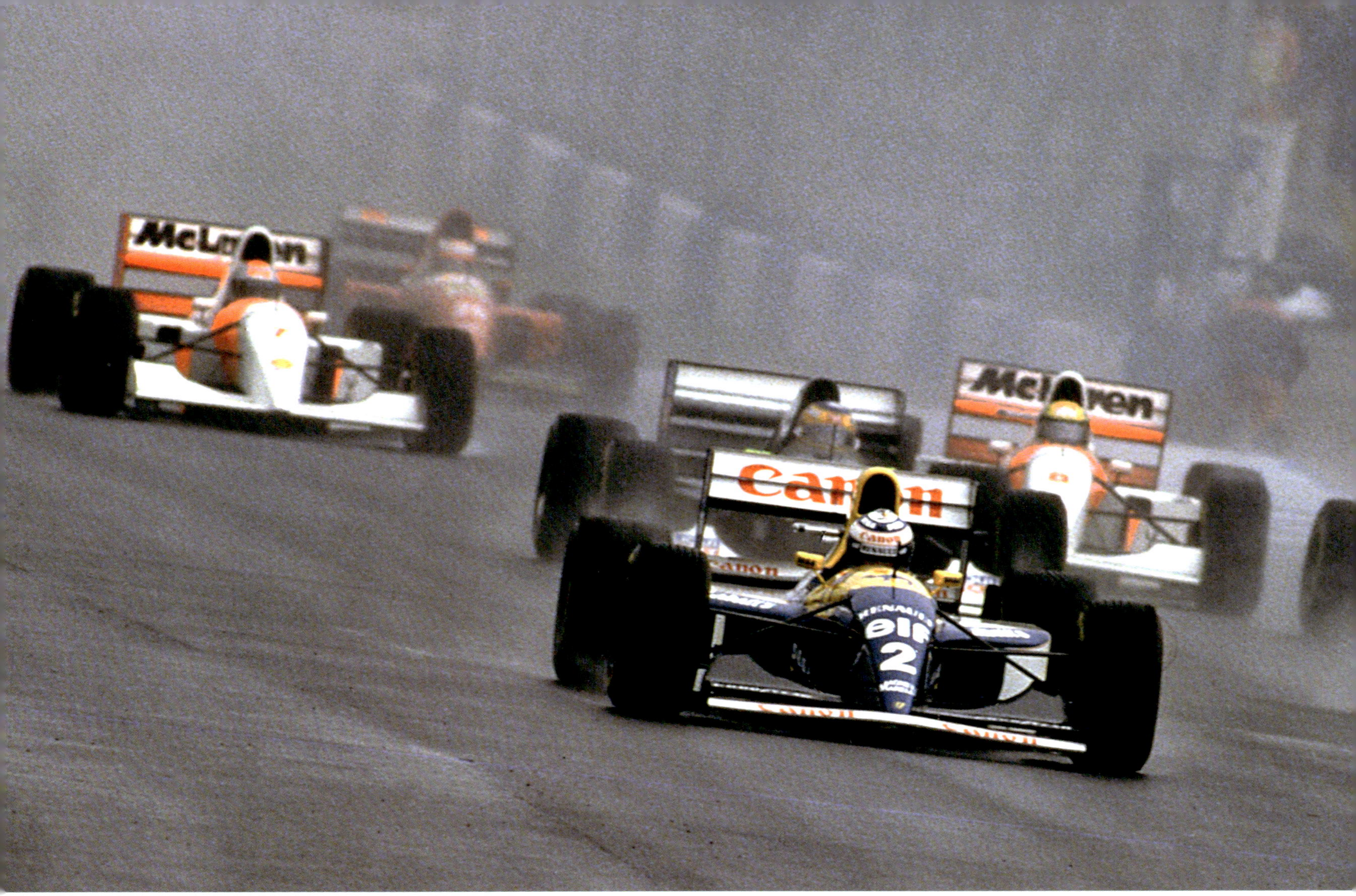

EUROPE GRAND PRIX: DONINGTON PARK'S LESSON

Motivated by his home win at the previous round, Senna knows that success at Interlagos cannot hide his McLaren's weaknesses in relation to the Williams's. The Brazilian media wonders whether Senna won't be praying to São Pedro at Donington. For the Brazilians, it is indeed this saint who "commands" the weather... "Rain gives us a chance of winning the race, because it nullifies the acceleration advantage of the Renault engines," Senna reasoned. His prayer was answered in practice when he set the fastest provisional time. But in qualifying, it was dry in Derby. Senna and his McLaren could only manage 4th place, just behind Schumacher. Prost and Hill were on the front row, but the Frenchman was two seconds ahead of Senna. The Brazilian press even spoke of a "Williams massacre"—that's something!

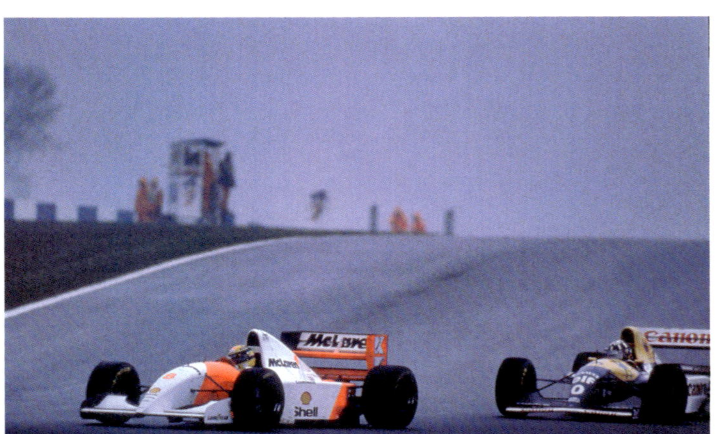

Bottom: It is not a problem for Senna to overtake Damon Hill at Hill's home circuit in the rain. The Brazilian leads from the first lap of the race.

With Princess Diana looking on, Senna gives everyone a driving masterclass. For, although it had stopped raining, the English track was still wet. At the first corner, Senna is 5th, overtaken by Karl Wendlinger. But a few seconds later, the Brazilian manages to overtake Schumacher, then the Austrian. Hill receives the same treatment a few corners later. The McLaren seems to be going at full speed on this wet track. On the penultimate stop, Senna overtakes Prost and ends the first lap in the lead. In the space of a minute and a half, he overtook four rivals. "I did what I had to do: try my luck," he said at the finish about this magic trick. The gap between Senna and the Williams drivers is increasing lap by lap. For once, the Williams team was at a loss, even though it had hired a weather advisor... who caused confusion! "Every time he announced something, the opposite happened. And I hold the record for the most tire changes in a race: seven, including six against the clock," Prost would later recount with a smile in a documentary about the Brazilian.

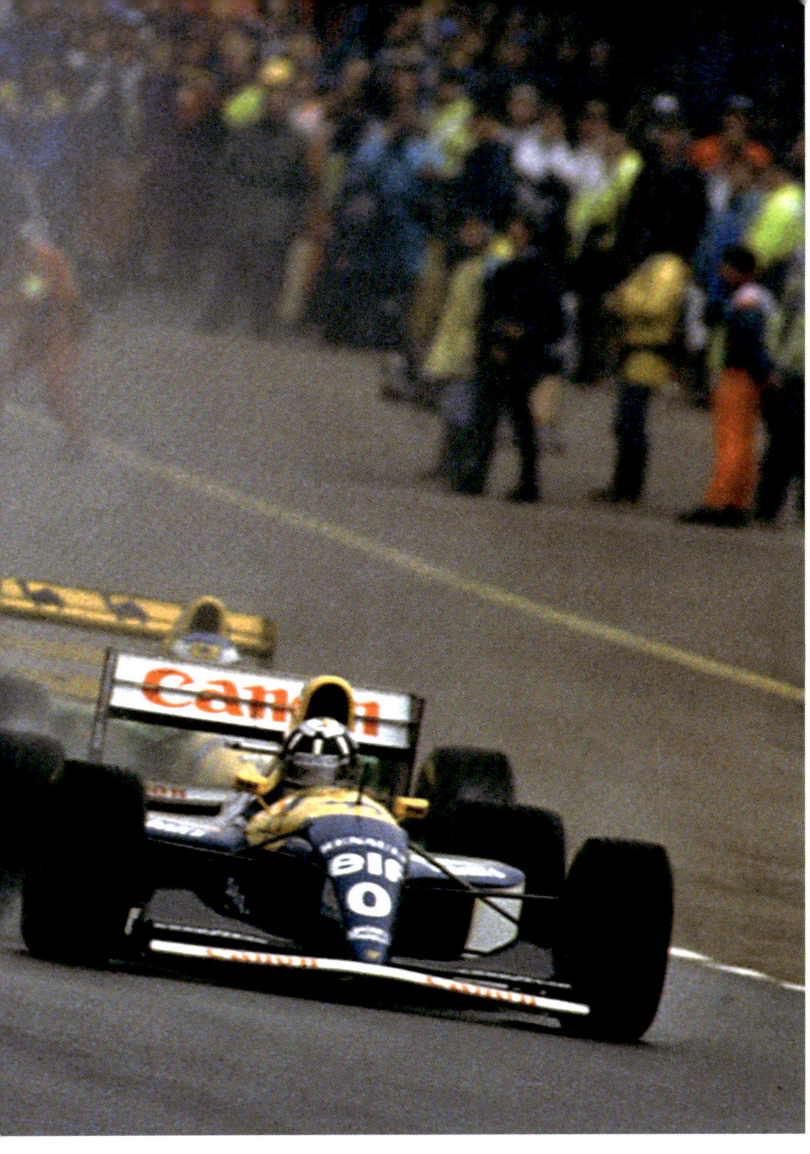

Starting from 4th place on the grid, Senna is in a potentially difficult position at the start of the 1993 European Grand Prix at Donington Park.

On lap 57, Senna sets the fastest lap of the race... in an unconventional manner. He announces that he's returning to the pits, but his radio crackles, and his team doesn't understand him. As a result, the mechanics weren't ready, and Senna decides not to stop. He knew that the pit lane was a shortcut, and at the time, there was no speed limit. And so it was that the driver completed his lap in 1'18"029, before racing to victory!

On the podium, Senna receives a trophy in the colors of the blue hedgehog Sonic, the game console manufacturer Sega being the title sponsor of this European GP. Rather comical, given that Sega is also a major sponsor of Williams. For the record, the trophy disappeared for a long time, until McLaren revealed in August 2023 that it was indeed being kept in Woking. At a press conference, Prost—who had finished 3rd behind Senna and Hill—complained about the way his Williams was running. This prompted the Brazilian winner to ask ironically: "Do you want to swap cars?" A harbinger of things to come in 1994.

The hilly circuit of Donington Park is an ideal setting for a driving lesson by Senna in 1993.

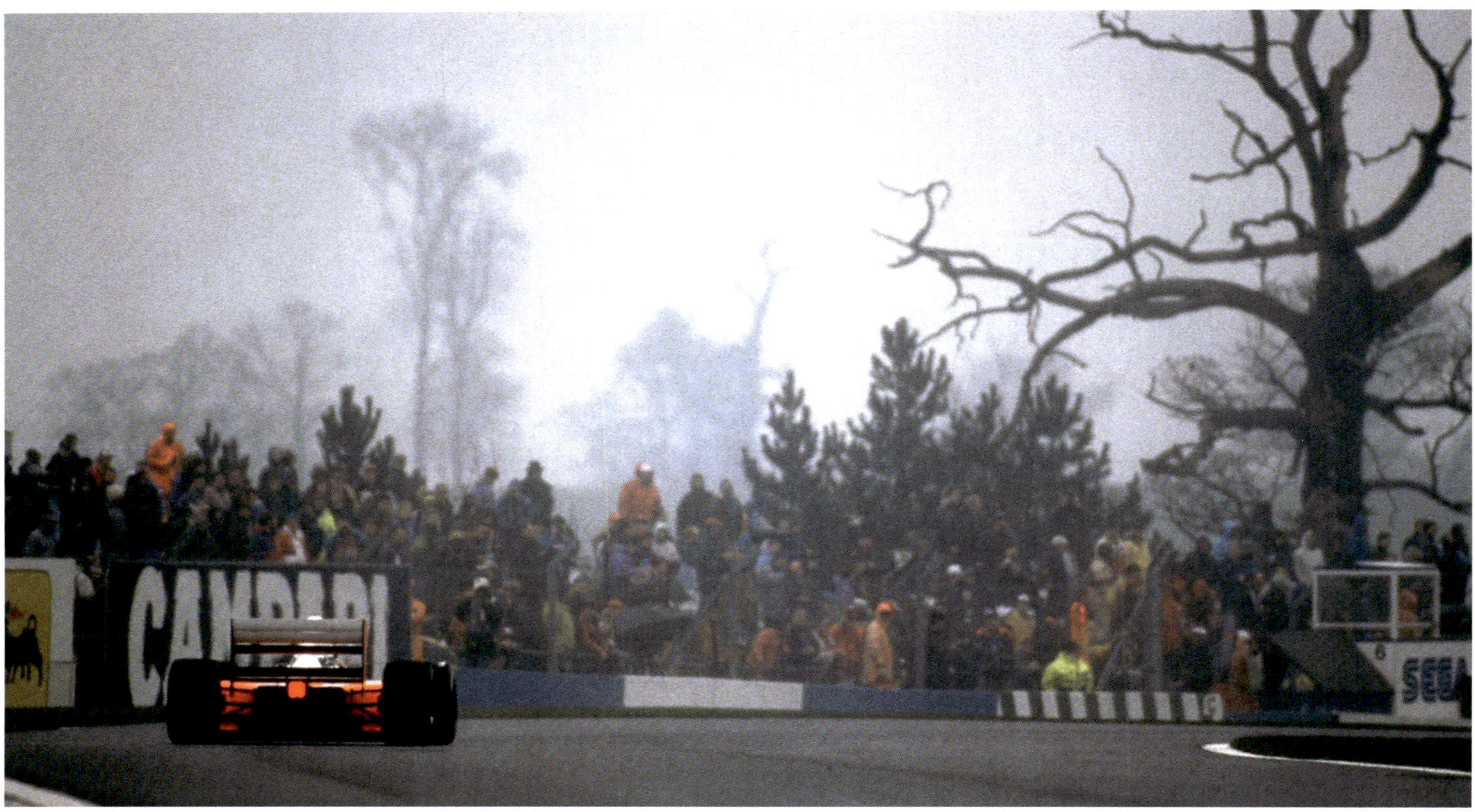

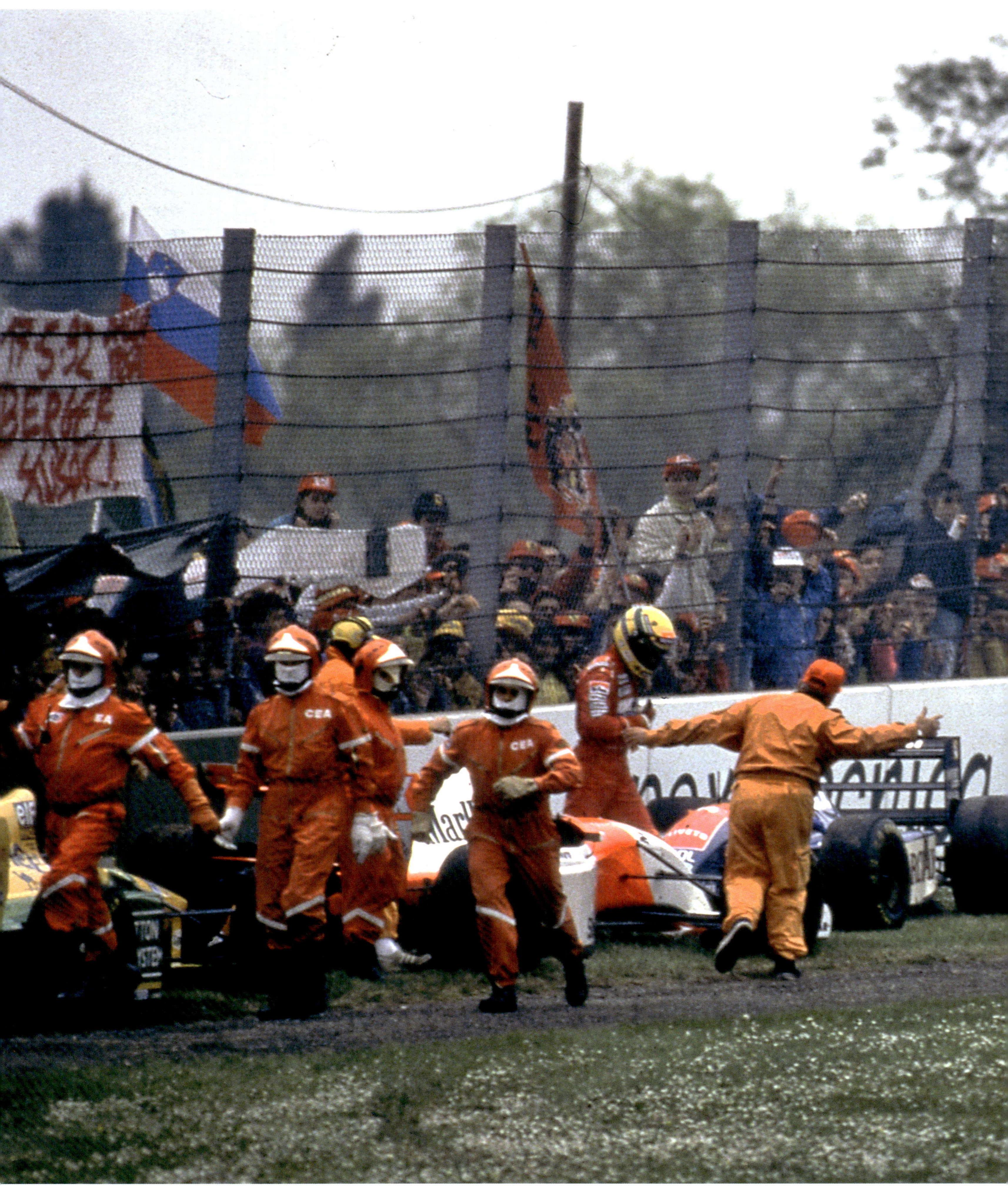
CEA
CEA
CEA

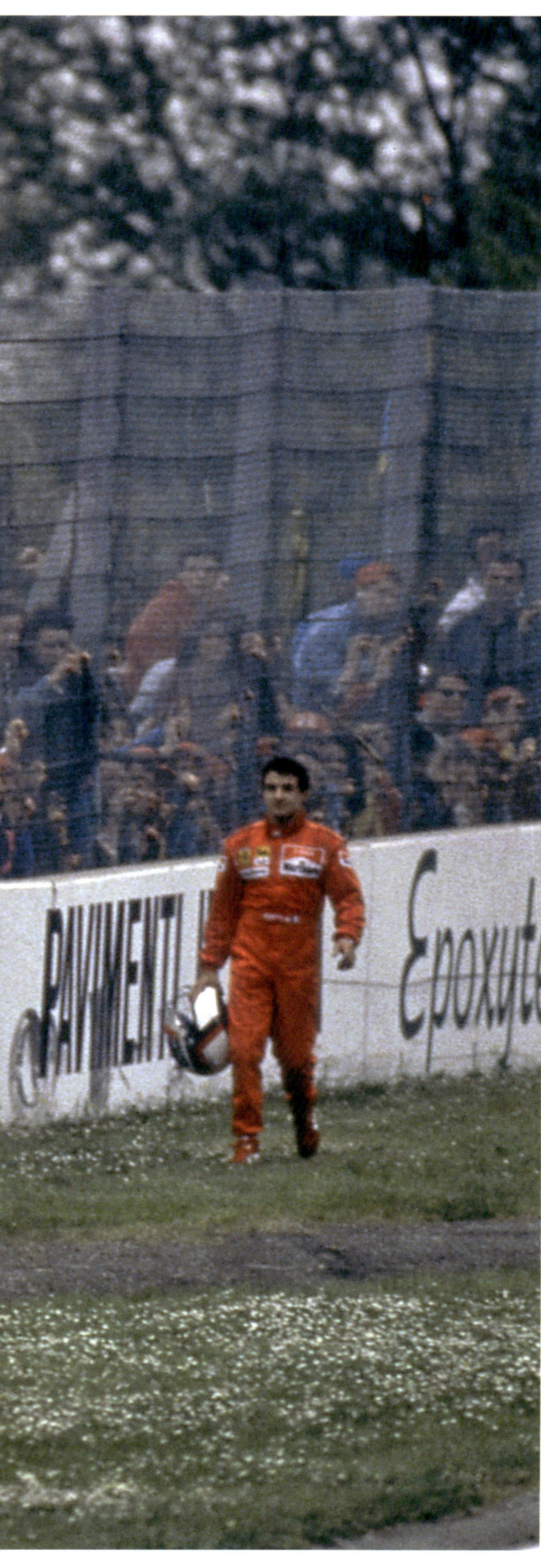

BEHIND THE SCENES IN THE PADDOCK

"NO MONEY, NO RACE": ONE MILLION EACH RACE

One million dollars per race disputed. Sounds crazy? It is! Yet that's how much Senna managed to negotiate with McLaren and Philip Morris to continue racing for his beloved team. The Brazilian was very tough on business. Dr. Jacques Dallaire, who was close to the Brazilian, recalls a discussion on the subject: "He told me: 'I don't care about money. What matters to me is to know what my value is in their eyes. And money is an indicator. I want to know how much they really want me.'"

Following Honda's departure, Senna was less than enthusiastic about the idea of driving a Ford-powered car. At the beginning of 1993, a summit meeting took place at the Swiss offices of Philip Morris. Ron Dennis, Julian Jakobi, and Senna took part. Ron Dennis announces that he has five million dollars at his disposal. Jakobi remembers the driver's almost instinctive remark: "Then Ayrton said, 'That's fine. I'll do the first five races, and that's it.'" Senna later invites Philip Morris members to respond and says: "If you find you have more money later, we'll discuss additional races after the first five." The million dollars per race was finally acquired.

In the signed contract, a clause is added to the effect that the money must be transferred to Senna's bank account on the Wednesday before each race. Fábio Machado, the Brazilian legend's cousin and manager, was in charge of informing the driver of this bank transfer. If the transfer had not been made, Senna had a ready-made reply: "No money, no race."

Even though most Italians have eyes only for Jean Alesi and Ferrari, several tifosi cannot help but admire Senna.

MONACO GRAND PRIX: SENNA 6 – PROST 4

The Monaco Grand Prix is the other race that Senna absolutely wants to win, every year after the Brazil Grand Prix, and Prost's domination does nothing to change his motivation—quite the opposite, in fact. A big crash at high speed on Thursday, in the Sainte Dévote corner, ends with a bandaged thumb due to bad steering wheel feedback. Saturday qualifying sees Senna take 3rd place on the grid, behind Prost and Schumacher. Fate was to give him a helping hand...

At 3 p.m. on Sunday, Prost gets off to a better start than Senna, but the stewards immediately judge that he has anticipated him a little and give him a 10-second penalty. He returns to the pits in the lead to serve his stop-and-go, but his Williams stalls. Farewell to the dreams of a 5th victory in the principality, following in the footsteps of Senna and Graham Hill. A boulevard opens up before the wheels of the Brazilian, who makes no mistakes and takes full advantage of the opportunity. It's his 6th victory in Monaco and a new record too, and Damon joins him on the podium to congratulate him. At the press conference, Alain Prost proclaims: "I'm not a start thief; I know the difference between red and green." He also has a good excuse, of a technical nature: "Our carbon clutches lack consistency in their operation." Ayrton didn't care and spent the evening at Jimmy's with his new partner Adriane Galisteu, a 20-year-old supermodel. Maybe because it was such a good weekend, he proceeds to take over the World Championship lead from Prost by five points (42 to 37). To be continued.

Below: In Monaco in 1993, Senna wins for the sixth time on the streets of the principality—a record that no one has yet managed to equal.

Following double page: Like an impressionist painting, Senna's McLaren blends perfectly into the scenery of circuits worldwide.

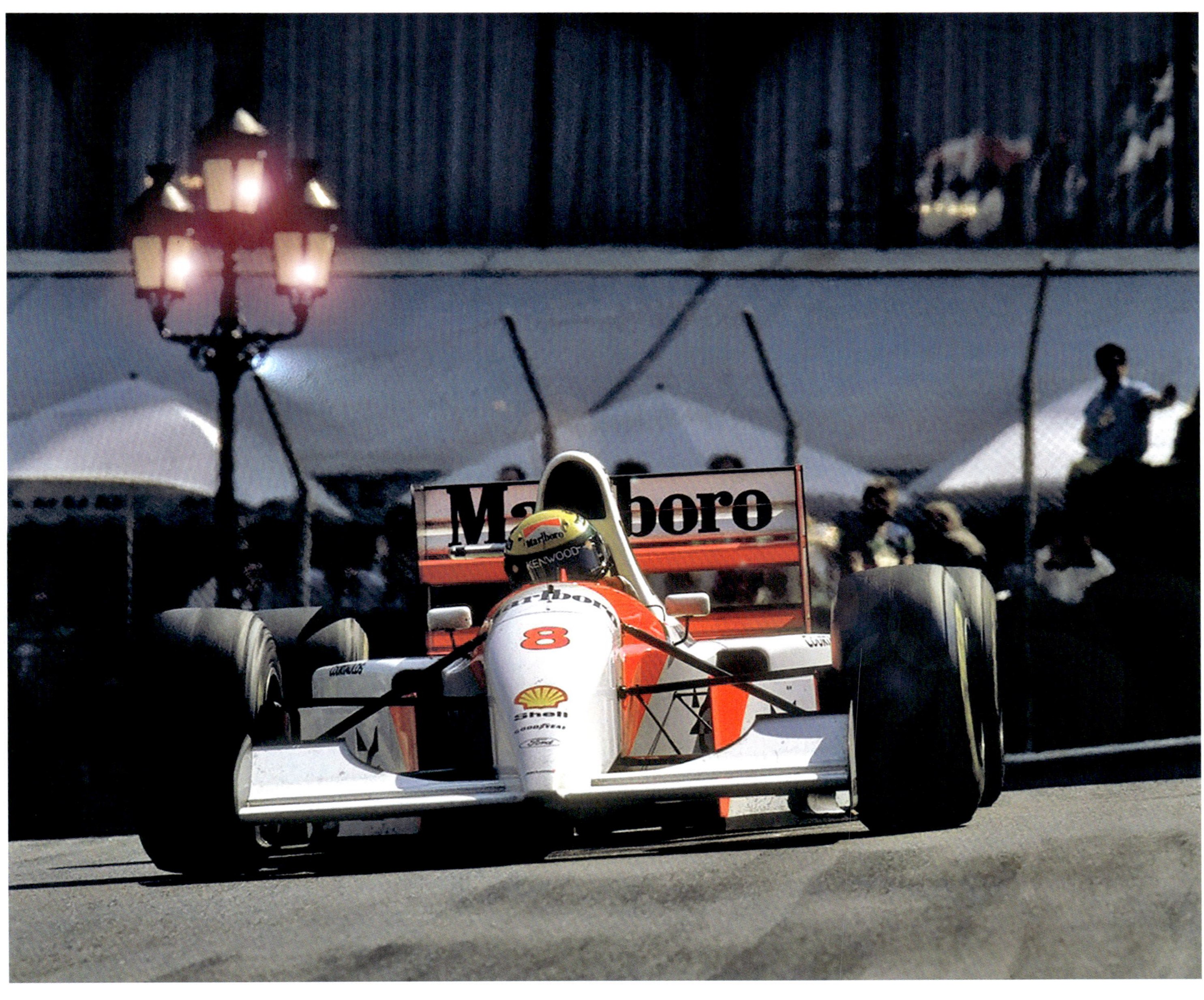

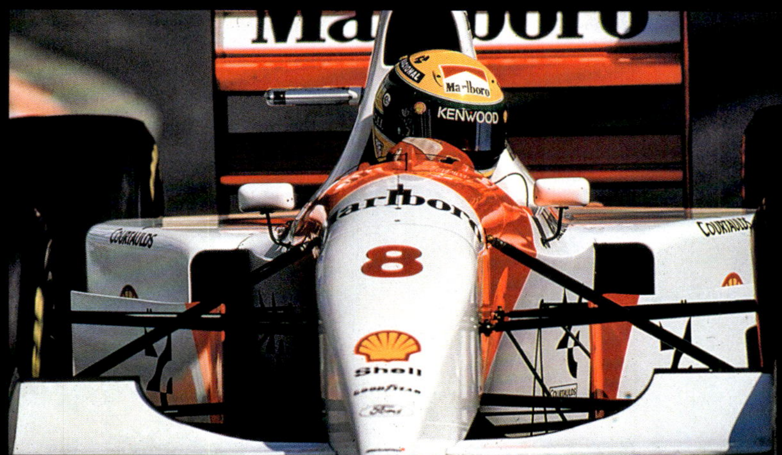

THE CAR: MCLAREN MP4/8

Underpowered—because it was equipped with a "customer" Ford V8—the MP4/8 will be remembered as the last McLaren driven by Senna. Honda left F1 at the end of 1992. After months of doubts, Senna decided to stay on for one more season with the team where he had won three world titles. During the first private test at Silverstone on March 3, 1993, Ayrton was surprised by the engine. Very sure of himself, he even said to Ron Dennis: "This engine is great. We can win with this car." In reality, this remark was surprising: the American V8 only developed 680 horsepower, whereas the Renault engine at Williams provided an extra 80 hp. Except that the McLaren MP4/8 was well-born, as well as ultra-sophisticated. According to Ron Dennis himself, it's "one of the best McLarens ever."

Steve Hallam, a McLaren engineer at the time, explains the role played by Ayrton Senna in the car's development: "The collaborative work to develop it was strengthened by his understanding. And his competitive instinct enabled him to make the most of it. I think the intelligence he had, as an individual, contributed to the development of this car. He was putting into words what all of us engineers were trying to code into the internal software of this single seater, to improve its performance."

Active suspension, traction control... even the gearbox has been automated. A device—designed for American Michael Andretti from the CART championship—that Senna never wanted. Steve Hallam recalls: "Ayrton tested this feature and always chose not to use the automatic gearbox. That was his driving style: he wanted total control of the car's downshift." Designed by Neil Oatley, this MP4/8 helped Senna win at home, at Interlagos, and sublimate at Donington Park. For the record, every time the Brazilian won, McLaren displayed a sticker on the cockpit showing a hedgehog running over it: a way of mocking Williams, its sponsor Sega, and its mascot Sonic. At the wheel of the MP4/8, Senna also won in Monaco, Japan, and Australia, in Adelaide, ahead of Prost. This 41st victory was also his last.

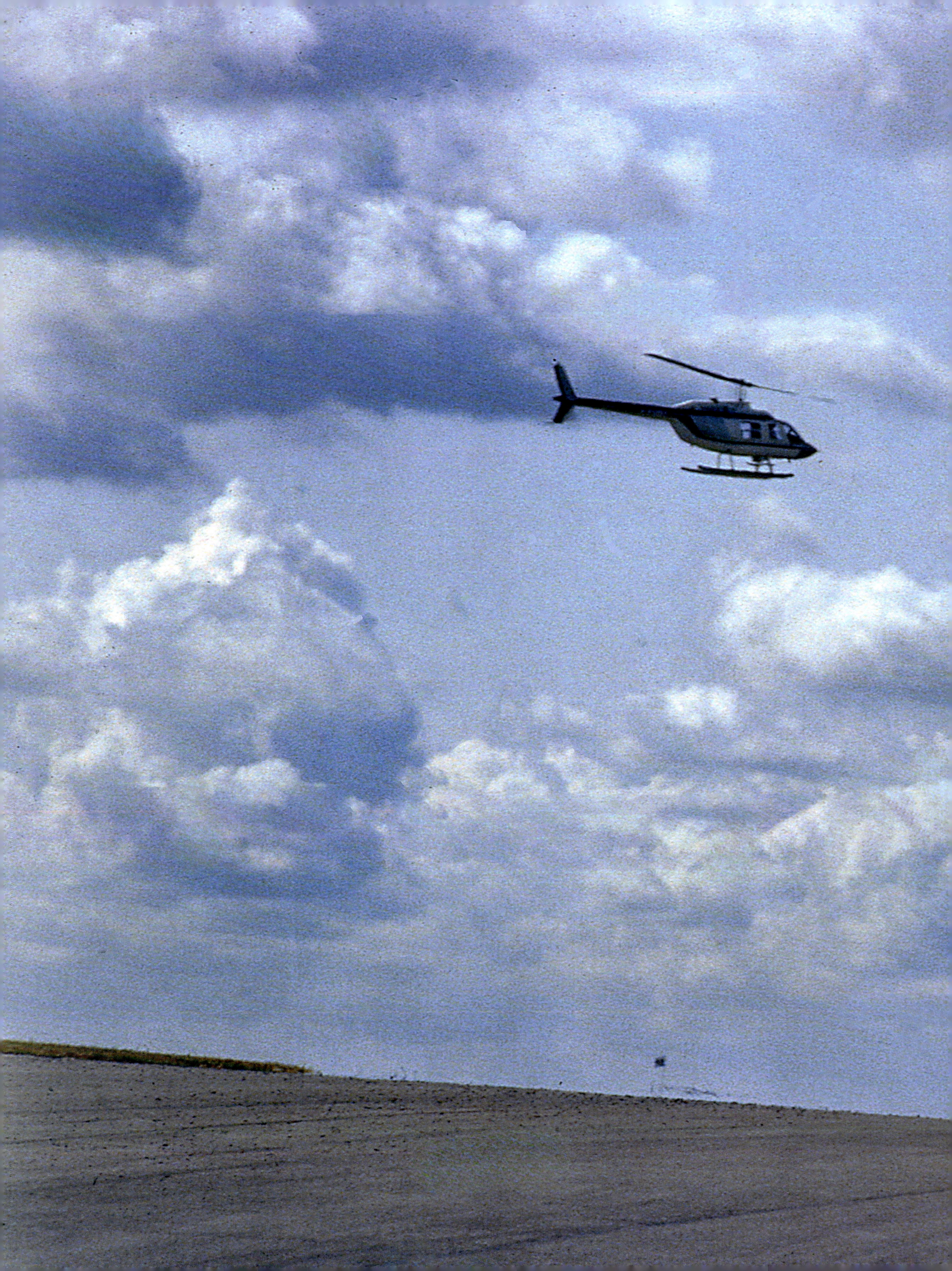

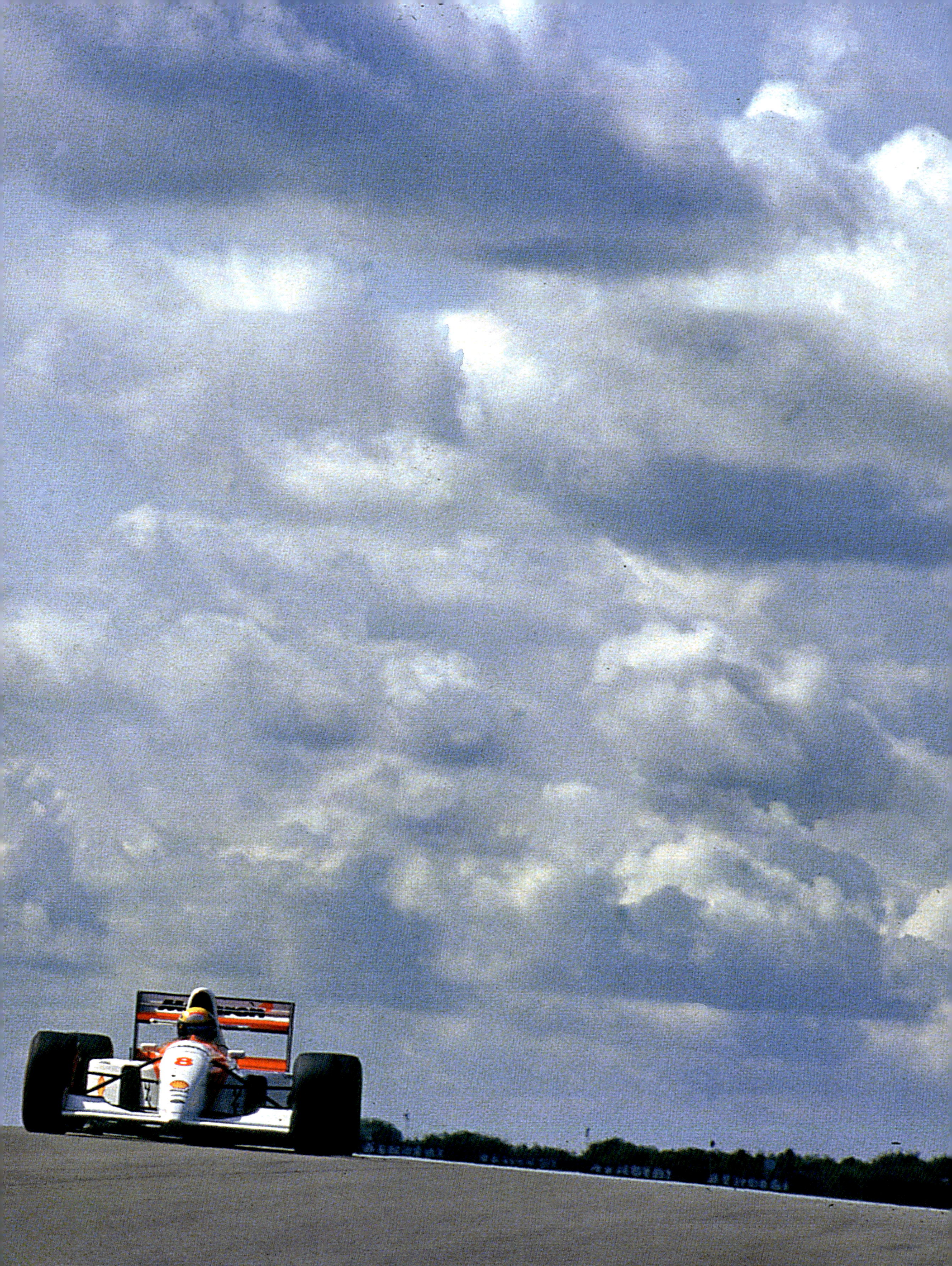
8

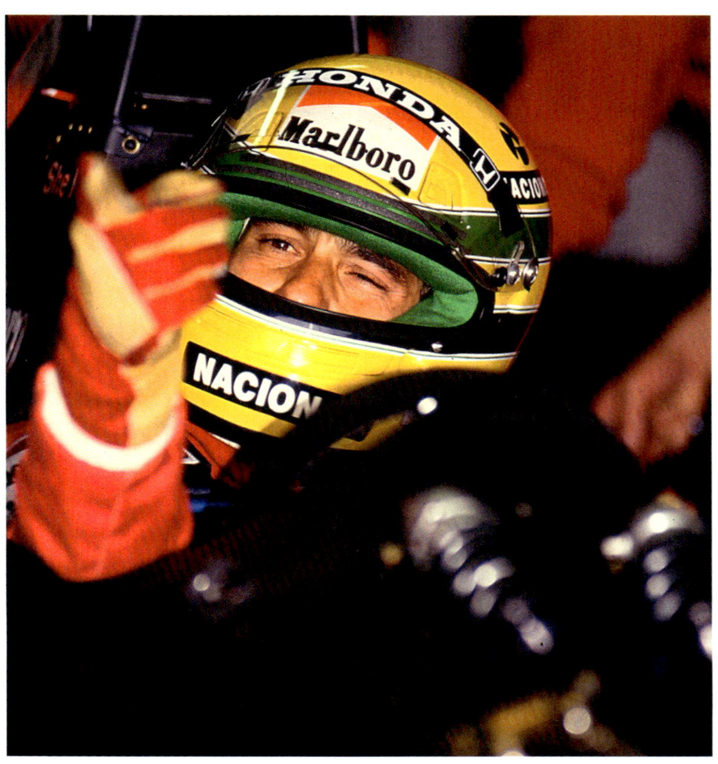

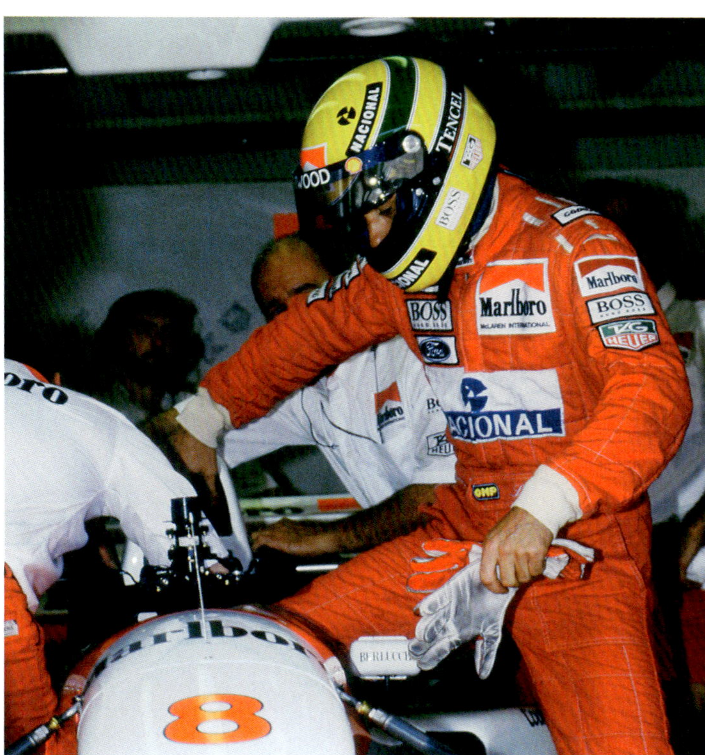

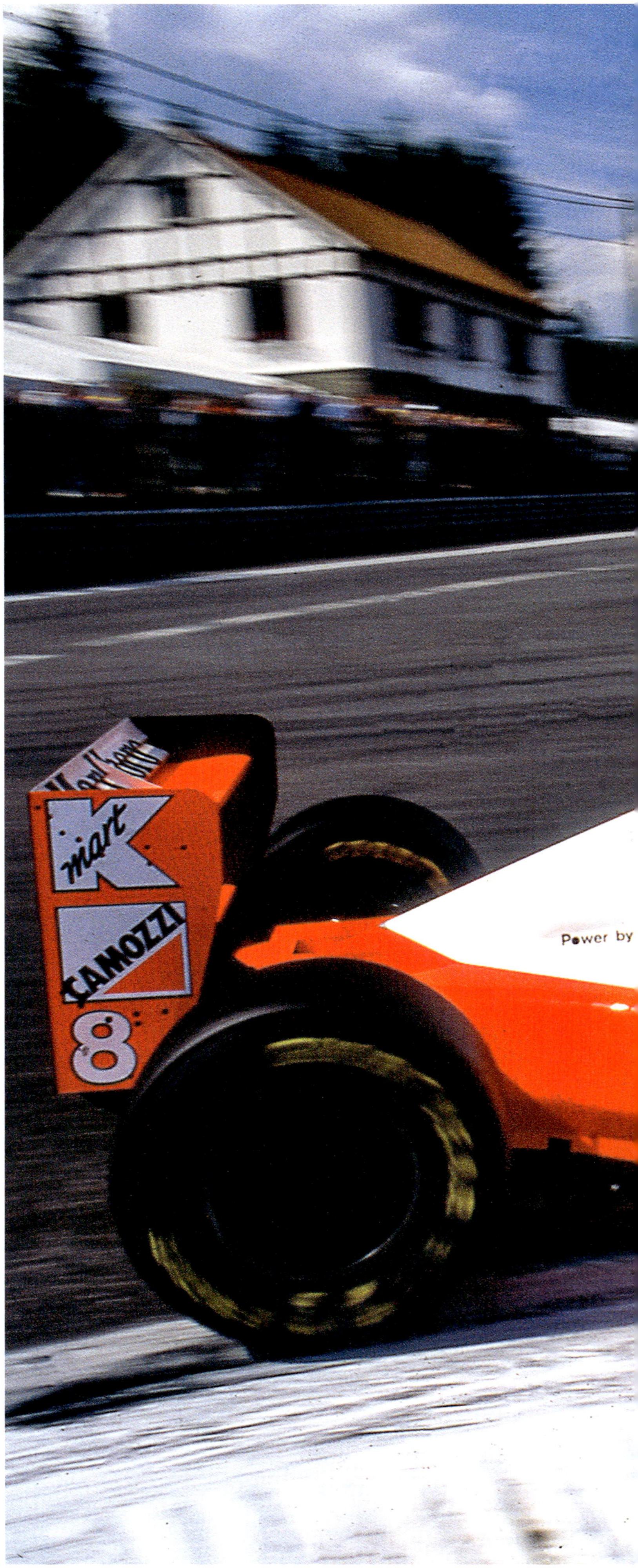

Top left: Minutes before embarking on a timed lap, the Brazilian requests final adjustments to the settings of his race car.

Bottom left: Senna takes his place in the bucket seat of his 1993 McLaren and is determined to make the most of his Ford engine.

Right: Although photogenic at the La Source hairpin on the Spa-Francorchamps circuit, the McLaren MP4/8 does not allow Senna to do better than 4th in the 1993 Belgian Grand Prix.

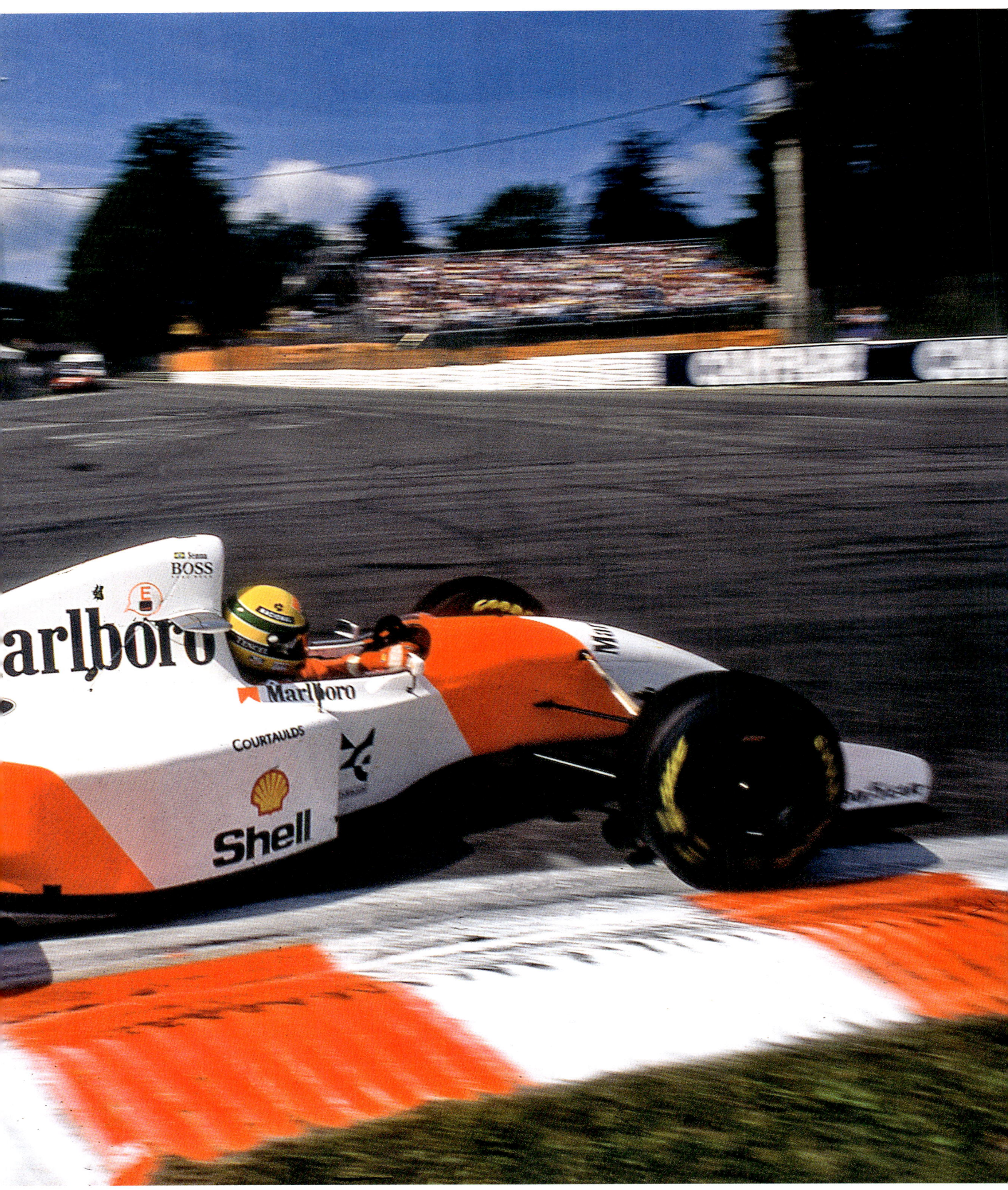
Senna
BOSS
arlboro
Marlboro
COURTAULDS
Shell

SENNA VS. PROST THE FIGURES

During their seasons of rivalry in F1 (from 1984 to 1991, and again in 1993), Senna and Prost battled it out mercilessly, enabling F1 to write some of the greatest pages in its history. The Frenchman's overall record (victories, podiums, fastest race laps) was in his favor, but it was in the Brazilian's in terms of pure performance (pole positions).

1984-1993*	VICTORIES	PODIUMS	POLE POSITIONS	BEST LAPS	TITLES
SENNA	38	73	61	17	3 (1988, 1990, 1991)
PIQUET	42	89	23	33	4 (1985, 1986, 1989, 1993)

*Without season 1992 (Prost's sabbatical)

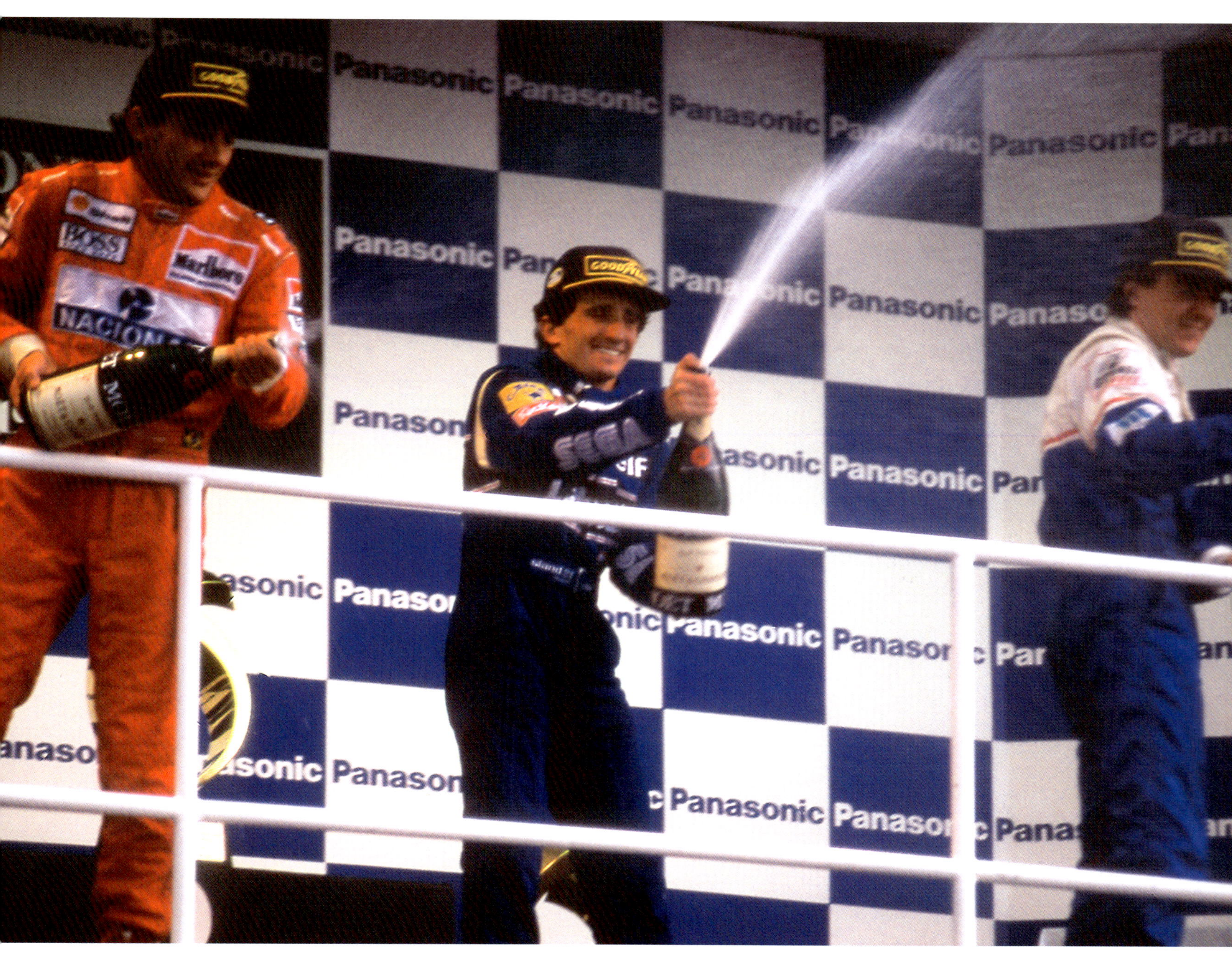

THE MAIN CHARACTERS

ALAIN PROST, THE LEGENDARY RIVAL

The intense rivalry between Ayrton Senna and Alain Prost has no equal in the history of F1 since 1950. Fans of all ages still talk about it today, 30 years on, as if it were yesterday, even though some of them weren't even born to witness those nine intense seasons, during which the Brazilian and the Frenchman won more than half the Grands Prix on the calendar (80 out of 144), and seven world titles out of the nine at stake. So, inevitably, on the day it all comes to an end, emotions run high on both sides.

Flashback. It's November 7, 1993, in Adelaide, Australia. Senna completes his lap of honor by waving a Brazilian flag, as he often does when he wins in F1. It was the 104th victory for a McLaren in F1, enabling Ron Dennis's team to overtake Ferrari in the record books. Senna, Prost, and Hill, the top three finishers, meet up with Ron Dennis in the cool-down room before taking to the podium. Ron greets Alain and says a few words in his ear, then does the same with Senna. The hilarious Brazilian revealed that his boss had asked him if he'd changed his plans for 1994. "That's what he just told me too!" exclaims Prost. The mood is generally upbeat. Senna extends his hand to Prost, who, after a brief hesitation, agrees to shake it. The gesture could not be more sincere, as both men are unaware that they are being filmed by a camera.

The podium ceremony is overwhelming and perfectly staged. Twice, Senna invites Prost to join him on the top step, in front of a delighted crowd. They exchange a second handshake. They make peace. Prost didn't win, but he is a world champion for the fourth time. And everyone knew that Senna was about to succeed him at Williams: the announcement had been made a month earlier. Senna struggles to hide the tears that cloud his eyes. He knows that a whole part of his sporting career is coming to an end.

A few moments later, the two meet again at the press conference. Smiling at each other, they show their complicity and agree to draw a line under the past. "We have to focus on this sporting image," says Prost. Ayrton and I had some good times together, especially in 1988. "With my departure, it's preferable to retain only the good memories, the good aspects of our sporting rivalry." Senna interrupts him: "At McLaren, the biggest problem we had was that Alain wanted to leave the circuit as soon as possible to go and play golf! Impossible, because I made sure the briefings lasted for hours! He kept saying to me: 'Come on, let's stop, I want to go golfing! I remember it perfectly!'" Then the Brazilian turns serious again and adds: "What can I say today? Our attitude says more than any words we might utter, more or less skillfully. Only gestures really count. It was a beautiful podium. It reflected my feelings. His too, I think."

It's the end of the final chapter in the most fascinating rivalry in F1 history. The most beautiful, the most intense, the most violent, the most irritating too. Prost, a little disoriented, had to train and reinvent himself. Senna, deprived of his best enemy, embarked on another chapter in his life against a rising generation of young wolves: Mika Häkkinen, Jean Alesi, Damon Hill, and, above all, a gifted and stubborn German, ready to do anything to win, Michael Schumacher.

Prost and Senna are together on the top two steps of a podium, which happens six times in 1993.

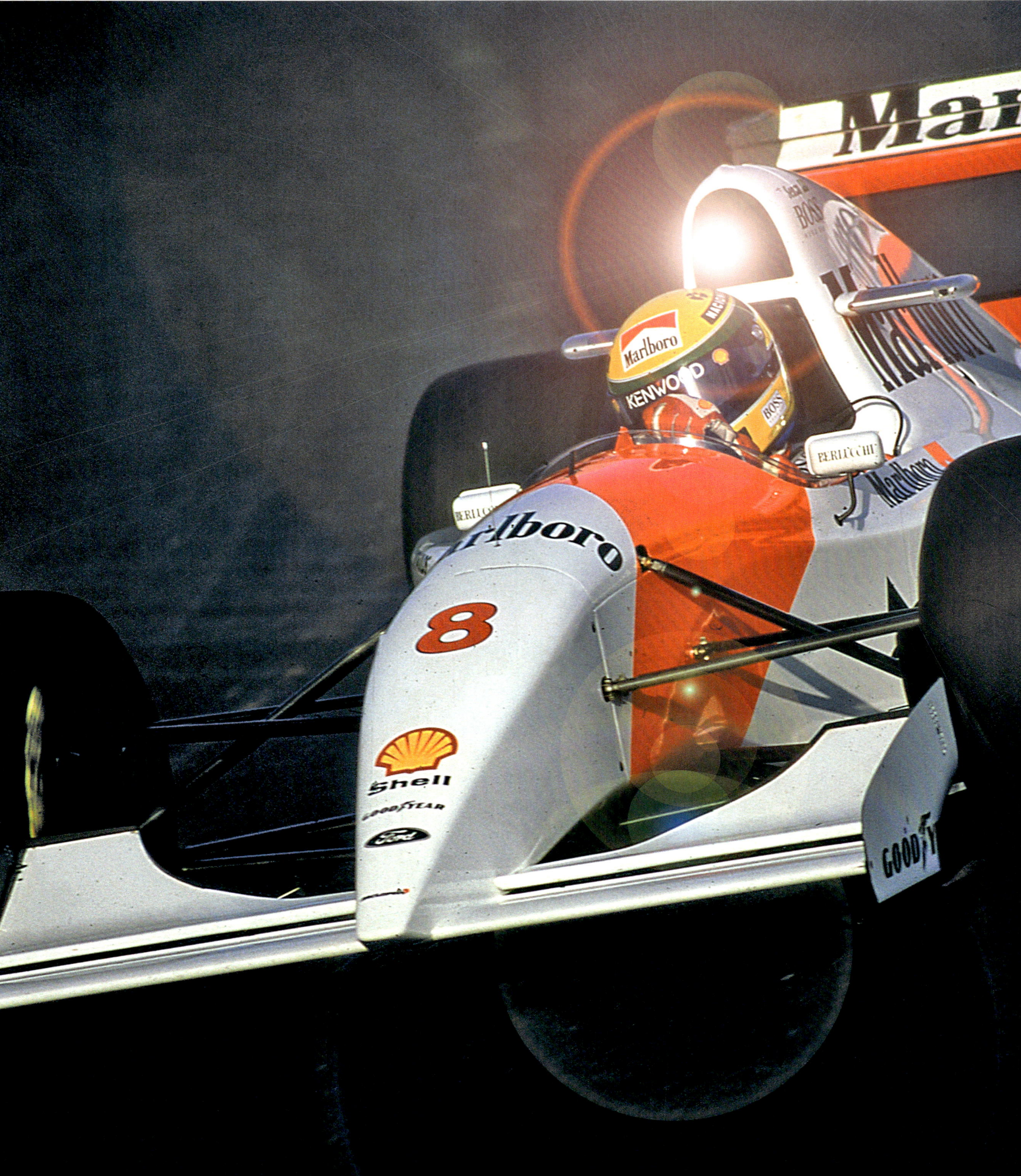

Marlboro
KENWOOD
BERLUCCHI
8
Shell
GOODYEAR

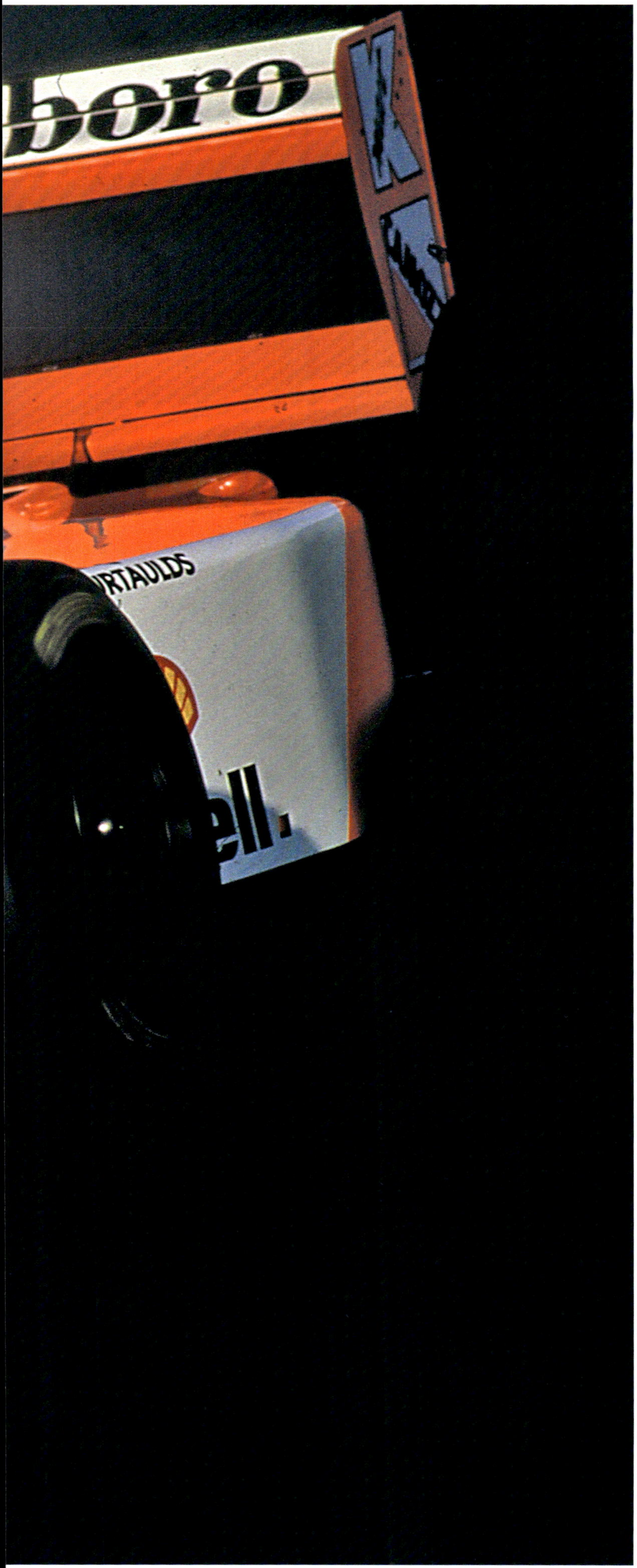

The 1993 season is Senna's last with McLaren before his move to Williams Racing.

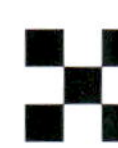

AGAINST IRVINE IN JAPAN

With Prost having secured his 4th world title with a 2nd place in Portugal, the last two rounds of the season are of limited sporting interest. Except for Ayrton Senna, who wants to finish 2nd in the championship behind Prost by winning again in Japan if possible, and Eddie Irvine, the young Jordan driver, making his F1 debut.

Less than an hour after the end of the Suzuka race, the Brazilian winner was still pale with anger. He storms past the pits, amid the mechanics packing up their equipment. His track engineer, the perpetually bad-tempered Italian Giorgio Ascanelli, tries to follow him through the maze of boxes, tires, and single-seater parts.

At a brisk pace, the driver climbs a few steps and enters the Jordan team's private premises. It's as if he's bursting into a Dublin pub just after leaving the office. The beer is flowing, and the atmosphere is smoky. Among the many people present, he recognizes a friendly face, that of Rubens Barrichello, who is also making his F1 debut with Jordan, like Irvine at this race. It's not for him that Senna has come. He's looking for Eddie Irvine, whose face he doesn't even know, to explain to him how things work in F1: the exuberant young Irishman overtook him when he was a lap behind, then slowed him down, corked him up. A real crime of lèse-majesté! Senna shouted at him, then began a surreal dialogue, interspersed with insults, threats, reprimands, and name-calling. In the end, he shoves his fist in his face. Welcome to the club!

AUSTRALIA GRAND PRIX: GOUNON DISCOVERS SENNA... AND TINA TURNER!

In Australia, to wrap up the 1993 season on a high note before leaving for Williams, Senna did well: pole position—the 62nd of his career—and victory—his 41st in F1—accompanied by a well-deserved 2nd place in the F1 World Championship. On the podium and at the press conference, he reconciles with Alain Prost, his historic rival (see below). In the front row was a young driver, Frenchman Jean-Marc Gounon, making his F1 debut and not missing a beat. From the qualifying session to the Tina Turner concert...

In Australia, Senna secures his 41st and final victory in F1 (and the 104th for McLaren) to end his adventure ahead of Prost—an ultimate summary of their rivalry.

Far right: Senna wore the red and white combination of the McLaren team for six years, from 1988 to 1993.

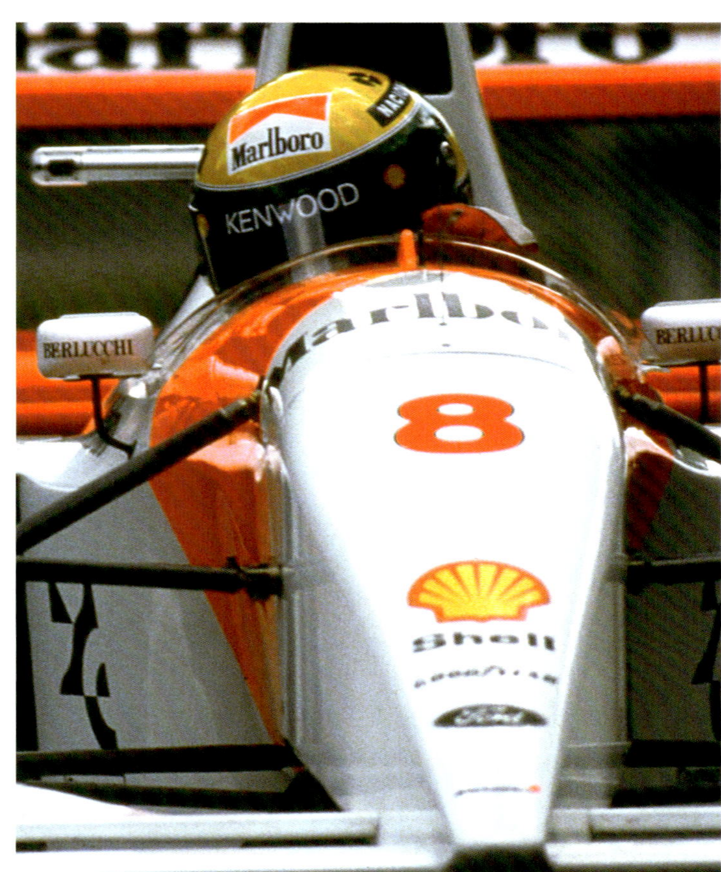

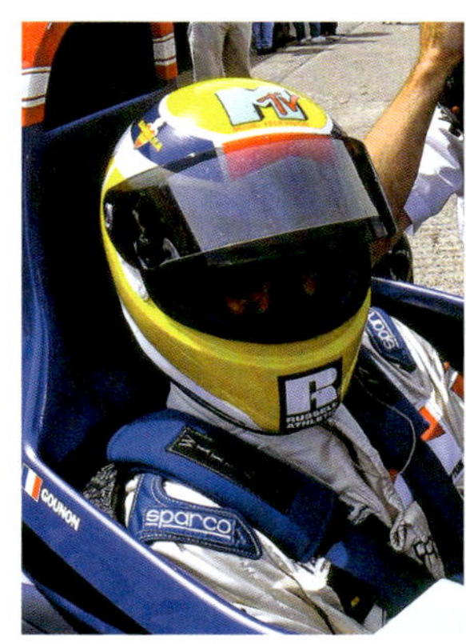

JEAN-MARC GOUNON

Jean-Marc Gounon recalls: "I'm on my qualifying lap, and just as I start down the straight, I see a McLaren coming up behind me, wearing a yellow helmet. It's Senna. I let him behind me all the way down the straight; he comes back on me; I get off the ideal trajectory and let him go by. I don't really care about it, and it's Ayrton Senna. I do my job; I finish my lap. Nothing happens. The next day, it's a city circuit where everything is pre-assembled, including the toilets. It's a huge pisspot, everyone comes there, and just before the Grand Prix, a guy taps me on the shoulder. It's Senna. He says, 'Listen, thank you for yesterday. That was a nice thing you did. If you need anything in this world, you come and see me.' Fuck (sic). I say thank you, even if it seems normal to me. The guy's a world champion with McLaren, he's on pole, and he comes to see me, a beginner. I thought he was a great guy. I saw that he wasn't just a driver."

After the race, a concert was organized by Foster's beers, the sponsor at the time. All spectators were invited free of charge. Gounon continues: "The concert that year was Tina Turner. I'll remember it for the rest of my life. Senna had won the race, Prost was already the world champion with the Williams and had finished 2nd, both of them on the podium. At the concert, we're all invited to come to the back of the stage to watch Tina Turner sing up close. And there are 200,000 spectators, a veritable human tide—a bit like at Le Mans around the podium. Tina Turner sings, and at one point, between songs, she comes to the back of the stage and takes Senna by the hand, then starts singing "Simply the Best." She did the whole song with Senna's arm raised beside her. It was incredible, unreal."

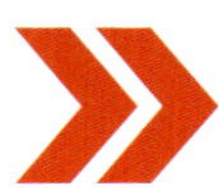

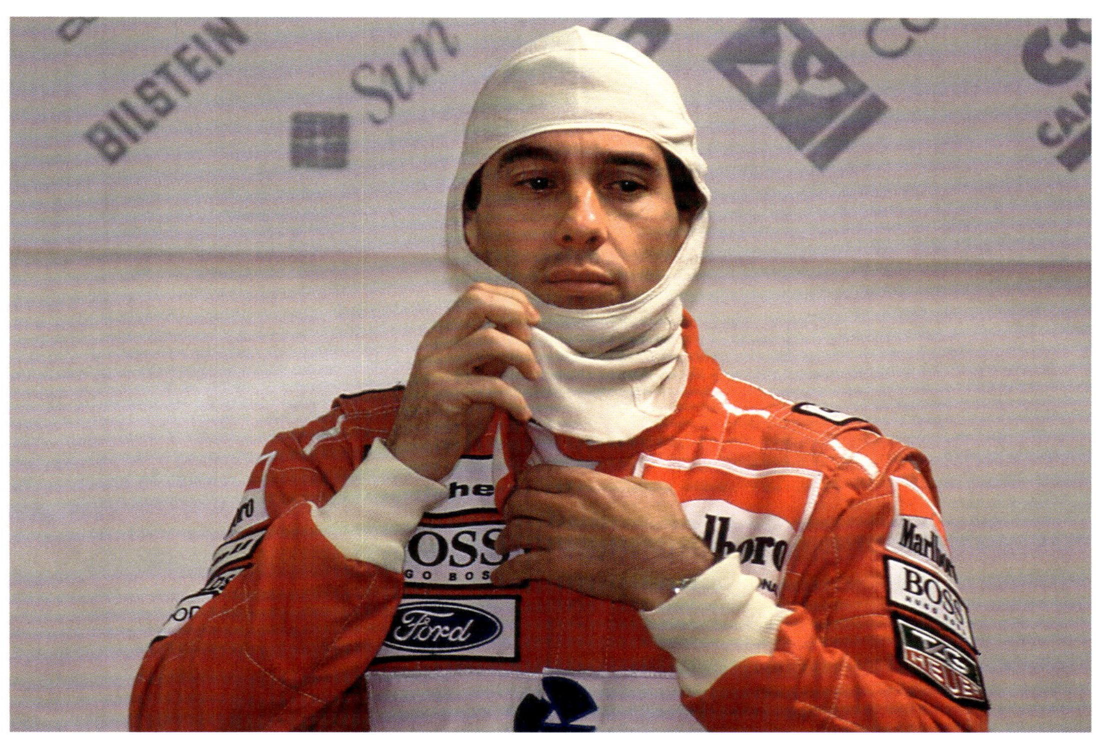

THE 1993 SEASON IN FIGURES

GRAND PRIX	QUALIFIERS	RACE
SOUTH AFRICA	2ND	2ND
BRAZIL	3RD	VICTORY 37
EUROPE	4TH	VICTORY 38
SAN MARINO	4TH	DNF (SUSPENSION)
SPAIN	3RD	2ND
MONACO	3RD	VICTORY 39
CANADA	8TH	18TH (ALTERNATOR)
FRANCE	5TH	4TH
GREAT BRITAIN	4TH	5TH (OUT OF FUEL)
GERMANY	4TH	4TH
HUNGARY	4TH	DNF (THROTTLE)
BELGIUM	5TH	4TH
ITALY	4TH	DNF (CRASH)
PORTUGAL	4TH	DNF (ENGINE)
JAPAN	2ND	VICTORY 40
AUSTRALIA	POLE POSITION 62	VICTORY 41

2ND IN FORMULA 1 WORLD CHAMPIONSHIP
(73 POINTS, 5 VICTORIES, 7 PODIUMS,
1 POLE POSITION, 1 BEST LAP)

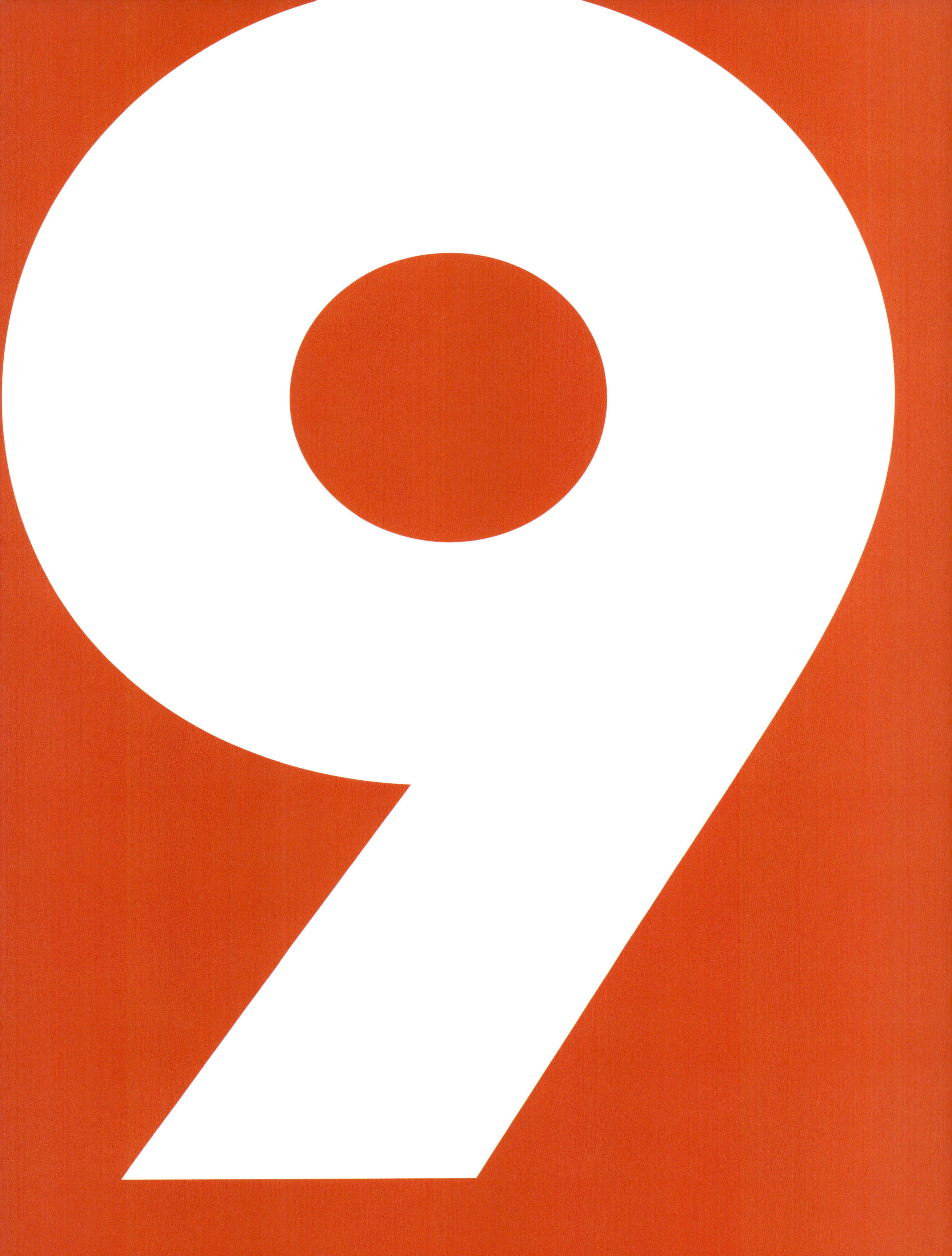
9

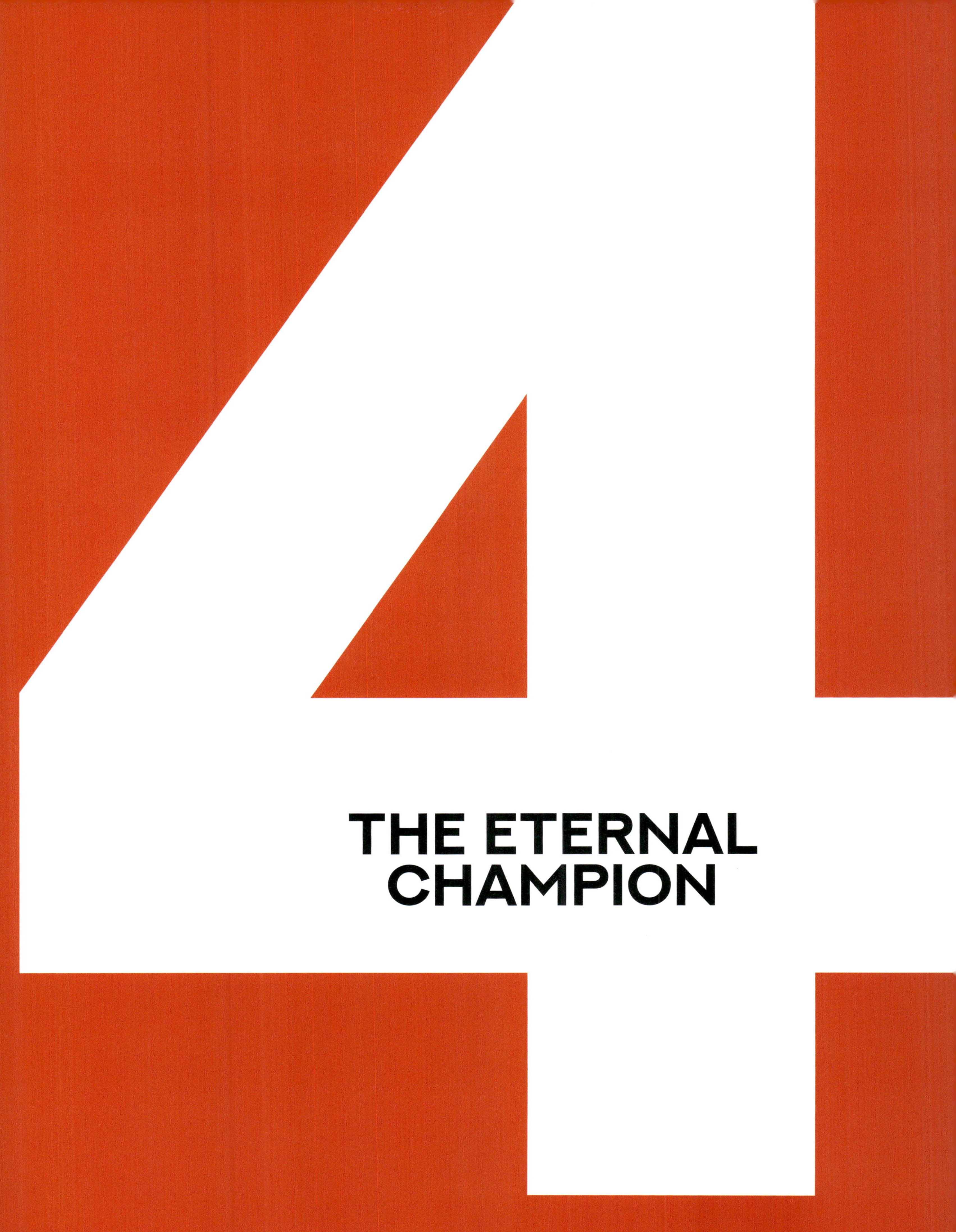

4 THE ETERNAL CHAMPION

THE LAST THREE RACES

THE 1994 FORMULA 1 SEASON PROMISED MUCH, BUT IT LASTED JUST THREE RACES FOR AYRTON SENNA—THE LAST THREE RACES OF HIS CAREER AND HIS LIFE.

Having moved to Williams, the best team at the time, the Brazilian was the favorite to succeed Alain Prost on the world championship podium. He showed that he was still the fastest in terms of pure performance, winning the first three pole positions of the year. Unfortunately, after having often benefitted from the favors of luck since 1984, he was unsuccessful. He failed to score any points at home in Brazil or at Aida during the Pacific Grand Prix. He lost his life at Imola due to a steering failure on his Williams. For three months, Ayrton had doubted himself, his talent, and his team. The Virgin's medal, given to him at the Paul Ricard Circuit by an elderly lady with a passion for F1, did not protect him.

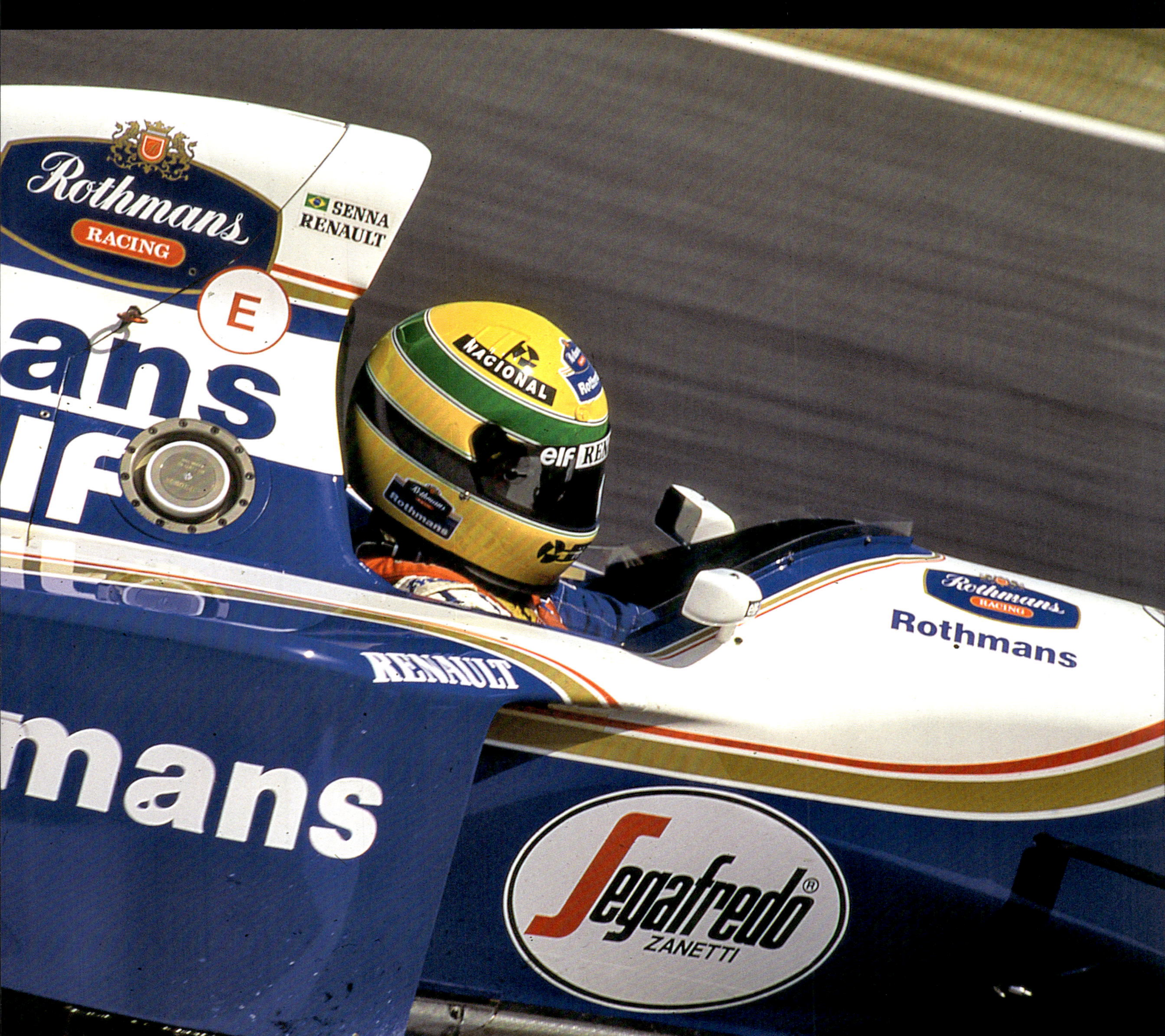
Rothmans
RACING
SENNA
RENAULT
E
NACIONAL
elf
RENAULT
Rothmans
RACING
Rothmans
Segafredo
ZANETTI

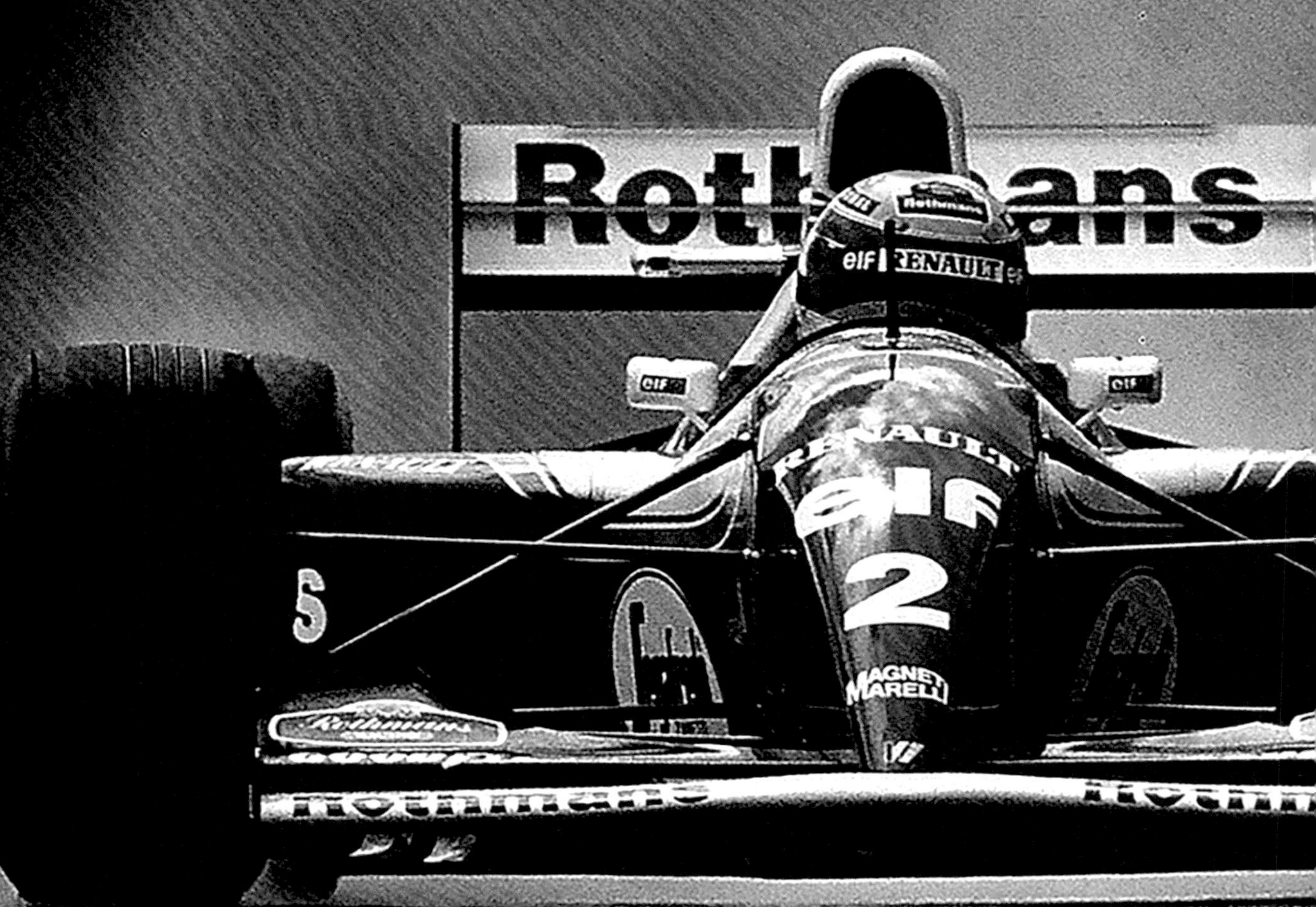
elf RENAULT
RENAULT
elf
2
MAGNETI MARELLI

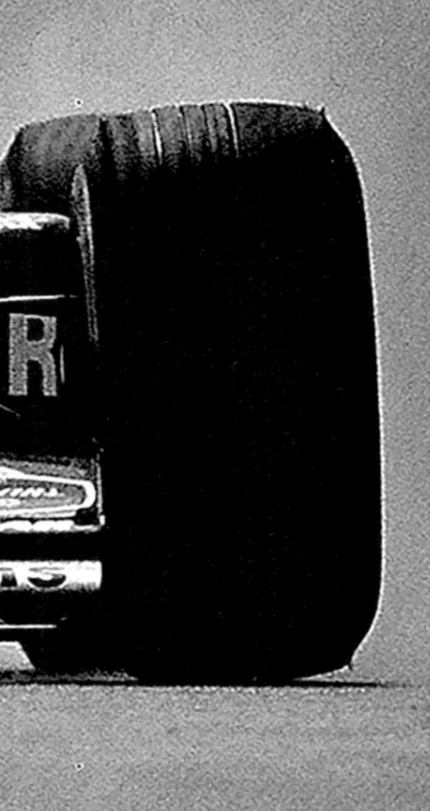

RACE AFTER RACE

1994

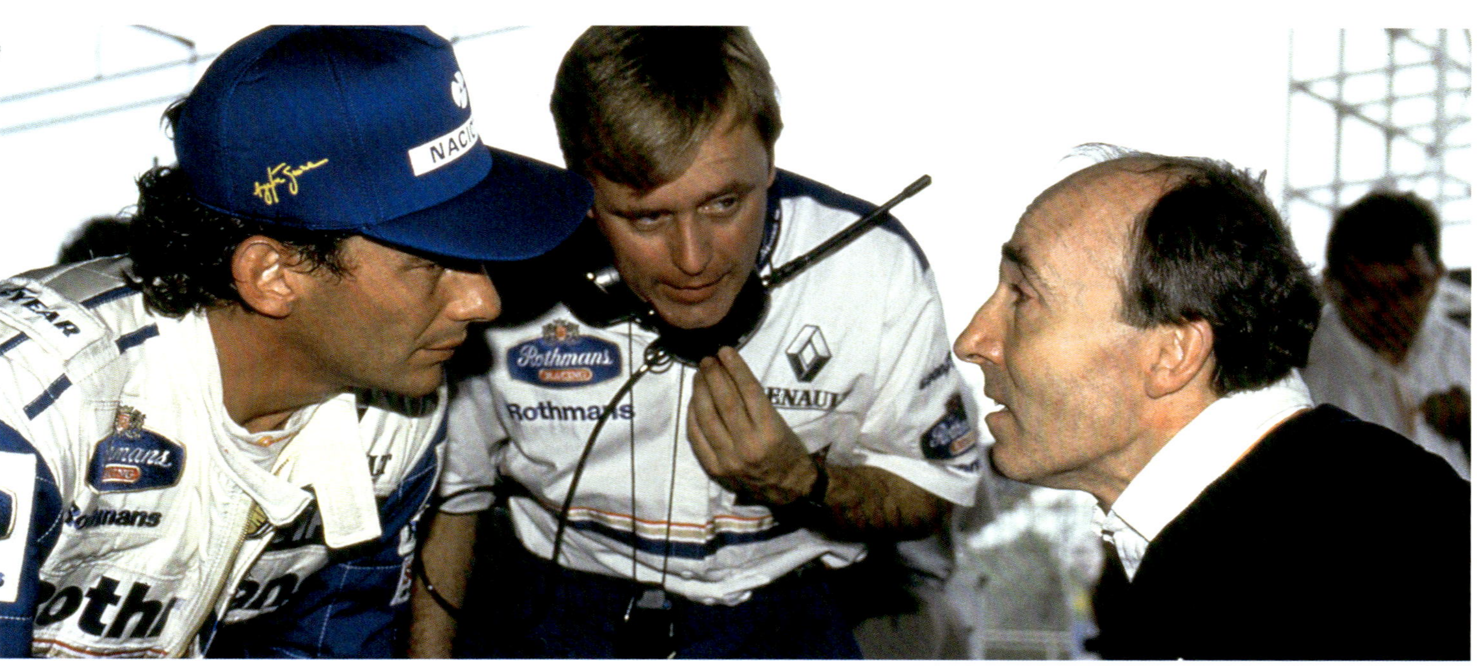

BRAZIL GRAND PRIX, INTERLAGOS: ALREADY SOME DOUBTS

It's his first F1 Grand Prix in a Williams, and Senna is worried. The new Williams-Renault is difficult to tune, with a very narrow operating window. He's uncomfortable in the cockpit, which hinders his driving. He also needs to become accustomed to a new atmosphere and new habits, and the mechanics and engineers are a little intimidated by his charisma and track record. Ayrton often interacts with his former rival, Alain Prost, who is now retired from racing. Prost is very attentive to the man who, after ten years of fierce battles, has become his friend. It's also the big return of refueling, reintroduced to contribute to the show. This is a new variable for the teams to master.

On Saturday afternoon, the qualifying ends in the rain. The local hero is once again in pole position in front of his home crowd. Although he feels his FW16 is too reactive and difficult to drive, he beats Michael Schumacher's ("Schumi's") Benetton and Jean Alesi's Ferrari. On Sunday, Senna gets off to a good start and leads into the first corner. By lap 3, he has a three-second lead, and by lap 4, a four-second lead, already a small advantage over the Schumi-Alesi duo. By lap 10, however, the young German, Schumacher, is back within two seconds of Senna and starts to

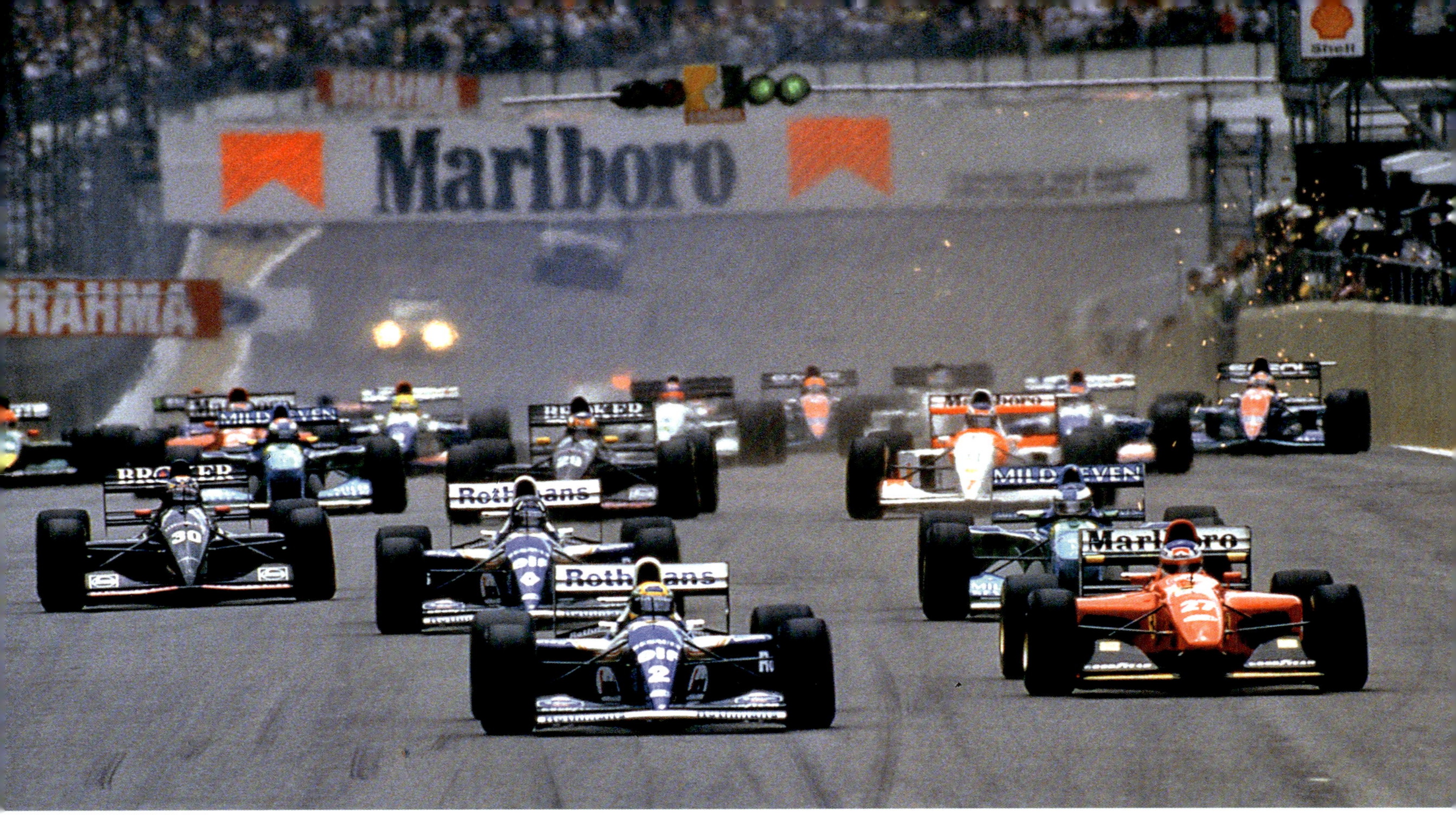

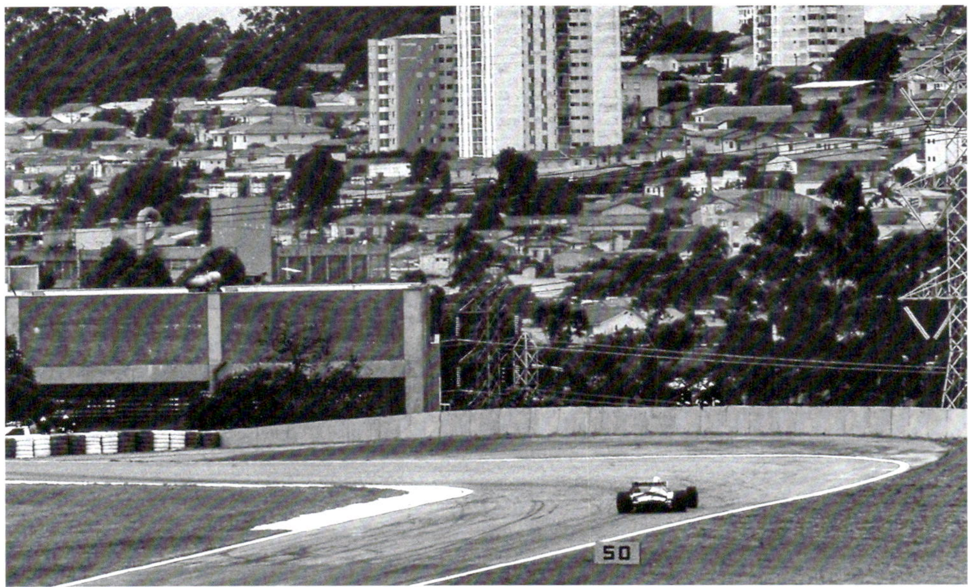

Far left: Ayrton Senna and Patrick Head, Williams' technical director, exchange words with Sir Frank Williams, the founder of the English team.

Top: The Interlagos circuit in São Paulo often sees eventful starts.

Bottom: In front of his home crowd, the first Grand Prix of the 1994 season in Brazil concludes with a spin for Ayrton Senna and a victory for Michael Schumacher.

put pressure on him. By lap 18, he is down to a one-second lead, and Alesi has stalled. On lap 22, both drivers return to the pits to refuel and change tires. Benetton's mechanics are quicker than Williams', and Schumi emerges ahead of Senna.

The gap widens—six seconds on lap 42—before the second pit stop. Senna comes back towards the end of the race until a rare mistake occurs on lap 56. He is caught out and spun. The Renault engine in the Williams stalls. He calls the stewards for help, but they are not allowed to intervene. Magic Senna is out of the race. He returns to the pits to applause, but it's Schumacher who wins. Some of the fans have already left the circuit. Second on the podium is Damon Hill, also in a Williams. He is exhausted by the difficulties he had controlling his car. The podium is completed by Alesi. After the finish, Senna takes responsibility for his driving error: "We didn't manage to set our car up properly for this circuit. There was nothing we could do. When I made my mistake, I was really on the edge of my seat." There is no longer active suspension on the Williams cars, as it has been banned by the new regulations. It was one of the British team's major assets.

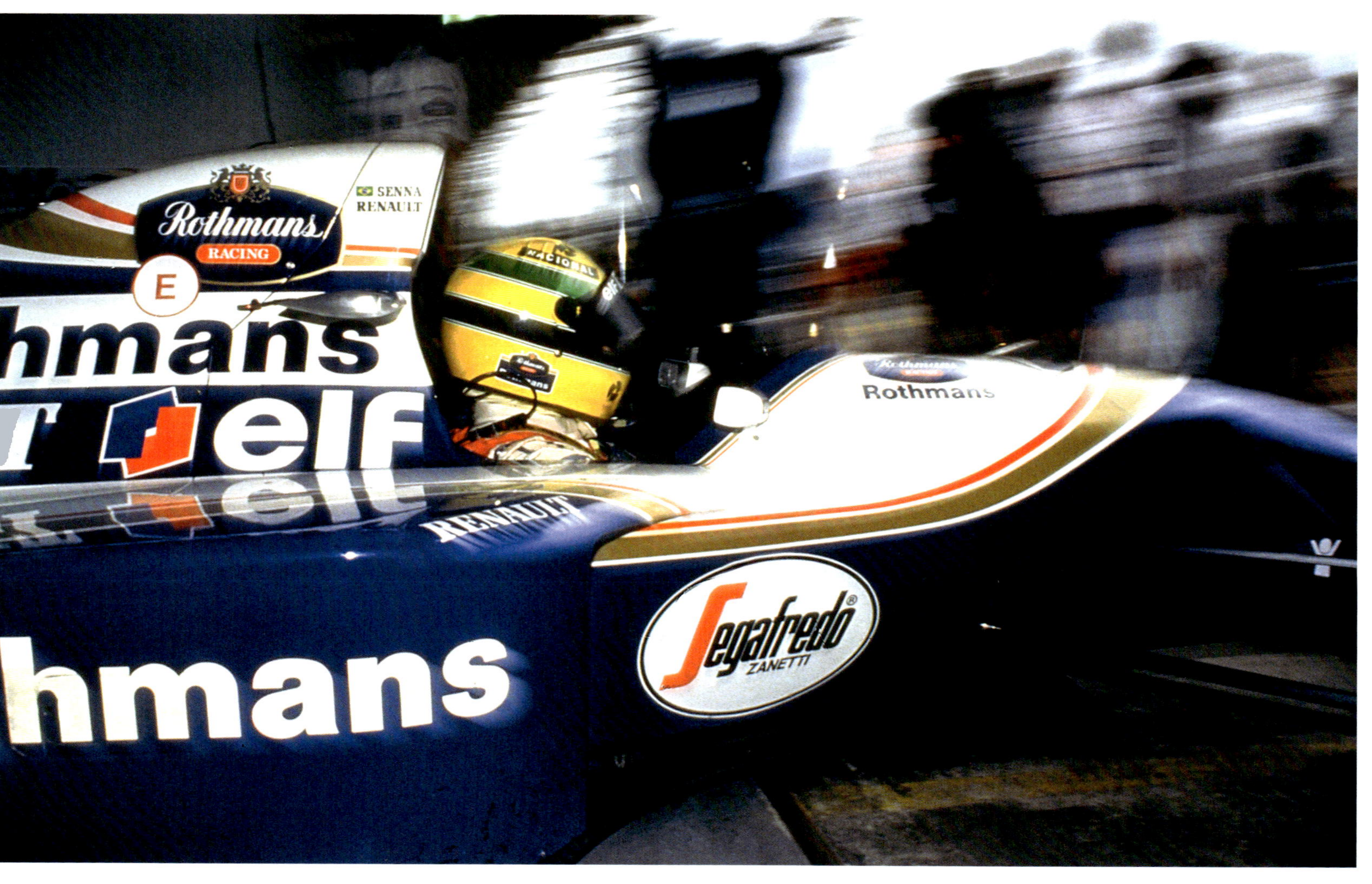

At Williams Racing, Senna aims for a fourth world title, like Prost. However, he does not feel confident in the Williams FW16 at the start of the season.

SENNINHA—SENNA'S ONLY "CHILD"

On January 28, 1994, Ayrton Senna announced in a video the "birth" of a little comic character who looked exactly like him: Senninha. Born from the imagination of Rogério Martins and Ridaut Dias Jr, this intrepid and combative (but impatient) youngster was always surrounded by his group of friends and wearing his yellow helmet, just like the real Senna! The first comic book about Senninha came out in March 1994 and was distributed free of charge to schools in Brazil. Initially, Senninha drove an entirely blue car as a reference to the Williams racing team, and after Senna's death, the character was portrayed in an all-red suit. "This is his iconic tunic. The one people associate Ayrton with," said Marcio Petta, a member of the Instituto Ayrton Senna, the foundation set up a few months after the tragedy by the champion's sister, Viviane.

Little Senna still lives on across a variety of media almost thirty years after his creation. He is a valiant character who is proud of his Brazilian nationality. Although the comic strip no longer exists in its original form, Senninha is now available in video games, cartoons, and derivative products. Sandals bearing the character's head are very popular in Brazil, and even pizzerias bear his name! Ayrton had great faith in Senninha and was proud of the little character who bore his features. The story goes that, on May 1, 1994, the Brazilian champion wore a T-shirt with the name and image of Senninha under his blue and white Williams racing suit. A child, forever.

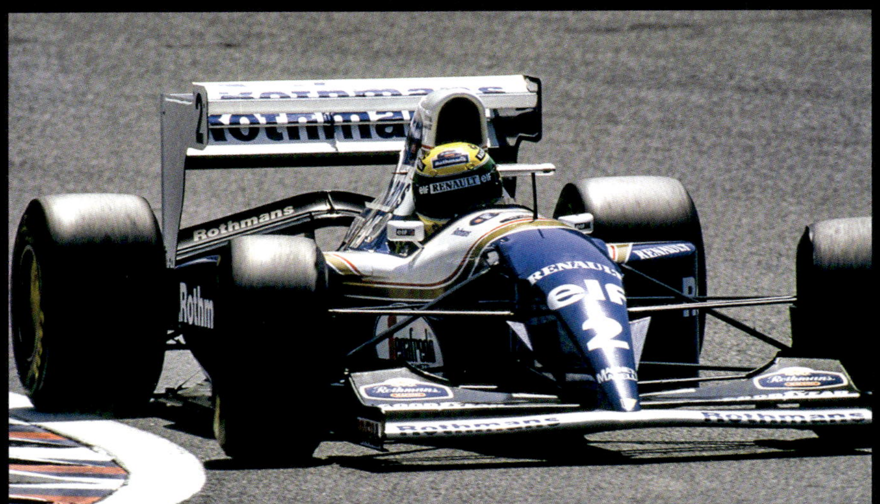

THE CAR: WILLIAMS FW16

At the time of Senna's official move to Williams, the French press spoke of the "marriage of the century." The FW16 was supposed to be the wedding ring on the Brazilian's finger. But the relationship between the driver and his car was more like "Je t'aime, moi non plus." In 1994, refueling returned, and electronic aids such as launch control were removed, as were active suspension, anti-lock brakes, and traction control computers. The FIA intended to emphasize the performance of the drivers rather than that of the electronics specialists. Unluckily, this is—in part—what had made Williams so dominant in previous years.

The FW16 was an evolution of the 1993 model. The bodywork had been reworked and the pontoons raised. At the rear, it featured the powerful Renault V10 RS6 engine, but that was not the problem. This Williams model proved to be unpredictable. Adrian Newey, in charge of the car's design, explained, "I had negotiated the return to passive suspension badly and designed a car that was aerodynamically unstable. At the wheel, Ayrton tried things that the car was not capable of doing." Despite this adversity, Senna managed to secure the last three pole positions of his career. On each single lap, he proved that he was the best, even if the car's handling was questionable. His spin in Brazil was a prime example. The interventions of Technical Director Patrick Head and Newey did nothing to change this. Senna would never feel at ease in the cockpit of the FW16, which would carry him to his doomed fate on May 1, 1994. Nevertheless, its improved version, the FW16B, enabled Damon Hill and David Coulthard to take the Constructors' World Championship from Benetton—the third in a row for Williams since 1992.

PACIFIC GRAND PRIX, AIDA: DISAPPOINTMENT, YET AGAIN

The second round of the season is scheduled for Japan, where Senna is still—more than ever—an absolute idol for F1 fans. Before arriving in Aida, he takes a trip to Disneyland, Tokyo, with his friend, Rubens Barrichello. Meanwhile, in England, Adrian Newey is working on a new front end for the FW16, which is due to appear at the San Marino Grand Prix. Once again, his top driver gets the job done—pole position, as in Brazil, ahead of Schumi, the young championship leader.

Schumacher gets off to a good start as Senna's rear wheels spin. Häkkinen also gets off to a good start in his McLaren but hits Senna's Williams on the inside of the first corner. The FW16 spins and is hit by Nicola Larini's Ferrari, which is unable to avoid him. Senna emerges from his cockpit, stunned by this latest mishap. Schumacher wins again without too much difficulty, and Senna is disappointed: "This car isn't as good as I'd like it to be. I can't drive it the way I'd like to. To stay on the razor's edge for one or two laps to go for pole, fine. But not for the whole distance of a grand prix." Once again, the switch back to conventional suspensions—the "active" version having been banned—may explain the difficulties experienced by Williams, which was the most skilled team in this highly specialized field.

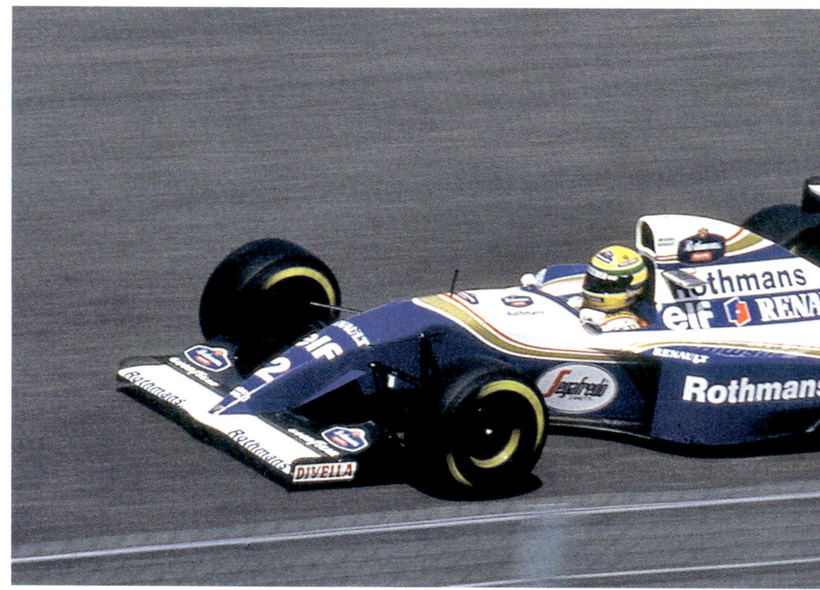

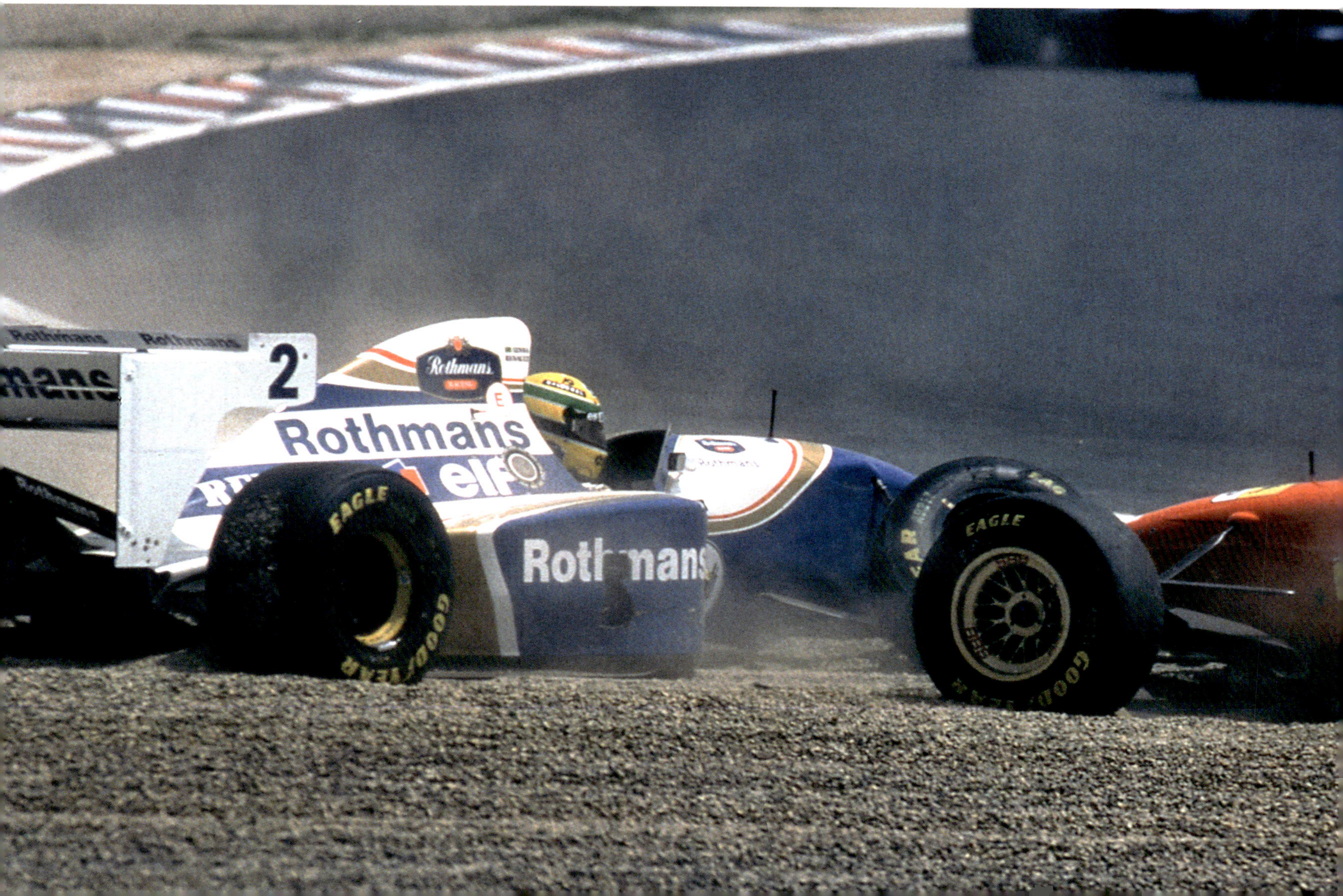

Top: For many observers, Senna's arrival at Williams in 1994 is considered the marriage of the century but turns out differently.

Bottom: At the Pacific Grand Prix, Senna's race ends at the first turn of the first lap after a collision with Mika Häkkinen, the Brazilian's short-lived teammate at McLaren during the previous season. He is then hit by Nicola Larini's Ferrari.

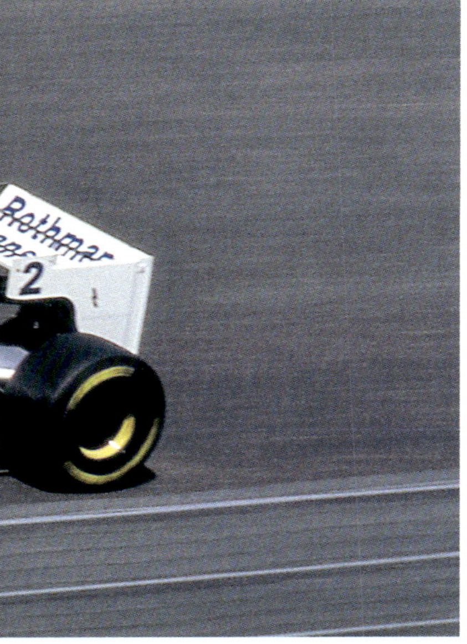

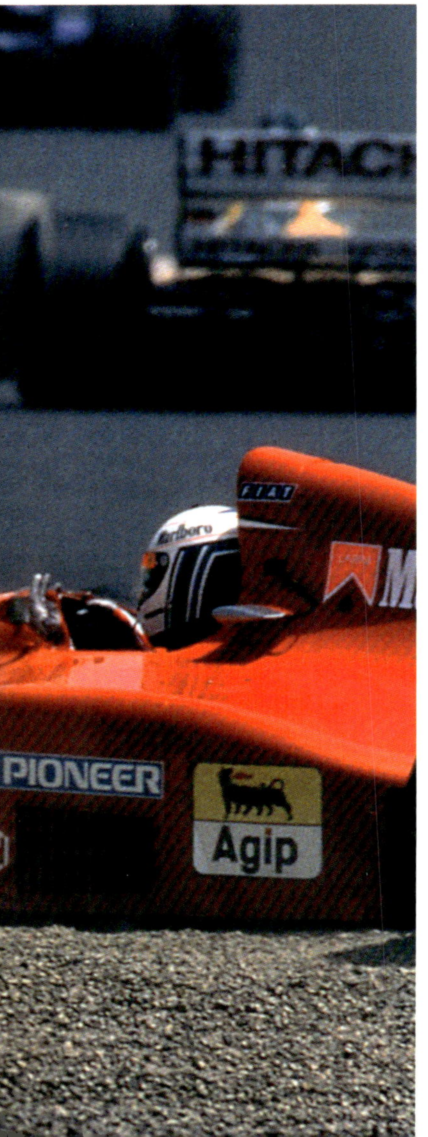

THE MAIN CHARACTERS

MICHAEL SCHUMACHER, THE DARING GERMAN

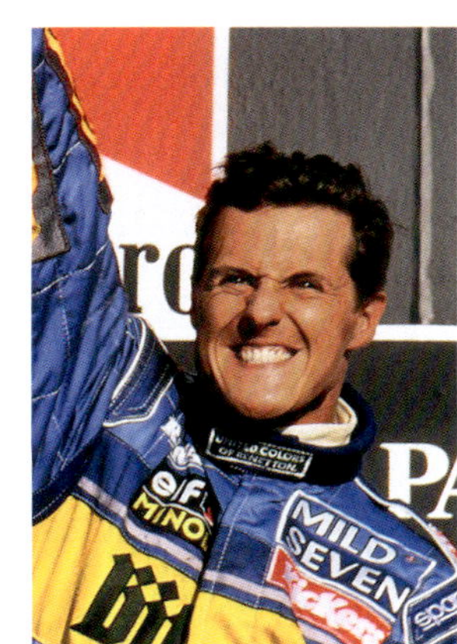

At the beginning of 1994, Michael Schumacher was known as a fast, intrepid driver who shook up the established order. But he wasn't yet the man with seven world titles—far from it. The 25-year-old had only two-and-a-half F1 seasons under his belt. Even so, he already had 17 podium finishes to his name, including two victories. His talent attracted attention but also criticism. Senna was not a fan of the German's driving style, which was a little too aggressive for his liking. The two men had already clashed at Magny-Cours in 1992, and a heated discussion had ensued. "Ayrton tried to put Michael in his place a few times on the circuits. Michael was disappointed. He didn't think it was very respectful," said British engineer Ross Brawn in a documentary about the German—a commonly held view of the Brazilian during his early days.

Before the 1994 season even kicked off, the duel had begun to take shape. On the car side, the Italians from Benetton competed with Williams, and the start of the championship quickly turned in favor of the Italian team led by Flavio Briatore. On his rival's home turf, Schumacher had set the tone and won with great skill. He did the same at Aida in the second race, which led Senna to question the legality of the Benetton B194. The three-time world champion believed it was equipped with illegal traction control. After an investigation by the FIA, Senna's theory was refuted, but skepticism remained.

After the Imola tragedy, Schumi became the F1's new figurehead. But the Brazilian's death still lingered in the back of his mind. A few weeks later, as he circumnavigated the Silverstone Circuit in a production car, he was disturbed by some of the curves: "I thought, 'Here is a place where you can kill yourself, at this place too. There are so many places where you can crash and kill yourself instantly.' That's the only thing I was thinking about." After winning the world championship for Benetton in 1994 and 1995, Schumacher joined Ferrari to continue building his legend despite the Tifosi's initial disapproval. In 2000, he won in Italy and matched Senna's 41 victories. A journalist mentioned this similarity in a press conference. The German, who had seemed cold, arrogant, and distant, broke down in tears, overwhelmed by emotion. At the end of the year, he clinched a third world title, like Senna before him, and brought Scuderia Ferrari back to the top—a dream that the Brazilian was never able to realize.

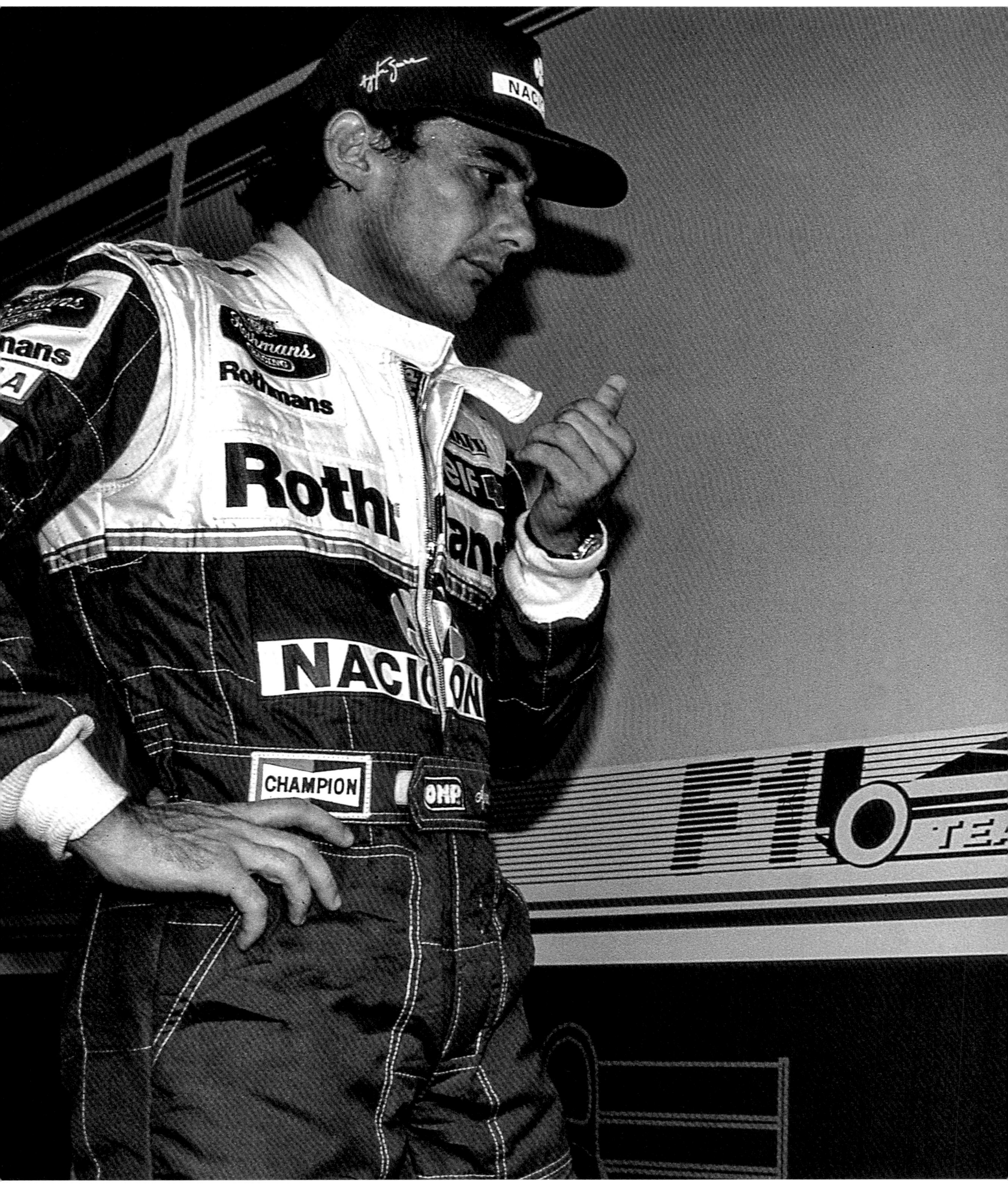

Rothmans
Roth
CHAMPION
OMP
F1

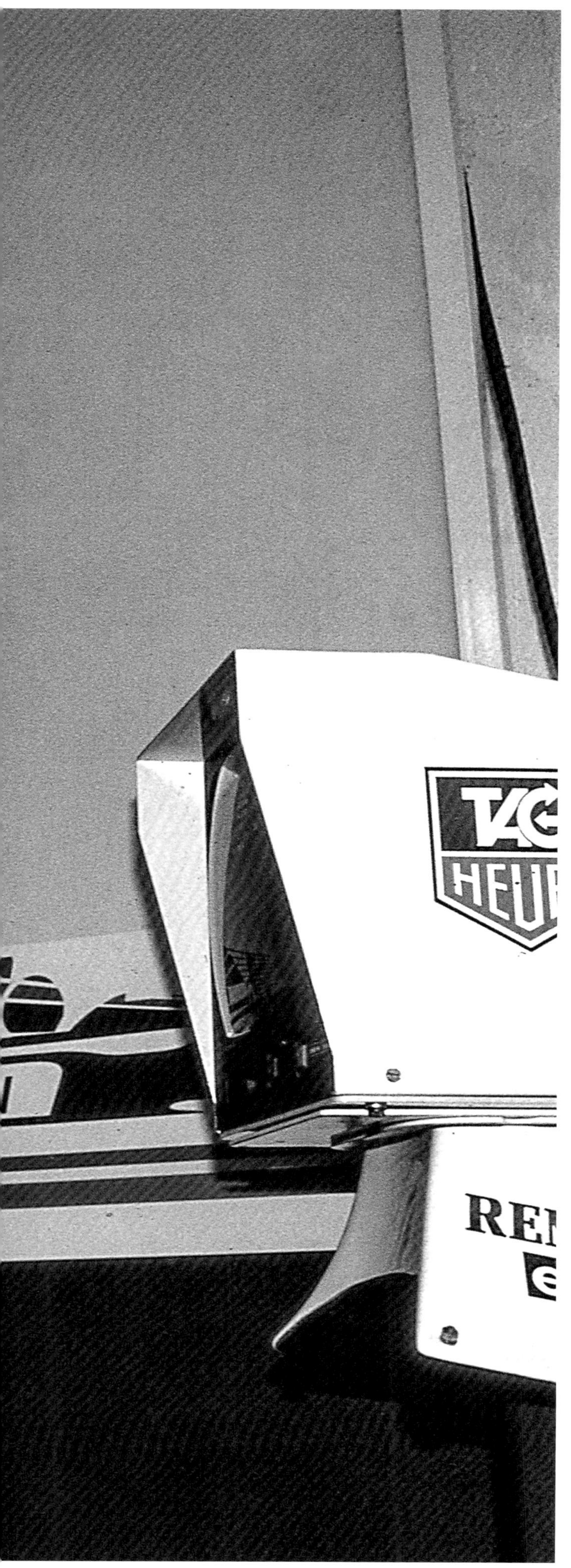

A special hello to my friend ... to our friend Alain. We miss you, Alain.

AYRTON SENNA

SAN MARINO GRAND PRIX, IMOLA: THE TRAGEDY

San Marino is the first European round of 1994. Senna is determined to shine and catch up with Schumacher, who leads 20 points to zero. Squeezed into a cockpit he finds too cramped, the Brazilian secures provisional pole on Friday, but his young friend, Barrichello—a Jordan rookie, takes off and crashes into the tire wall at 220 kilometers an hour. He breaks his nose and suffers more from fear than harm. The next day, as Austrian Roland Ratzenberger attempts to qualify, the wing of his Simtek-Ford comes loose a few meters before entering the Gilles Villeneuve curve. At 315 kilometers an hour, he hits the wall, and it's all over. Death strikes F1 for the first time since May 14, 1986, when Elio De Angelis died on the Paul Ricard Circuit. Senna sees Ratzenberger's crash from the screen in the Williams pit and goes to the scene. His friend, Dr. Sid Watkins, suggests that he end his race weekend. "Sid, I can't give up. I've got to drive tomorrow," replies the Brazilian. It's his 65th pole position, and he's determined to honor it. The next morning, he is TF1's luxury consultant for the circuit tour. Before starting, he lets slip a token of his friendship for Alain Prost, who is about to comment on the race: "A special hello to my friend ... to our friend Alain. We miss you, Alain."

On the grid, before taking the start, Senna looks worried and disturbed. This is unusual for such a meticulous, focused man. The start is marred by a collision between JJ Lehto and Pedro Lamy. The debris and a wheel fly into the crowd, hitting spectators, and the safety car comes out of the pits. When it re-emerges again at the end of lap 5, Senna is ahead of Schumacher. At the end of lap 7, seven seconds after crossing the timing line, he plunges into the Tamburello curve. Senna's Williams FW16 slams straight into the tire wall. The accident plunges Brazil into grief. And leaves 160 million Brazilians without their hero.

Beaten by the Benetton-Ford team, Senna has doubts about the legality of certain elements of Michael Schumacher's car.

PARADOX AND TRAGEDY

At 2 p.m., the European F1 season kicked off. But a collision occurred within the first few meters. Pedro Lamy and JJ Lehto left a lot of debris on the grid, and a wheel flew off, hitting nine spectators. The safety car was brought out. Comas damaged his Larrousse when he ran over the pieces of carbon and aerodynamic components. His return to the pits for repairs was a necessity.

In the meantime, mondovision viewers and on-site spectators had their eyes riveted to the giant screens that showed images of Tamburello. A drama was unfolding. The unbelievable had happened: Senna had crashed; the red flag was waving. Comas, who was at the end of the pits, was curiously allowed back on the track. He immediately arrived at the cursed curve and saw the fallen idol lying on the track. It was a dramatic event he witnessed with the other drivers. He recalls the episode painfully:

"I was paralyzed, I felt an intense sensation. I was staring at his body lying inert on the ground and at his helmet in the ambulance. I immediately understood [that Senna had died], and at that moment, I felt like an energy being released, escaping from his body. His soul was flying away as if after a blast, causing an immense release of energy. From that moment on, my relationship with Formula 1 beyond changed."

Erik Comas recovered from this tragedy with great difficulty, leaving F1 at the end of the 1994 season. He moved to Japan for eleven years to clear his mind and notched up numerous successes in the famous Japanese Super GT Championship. Deep down, he would always have very personal memories of the legendary Brazilian champion.

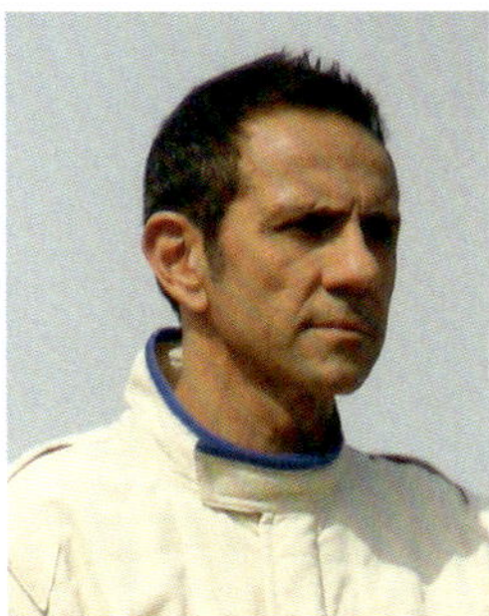

ERIK COMAS: "LIKE SOME ENERGY DISSIPATING"

On May 1, 1994, in Imola, the drivers met at 8:30 a.m. for the traditional briefing before Erik Comas took the start in a Larrousse. He said:

"The atmosphere is heavy and unbreathable. Ayrton is troubled and scarred by Rubens Barrichello's accident and Roland Ratzenberger's death. He tells me, 'It's a disaster and we're vulnerable. We need to have a meeting before Monaco, with the other drivers, to talk about circuit safety.'"

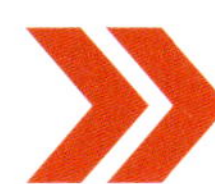

Top: On May 1, 1994, the San Marino Grand Prix starts at 2 p.m. at the Imola circuit.

Middle: Senna secures the 65th pole position of his career at Imola with a successful lap on Saturday, a day marked by the death of Austrian Roland Ratzenberger during qualifying.

Bottom: After Senna's accident at Tamburello Corner, the red flag is waved, and the race is stopped. Michael Schumacher leaps out of his Benetton and heads toward his team's pit to find his team manager, Flavio Briatore.

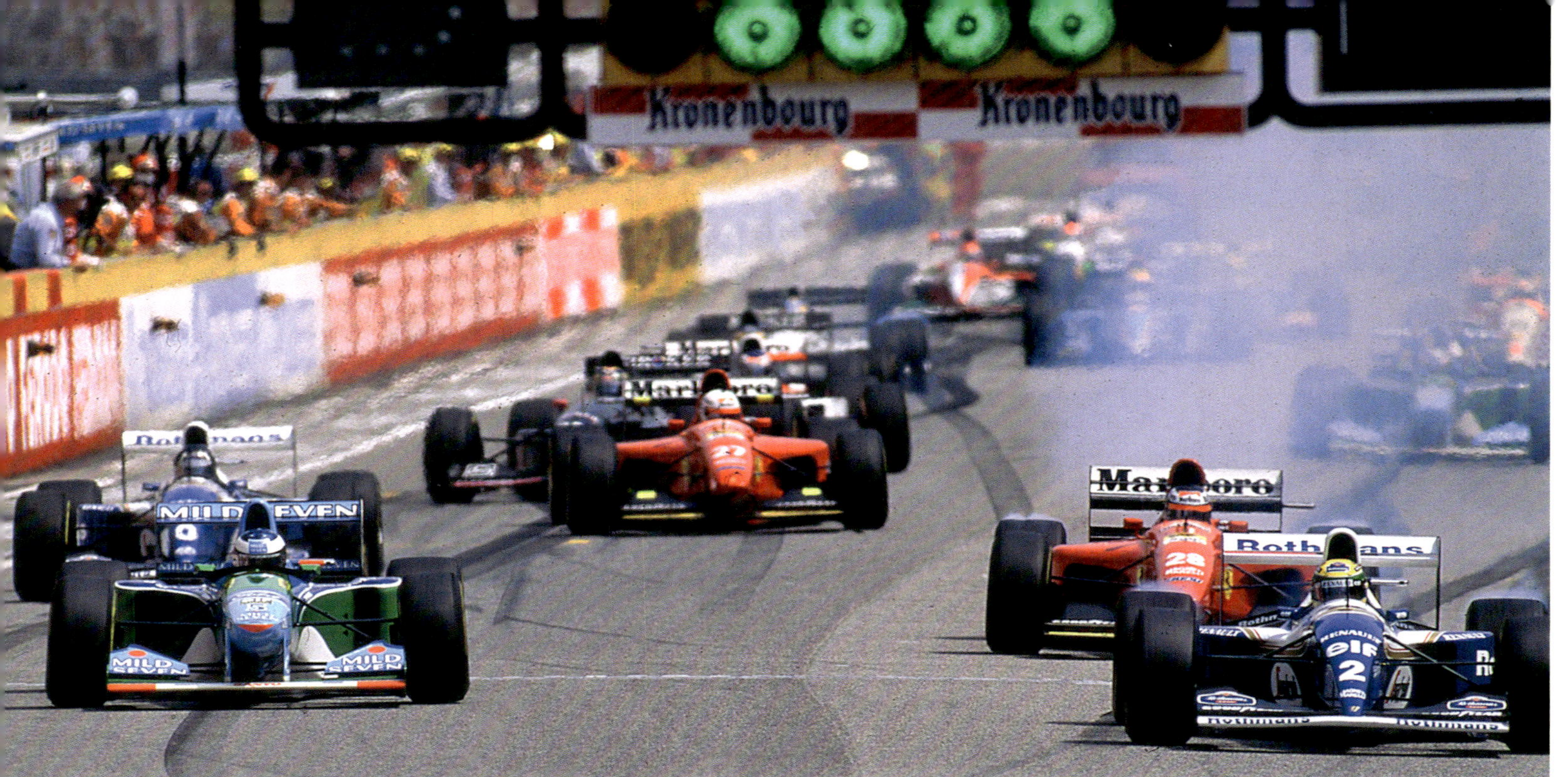
Kronenbourg
Kronenbourg
MILD SEVEN
elf

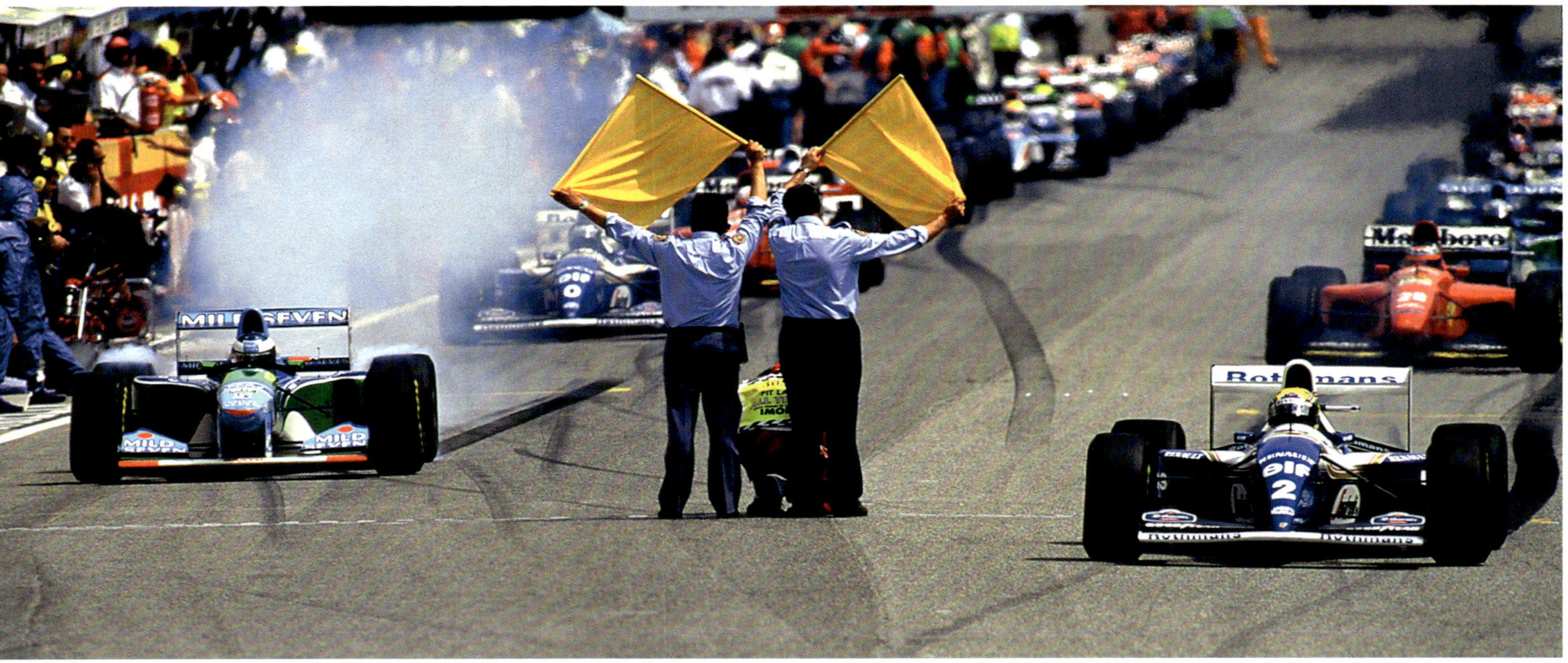
MILD SEVEN

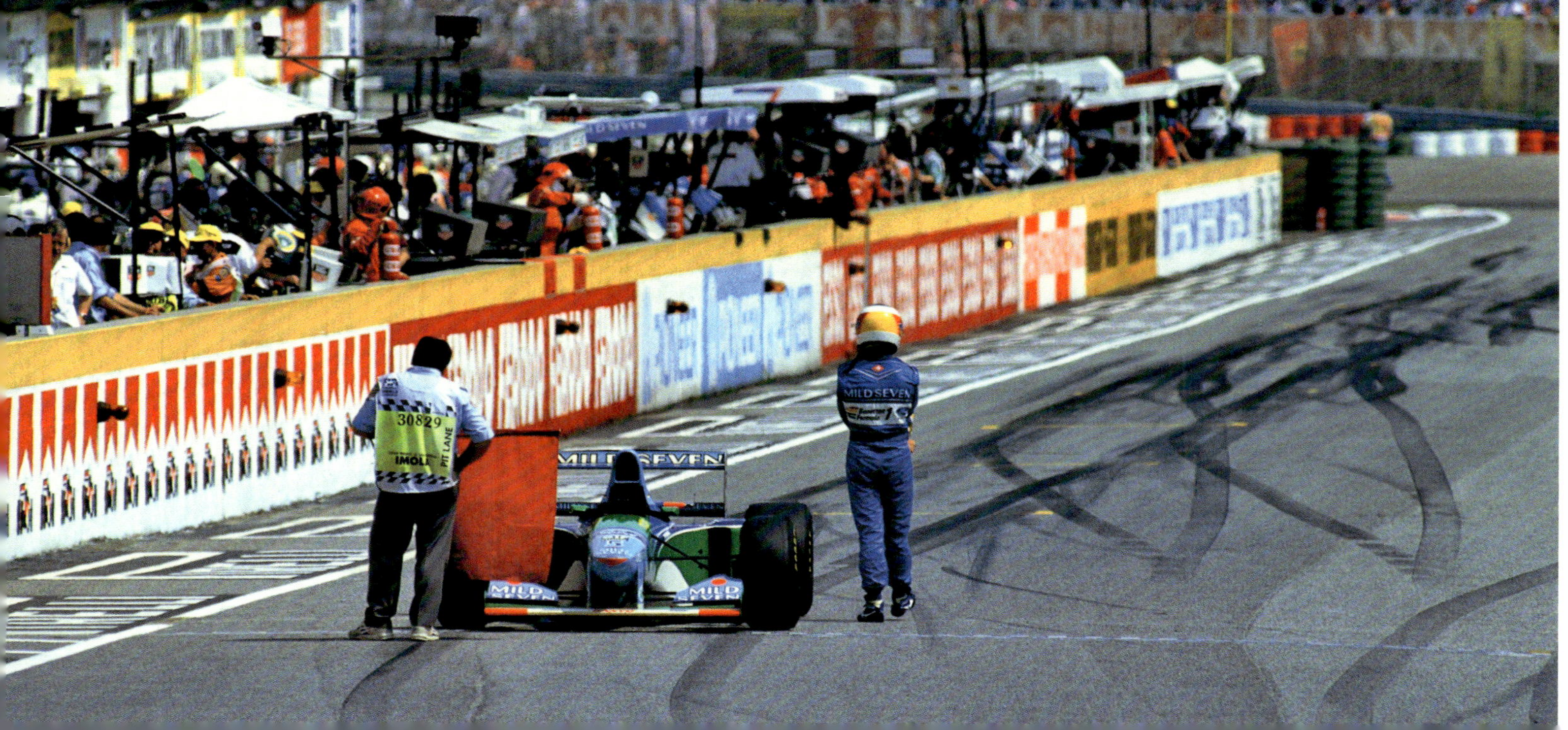
30829
IMOLA
MILD SEVEN

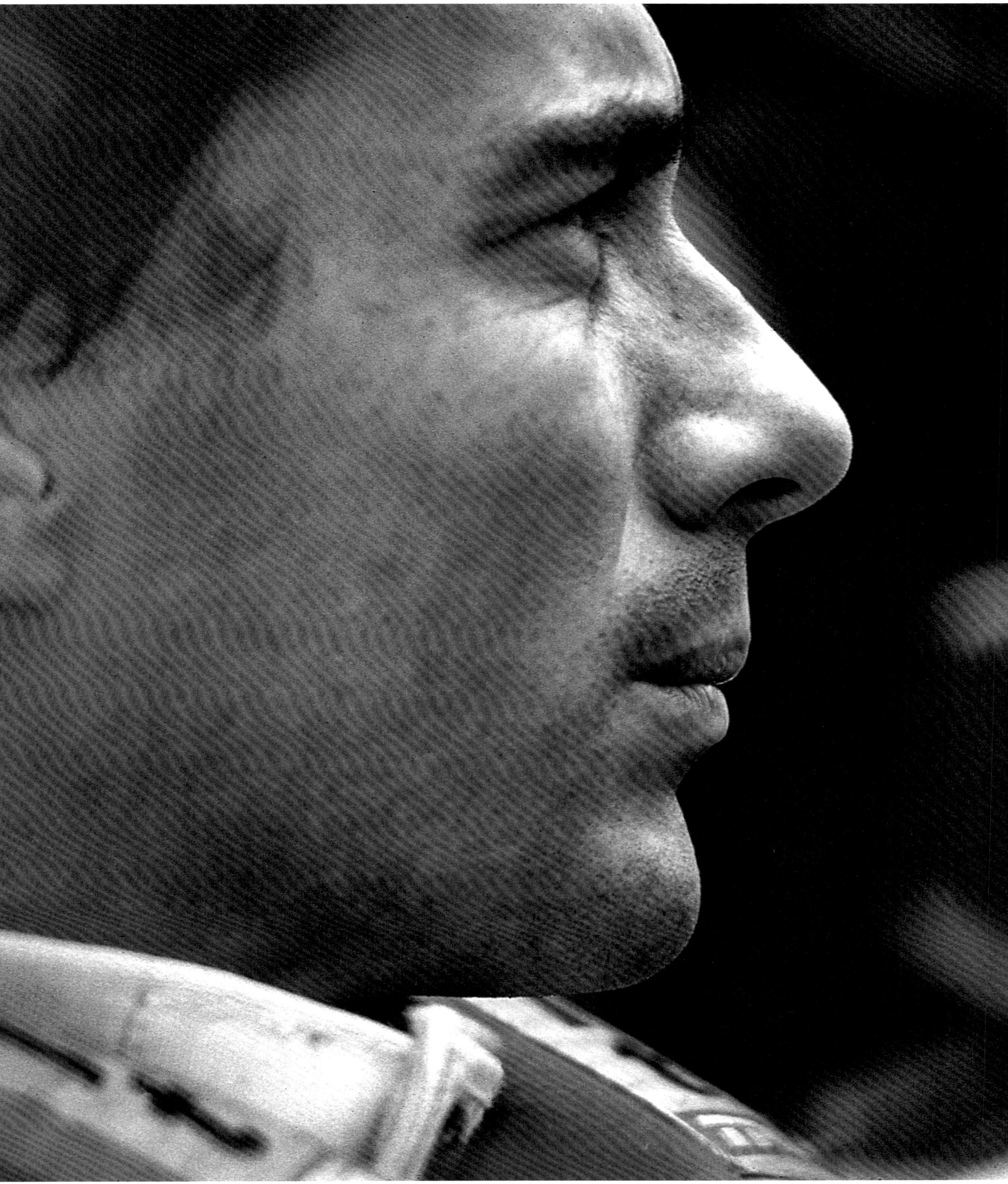

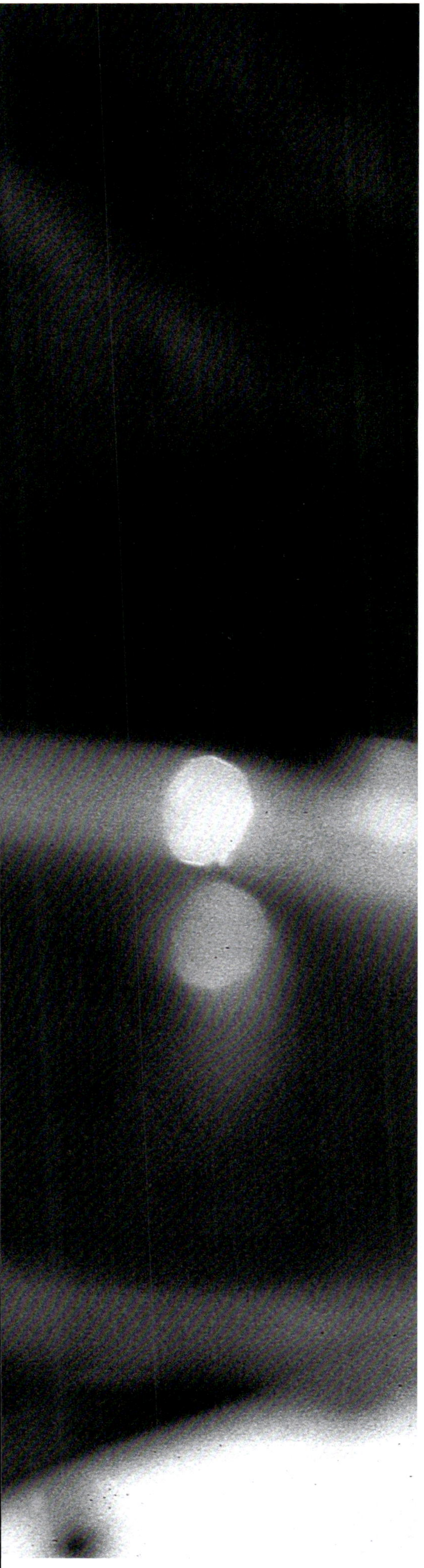

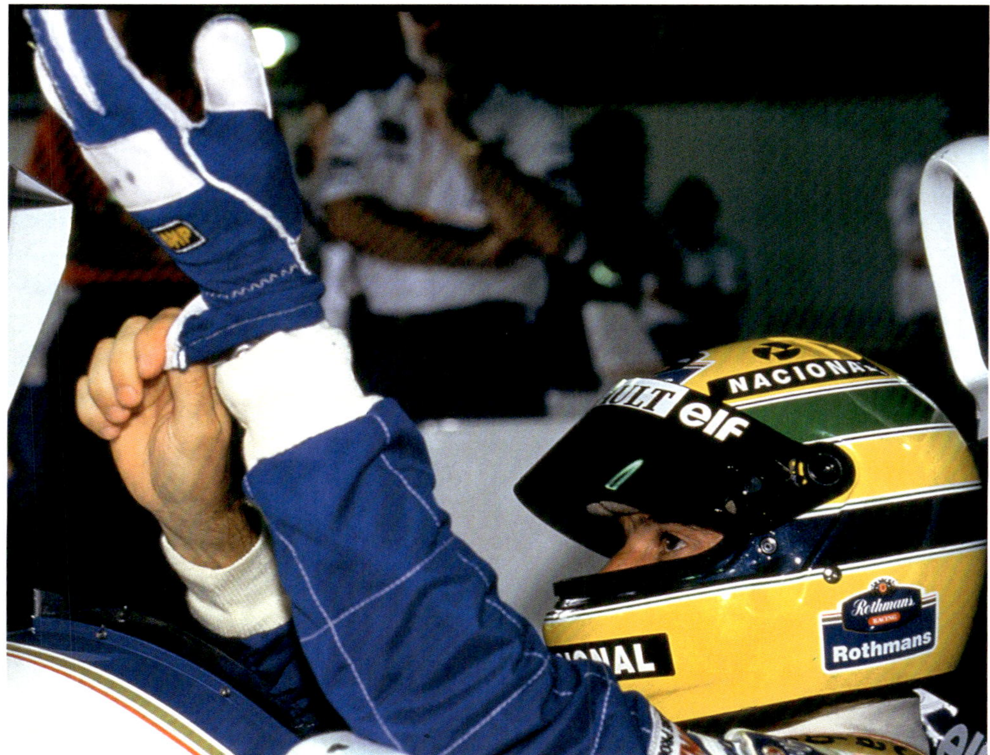

Just minutes before the start of the 1994 San Marino Grand Prix, Senna is so disturbed that he leaves his helmet in front of him on the grid—a significant detail, as the Brazilian has never done this in ten years of F1.

Despite the challenges posed by his car's behavior, Senna manages to exploit the qualities and power of the Renault engine and win three pole positions in three races.

SENNA'S LAST THREE POLES

1994

GRAND PRIX	QUALIFIERS	OUTCOME
BRAZIL	POLE POSITION 63	DNF (SPIN)
PACIFIC	POLE POSITION 64	DNF (CRASH)
SAN MARINO	POLE POSITION 65	DNF (CRASH)

IMOLA 1994, BY DOMINIQUE LEROY

In 1994, photographer Dominique Leroy worked for Elf, Williams' major partner, and was following Ayrton Senna's every step. Leroy was present at the Imola Circuit to witness a weekend like no other.—the most tragic in F1 history. Thirty years on, it's still etched in his memory.

THURSDAY, APRIL 28, 1994: A WONDERFUL DAY

"After an eight-hour freeway journey from Nîmes, I arrived in Imola with my colleague and friend Alain Patrice. By 4 p.m., we're hard at work at the circuit. I move fast: I have an appointment to take photos of Ayrton. I'm under contract with Elf, a privileged position I hold dearer than anything else because this driver is my driver—I've been following him since 1983, a year before he entered F1, and this year my contract will allow me to follow him everywhere.

"He arrives, calm. Each time, his presence liquefies me. I immediately find myself in a bubble detached from everything and everyone—except the clouds, and I'm on it. That day proves even more incredible: Ayrton calls me and, smiling, hands me one of his helmets in its original cover. 'It's for you'—nothing more. I'd asked him for it in Brazil, but no action had been taken, so this is a huge moment of amazement (and gratitude!). I'm talking and talking, not knowing what I'm saying, so stunned and moved. I finally manage to stammer out a request for him to sign this helmet for me, for us to take a photo, for us to take a little time (not for Elf—just him and me). He smiles approvingly but adds apologetically, 'We'll do all that after the race. Right now, I'm going into the briefing, I can't.' That

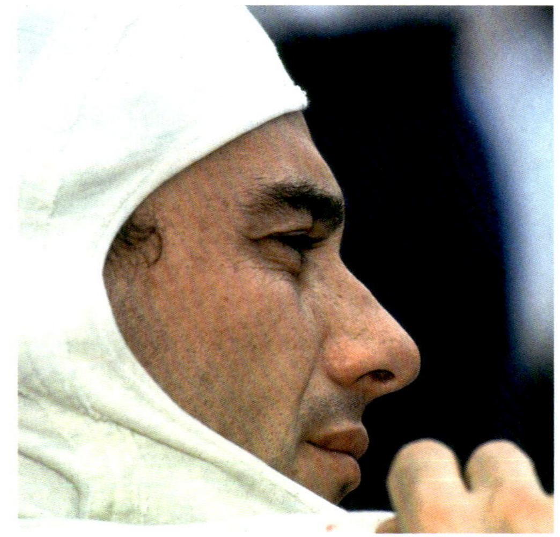

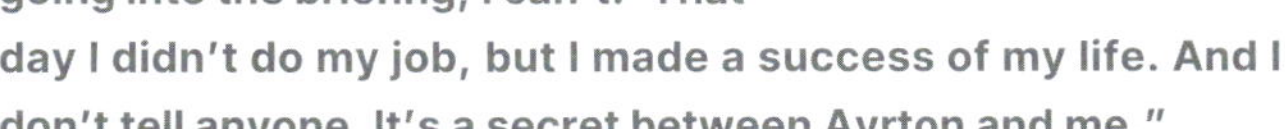

day I didn't do my job, but I made a success of my life. And I don't tell anyone. It's a secret between Ayrton and me."

FRIDAY, APRIL 29, 1994: AN ATROCIOUS DAY

"In the early afternoon, it's time for testing. Rubens Barrichello took off in his Jordan-Hart. He's going fast, very fast—too fast! But he realizes it too late, and the car takes off, hits the cables of the protective fence, rolls over twice in the air, and falls on its side. The impact was so violent that nobody could breathe. Nor, apparently, was Rubens! He's inert, his face bloody. Fortunately, no further harm was done. Ayrton himself rushes to the news. Phew! All's well. The day goes on, calm returns … and so does routine."

SATURDAY, APRIL 30, 1994: A HORRIBLE DAY

"Last practice session—the left flap of Roland Ratzenberger's Simtek flies off. The car goes mad and crashes into the wall. I didn't take a photo but recorded the image on the screen, the driver's head wobbling, sagging, and not moving—live death. Now Italian law dictates that a death on a circuit must stop the event and trigger an investigation. The crash occurred at 2:18 p.m. The official time of death was 2:30 p.m. at the Bologna hospital because 'the show must go on.' But not for Senna, who did not take the wheel again (nor did Schumacher and others). He's broken down, in tears, really worried, and he wants to understand.

"His generation of drivers hasn't had a fatal race accident since Riccardo Paletti, just after Gilles Villeneuve, in 1982. They all trust the engineers and mechanics, the cars and circuits, and themselves. Ayrton goes to see Jean-Marie Balestre, President of the FIA and loses his temper. Circuit safety is at the heart of the dispute. That evening, he requisitions a vehicle to go to the scene of the accident. He wants to see for himself and understand what happened to his friend. The officials dismiss him and give him a reprimand—an official one.

"For my part, I'm devastated. Until then, I'd only witnessed one fatal accident on a grand prix weekend, that of Peterson in 1978, and I was only in the stands at the time. I was dazzled and horrified by the horrifying fire, the never-ending flames. That day, we all wore a kind of leaden blanket on our shoulders. Death hovered over the Imola Circuit: Barrichello came very close; Ratzenberger succumbed. Like everyone else, I prefer to go to bed early because I'm at a loss for words and don't understand what I'm doing here."

SUNDAY, MAY 1, 1994: THE WORST DAY

"After yesterday's tragedy, everyone is in a daze. Ayrton included. He passes furtively through his stand, looking grim, his expression tense. Because of my Elf contract, I've been following him for several months, and I've never seen him like this. Before the start, like many others, I noticed something totally unusual. Alain Prost was also astonished and mentioned it on television: While waiting for the first green light for the warm-up lap, Ayrton took off his helmet and balaclava, something he never does! Sitting in his cockpit, his gaze is fixed and tense, his jaws clenched. I click, unknowingly snapping a historic shot that will never fade from my retinas. For a quarter of a second, I think: 'He doesn't want to go.' But it's so inconceivable … I notice that he takes a long time to put his helmet back on.

"I chose to go up to the grandstand. The atmosphere is heavy. In the television multilanguage feed, I hear that Ayrton, in a state of shock, almost didn't race. He gave in because Balestre promised greater safety on the circuits. It's time for the start. Ayrton took the lead from pole, while Lehto, in third place in his Benetton, stalled and was hit by Lamy. The impact was violent, and pieces of cars flew off—debris everywhere. I take photos from the grandstand and, of course, even more of what has just happened. I press the shutter release as if to exorcise a fatal sequel. Phew! Neither of them is hurt. But it's still a lot to take in for this fucking weekend!

"For the second start, I'm lowered to the ground. The big screen showed me the first images of the drama that had played out of my sight. And in front of me, the red flags waved and immediately stopped Schumacher, who was in the lead at the time. I understand that it's Tamburello, a stone's throw away. I run, and like three of my colleagues who have arrived just as fast, I release the shutter. Again and again, I press the button on my camera. Photography has robotized me. But suddenly, my brain takes over with a single message: 'Stop! I must stop! This is horrible. I can't photograph this!' None of the four of us would publish one of these appalling photos, which can make you a millionaire. I'm not an unworthy paparazzi. The publisher employer of one of us put them in a safe. I burned them. Keeping them would have burned me.

"The show must go on. Maybe. But right now, I'm in tears! The drivers still racing have probably been reassured about Senna's condition. But the black series continues! Just before lap 50, Michele Alboreto—such a close friend of Ayrton!—left the pits with a loose wheel, which flew off and mowed down several mechanics. Some injuries, but no one in serious danger. Another 'oof.' I record, but I don't care. Schumacher wins, but I don't care. There's no champagne on the podium. And not even an effusion between the winners of these three morbid days, but I don't care! I'm somewhere else. And I'm going further away—away from this cursed place. With me, this helmet under my arm, so precious that I want to cherish it, to kiss it. No one else will ever have it. It saves me from this weekend of the apocalypse. As Alain and I head back to Nîmes, the onboard radio announces Ayrton's death."

AUTOSPRINT INVESTIGATION

In the aftermath of Senna's accident, newsrooms around the world turned their attention to Imola. They had only one question on their minds: Why did the Williams car go straight into the Tamburello curve? The Italian magazine Autosprint was the first to get to the bottom of this question. On Monday, May 2, 1994, the editorial team gathered at its offices in San Lazzaro di Savena. Angelo Orsi, the magazine's photographer, displayed the photos of the accident that were taken the previous day on an overhead projector. Gabriele Tarquini, a former F1 driver, called out to the editorial team when, in the Rai images, he noticed an intriguing unidentified object next to the cockpit of Senna's Williams.

The editors consulted the pictures again: It was the steering column of the FW16. The journalists assumed that it had been cut by the medical team to remove the driver from the cockpit. But it just so happened that Dr. Domenico Salcito, who was assisting Senna's friend, Dr. Sid Watkins, at the scene of the accident, was in the magazine's office that day. "We didn't touch or see the steering column, which was lying on the floor as soon as we started working on it. It was strange," he recalled in the magazine's 2019 article.

Gradually, Autosprint—renowned for the technical quality of its analyses—was able to discover the cause of the accident. On May 10, they published the evocative front-page headline "The suspect," accompanied by a photograph of the infamous detached steering column. The investigation launched by the magazine and the ensuing high-profile trial revealed that the accident had been caused by a broken steering column. The column had been modified at Senna's request, as he wished to be more comfortable in the cockpit of his car. Ayrton Senna died as a result of a blow to the head from a suspension arm.

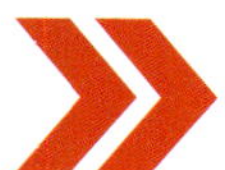

Following double page: The Williams FW16 is the last F1 car driven by the Brazilian.

ACKNOWLEDGMENTS

Writing about Ayrton Senna is both a chance and a privilege. This book you are holding could never have come to fruition without the invaluable support of people who are now very dear to us. At Glénat, first and foremost. In pole position, a big thank you to David Kings and Sophie Lecompte. Their advice, guidance, and support during the book's writing meant a lot to us. A special thanks also to Sophie Legras for the finalization of this work.

I have immense gratitude to the individuals approached for this book who agreed to discuss the man Ayrton Senna was and delved into their memories. At Lotus in Norfolk, Bob Dance and Chris Dinnage. In Italy, thanks to Leo Turrini and Mike Wilson. On the North Carolina side, sincere thanks to Jacques Dallaire and Steve Hallam in California. Also, in São Paulo, eternal thanks to Nuno Cobra. Thanks also to Sidineia Schwarzwalder and Pamela Jansen for the multiple connections.

To Helena Santos Hortz, who has been immensely generous. Her assistance in navigating texts in the language of Vasco de Gama and her help in various interviews in Brazil are priceless. Muito obrigado a você.

To Dominique Leroy, thank you for your trust and collaboration in this adventure. To Richard Micoud from the Automobile Club de Monaco. To Grégory and Loïc, and Formula 1 and fast sports enthusiasts. To our parents, families, friends, and colleagues of Thomas at Silverstone in Monaco, whose support and enthusiasm are unwavering. To Victoria and Sylvain.

Daniel Ortelli et Thomas Woloch

A big thank you to all those who made the realization of this book possible, starting with the drivers with whom I have been able to forge a deep friendship: Jean Alesi, Gerhard Berger, and Thierry Boutsen. Their testimonials published in the preface touch me particularly.

Thanks also to the playmates who accompanied me to conduct interviews with many Formula 1 actors: Jean Claude Azria and Bruno Bonizec.

I want to express my gratitude to the following individuals for their valuable contributions: Patrick Behar, Denis Chevrier, Jean-Jacques Delaruwière, Steve Domenjoz, René Fagnan (especially for the shots in Detroit in 1986), Richard Micoud, Raymond Papanti, Didier Paris, Pierre Van Vliet, Anaïs Monells, Anne Rol, Marion Yvora, Jean-Michel Tibi, Guillaume Zazurca, and Stéphane Zuber.
A special thanks to Anne-Laure Chambert-Protat and her daughter Coline.

To my partner, Theresa Revoil, who supported me throughout the stressful moments. Finally, thanks to the Glénat team and my coauthors, Daniel and Thomas, who have taken up the torch so dignifiedly to write a text worthy of this grand champion. Bravo to them!

Special thanks to René Fagnan for the photos on pages 15 (B), 17, and 36; to Renault Sport for the photo on pages 34-35; and to Honda for the photos on pages 72, 73, 109, and 164.

A big thank you to Grand Prix Photo, which has long showcased Dominique Leroy's work. Except for the photos mentioned above and the photos on pages 4, 5 (M), 14 (T), 27 (T), 48, 63, and 216, all the photos in this book are now available on www.grandprixphoto.com and www.dominiqueleroy.art.

Dominique Leroy